D1032174

PARADOXES OF CIVIL SOCIETY

"The resurgence of interest in the concept of civil society among political scientists and social theorists has permeated the language of historians during the past decade—bringing with it the familiar dangers of inflation, confusing eclecticism, and misuse. This volume ... grounds the discussion in an impressive series of carefully delimited essays, contextualizing the category in rich and illuminating ways. Frank Trentmann's team eloquently brings theory and history together."

Geoff Eley
Department of History
University of Michigan

PARADOXES OF CIVIL SOCIETY

New Perspectives on Modern German and British History

Edited by

Frank Trentmann

Berghahn Books
NEW YORK • OXFORD

Published in 2000 by **Berghahn Books**

© 2000 Frank Trentmann

Library of Congress Cataloging-in-Publication Data

Paradoxes of civil society : new perspectives on modern German and
British history / edited by Frank Trentmann.
        p.   cm.
    Includes bibliographical references and index.
    ISBN 1-57181-142-7 (alk. paper)
    1. Civil society.   I. Trentmann, Frank.
JC337.P37   1999   99–35022
301—dc21   CIP

British Library Cataloguing in Publication Data

A catalogue record for this book is available from the British Library.

Printed in the United States on acid-free paper.

CONTENTS

ACKNOWLEDGMENTS

THE COMPLETION OF THIS VOLUME offers a welcome occasion to thank several people and institutions for their kindness and assistance. About half the essays grew out of earlier presentations at a three-day workshop on civil society in Germany and Britain at the Center for European Studies at Harvard University. This interdisciplinary conference would not have been possible without the support of the center's staff, its director Charles Maier, and Abby Collins, as well as a grant from the Programme for the Study of Germany and Europe. Special thanks must go to Steven Young, who helped me conceive and organize the workshop, and to Susan Pedersen and David Blackbourn, who offered generous advice in the planning and selection process, and, later, acted as model commentators. Many thanks also to Geoff Eley, Tom Ertman, John Hall, John Keane, and Dieter Rucht for their perceptive comments. At Princeton University, my colleagues and students have helped me sharpen my thinking about civil society. In the final stage of production, Meg Turner provided invaluable assistance with house style and index. At Berghahn Books, Janine Treves was a model editor. My final thanks, however, go to the contributors for their patient labours and for many constructive discussions in the last couple of years that have made this a genuinely collective, interdisciplinary effort.

PREFACE

The essays in this volume represent an emerging second generation of scholarship on the idea and historical development of
civil society. It is second generation, in one sense, because a number
of contributors are young scholars whose essays emerged from the
conference that this volume's editor, Frank Trentmann, helped con-
vene under the auspices of the Harvard University Center for
European Studies. It is second generation in a metaphorical sense
because the concepts of civil society examined by the authors are
more complex, indeed contradictory, than the challenges to repressive state socialism that beckoned to intellectuals, East and
West, in the 1980s. The transformations in Eastern Europe, after all,
helped make the intellectual fortune of the idea of civil society. But
the civil society invoked in the magical moments around 1989 had
far fuzzier content than the closer examinations in this volume
allow to persist.

Probably a renewed scholarly and political interest in civil
society would have emerged by the late 1980s even had the opposition leaders in communist Eastern Europe not made it central to
their aspirations in the late 1970s and 1980s. Welfare states in the
West had apparently encountered their own limits in supervising
bargains among social groups. A new political movement around
issues of ecology, gender, and "identity" was strongly underway.
Social scientists who had called for "bringing the state back in"
would have scurried to bring society back in. And in Eastern
Europe, as for so many Western analysts of the great transformations of 1989, the idea of civil society beckoned as a realm—indeed
a metaphorical location—that might cast loose the suffocating
control still maintained (but more and more precariously) by late
communist regimes. Churches, universities, and independent labor unions had long advocated change; the new social movements
encompassing women, environmentalists, and nuclear protesters
were emerging in Eastern Europe as well. The task for those who

led the transformations of 1989 was to draw on their potential strength or to resuscitate them to change the state. And for many years into the decade of the 1990s, the evocation of civil society cast a warm glow, an instinctual approval of a richly textured social life that let individual personality develop and resist authoritarian manipulation from "above."

As the contributors to this volume show, many ambiguities were present in this appeal. Civil society described a realm of associations—the layer of supposedly non-coercive organizations located between the family and the state or the state party. Civil society was also an aspiration, a target for political education. A major question arose very quickly both in theory and practice, and it is the merit of this collection to focus on it at several key points. Was the market or capitalism the major component of a robust civil society; or might market relations undermine the sociability needed for civil society to prosper? The market was an arena where purchasers and sellers met out of mutual uncoerced interest. Since state coercion was absent (at least in everyday transactions, although the ground rules had to be established by politics), and individuals could develop their skills, the capitalist market society was an important component. The whole tradition descending from Scottish Enlightenment thinkers and prevalent in the West answered the question affirmatively. As we contemplate the inroads of globalization, the possibility of a less cheerful answer also emerges. In theory, civil society included economic associations and market relationships. The contributors in this volume provide the bases for an informed debate, which will doubtless become more urgent in the century ahead.

John Hall—the elder statesman in this gallery of young scholars—insists on the idea of civility as a component of civil society. Civility spotlights the quality of associational life, not just its presence; it suggests mutual respect and the capacity to listen—the temperamental mood in which the Habermas concept of rational discourse and conversation can take place. Civility guarantees the possibility of the "public sphere," that ambiance of reading and opinion formation on the part of a genteel educated class, which seemed so central to the spread of Enlightenment in Central Europe. But civility was also advanced—so the philosophers of the Scottish Enlightenment insisted—by economic development. With wealth and manufacturing came refinement, manners, and the abandonment of violence. Nor was this a development that depended primarily on the refinement of the aristocracy as Elias might suggest, but rather on the spread of gentry and middle-class businessmen. As other contributors suggest, the roles constructed for men and women became of fundamental importance in determining the advances and the limits of sociability.

Frank Trentmann's introductory essay admirably covers the diverse strands of argument and the wide range of issues that the contributors to this volume take up. Together, they advance our historical and political understanding of one of the key orienting concepts of our own historical era. Together they reveal that the idea and the reality of civil society is far more complex than we believed when we all first took it up, cheered by its optimistic premises for our collective life. We emerge from this book less certain, more chastened, but also better able to navigate intellectually during the political debates that loom ahead.

Charles S. Maier

Krupp Foundation Professor of European Studies
and Director of the Minda de Gunzburg Center
for European Studies, Harvard University

PART I

INTRODUCTORY PERSPECTIVES

INTRODUCTION

Paradoxes of Civil Society

Frank Trentmann

C IVIL SOCIETY HAS LIVED a perplexing double life. From its evolution in early modern Europe to its contemporary revival, "civil society" has always stood both for norms and for social realities. On one hand, it has been tied to ideals of civility, toleration, and peace, to theories of society as a self-regulating body, distinct from the state. On the other hand, beginning in eighteenth-century Britain, the term also came to describe a new kind of society, a body with its own heart and soul, composed of a growing plethora of clubs and associations, coffeehouses and Masonic lodges, public parks and libraries, where people could come together voluntarily as independent persons, irrespective of social rank, belief, or profession, to read and talk, to study and socialize, to exchange ideas or to drink and play games, to organize self-help for members or charities for the community. Civil society came to denote not just an ideal but also an expanding social reality, rooted outside the state and freed from the traditional ties of church, estate, or corporation, and, instead, based on principles of self-government, equality among members, and openness to all, allowing members to fashion their selves, to create group identities, and to "improve" society.

The modern history of civil society has been a story of dynamic tension between these two lives, for ideal and praxis never found a perfect fit. Unlike some recent propagators, early theorists were always aware of the gulf, even the contradictions, between the two. Civil society, Adam Smith already recognized, was a sphere of exploitation as well as sociability. Likewise, few members of voluntary societies had any illusions about civil society being an accomplished fact. Indeed, part of the enthusiasm driving associational life came from the conviction that civil society was an ongoing project that required commitment, time, and money from its proponents—and "civilizing" lessons for its "rude," "barbarian" "objects." Civil society, then, is historical, in a dual sense. It is not a universal phenomenon but the product of European history. Equally important, it was tied to a teleological vision, one that drove its members to attain civility for themselves and to disseminate its principles more broadly. The social realities and ideals of civil society flowed in and out of each other. They therefore need to be analyzed together, not only to highlight the continuous discrepancies between theoretical promise and social deficit but because it was in the bosom of associational culture that ideas of societal emancipation and improvement were shaped, creating new forms of collective identity among the members of a club while simultaneously providing new visions and means of organizing society at large, at home and abroad.

Whatever we think of the recent wave of Western agencies and programs promoting civil society, it is important to recognize that this is nothing fundamentally new. From its birth in eighteenth-century Britain, civil society combined a prescriptive and expansionist with an emancipatory momentum. It was a popular, applied science, informing views about "how society should work" as well as "how society worked." This increasingly complex and differentiated network of social agencies and relations, for all its appeal to equality and intelligence rather than rank or privilege and its quasi-democratic mechanisms of self-government, was nonetheless tied to values and practices with hierarchical and exclusionary elements. If for many groups the expansion of civil society opened doors into a new world of freedom and plurality, its normative, prescriptive qualities often suspended its core values of tolerance and mutual recognition when it came to those groups marked out as living in a sort of prehistory to civil society. Just as "civility" depended on the discovery and categorization of "rude" or backward forms of social life, so the project of extending civil society went hand in hand with an identification of "lower" types of social relations. Here lies the central historical paradox of civil society.

Multiple Meanings

This opening essay, by bringing together theoretical ideas and historical analysis, will work toward a framework for exploring this paradoxical relationship. Civil society has had very different meanings for theorists, sociologists, and historians, meanings that often have stood in the way of a critical dialogue. The following sections outline some preliminary analytical criteria to prepare for the more substantive task of engaging historically with core theoretical issues: the relationship between associations and democracy; between sociability and public sphere; between civil society and religion; and between civil society, nation-state, empire, and capitalism.

Few historical concepts can rival the dramatic reversal of fortune that the idea of civil society has undergone. A central notion in Western history until the turn of the twentieth century, it disappeared from the political and academic vocabulary in the age of totalitarian ideologies. It was in the battle against dictatorship and totalitarianism in the 1970s and 1980s that new social movements in South America and Central Europe rediscovered the idea. Fashionable today in liberal, conservative, and postsocialist circles alike, civil society has found its way into corporate boardrooms as well as into the language of liberation movements; it has even made a guest appearance in academic satire.[1] Civil society, it seems, is everywhere—so much so, that, like a gas, it is difficult to grasp. So what exactly does it mean? Where did it come from? Who belongs to it, and who does not? And how much of a "good thing" is it?

Some analysts like to measure civil society by counting associations and, along with Robert Putnam, predict a positive correlation between their density and the vitality of democracy.[2] Others have focused on the habits and values fostered by different bodies, some more civil than others. This perspective emphasizes the evolution of a flexible and tolerant mode of behavior, the creation of what Ernest Gellner called "modular man," who has the ability to join (and leave) multiple associations without binding himself to a totalizing way of life.[3] In politics, the concept has played an equally wide range of roles. For central European dissidents, civil society promised "anti-politics," captured in Václav Havel's call for "living within the truth" with oneself and with tolerance toward others: a personal ethics linked to a vision of society as not just independent from the state but opposed to it.[4] By contrast, the "associational democracy" championed by British and American progressives calls for more bridges between civil society and state.[5]

There is similar disagreement over whether the market economy and business associations should be counted as part of civil society.[6] Finally, there is the question of whether civil society has a global affinity with peace, democracy, and human rights, or is yet another Western disguise for promoting individualism and market capitalism by other means.[7]

The multiple, often contradictory definitions of civil society today are testimony to the ongoing tension in the double life of civil society as both prescriptive ideal and social reality. It is important here to separate analytical criteria from political judgement. To historicize the interplay between associations and ideas of societal self-regulation as they emerged in modern Europe does not require endorsement of a European path. At a time when women's movements, student groups, workers, and others in Asia, Africa, and Latin America are fighting states for greater societal autonomy, it is not entirely persuasive to reduce the present debate about civil society into a "vogue predicated on a fundamental ethnocentricity."[8] In reaction, Chris Hann has turned to a broad, universal definition of civil society that encompasses cooperation within all human societies at all times; but this is to throw the baby out with the bathwater, for the analytical merit of the concept is precisely that it helps to distinguish one particular type of social relations from others. The same problem arises where the concept is stretched so far that any social act counts as long as it is taking place outside the state and family. "Civil society," Tester has written, "is about what happens to us when we leave our family and go about our own lives. It is about the relationships I have with my colleagues and the person who crashed into my car."[9] There is good reason to be skeptical of such a conflation of civil society with all forms of the social or with "modern society."[10] As John Hall emphasizes in this volume, "civil" is an all-important adjective referring to distinctive types of social arrangements taking shape in early modern Europe that prized openness, equality, and tolerance and thus broke with earlier, more closed social worlds organized around rank, religion, guild, or clan.[11]

Students need not feel discouraged by the proliferation of competing definitions and agendas. After the Napoleonic wars, the German conservative Karl Ludwig von Haller thought it "desirable if the expression *civil society* ... could be banned from learning altogether."[12] Haller rejected the view of civil society as an association of free individuals that existed prior to the state, defending instead the older classical equation of the two (*societas civilis sive res publica*). It was precisely the conceptual discovery of the social as distinct from the political that made it possible to problematize the relationship between civil society and the state—and many current approaches can be traced back to early answers to this problematic, such as Thomas Paine's antistatism in the late eighteenth century and G.W.F. Hegel's incorporation of civil society into the state a generation later. Rather than crystallizing into a single master definition, then, the modern history of civil society is an unfolding dialogue between different imaginaries of the social. The dialogue rests on a shared recognition that society has its own life with roots outside the state and a shared interest in the mechanisms and values that make society work, not on any programmatic, let alone ideological, agreement on its relationship to state and economy.

At its most fundamental, the multiplicity of meanings reflects an important part of civil society's historical essence as a flexible, procedural understanding of social relations rather than a full-fledged ideology. Civil society emerged prior to the nineteenth-century ideologies of liberalism, socialism, and nationalism—and its decline, which still awaits much-needed study, probably has as much to do with liberal universalism and statism in the West as with totalitarianism in Central and Eastern Europe.[13] In the last two decades, as the universalist, individualist claims of liberalism came under pressure from value pluralism and as the totalizing vision of socialism became tainted with statism, anonymity, and intolerance, civil society came to offer an attractive, nonideological guide for Western postliberals and postsocialists alike, because it held out a procedural arrangement allowing people with different beliefs to coexist peacefully.[14] It was this tolerant spirit that appealed to social movements on either side of the Iron Curtain. Instead of a positive program of capturing the state, civil society is about imposing limits on the state, preventing any single group or ideology from dominating society, and, thus, preserving open spaces for diverse views and interests.

Such a turn to the procedural qualities of civil society is a helpful starting point for critical inquiries into the history of civil society. It avoids the elusive search for one ideological master narrative as well as the teleological temptation to reduce associational life into a mere prehistory of Western democracy. Instead, it opens up for investigation the modus operandi of civil society in different historical settings. This procedural point of view breaks with those popularizers in whose hands civil society is turning into a warm and cuddly thing, a new all-embracing sociopolitical program. As John Keane has rightly warned, civil society's most dangerous friends are those who are trying to sell it as an ideological vision for the future and, thus, risk repeating the mistakes of statist ideologies.[15] The procedural nature of civil society, by contrast, might be compared to an ideal public park, open to all members of society at all times, where people freely join and leave different groups at play, organize their activities on a voluntary and equal basis, where all show a mutual recognition of each others' tastes and activities. Here the subject of inquiry is not motivating interest, whether members play chess or football, or prefer to watch from a bench, nor whether some teams pursue competitive sports while others play free-floating pick-up games without score; instead, it is how these activities are organized by members, how much they are able to pursue a variety of interests without becoming the prisoner of any one group, whether they act with respect toward the opposing team, how they behave toward other park users, and whether they do their bit to keep the park clean, green, and open.

Of course, there is no such thing as a civil society without some conflict and inequality, just as there are no parks without restrictions (e.g., pertaining to time, nudity, pets), physical violence, conflict between users, individuals who would like to control the park for their uses alone or who work to have all games abolished on Sundays, or simply individuals who leave their trash behind. Still, just as some parks approximate the ideal more than others, so some societies have a larger arena distinct from the state and a more pluralist outlook. In modern history there has been a wide spectrum of positions between the politics of difference and open persecution; a club might have no objection to members with different religious faiths but still draw a line at atheists; an association might respect a variety of political opinions but exclude women; members of a philanthropic society might work hard to strengthen societal autonomy by organizing poor relief but equally hard to keep out Jews and foreigners. Instead of the tendency to use civil society as a simple pass/fail test, then, it might be helpful to differentiate between types and degrees of civil society, and to historicize the extent of tolerance, pluralism, and self-regulation at work within and between groups as well as between societies.

Beyond *Bürgertum* and Liberalism

Given the rivers of ink that recently have been poured into the advocacy of civil society at present, we know surprisingly little about its workings in the past. Few historians have engaged directly with the perspectives opened up by the rediscovery of civil society. Older methodological concerns about class and ideology have made it difficult to absorb a way of viewing civil society that looks beyond its older equation with liberalism or its Marxist reduction into bourgeois capitalism. Historiography has been dominated by two rather separate enterprises. One has traced the evolution of the concept from the perspective of a high intellectual history of ideas, examining the gradual separation of state and society in the seventeenth and eighteenth centuries, the contribution of the Scottish enlightenment, and the transformation of the idea of civil society in liberal, conservative, and socialist thought in the nineteenth century.[16] This approach has tended to produce a picture of civil society as a sophisticated conversation between great thinkers. This discussion, however, has taken place in virtual isolation from the "real" transformation of civil society at the grassroots.

What we know about this latter dimension for Germany and Britain has been mainly a by-product of research into the history of the middle classes, in particular their associations.[17] The leading questions here have addressed not the modus operandi of civil society but class formation. German historiography in this respect has been driven by the debate about Germany's pathological path, or *Sonderweg*, to modernity and Nazism, purportedly caused by a deficit of liberalism attributed to a weak middle class. Major research projects have confronted this sociological notion, documenting both the continued importance of the older *Bürgertum* into the nineteenth century[18] and the special contribution of the *Bildungsbürgertum*, an educated elite with particularly close ties to the state.[19] If the economic bourgeoisie perhaps played a lesser role in Germany than in Britain, the ghost of the missing middle class has clearly been put to rest.

From the perspective of civil society, this historiographical preoccupation with the middle class has been a mixed blessing, not least because of the ambiguous use of the German term for civil society, *bürgerliche Gesellschaft*, a term partly derived from *Bürger*— referring alike to citizen and bourgeois, as well as to the older privileged burghers of towns, and excluding the lower middle classes. It has facilitated a corruption of the concept whereby bürgerliche Gesellschaft becomes little more than the society of the educated and better-off male members of the middle class, or simply synonymous with Bürgertum.[20] Civil society thus finds itself in a sociological straightjacket. No doubt, this small group played an important role in the creation of civil society, but this does not mean that civil society is little more than its extension.

The subordinate treatment of civil society as a chapter in the history of the Bürgertum has been exemplified by the rich literature on associations (*Vereine*). Voluntary associations were the birthplace of the new group, for it was here, as Thomas Nipperdey emphasized, that the "process of individualisation, decorporation, and emancipation" from the traditional world gathered momentum. There is a temptation to paint a heroic picture of associations as the vehicle of emancipation, steered by an emerging middle class across the barriers of privilege, estates, and ignorance, a vehicle that in the nineteenth century opened its doors to the working class, carrying an ever greater number along the road of equality, merit, and democracy. This progressive narrative was, of course, the mantra of many early liberals but it becomes more problematic once the focus of analysis moves to modes of exclusion and inclusion and to the question of the degree to which clubs fostered a "politics of difference" and civility outside the clubhouse as well as within. As the number of loyalist associations in late-eighteenth-century Britain makes clear, civil society was from the beginning open to a range of ideas and groups, and not the sole province of middle class or liberalism, let alone democracy. Without the analytical separation of civil society from a particular political ideology and sociological constituency, there is a danger that the myth of a natural affinity between the middle classes and liberal democracy will be reintroduced by the back door.[21]

This volume is an attempt to loosen this straightjacket and to further dialogue between historians and theorists of civil society. It is designed to add some historical complexity to the sometimes abstract picture painted by the theorist and, equally, to suggest to the historian some new ways of looking at an old term. The different essays develop new perspectives on the modus operandi of civil society, from its rebirth in the eighteenth century to its crisis in the early twentieth century. They come from different directions, bringing together historical, theoretical, and sociological inquiries into the evolution of the ideal and into the social, cultural, and political relations distinguishing the praxis of civil society. The focus on modern Germany and Britain partly reflects the centrality of the concept in the history of these two societies, but it also results from the fact that a lot of original work has been concentrated here. Existing historiography on associations, liberalism, and the middle class, whatever its methodological constraints, has offered important jumping-off points in this respect. Yet, if the goal of this volume is not to establish some new metanarrative of civil society, neither is it to offer a new aggregate national evaluation of

"Germany versus Britain" concerned with the Sonderweg. Rather, the essays develop a number of fresh perspectives about different dimensions of civil society at work within each nation as well as between them. These interpretive perspectives could well be extended to other historical contexts.

Three shifts in focus emerge. First, the inclusion of neglected groups creates a broader, more critical picture of civil society. Several chapters widen the scope of inquiry by examining the self-organization by groups that at the time were treated as "objects" of improvement or as enemies of civil society such as prostitutes and peasants. The focus on the interaction between groups with competing views of civil society shifts attention toward the broader issue of reciprocity: the degree of mutual recognition and plurality between social groups as well as within their own associations. While these essays bring into the discussion groups normally considered outside civil society, others reinterpret more traditional subjects in terms of gender, nation, and empire. This second shift is reflected here in original inquiries into the place of women in eighteenth-century conjectural histories, the role of masculinity in patriotic associations, and the relationship between women and empire in missionary societies. Finally, the volume takes a broader look at the idea of the distinction between civil society and state, complementing studies of high theory with examinations of the role of the idea in society and political culture. On one hand, the analysis of the role of "the public" in Kant's theory of civil society can be read in parallel with the chapters on rural publics and with a social history of semiofficial projects to foster civil society through the creation of public "intelligence" in provincial everyday life. On the other hand, the relationship between civil society and political economy is taken up first with regard to Smith and Hegel but then extended to popular radicals, liberals, and socialists. Here, at the level of political culture, ideas had profound implications for the praxis of civil society. Whether society was imagined in terms of connection or opposition to the state, of relative autonomy or embeddedness in the economy, influenced whether the political strategies of social movements would target the state or were more defensive, concerned with preserving social spaces of self-regulation against encroachment. As the studies of Free Trade and social policy toward war veterans highlight, the politics of civil society helped shape both political economy and social services, structuring institutional relations between state and social actors, and creating notions of rights and entitlements vis-à-vis the state as well as different degrees of tolerance and trust between social groups.

Associations, Plurality, and Democracy

Soon after the rapid growth of the first voluntary societies in early eighteenth-century Britain, commentators began to see them as embryonic models of a new society. David Hume, in his *Enquiry Concerning the Principles of Morals* (1751), thought that clubs might well be studied as microcosms of social morality and cohesion. More recently, political scientists have taken this line of reasoning in a political direction, linking associational life to democratic stability. The decline in the number of intimate associations, such as bowling leagues, Putnam has argued, should not be viewed merely as a shift in leisure activity but as an alarming portent of a decline in social trust, civic engagement, and ultimately, in democratic spirit. Inevitably, such approaches to civil society rest on highly positive assumptions about past associations; in its communitarian version, this becomes a new kind of *Kulturkritik*, tying associations to a vision of small, intimate communities with a shared sense of morals as opposed to the helter-skelter of global cities and telecommunications, of violence, anarchy, and a multiplicity of values. Voluntary associations are praised for creating horizontal ties between different members of the community in an atmosphere of equality. They are likened to schools in the democratic arts of discussion, compromise, voting, and self-government. Associations, in this view, teach individuals to cooperate, to trust each other, to tolerate rival views, and to resolve differences peacefully; that is, they create the "social capital" and civic engagement necessary for a healthy democracy.[22]

This line of reasoning has an influential ancestry in nineteenth-century liberal thought, particularly Tocqueville's observations on the role of clubs and churches in *Democracy in America* (1840–5). The idea also became a central part of some movement cultures. For the thousands of married women in Britain who joined the Woman's Cooperative Guild around the turn of the twentieth century, for example, the "coop" was a lesson in democracy, providing experience in public debate and speaking, electing officials and becoming representatives at national congresses—a "fine training ground for national citizen work," as the secretary tirelessly emphasized.[23] Yet, how typical are such examples? Does the history of clubs and associations bear out the idea of a correlation with social cohesion and reciprocity, or even further, with democratic habits? In other words, is the liberal idea of association a methodologically useful ideal-type that abstracts from historical development, or is it merely a figment of the theoretical imagination?

Associational life expanded in four overlapping waves. The first wave started early, if slowly, in the seventeenth century with the emergence of language societies (Fruchtbringende Gesellschaft, Weimar, 1617) and learned societies (Royal Society 1660; societas ereunetica, Rostock, 1622), gathering momentum in the early and mid-eighteenth century, with the proliferation of urban clubs (The Ugly Face Club, Liverpool), music societies, horticultural groups, debating clubs, proprietary libraries (Liverpool, 1758), and, finally, reading societies, the most numerous type in Germany, where some 50,000 gathered regularly in *Lesegesellschaften* by the late eighteenth century. If culture and communication pushed the first wave, the second was propelled by improvement, philanthropy, and public welfare. The coming of this next wave is already apparent in the foundation of the Grand Lodge in England in 1717 and the subsequent expansion of freemasonry into a European network whose raison d'être was to spread enlightenment, foster civic engagement, and create a universal brotherhood. Its primary types, however, emerged after the middle of the century. These were the "friendly society" in Britain, aiding the poor and sick, widows and prostitutes, and the philanthropic society in Germany, such as the Patriotische Gesellschaft in Hamburg (1765), whose functions ranged from aid to sailors to the improvement of fire engines. This second wave crested with the expansion of self-help associations, humanitarian groups, and charities in the mid- and late-Victorian period. Many now developed international networks as well, such as antislavery movements, peace societies, and the federation against vivisection. A third wave, overlapping with the previous ones, was made up of political groupings and what is now called interest groups. In Britain, political clubs reach back into the late seventeenth century (Whig Ribbon Club), a good century before the emergence of Jacobin clubs in Germany. The nineteenth century also witnessed the expansion of professional associations, trades unions, and business associations.

Many of these associations continue to this day, but they clearly have been overwhelmed by a final, tidal wave that has swelled since the mid- and late nineteenth century: leisure clubs and lifestyle societies. This is the era of popular sport clubs, youth movements, hobby clubs, and saving societies. This tidal wave was particularly pronounced in Germany. In cities like Munich and Hamburg, associations mushroomed in the second half of the nineteenth century, from a few hundred to three thousand and six thousand respectively, a trend that was interrupted by wars and Nazism but resumed in the 1950s, when over half of Germans belonged to some Verein, primarily sports, savings, and singing clubs. Whereas the clubs and societies of earlier waves expressed a belief in bringing together members with different interests and backgrounds to advance enlightenment and harmony—Harmonia and Concordia were popular names in Germany—this new associational world was increasingly subdivided by class and identity, ranging from workers who set up their own chess club to those men in Hamburg in 1900 whose interests could no longer be satisfied by a general zoological society, nor even by the more select Friends of Birds, but required nothing less than the founding of the Friends of the Canary.[24]

These overlapping trends in the nature and numbers of associations apply to both Germany and Britain, but there are important national differences. Germany followed British developments, but more slowly and selectively. Much of German club life was imported from Britain through Hamburg, which functioned as a kind of associational *entrepôt*, giving a home to the first lodges and the journal *Patriot* (1724), which copied the culture of sociability pioneered by the British *Tatler* and *Spectator*. In commercial life, consumer culture, and general literacy (50 percent in 1750), Britain was several steps ahead of Germany. The *Tatler* was read by artisans. Provincial subscription libraries included hosiers and rope makers as well as merchants and attorneys, as in Liverpool in the 1760s. Subscription concerts, and music and historical societies sprang up in Hanoverian England; most German cities would see them only after the turn of the nineteenth century.[25] Until the 1830s, German clubs remained the preserve of a much smaller elite. In masonic lodges, lawyers, merchants, academics, and a few nobles continued to dominate, as Robert Beachy shows in his chapter on Leipzig in this volume.[26] Vereine often had no artisans or small traders at all or, as in Frankfurt am Main in the 1810s and 1820s, they were underrepresented, with less than 5 percent.[27] By contrast, there were over nine hundred benefits societies in London alone at this time, drawing in more than a quarter of the male population. Nor was this a metropolitan peculiarity. In Norwich, every fifth male was a member of an association by 1750. By 1815, 8 percent of Britain's population belonged to a friendly society.[28]

These numbers reflect not only the broader social spectrum of associational life in Britain but also more extensive self-regulating mechanisms at work. In Sheffield in the 1780s, the fifty-five sick clubs paid out more than did parish poor relief. By then most towns had set up hospitals sponsored by public subscription, while countless local voluntary organizations provided refuge for prostitutes or aid to poor pregnant women. Instances of this are, of course, not entirely missing in Germany. Yet—and here quantity becomes quality—the various philanthropic societies acted on a considerably smaller scale and represented an elite, not a mass, movement. In the establishment of hospitals in eighteenth-century British towns, artisans were not only beneficiaries or "objects" but active participants and subscribers.[29] If anything, this trend was reinforced in the Victorian cult of charities. By the late nineteenth century, the annual receipts of charities in London were bigger than the budgets of many European states. And, as Frank Prochaska has emphasized, this was not only because the middle classes spent more on charity than on any item in their budget other than food but because many charities were organized by, as well as for, the working classes.[30] In short, societal self-organization occupied a larger terrain in Britain.

What is the relationship between the expanding network of voluntary associations and self-regulatory practices, on one hand, and civic politics, reciprocity, and social trust, on the other? Most directly, the politicization of civil society advanced earlier and faster in Britain than in Germany, favored by a lack of censorship of associations, the earlier erosion of guilds, the influence of a language of "rights," the emergence of urban popular politics after the civil war, and the growing importance of Parliament after the Glorious Revolution. The Kit-Cat Club (1696) was founded by aristocratic members of the Whig Party, the Society of Supporters of the Bill of Rights—the first modern radical movement—half a century later, soon to be followed by other groups calling for political reform. With the exception of the smaller Jacobin clubs in the 1790s, German bodies were distinguished by their apolitical view of civil society: they saw their mission as complementing their states by improving the local infrastructure and gathering information to assist official knowledge, not as opposing or eliminating government. Administrators played a disproportionate role in German clubs, and confidence in enlightened reform absolutism remained high. In Thomas Paine's popular radical writings, by contrast, the advance in societal self-organization became tied to a political vision of freeing civil society from the state altogether and superseding government as far as possible.

These are examples of the political contingency of associational life, however, not evidence for two narrow, national paths of civil society. Radicalism was merely one voice in the British debate about the relationship between state and civil society. To include other voices shows the fallacy of positing a functional link between associations and democracy. Edmund Burke, Paine's target, expressed an older political understanding of civil society that retained considerable support. In his *Reflections on the Revolution in France* (1790), he defended civil society as an "off-spring of convention" with religion as its basis. There was no room for ideas of prior universal rights or for tolerating dissenting communities as voluntary associations.[31] At a popular level, this brand of loyalism was, if anything, more widespread than any radical understanding of civil society. The association movement in the 1790s was fueled by a concern for conserving political structures and social order. The Proclamation Society's attacks on Paine and his publisher illustrate the spectrum of political uses of the associational medium. Most associations spoke the language of persecution, not pluralism.

The variety of political directions taken by nonpolitical clubs suggests the need for a more rigorous analytical distinction between an association's internal practices, its external relation to society, and the role of ideas and values mediating between the two. The neo-Tocquevillian view of associations as "nurseries of democracy" has rested on an assumption that the experience of equal, reciprocal relations within an association spilled over into attitudes toward society at large. In a study of eighteenth-century Masonic lodges, for example, Margaret Jacob has presented these groups not only as elements of a new civil society but as "invariably civic, hence political, and most frequently progressive and reformist."[32] Clearly, the temple exposed members to a new atmosphere of equality and democracy, but why presume that masons wished to apply these principles to the rest of society or the state? Most individuals in modern societies belong to a variety of groups and have a kaleidoscopic view of the world that reflects multiple, even contradictory allegiances rather than a single, magnified version of their relations within a single group; in Northern Ireland today, Protestants and Catholics cooperate peacefully in pigeon clubs but attack each other during Orange parades and republican demonstrations. There should be nothing surprising about individuals enjoying democratic rights within a club but having no interest in extending the same rights to the body politic. Many lodges saw no contradiction between their own crypto-democratic constitutions and hero worship of absolutist militarist princes, like Frederick II. In the English Midlands, lodges moved effortlessly from mid-century reformism to turn-of-the-century loyalism.[33] Voluntary organizations can serve as schools of mutual recognition and constitutional government, but they can also suppress others' political efforts, as when voluntary yeomanry attacked protesters gathered in St Peter's Field in Manchester in 1819, killing eleven and wounding hundreds.

Equality, openness, and reciprocity within associations ought to be treated as historical problems rather than inherent properties present from birth. The masonic lodges illustrate the Janus-faced nature of early voluntary gatherings. Democratic and equal in terms of the voting rights of members and the suspension of their outside rank, denomination, or profession, freemasonry nonetheless remained hierarchical and elitist. Criticism of lodge affairs was not discussed democratically but had to be referred to the *Meister vom Stuhl*, an unelected officer. Membership was socially exclusive. Above all, the temple not only was a site of enlightenment but promoted secrecy, encouraging deception as much as transparency. The elitist sense of superior virtue did not translate well into respect toward those outside the temple.[34] Other associations retained certain corporate features well into the nineteenth century; the Berlin *Korporation der Kaufmannschaft* preserved exclusive tax and discounting privileges for its merchant members and was ruled by a body of elders as late as 1870. It is too simple to presume a clear-cut divide between "modern," open, democratic associational life and a "traditional" caged corporate society.[35]

Plurality and inequality, tolerance and discrimination went hand in hand in associational life. To acknowledge this is not to diminish the significance of new spaces for peaceful meetings and discussions between individuals with different opinions, beliefs, and backgrounds—between Anglicans and nonconformists, aristocrats and merchants, radical believers in collective property and defenders of private property. If not entirely free from aggression, these spaces contributed to a new ability to live with difference.[36] Most societies explicitly barred politics as a subject of conversation in order to keep open channels of discussion on other subjects.

Nonetheless, it is misleading, I think, to view historical limits to equality and reciprocity merely in terms of externally located aberrations from a "natural" ideal, such as the impossibility of attaining truly meritocratic associations in a class society. Were not some of these inequalities inherent, built into the constitutional framework of clubs? In early nineteenth-century German Vereine, the neo-humanist ideal of *Bildung* or self-cultivation rather than rank or wealth was always checked by high membership fees; in a typical club like the Aachen Casino, admission fees alone were the equivalent of one-third of a skilled worker's annual income. Several societies came to openly acknowledge the social boundaries in which the supposedly classless pursuit of Bildung took place; Harmonie, in Nuremberg, amended its statutes in 1829 to limit membership to aristocrats, government officials, academics, artists, merchants, and industrialists.[37] The search for social distance also lay behind the expensive creation of club gardens, for public gardens, according to the Munich Museum, were "no proper [*schicklich*] place of leisure and relaxation for the more polite world [*feinere Welt*], because of their all-too mixed class of visitors."[38] British associational life had more openings for the educated artisan and shopkeeper, but inequalities and contradictions existed here as well. In Birmingham in the 1840s, the Botanical and Horticultural Society was deeply divided about the issue of popular access to its gardens, torn between the universalist language of improvement and benevolence and the social anxieties of many middle class members; in 1846 entry procedures were liberalized but not without a wave of resignations in protest.[39] The model of the subscriber democracy, the predominant type of association in Britain from the 1780s on, gave rise to patronage societies as well as self-help associations. The first tended toward oligarchy and a clear division between the small elite of trustees and the majority of hard-working inferiors. Few artisans, workers, or small traders had the time, money, or status to be appointed to positions of influence. The patronage society, as R. J. Morris has argued, offered "the perfect compromise between middle-class people striving for self-respect and independence, and the reality of the hierarchical society with its massive inequalities of wealth and power, even within the middle classes."[40] This glass ceiling was frequently complemented by a double vision. Eager to extirpate drinking among the ignorant, mechanics institutes prohibited alcohol to workers but served wine to the more enlightened patrons. Similar conflicts arose over the control of resources and communication, such as the choice of books and newspapers worthy of acquisition for the library.

* * * *

THE MOST POWERFUL DIVIDE between inclusion and exclusion, however, came to run along gender lines. Rather than witnessing some gradual realization of the egalitarian potential of associational life, the 1780s–1830s were decades in which numerical expansion was complemented by gendered reconfiguration. There was nothing inevitable about this. Early clubs and societies had not been havens of gender equality—the Kit-Cat Club mixed Whiggish principles with pornographic verse, while Wilkes's popularity among radicals rested partly on his misogynistic *Essay on Woman*.[41] Yet, in the eighteenth century, women's role in civil society was not premised on a clear-cut separation between public and private spheres, either in theory or in social practice. Mary Catherine Moran shows in this volume that early writers like Lord Kames and John Millar rejected the classical dichotomy between public and private and introduced "society" as an intermediate sphere in which women played a constitutive role in the exchange of views and, thus, in the very creation of civil society.[42] Early lodges accepted women.[43] Women attended literary societies and were included in informal conversational and debating societies like the Kränzchen and the semipublic salons run by Jewish women in late-eighteenth-century Berlin.[44] Nor was this simply a feature of middle- and upper-class life. Eighty-two female friendly societies were active in London in the 1790s.[45] Throughout the eighteenth century, communities had organized self-help organizations that included or were run by women.

By the early nineteenth century, this fluid and informal world had given way to a more formal, institutionalized, and male-dominated network of societies that demarcated separate subjects and functions for women.[46] Just as women's active role in public culture as playwrights or actresses became suspect, women were now debarred from most associations, except as spectators or in charitable activities fit for "feminine virtues." Philosophical and debating societies normally excluded women. Some Mechanics Institutes allowed men to bring women along to lectures, as in Colchester after 1835, but most literary societies denied women even this passive role; the Anglican Literary Institute did not allow women until 1888. Reading societies in Hamburg had only three women from the 1790s to the 1860s. Popular leisure clubs began to open their doors to women in the late nineteenth century, but mainly as passive members; for many, voting rights or access to committees came only after the First World War. Women's more active engagement took place mainly in areas in which public involvement appeared as a symbolic amplification of domestic virtues or around those "feminine" subjects where men would not tread. If the groups mobilizing against slavery or drink were examples of the former, lying-in charities represented the latter. An early separate organization was the Female Society for the Relief of British Negro Slaves in Birmingham (1828), which, significantly, met in private homes. Female involvement was not entirely static and could contest the gendered boundaries of civic engagement; but ultimately, as Davidoff and Hall have stressed, "the male and female philanthropic worlds remained substantively different and when women moved in it was usually because men were moving out into new concerns."[47]

This trend resulted from a series of mutually reinforcing developments: evangelicalism's emphasis on purity and domesticity, the decline of women's independent status in business and property, the Victorian cult of respectability, and the equation between masculinity and public rights. The move of most societies and clubs from the informal world of coffeehouses, inns, and taverns to public buildings with committee rooms, treasury, and formal annual meetings exacerbated this trend, because it was men who had legal, fiscal, and rhetorical training. New notions of sexuality and civil society stood in a symbiotic relationship in late eighteenth- and early nineteenth-century Germany, too. Here the shift away from absolutist notions of the state as the final arbiter of moral relations was driven by what Isabel Hull has identified as a prescriptive "sexual self-image of civil society." Agency, creativity, and independence became associated with men, whose sex drive was revalued as a source of productive energy that could be domesticated for the productive welfare of civil society, whereas women became sexual derivatives, not entirely passionless but dependent means to the greater happiness of husbands and future citizens. The transfer of morals to civil society went hand in hand with a masculine definition of citizenship and the creation of gendered rights in a new private sphere; for example, in questions of out-of-wedlock pregnancy, fathers, but not mothers, were protected against legal intrusion by the state.[48]

Associational culture more generally bore the stamp of the new culture of masculinity. Freemasonry came to evolve around rituals of masculine virtue that celebrated the natural union between civic engagement, economic independence, and being a man and a "brother," a language that would inform the discourse of political reform and labor movements in the nineteenth century. Although originating within the middle classes, the culture of domesticity ultimately came to restructure the workings of civil society across the class spectrum. This involved not only social control "from above" but a radical political strategy from below, as artisans in Britain came to emphasize their own manhood and independence as responsible patriarchs in campaigns for the vote and a bread-winner's wage.[49] In nineteenth-century Germany, as Dan McMillan argues in his chapter on the gymnastics movement, the cult of masculinity left an equally significant legacy on the relationship between state and civil society, for the organic equation between manhood and nation-state left little room for pluralist politics.[50]

* * * *

THE EXPANSION OF ASSOCIATION AND SELF-COORDINATION, then, was accompanied not just by the demolition of external constraints imposed by state, church, and corporation but by the construction of internal barriers to access. The historical interplay between self-regulation and reciprocity was not free from ambivalence and conflict. It might be well to distinguish more carefully, on one hand, between self-regulation and plurality and, on the other, three more demanding elements of recent definitions of the concept: that civil society is an open, egalitarian setting; that it has a self-sustaining equilibrium; and is a "cool" concept that favors toleration.

Civil society, Michael Walzer has written, challenged the "singularity" of totalizing visions of life, like nationalism or socialism, without imposing one of its own, making it merely a "setting of settings: all are included, none is preferred."[51] The historical proponents of civil society might have agreed with the first, negative half of this proposition, but openness was always qualified by new and often conscious strategies of exclusion and preference across society.

The idea of a self-sustaining equilibrium underlies Dahrendorf's picture of a "creative chaos" of associations that protects groups against both the state and "monopolistic claims by self-appointed minorities and indeed majorities."[52] Again, there is some truth to this picture. The multiplicity of associations in Victorian Britain is an example of civil society offering a space for coexistence between different religious and ideological groups that might have come to blows under an alternative scenario of state intervention and its attendant struggles to capture state power to advance particular interests. Yet the absence of a monopoly by any one group is not the same as pluralism safeguarding all others. Britain's associational landscape was not a level playing field. Much of the energy generated within civil society flowed into a series of associations that perhaps had distinct purposes and members with different party allegiances but whose membership and moral outlook more or less converged in the evangelical and humanitarian oligopoly of sabbatarians, teetotalers, and the Royal Society for the Prevention of Cruelty to Animals (RSPCA); by the turn of the twentieth century, the temperance movement alone had half a million activists. While some historians have traced the "roots of consensus" in Britain to these nonviolent reform movements,[53] it should be equally clear that, whatever art of compromise these movements developed, civil society, left to itself, did not naturally tend toward a "creative chaos" of pluralism and tolerance. Sabbatarians used their moral and judicial power to stop the poor from shopping on Sundays as well as others from drinking, swearing, or enjoying cruel sports. The RSPCA had its own inspectors and system of enforcement, and it was partly thanks to the organization's vigilance that hundreds of thousands of fines and several thousand prison sentences were issued every year in mid-Victorian Britain for offenses under the Lord's day observance act, licensing act, and similar legislation.

That the associational structures allowing society to regulate more and more of its own affairs could be transformed into instruments of policing points to the significance of distinguishing between the institutional body of civil society and the values flowing through its veins. Associations and civility can pull in different directions. We should be wary of conflating the non-ideological culture of a civil society with the existence of clubs or new social movements simply because they are voluntary, self-governing, and without a totalizing vision. Civil society is the enemy of totalitarianism, but this does not mean that all voluntary associations favoring societal autonomy are automatically champions of civility.

Civil society has been described as a "cool concept," in contrast to the heat required by ideologies based on class or national solidarity.[54] It requires tolerating other ways of life, not embracing them, let alone a passionate feeling akin to the "love of the fatherland." Walzer has taken this notion one step further and argued that civil society offers an alternative to the all-absorbing visions of life propagated in socialism, capitalism, and nationalism precisely because it is "local, specific, [and] contingent" and fosters an outlook where the "good life is in the details"—so much so, he concludes, that it has difficulty attracting enthusiasm, for its typical activities are small-scale and "seem so ordinary."[55] Historically, this is a problematic thesis. The scale of activity does not determine whether members' outlook is imperialist or self-limiting. There has been a temptation to portray associations as narrow but nonetheless beneficial microcosms of civic life, like the bowling leagues invoked in the American literature. In fact, the late-nineteenth-century tidal wave of ever more differentiated clubs with ever more specific interests produced two diverging trends. First, a large number of clubs continued to view their local activities as part of a larger vision, as when, for example, the Hamburger Sport Verein, in its anthem, dedicated "our ardent efforts to Germany, holy land of love."[56] The second trend was toward over-identification with a particular issue, inspiring either a retreat from civil society into the reclusive small world of like-minded peers and *Vereinsmeier* or a missionary zeal to disseminate one's own values and habits to the rest of the community.[57] These practices might stop short of the ambitious totalizing visions of modern ideology and even be deeply antistatist, yet they introduced a tension between plurality and conformity. This is the world of the teetotaling activist and the moral improvement society, which is hardly as dangerous to civil society as Hitler or Stalin but still undermines tolerance and social trust. There are hotter members of associational life, then, as well as colder ones.

Civility, then, needs to be historicized more subtly, not treated as a clear-cut component that civil societies either possess or do not. The acceptance of nonviolent, noncoercive social relations can come in different forms and different degrees. For example, about one million mothers and children attended weekly mothers' meetings in late-nineteenth-century Britain. These were voluntary gatherings, organized by middle-class women, providing tea and clothes for the poor in exchange for the poor listening to Bible stories and lessons in benevolence. For some, philanthropy might have been the "tap-root of female emancipation" (Prochaska) but for others it involved the denial of reciprocity and independence. Many working-class women experienced these meetings as oppressive and humiliating. "[L]adies came and lectured on the domestic affairs in the workers' homes that it was impossible for them to understand," one woman recalled. "I have boiled over many times at some of the things I have been obliged to listen to, without the chance of asking a question." She subsequently joined the Woman's Cooperative Guild, where "we always had the chance of discussing a subject."[58] Julia Roos's discussion of prostitution and social policy in Weimar Germany reveals the importance of an "outcast civil society" that offered prostitutes opportunities for self-organization, challenging the norms of respectability upheld by middle-class feminists as well as by men. Such spaces for voluntary organization and resistance, she concludes, cannot be satisfactorily understood in terms of Michel Foucault's negative view of civil society as a site of repressive "bio-power" and normalization.[59] Here are instances, then, that point to the important condition of flexibility in civil society, a kind of internal safety device that stops groups with universalist ideas from monopolizing social relations and preserves a space for movement, as Keane has recently reemphasized.[60] To recognize that the multiplicity of voluntary associations keeps the river of social relations from freezing is very different from suggesting a positive correlation between the density of associations, social trust, and democracy. For all its emancipatory dynamics, the increasingly self-regulatory and self-governing world of associations did not naturally generate civility. The pluralism it fostered was that of an inegalitarian "politics of difference."

Sociability and the Public Sphere

Focusing on the interplay between inclusion and exclusion, emancipation and discrimination, and self-regulation and policing also casts a new light on the relationship between civil society and the public sphere. It will be apparent from the above that much of the social praxis of associations was taking place in public spaces, such as the coffeehouses and taverns that functioned as meeting places for clubs and societies from the late seventeenth century on. In Jürgen Habermas's influential writings, these spaces exemplify a theory of civil society as a network of associations anchoring the communicative structures of the public sphere in the private "lifeworld," the sphere between state and economy.[61] This account of the public sphere has sparked several critiques, challenging its normative assumption that conflict is resolved discursively and emphasizing the historically gendered essence and the multiple and competing, rather than uniform, forms of the public sphere.[62] Equally important, Habermas's understanding of the public sphere and its shared politics of public reason is tied to a debatable view of civil society and its communicative nature.

In *Between Facts and Norms*, Habermas has offered a sustained discussion of the functional relationship between civil society and political public. His guiding question is how democracy and societal integration will be able to resist the centripetal force of the increasingly differentiated and distant systems of politics and economy. Free associations play the crucial role of antennae, picking up signals of societal problems from the private sphere and, after turning them into a clearer frequency, transmitting them to the public. Civil society thus acts as a "warning system" for the democratic process, bridging the gulf separating bureaucratic politics from social problems at the grass roots.[63] In addition to a liberal constitution and an intact private sphere, this view highlights as an important precondition the defensive, self-limiting self-understanding of civil society that is often attributed to new social movements. In contrast to totalizing ideologies, a lively civil society keeps open the many private sources of public opinion and social solidarity. Associations that are not simply interest groups but are consciously engaged in the critical work of the public play a dual function, transmitting social problems to the political system and, in the process, strengthening civil society.[64] This theoretical approach encourages a historical view that sees a functional correlation between civil society, discursive communication, and a democratic public sphere. For Klaus Eder, for example, associations emerging in the eighteenth century mirrored the "modern" principles of discursive communication, based on equality, impartiality, and the resolution of conflict through critique.[65] They were sites of a modern learning process based on reflexive communication, that is, a process in which people communicated about communication.

Neither Habermas nor Eder are unaware that associations have not always lived up to these criteria. Yet the question remains whether historical studies should treat such failures as pathological aberrations or should altogether revise the theoretical picture. We have already seen the limits to openness and democracy in early clubs and associations. Before the sobering impact of evangelicalism in the late eighteenth century, excessive drinking, blasphemous songs, and violent brawls (including murder) were common sights in clubs and coffee houses—hardly an atmosphere conducive to critical reason.[66] Here it may be helpful to briefly explore three further challenges to the Habermasian concept of the public sphere, turning toward the more ambiguous genealogy of the public sphere, the understanding of "public opinion" by early propagators of civil society, and the centrality of alternative nondiscursive modes of interaction, particularly sociability.

The social history of civil society appears in a very different light once it is conceptually separated from a public sphere defined by discursive communication and disinterested reasoning. As Ian McNeely argues in this collection, Habermas's focus on critical reason means that the "public" becomes removed from social interests and practical concerns. By contrast, McNeely points to practical information as a catalyst of social knowledge and political consciousness. His analysis of intelligence gazettes in late eighteenth- and nineteenth-century Württemberg shows how patterns of civil society emerged gradually, not as the product of ideological forces, nor from within a disinterested, reasoning public, but as the result of a transformation of practical knowledge (initiated by the state) into new forms of social communication (outside the state). From this perspective, "civil society's origins in the state ... were less the signs of weakness and dependence than the source of initiative and dynamism."[67] John Abbot, in his discussion of Altbayern, finds much support for the idea that a weak civil society might result from a weak rather than a strong state.[68] When a public sphere finally emerged late in the nineteenth century in this rural Bavarian province, it followed on a dramatic expansion of newspapers first set in motion by the Catholic Church.

At the level of intellectual history, the idea of "public reason" played an important role in the eighteenth-century transition from the older notion of societas civilis as a governed body of people to the new concept of civil society as outside the state. In a close reading of Immanuel Kant, Elisabeth Ellis shows how the idea of "publicity" mediated between questions of universal standards and practical politics. Kant offered a picture of civil society constituted as a public sphere. In the course of the French Revolution, his thinking about the public's disinterestedness and its role as the authoritative source of political judgement introduced an important divide between the communicative structures of civil society and the political process of the state. For Kant, as for Habermas, the public sphere sends signals to the state, but without immediate influence on political action. "What insulates the authority of the public sphere from the potentially corrupting influence of its practical effects," Ellis emphasizes, "is that, given the slow pace of reform, participants in the public sphere will be unable to observe any direct results of their suggestions."[69] This, then, is a different mechanism from that envisaged today, in which new social movements transmit issues of common interest via the public sphere with the distinct expectation of achieving quick reforms.

If Kant's civil society achieved its status as a separate public sphere by divorcing its universal interest in reason from the political claims of its social interests, a second European current was increasingly skeptical about "the public." This trend was particularly pronounced in the Scottish Enlightenment and reveals the danger of presuming a natural affinity between "public" and civil society. It is perhaps symbolized by the changing location of the "impartial spectator," the observer invoked by Adam Smith to explain how it was possible for individuals in increasingly complex commercial societies to think beyond the narrow confines of their own personal worlds. The ability to imagine oneself in someone else's shoes created reciprocal bonds of sympathy. Initially the impartial spectator had been presented as a universal feature located in public opinion, but in the sixth edition of *Theory of Moral Sentiments* in 1790 it became internalized within the self, a reversal that reflected growing doubts whether most people possessed the mental and emotional capacities for sympathy and, ultimately, civility.

Emotion and sociability, not universal reason and discursive communication, were the lifeblood of the most influential theories of civil society in the eighteenth century. Like contemporary theorists of the public sphere, eighteenth-century Scottish philosophers were preoccupied with the question of how an increasingly differentiated society managed to remain integrated and harmonious. Yet these philosophers' turn to sentiment and psychology rather than discursive theory meant they imagined civil society very differently. Instead of aspiring to create a consensual, public-oriented will through critical reason, Hutcheson and Hume turned to communication as a means of moral and emotional exchange, that fostered social bonds and friendships and cultivated manners and moral taste. This was not a world of lofty, disinterested individuals reasoning, but of people longing for moral and social approval, driven by sentiment and jealousy as much as intellect. Through social conversation, individuals were able to enter a common realm of moral judgements and refine their senses, affections, and benevolence, creating a harmonious network of social relations. Communication was relational, concerned with pleasing others and being admired, not with universal principles. The club established a cultural universe separate from the polity. Civil society's emphasis on emotional exchange rather than on critical reasoning or the public display of civic "virtue" was reflected in a more fluid treatment of private and nonprivate relations as mediums of sociability. Intimate bonds of love relationships and the civil manner of small talk merited as much attention as public debate.[70] While Smith and others recognized the need for a state and "police" as external checks on the imperfect workings of civil society, internally sociability was divorced from virtue and polity.[71] The *Tatler* and the *Patriot* spoke the language of sociability in articles about nonpolitical subjects in a variety of genres, from works of imagination to satires, from portraits to accounts of dreams. From this perspective, the Habermasian concern with a unified public sphere with a political will may well have more in common with civic humanism's older political language of virtue than with the new language of civil society, which turned away from an all-encompassing view of individuals as political animals to rediscover them as sociable beings with different tastes and moral judgements.

Whatever we think of the normative ideals of theories of the public sphere, from a historical perspective they fail to encompass much of the intellectual and cultural work of civil society. Sociability was the lifeblood of most clubs and associations, where members came to chat, play cards or billiards, listen to music or a reading, and make connections, as well as study the newspaper and discuss common affairs. Putting sociability rather than discursive communication at the center of analysis helps bring into sharper focus the prescriptive and often paternalistic dynamics of civil society. Civil society (then and now) not only functioned as a positive "warning system," recognizing social problems in the private world and transmitting them to the public. It was also a source of social power and cultural norms. Arguably, the outward-directed goals of politeness and creating a good impression, together with the emphasis on moral judges, from the outset infused sociability with paternalism. Civility, then, had costs as well as benefits, individually and collectively. The cult of politeness can be seen as one chapter in the larger civilizing process analyzed by Norbert Elias. Elias charted the growing concern with manners since the late Middle Ages and the parallel monopolization of violence by the state.[72] It is debatable, of course, whether modern civil society has seen a decline of violence, but his main observation, that a shift from physically expressive to mannered conduct held psychological consequences for individuals, remains significant. Politeness, the eighteenth-century language of civil society, required constant self-control and self-interrogation, partly for the sake of refining oneself, but partly to fulfill that other criteria of sociability, shaping one's behavior with a view to its effect on others. Examining oneself in the omnipresent mirror of civil society produced anxiety and confusion about identity.

If anxieties about one's own civility spurred individuals' quest for refinement through diaries or schemes of self-improvement, some of these doubts could be put to rest by demonstrating one's civility to other, less fortunate groups. Civil society lived by a certain psychological balance of trade. The persistence of violent forms of behavior, such as blood sports, and of entire alternative cultures gave middle-class associations the opportunity to mix benevolence with a reassurance of their own civility. Inevitably, such efforts did not stop at the door to the private sphere. In nineteenth-century Leeds, for example, the Infant School Society saw working-class parents as "lamentably incompetent to the great work of early intellectual culture and discipline," and a temperance society held that the "extirpation of intemperance amongst the operative classes would place them in a condition to receive cultivation analogous to that which soil presents to its first cultivator."[73] Housing reform movements, in particular, often ran roughshod over working-class culture and invaded the home itself to enforce new rules of behavior. That civil society has the potential to communicate social problems to the public, then, should not blind us to the ways in which associations and social movements themselves have posed threats to a private sphere, undermined social solidarities, and used civility in defiance of equality and impartiality.

Civil Society and Political Economy

If sociability became one way of imagining how civil society was able to recycle itself as an integrated system in relative autonomy from the state, it was complemented by another, that of political economy and its account of the self-regulating nature of the economy in a commercial society. It may be worth noting that, with a few exceptions,[74] political economy has lost this foundational position in the recent revival of the concept. There are political and ideological reasons for this marginalization. In Central Europe and Central and Latin America as well as in new social movements in the West, civil society was heralded as a post-Marxist alternative to global capitalism. As much as civil society here was antistate, so too was it antimarket, a point of view given considerable prominence by Havel, who advocated it as a way of transcending consumerism and totalitarianism.[75] Likewise, Habermasian theories, by linking civil society to the "lifeworld," tend to position it outside and against the systems of economy and state.[76] Instead of speaking of the "apolitical" thrust of the recent wave of civil society, it would be better to refer to its "apolitico-economic" outlook. This is doubly unfortunate, perhaps. For it has meant not only that the politico-economic dimension is undertheorized in accounts concerned with the present but also that it is frequently lost from sight as a dynamic force in the historical evolution of civil society. Yet, in addition to playing a crucial role in the conceptual history of civil society, political economy came to function as a kind of applied knowledge that helped transform socioeconomic realities. Most fundamentally, popular ideas of political economy were an important part of how social movements understood themselves and the past and future of civil society, and, through their actions, contributed to the relationship between state and economy. Good reasons exist, therefore, to reintegrate political economy into the study of the ideas and praxis of civil society.

In eighteenth-century theories of civil society, a striking symmetry is noticeable between sociability and a commercial economy as mechanisms of societal self-coordination. Just as politeness and conversation wove a web of mutual recognition and social trust, so the market came to be seen as a site of reciprocal interests and social learning. The market was a forum of social as well as capitalist exchange, in which people, through their material needs, were brought together in a type of communication that taught them a sense of themselves as well as respect for others. In his theoretical analysis of Hegel and Smith, Rupert Gordon shows the continued importance of the market as a noncoercive agency of social learning and self-cultivation, or Bildung, into the early nineteenth century.[77] To treat other people in a market exchange as means for satisfying one's own interests was also to recognize one's dependence on others. In this way, the market, like the association, was seen as a school teaching daily lessons about mutual recognition. If the "system of needs" instilled a mode of self-regulation in civil society, this did not mean it worked without generating social inequality and conflict. What it did mean, however, was that poverty could be conceptualized as a "social question," that is, as a collective problem *for* civil society, rather than as a purely material condition or fate concerning the individual.[78] The social reading of the market, then, endowed members of civil society with social rights and obligations.

The theoretical presentation of the economy as a self-regulating system based on market exchange and the division of labor had profound implications for the praxis of civil society. The pioneers of political economy consciously engaged in prescriptive science, seeking to make visible to legislators a pure system yet to be realized, rather than giving an account of present economic reality.[79] If the market identified by Smith did not yet exist, there emerged authorities, reared on political economy, who worked hard to establish it. Commercial society became the highest "natural" stage of historical development. This inevitably necessitated the interventionist reordering of social relations at home and in the empire to create a civil society that could work in accordance with the abstract principles of the market. In late-eighteenth-century London, to take just one example, the River Thames Police was set up to "realize" the true labor market held necessary for a well-ordered civil society and, in the process, came to determine who received wages and who was prosecuted for taking customary forms of payment, such as direct appropriations. Thus in the name of civil society, the first police force in London under central state authority was created. Applied political economy created a "civilizing" language that legitimated intervention for the sake of "human improvement" and at the same time identified older social customs as barriers to the realization of civil society and as expressions of the "unruly passions" and "rapacious desires" characteristic of "half savages."[80]

If the ideal of civil society was no mirror image of existing social relations, indeed, if it could be linked to the suppression of customary practices, how did the idea manage to maintain significant cross-class support well into the early twentieth century?

Historically, the interesting question is not so much that some theorists, like Marx, sought to expose the capitalist bourgeois base of civil society but that a more positive view remained popular. There were many middle-class initiatives, such as building and saving societies, to disseminate among the lower classes the economic virtues needed in a civil society. More telling than such efforts from above, however, is the popular debate about civil society and voluntarism among radical movements and new progressive and socialist groups in the second half of the nineteenth century. This debate reveals the possibility of endowing civil society with popular democratic visions and transcending its liberal connection with competitive capitalism.

Ideas of political economy and civil society were as tightly interwoven in popular culture as in high theory. Different understandings of the economy were connected to different views of social development in German and British popular radicalism. These, in turn, favored different political strategies toward other social and political groups and different constellations between civil society, state, and economy. In Hamburg, Madeleine Hurd's chapter shows, the social vision of the radical *Mittelstand* evolved around independent work and was anchored in the guild as the crucial agency of social cooperation and political education.[81] This vision favored corporate occupation over dependent wage labor, and it looked with suspicion toward the liberal program of separating civil society from polity and economy and establishing Free Trade. In Britain, by contrast, radicals and liberals joined forces around Free Trade, a union perhaps eased by the earlier disappearance of guilds but consummated through the language of consumption and civil society, as I argue in my chapter.[82] This envisaged a positive affinity between Free Trade and the democratizing influence of voluntary organizations and pictured Free Trade not as an agent of materialism but as an arrangement strengthening social trust and self-regulation within civil society and shielding it against the forces of oligarchy, bureaucracy, and large-scale organized capitalism. In contrast to the citizen-worker, British progressives imagined a "citizen-consumer."

There are, then, good reasons for being skeptical about approaches to civil society that see it entirely as outside or even opposed to economy and state. Rather than being antennae communicating social problems resulting from the impact of outside systems, social movements played an active role in shaping both the infrastructure of political economy and the workings of the economy itself, whether through the influence of the labor movement or the redistribution of income channeled through charity organizations. This has implications for our understanding of the changing place of civil society in the twentieth-century expansion of welfare state capitalism. As the chapters on British socialism and welfare provisions in Weimar and 1920s Britain suggest, national legacies of institutional structures and economic development played a role that was far from decisive, let alone deterministic. Mark Bevir's chapter highlights how different intellectual critiques of the market among British socialists structured their approaches to the institutional reconfiguration between state, society, and economy.[83] Whereas the Fabian critique of liberal political economy pointed toward statist reforms, ethical socialism favored a transformation of civil society from within, by substituting a cooperative spirit of love and equity for the erosive force of the market. For Imperial Germany, there can be little doubt about the highly modern features of the emerging welfare state, in which the industrial mentality of bureaucrats meant that social provision was tied to industrial capitalism.[84] Yet, as Deborah Cohen's chapter on disabled veterans after the First World War shows, the precise relationship between voluntarism and statism was neither fixed nor inherited but initially was fluid and ultimately was determined by the ideas and interests of the new democratic state. In contrast to the dominant role of voluntary societies in the treatment of disabled soldiers in Britain, in Weimar the state effectively eliminated the many philanthropic bodies that had sprung up during the war.[85] These different strategies of social reconstruction carried implications for the reconstruction of social trust and political legitimacy. Whereas voluntarism in Britain tied veterans to the rest of the public and shielded the British state from criticism, the statist monopoly in Germany, though offering better material terms, eroded social solidarities and politicized veteran groups into powerful critics of the new democratic state.

Voluntarism and statism were not exclusive national paths, however. For many Liberals and Laborites in early twentieth-century Britain, the future lay with a combination of state intervention and voluntary association—a "third way" that, in contrast to recently revived versions, included economics as well as social relations, as in the coexistence of nationalized industries with cooperative trade and market. For Philip Snowden, chancellor of the exchequer in the first two Labor governments (1924, 1929–31), the expansion of voluntary association followed an evolutionary law that proved people were associational beings and that cooperation and mutual aid ultimately won out over anarchic competition. There was no inherent conflict between state assistance and voluntary effort as long as state provisions were not simply doles or demoralizing charity from above that suppressed the necessary "sense of individual responsibility or the response of reciprocal effort from those upon whom the benefits are conferred."[86] The four million people in friendly societies with accumulated funds of £45 million, he emphasized, showed an increase of 25 percent since the Edwardian social reforms, evidence that state provisions could supplement voluntary organization and individual effort instead of displacing it.

Britain's transformation from the most voluntarist into the most statist welfare system in the 1940s and '50s underscores the contingency of state/civil society relations. It would be misleading, however, to see this as an illustration of some more general absolute decline of civil society. As in Germany, the number of voluntary associations in Britain today exceeds that of previous centuries and the voluntary sector remains large. Rather, several overlapping developments have undermined the independent function and autonomy of civil society as a central site of self-organization and social life. The expansion of commercial consumer culture started cutting into the instrumental function of many associations as cultural providers of sociability and entertainment, a trend that has been traced to the late nineteenth century.[87] Where civil society retained most of this function, it become divorced from general, public-oriented societies and attached to more particular lifestyle, identity, or single-issue movements, such as nature movements or Real Ale societies. The increasingly compartmentalized structure of civil society might also explain how participation in voluntary association has remained high while political engagement has been falling in recent decades. At the same time, as Jose Harris has put it, "the private self-governing pluralism of Victorian society" gave way to "the competitive client pluralism of the later twentieth century," where voluntary societies became coopted by the state or sought to control public provisions.[88] No doubt Snowden and Beveridge, the liberal father of the British welfare state constructed during the Second World War, would have been shocked to see Britain develop into the most centralized and statist social service system of all. But their insistence in the first half of the twentieth century on the need for calling in the state to assist voluntary agencies suggests that it is a dangerous fallacy today to presume a stark choice between civil society or a statist bureaucracy or to think that it is possible to revitalize civil society on the cheap without a commitment to state intervention in social and economic relations.

Religion, Nation, and Empire

Much of the recent focus on democracy and the public sphere has taken a domestic view from within what are deemed essentially "modern" societies. Not only do these approaches single out the secular, critical, and reflexive aspects of group relations, but, by favoring domestic perspectives in which the subject is located at the social grass roots and separate from state and economy, they make it difficult to analyze civil society in relation to large-scale, international phenomena. Let us now move toward a more macro-historical plane of interpretation to bring into view the interdependent relationship between religion and civil society and to situate it within the contemporaneous processes of nationalism and imperialism.

Well into the twentieth century, religion played a significant role in shaping the ideal of toleration and in providing the main setting of associational life, through churches, charities and missionary movements. On a larger scale, Charles Taylor has argued, the "bifocal" nature of Western Christendom was a distinctive factor favoring the development of civil society in Europe.[89] The concept of two swords (temporal and spiritual) made it easier to view society as distinct from politics. The peace of Westphalia (1648), which put an end to the Thirty Years War and religious strife, considerably improved the chances for civility. It would be overdeterministic, however, to view the final achievement of religious toleration as part of a sequence of Protestantism breeding modular man breeding civil society. Rather, here is an example of the importance of political skill in the evolution of civil society, a point Hall develops in his chapter. The passage of the Toleration Act in England in 1689, which applied to Dissenters (but not to Deists, Catholics, or Jews), was a very close shave.[90] What brought about the change was not a prior decline of antitoleration feelings, which remained strong into the early eighteenth century, but the necessities of *Realpolitik*. For William III, Jonathan Israel has argued, toleration was "something basically political" and had less to do with his Calvinism than with gathering the support of Dissenters and Catholics to the new crown.[91] If attacks on different believers did not suddenly stop, it was important that they no longer came from the state. Even English Catholics made the transition from oppressed minority to a patriotic part of the national community, a shift reflected in the increasingly popular choice of royal first names. Rather than growing out of a cultural shift, toleration was the result of political strategy, which set a new institutionalized frame for learning to live in peace with different denominations.

It is possible to find affinities between the cultural movement toward self and sociability, noted earlier, and the growing importance of associational life and religious developments in non-conformity in Britain and pietism in Germany from the late seventeenth century. The preoccupation with the individual self and the accompanying critique of ecclesiastical authority led to an emphasis on choice and free, voluntary gatherings. Pietism fostered a concern with sensibility, sentiment, and subjectivity, the three "S's" driving the new culture of sociability. How should we link the politics of toleration and the new religious culture of voluntary association in the history of civil society? Rather than simply joining forces in a combined attack on intolerance, Protestantism and associationalism together carved out an ever expanding universe for civil society while at the same making the boundaries of that universe more rigid, universalistic, and, for many groups, impermeable. An example of this ironic relationship can be found in Róisín Healy's examination of the debate about anti-Jesuit legislation in Imperial Germany, where religious intolerance was justified in the name of civil society.[92] Even in eighteenth-century Scotland, fear of fanaticism and arguments for difference were opposite sides of the same coin; Hume and Smith had little sympathy with associational self-government when it came to the Popular Party clergy, for they were convinced it would breed fanatical clergymen.[93] More generally, the marriage of thoughts about sin and salvation to the praxis of associational work turned the terrain of civil society into a testing ground for one's personal merit. Here, then, was a religious extension of the concern with outward "effect" characteristic of sociability. Within a voluntary group, it could encourage pressures for conformity rather than diversity, as the example of churches in colonial America amply testifies. For societies as a whole, the attainment of civility could encourage a paternalistic rather than pluralist attitude. It stimulated a never-ending search for "barbaric" practices from which civil society needed to be purged. The rhetoric of sin reinforced a hierarchical notion of contempt for groups outside civil society; indeed, reformers like Francis Place justified contempt as an incentive to advancement.[94] The pursuit of civility and the conversion of deviant lifestyles became mutually reinforcing, a trend that reached its peak with the belief that salvation was conditional, a belief that underlay evangelicalism, probably the single most powerful source of associational activism and societal reform and self-management in the Victorian period.

To recognize religion as an integral part of the modern history of civil society, then, puts a large question mark behind teleological accounts culminating in the progress of liberal democracy or "defensive" social movements practicing the secular art of "critique." For John Locke, the most famous advocate of toleration, civil society and belief in God were inseparable: to lack faith was to lack the ability to trust in human association—toleration, consequently, did not extend to atheists. Putting religion back into the study of civil society undermines the conventional thematization and periodization of the subject along the "modern" divide of the eighteenth-century. As Dominique Colas has argued, the preoccupation with the then-emerging conceptual separation of society from state deflects from an important continuity between modern and premodern thought: the opposition between civil society and fanaticism. This conceptual divide played an important role in the Reformation, informing Martin Luther's violent attacks on anabaptists and peasant rebels as fanatics who sought to overcome the distinction between the City of God and the Earthly City, thus challenging the divinely designed existence of civil society. The defense of civil society and its temporal laws, authority, and language against fanaticism, with its repression of all forms of representation and mediation, was in this case achieved at a tremendous cost of human slaughter. Yet, looked at from a long-term perspective, Colas uncovers a line of continuity between social movements' attacks on totalitarianism in the late twentieth century and earlier battles against fanaticism, for both were directed against enemies of "representation"—in the first case, the iconoclastic destruction of visual representation, in the latter, statist denials of the independent mediating function of political representation. In the *longue durée*, the conceptual pairing that emerges here is one linking civil society to a law-governed state, protecting the civil rights of its members against totalizing visions seeking to erase social spaces of representation and mediation.[95]

* * * *

IN THIS BROAD VIEW, what place should be accorded in this broad view to the rise of associations in relation to the rise of the modern state, a transformation that produced a fiscal-military imperial state in eighteenth-century Britain and nationalism and nation-state in Germany (1866–71)? Dahrendorf has stressed that civil societies remain "imperfect" as long as they are situated within national boundaries,[96] but this leaves open the question of the historical relationship between civil society and nationalism. One way to approach this question is to ask about historical sequence. As Hall emphasizes in this volume, it made a big difference that England had become an unitary state in the Middle Ages, whereas in modern Germany nationalism continued to "override civil politics."[97] This picture becomes more complicated, however, if we look beyond England to the making of *British* identity and even more so if we look at the frequent overlap between associations and nationalism. Again, it is necessary to recall the distinction between the space for pluralism afforded by civil society and the actual beliefs and practices of voluntary associations. On one hand, after the First World War, new internationalists looked toward civil society and transnational organizations as a way of taming nationalism by separating political citizenship from national identity— anticipating aspects of the more recent theoretical debate.[98] On the other hand, the opposition between nationalist ideology and local, nontotalizing views of the world within associations can be exaggerated. Modern Britain and Germany offered spaces for clubs conversing in Gaelic, Hebrew, or local dialect, but an even larger number of associations worked toward a more homogenous national identity. Language societies like the *Sprachgesellschaften* were vehicles of cultural nationalism committed to stamping out foreign words, Latin and dialect alike.[99] For Scottish Enlightenment thinkers, civil society went hand in hand with contempt for Kirk and Highland culture. Theirs was a project of "cultural manipulation," in John Dwyer's words, seeking to replace traditional identities with "a new vision of a harmonious, if hegemonic, British community."[100] In this sense, the language of civility functioned as a source of political stability, integrating new elites into the union between Scotland and England (1707) by promoting a new type of cultural homogeneity.

Adam Ferguson was keenly aware of this complex interplay when he observed in 1767 that "Without the rivalship of nations, and the practice of war, civil society itself could scarcely have found an object, or a form."[101] The need for national security created new public openings for talent. National rivalries prompted emulation. Patriotism created bonds of sympathy between private rivals. Without endorsing this positive evaluation, there is something to be said for viewing the agencies of civil society and nation-state as frequently reinforcing each other, not least because associations created a national infrastructure for communication and for imagining nationality, manifest in the German choral societies or the notion of muscular Christianity disseminated in England. Again, there are

countless illustrations of our earlier thesis that the broadening of
the space for societal self-organization and pluralism went hand
in hand with the drawing of more rigid boundaries of exclusion
and intolerance for outsiders. The late-nineteenth-century proliferation of anti-Semitic associations in Germany and chauvinist
militarist movements in Britain is well known, but it would be
wrong to see these entirely as pathological mutations from the
naturally pluralist or discursive path of civil society. In Britain,
the notion of civility was always buttressed by a fear of the violent
Irish. In Prussia during the Napoleonic wars, the newly founded
Deutsche Tischgesellschaft worked for the exclusion of Jews and
women from associational life. And a century earlier the Beefsteak
Club had organized a public fireworks display, in honor of Queen
Anne's birthday, portraying the bloody defeat of the French.[102]

Situating civil society in the context of empire, national identity,
and evangelicalism, then, provides a broader and more critical
standpoint for the comparison of Germany and Britain than that
offered by inquiries focused on the Sonderweg. These have been
preoccupied with the relative progress of liberal constitutionalism, a perspective that has often created an idealized children's
book image of "liberal England," blending out the interplay between imperial relations and domestic dynamics of inclusion and
exclusion. In fact, it is difficult to make sense of the comparative
nature of political culture without bringing together the domestic
and imperial dynamics of civil society. In the first place, as we
have seen, the project of civil society had an outward-directed
momentum that inspired efforts at conversion of the "sinner" and
"brute," both at home and abroad. Civil society became an export
staple. Members of Bible societies in early nineteenth-century
Britain were told that Hindus and Muslims were simply waiting
to be Christianized, the first step in a civilising mission. In the following decades the empire was perhaps the major setting for the
double-sided working of associational life. The imperial mission
offered greater self-organization and public empowerment to
those seeking to rise above their inferior position at home, but this
domestic emancipatory momentum was inextricably part of the
replication of hierarchy, inequality, and exclusion in social relations within the empire. In his discussion of foreign missions,
Steven Maughan unravels the interplay between evangelical religion, imperial opportunities, and domestic gender relations that
led to a dramatic extension of women's role in late-nineteenth-
century Britain.[103] Evangelical theology, fixated on gendered ideals
of respectability and separate spheres, assigned to Christian women

an important role in the improvement of manners and morals and came to legitimate spiritual work outside the home. Many Victorian women achieved a greater role in associational life through the missionary campaign to "regenerate" the family in the colonies, a task that involved the suppression of non-Western cultural practices. The empire occupied a central place in the imagination of women's movements in Europe before the First World War. In Germany, the debate about mixed race relationships in Southwest Africa offered a platform for many women to support their demands for more public rights by pointing to the special imperial contribution played by German colonial women, saviors of the German race from the unhealthy and barbaric family practices of African women.[104] British feminism was predicated on a cultural imperialism that invoked what Josephine Butler described in 1900 as Britain's "Christian and civilising power" and pictured a collective "Indian woman," a passive object silently waiting to be freed from the chains of barbarism by her more advanced metropolitan sister.[105]

* * * *

VICTORIAN FEMINISM'S EFFORTLESS COMBINATION of cultural imperialism, expanding self-organization, and demands for greater civil rights and equal sexual morality at home brings us back to the general problematic of the paradoxical historical relationship between the associational praxis and theoretical idea of civil society. There is no straight line between the number of voluntary associations and the level of plurality, social trust, and democratic engagement. Instead of abstracting universal norms and behaviors from common institutional features, a necessary first step in histories of civil society should be to situate associations in their social, political, and imperial contexts and to reconnect the internal culture of the clubroom to the external attitudes of its members toward the rest of society and the rest of the world. Bringing together theoretical and historical perspectives around the issues of association and democracy, public sphere and sociability, political economy and religion, nation and empire has offered some axes of interpretation for exploring the interplay between inclusion and exclusion, societal self-regulation and policing, plurality and conformity, and tolerance and intolerance. It is important to stress that these tensions were partly internal features of associational life and the idea of sociability. They were not simply manifestations of problems generated outside civil society. Civil society has not been some kind of Ur-democracy with the potential to act as a panacea for contemporary ills if developed at a distance from the evils of media culture, bureaucratic politics, and modern capitalism. The recognition of the contingent political and cultural dynamics of civil society may be distasteful to some current prophets. Yet it should not leave behind a sense of fatalism. Unlike totalizing ideologies, civil society worked as a fluid arrangement that, in addition to fostering conformity or inequality in some groups, also provided openings for challenges to insularity, intolerance, and discrimination. If it is illusory to hope that the paradox of civil society will ever be resolved, critical study can be helpful for revealing to us historical moments in which societal self-organization tended toward more, rather than less, civility.

Notes

1. Elaine Katzenberger, ed., *First World, Ha, Ha, Ha! The Zapatista Challenge* (San Francisco, 1995), 134f. Dietrich Schwanitz, *Der Campus* (Frankfurt a.M., 1995).
2. See Robert D. Putnam with Robert Leonardi and Raffaella Y. Nanetti, *Making Democracy Work: Civic Traditions in Modern Italy* (Princeton, 1993); Putnam "Bowling Alone: America's Declining Social Capital," *Journal of Democracy*, 6 (1995), 65–78.
3. Ernest Gellner, *Conditions of Liberty: Civil Society and Its Rivals* (London, 1994), 97ff.
4. Václav Havel, *The Power of the Powerless: Citizens against the State in Central-Eastern Europe* (London, 1985).
5. Joshua Cohen and Joel Rogers, eds., *Associations and Democracy* (London, 1995); Paul Hirst, *Associative Democracy: New Forms of Economic and Social Governance* (Amherst, 1994).
6. For the most substantive discussion in terms of a strict separation between civil society and economy, elaborating on Habermas, see Jean L. Cohen and Andrew Arato, *Civil Society and Political Theory* (Cambridge, MA, 1992).
7. Gary Brent Madison, *The Political Economy of Civil Society and Human Rights* (London, 1997); Augustus R. Norton, ed., *Civil Society in the Middle East* (Leiden, 1995); D. Strand "Protest in Beijing: Civil Society and Public Sphere in China," *Problems of Communism* 39 (May–June, 1990): 1–19; Deborah S. Davis et al., eds., *Urban Spaces in Contemporary China* (Cambridge, 1995); E. Gyimah-Boadi, "Civil Society in Africa," *Journal of Democracy* 7 (1996): 118–32; Chris Hann and Elizabeth Dunn, eds., *Civil Society: Challenging Western Models* (London, 1996).
8. Chris Hann, "Introduction," in Hann and Dunn, *Civil Society*, 1.
9. Keith Tester, *Civil Society* (London, 1992), 8.
10. See, e.g., the conceptual stretch in an interesting recent survey of civil society in modern Germany, which begins with Kant and ends with chapters on Nazi

Germany and the Holocaust: Lutz Niethammer, ed., *Bürgerliche Gesellschaft in Deutschland: historische Einblicke, Fragen, Perspektiven* (Frankfurt a.M., 1990).

11. See John Hall, "Reflections on the Making of Civility in Society," ch. 1 in this volume. See also John Hall, "Genealogies of Civility," in *Democratic Civility: The History and Cross-Cultural Possibility of a Modern Political Ideal*, ed. Robert W. Hefner (New Brunswick, 1998): 53–77.

12. Karl Ludwig von Haller, *Restauration der Staats-Wissenschaft* (1816), cited in James Van Horn Melton, "The Emergence of 'Society' in Eighteenth- and Nineteenth- Century Germany," in *Language, History and Class, ed.* P. J. Corfield (Oxford, 1991), 139.

13. This has not prevented spokespersons from claiming it as theirs alone or from reducing it to little more than a negative alter ego of their own utopia; if Ralf Dahrendorf's recent celebration of civil society as providing "the lifeblood of liberty" is a liberal echo of the first, Karl Marx's critique of the separate constitution of political society as part and parcel of the dissolution of civil society into egotistical bourgeois individuals, alienated from their own humanity as well as their community, remains the most powerful example of the latter. Ralf Dahrendorf, *After 1989: Morals, Revolution and Civil Society* (New York, 1997), 51. Karl Marx, "On the Jewish Question" (1844), in *Marx: Early Political Writings*, ed. J. O'Malley (Cambridge, 1994), 28–50.

14. See John Gray, *Post-Liberalism* (London, 1993), chs. 12, 14; Ernesto Laclau and Chantal Mouffe, *Hegemony and Socialist Strategy: Towards a Radical Democratic Politics* (London, 1985); Michael Walzer, "The Concept of Civil Society," in Walzer, ed., *Toward a Global Civil Society* (Oxford and Providence, RI, 1995), 7–27; John Keane, ed., *Civil Society and the State: New European Perspectives* (London, 1988), and John A. Hall, ed., *Civil Society: Theory, History, Comparison* (Cambridge, 1995).

15. John Keane, *Civil Society: Old Images, New Visions* (London, 1999); I would like to thank John Keane for sharing an earlier draft with me.

16. Manfred Riedel, "Gesellschaft, bürgerliche," in *Geschichtliche Grundbegriffe*, eds. O. Brunner, W. Conze, R. Koselleck (Stuttgart, 1975), II: 719–800; cf. John Keane, "Despotism and Democracy: The Origins and Development of the Distinction between Civil Society and the State 1750–1850," in *Civil Society and the State*, ed. Keane, 35–71; Istvan Hont and Michael Ignatieff, eds., *Wealth and Virtue: the Shaping of Political Economy in the Scottish Enlightenment* (Cambridge, 1983); Hans Medick, *Naturzustand und Naturgeschichte der bürgerlichen Gesellschaft: Die Ursprünge der bürgerlichen Sozialtheorie als Geschichtsphilosophie und Sozialwissenschaft bei Samuel Pufendorf, John Locke und Adam Smith* (Göttingen, 1973); Adam B. Seligman, *The Idea of Civil Society* (Princeton, 1992); Charles Taylor, "Invoking Civil Society" in Taylor, *Philosophical Arguments* (Cambridge, MA, 1995), 202–24.

17. For Britain, the best studies from this perspective are R. J. Morris, *Class, Sect, and Party: The Making of the British Middle Class, Leeds 1820–1850* (Manchester, 1990) and Leonore Davidoff and Catherine Hall, *Family Fortunes: Men and Women of the English Middle Class, 1780–1850* (Chicago, 1987).

18. Lothar Gall, ed. *Vom alten zum neuen Bürgertum: Die mitteleuropäische Stadt im Umbruch 1780–1820* (Munich, 1991).

19. Jürgen Kocka and Allan Mitchell, eds., *Bourgeois Society in Nineteenth-Century Europe* (Oxford, 1993); Kocka, ed., *Bürgertum im 19. Jahrhundert: Deutschland im europäischen Vergleich*, 3 vols. (Munich, 1988); H.-J. Puhle, ed., *Bürger in der Gesellschaft der Neuzeit: Wirtschaft—Politik—Kultur* (Göttingen, 1991). Cf.

Jonathan Sperber, "Bürger, Bürgertum, Bürgerlichkeit, Bürgerliche Gesellschaft: Studies of the German (Upper) Middle Class and Its Sociocultural World," *Journal of Modern History* 69 (1997): 271–97; Utz Haltern, "Die Gesellschaft der Bürger," *Geschichte und Gesellschaft* 19 (1993): 100–34.

20. Lothar Gall, e.g., speaks jointly of "Bürgertum, bürgerliche Gesellschaft," *Bürgertum in Deutschland* (Berlin, 1989), 80, see also 382ff.

21. See, e.g., the liberal and bourgeois criteria underlying Kocka's use of civil society in "The European Pattern and the German Case," in *Bourgeois Society*, eds. Kocka and Mitchell, 9, 17ff., 32. For an early critique of the mythical tie between liberal politics and bourgeoisie, see David Blackbourn and Geoff Eley, *The Peculiarities of German History: Bourgeois Society and Politics in Nineteenth-Century Germany* (Oxford, 1984); and, more recently, Geoff Eley, "German History and the Contradictions of Modernity: The Bourgeoisie, the State, and the Mastery of Reform," in *Society, Culture, and the State in Germany, 1870–1930*, ed. Eley (Ann Arbor, 1996), 67–103.

22. See Putnam, "Bowling Alone" and *Making Democracy Work*; Michael J. Sandel, *Democracy's Discontent: America in Search of a Public Philosophy* (Cambridge, MA, 1996); cf. the critical discussions in: Robert Kuttner, ed., *Ticking Time Bombs* (New York, 1996); Keane, *Civil Society*; Amy Gutmann, ed., *Freedom of Association* (Princeton, 1998); *Politics & Society* 24, no. 1 (March 1996). For associations as a crucial medium in the moral development of the individual, see also John Rawls, *A Theory of Justice* (Cambridge, MA, 1971), 471 f.

23. Margaret Llewelyn Davies, *Women as Organised Consumers* (Manchester, 1921), 8; for many it was a stepping-stone to local government and other types of civic engagement.

24. Herbert Freudenthal, *Vereine in Hamburg: Ein Beitrag zur Geschichte und Volkskunde der Geselligkeit* (Hamburg, 1968), 246. My discussion of associational life has especially drawn on the following: Peter Clark, *Sociability and Urbanity: Clubs and Societies in the Eighteenth Century City* (Leicester, 1986); Otto Dann, ed., *Lesegesellschaften und bürgerliche Emanzipation: Ein europäischer Vergleich* (Munich, 1981); Dann, ed., *Vereinswesen und bürgerliche Gesellschaft in Deutschland* (Munich, 1984); R. van Dülmen, *Die Gesellschaft der Aufklärer: Zur Bürgerlichen Emanzipation und aufklärerischen Kultur in Deutschland* (Frankfurt a. M., 1986). É. François, ed., *Sociabilité et Société Bourgeoise en France, en Allemagne et en Suisse, 1750–1850* (Paris, 1986); Gall, *Vom alten zum neuen Bürgertum*; W. Hardtwig, *Genossenschaft, Sekte, Verein in Deutschland* (Munich, 1997); Brian Harrison, *Peaceable Kingdom: Stability and Change in Modern Britain* (Oxford, 1982); D. Hein and A. Schulz, ed., *Bürgerkultur im 19. Jahrhundert: Bildung, Kunst und Lebenswelt* (Munich, 1996); E. Hellmuth, ed. *The Transformation of Political Culture: England and Germany in the Late Eighteenth Century* (Oxford, 1990); U. Im Hof, *Das gesellige Jahrhundert*; M. C. Jacob, *Living the Enlightenment: Freemasonry and Politics in Eighteenth-Century Europe* (Oxford, 1991); Paul Langford, *Polite and Commercial People: England, 1727–1783* (Oxford, 1989); R. J. Morris, 'Clubs, Societies and Associations' in *The Cambridge Social History of Britain, 1750–1950*, ed. F.M.L. Thompson (Cambridge, 1990), III: 395–443; R. J. Morris, *Class, Sect, and Party*; Nipperdey, "Verein"; Frank Prochaska, 'Philanthropy' in *Cambridge Social History*, III: 357–93.

25. John Brewer, *The Pleasures of the Imagination* (New York, 1997); Hein and Schulz, *Bürgerkultur*.

26. Robert Beachy, "Club Culture and Social Authority: Freemasonry in Leipzig, 1741–1830," ch. 6 in this volume.

27. Ralf Roth, "'...der blühende Handel macht uns alle glücklich...': Frankfurt am Main in der Umbruchszeit 1780–1852," in Gall, *Vom alten zum neuen Bürgertum*, 405f. There are regional variations, of course. In Wetzlar in the 1790s, e.g., the charitable Gemeinnützige Gesellschaft was opening up to artisans, who came to represent one-third of members (Hans-Werner Hahn, "Aufbruchsdebatte und Krise: Die Stadt Wetzlar," in Gall, *Vom alten zum neuen Bürgertum*, 296), but this was highly unrepresentative.

28. Clark, *Sociability and Urbanity*, 7; Morris, "Clubs," 417.

29. See Kathleen Wilson, "Urban Culture and Political Activism in Hanoverian England: The Example of Voluntary Hospitals," in Hellmuth, *Transformation of Political Culture*, 165–84; Clark, *Sociability and Urbanity*, 17f.; Morris, "Clubs," 403ff.

30. Prochaska, "Philanthropy," 358ff.

31. Burke, *Reflections on the Revolution in France [1790]*, ed. J.G.A. Pocock (Indianapolis, 1987), 52. For the following, see A. Mitchell, "The Association Movement of 1792–1793," in *Historical Journal* 4 (1961): 56–77; Linda Colley, *Britons: Forging the Nation, 1707–1837* (New Haven, 1992); and the loyalist primary sources in Gregory Claeys, ed., *Political Writings of the 1790s*, VII (London, 1995).

32. Jacob, *Living the Enlightenment*, 9; the unfortunate slipping back and forth between "civic" and "civil" reflects a confusion between the older political- and community-oriented outlook of civic humanism and the new Enlightenment language of civil society concerned with wealth and sociability.

33. See John Money, "Freemasonry and the Fabric of Loyalism in Hanoverian England," in Hellmuth, *Transformation of Political Culture*, 235–71; Jacob, *Living the Enlightenment*, 17f., 156.

34. von Dülmen, *Gesellschaft der Aufklärer*, 56ff.; Hardtwig, *Genossenschaft*, 309ff. Not all lodges were blind to confessional background.

35. As Hardtwig has shown for Germany in *Genossenschaft*, several medieval and early modern bodies pioneered individual aspects of free associations. Local societies of *Vertraute* (confidants) were forerunners of self-help relief organizations and fused associational and corporate elements; they were self-governing bodies with free membership but based on familial ties of cooptation. The *Schützengesellschaften* anticipated voluntary membership and held meetings that cut across estate, but they remained limited to citizens.

36. Spence's friendship with Whig engraver Thomas Bewick, whom he first met at the Newcastle Philosophical Society, included an incidence in which, as Brewer writes, "their differences led to a fight with cudgels in which the strongly built engraver gave the slender radical a terrible drubbing," *Pleasures of the Imagination*, 508.

37. See Lothar Gall, "Vom alten zum neuen Bürgertum," and Michael Sobania, "Das Aachener Bürgertum am Vorabend der Industrialisierung," in Gall, *Vom alten zum neuen Bürgertum*, 15, 225.

38. Cited in Michael Sobania's chapter in Hein and Schulz, *Bürgerkultur*, 175 (my translation).

39. Davidoff and Hall, *Family Fortunes*, 423f.

40. Morris, "Clubs," 413.

41. Katherine Wilson, *The Sense of the People: Politics, Culture, and Imperialism in England, 1715–1785* (Cambridge, 1995), 219ff.; Brewer, *Pleasures of the Imagination*, 41.

42. See Mary Catherine Moran, "'The Commerce of the Sexes': Gender and the Social Sphere in Scottish Enlightenment Accounts of Civil Society,'" ch. 2 in this volume.
43. Davidoff and Hall, *Family Fortunes*, 426; Jacob, *Living the Enlightenment*, 120ff.
44. Deborah Hertz, *Jewish High Society in Old Regime Berlin* (New Haven, 1988).
45. Anna Clark, *The Struggle for the Breeches: Gender and the Making of the British Working Class* (Berkeley, 1995), 34ff.
46. For the following, see Davidoff and Hall, *Family Fortunes*, ch. 10; A. Tyrrell, "'Women's Mission' and Pressure Group Politics in Britain (1825–60)," *Bulletin of John Rylands University Library* 63 (1980): 194–230; Freudenthal, *Vereine*.
47. Davidoff and Hall, *Family Fortunes*, 434.
48. Isabel V. Hull, *Sexuality, State, and Civil Society in Germany, 1700–1815* (Ithaca, 1996).
49. Clark, *Struggle for the Breeches*; Eugenio Biagini, *Liberty, Retrenchment and Reform* (Cambridge, 1992), ch. 3; James Vernon, ed., *Re-reading the Constitution* (Cambridge, 1996). For the portrayal of women as strikebreakers and wage-cutters in German trades unions, see Kathleen Canning, "Gender and the Politics of Class Formation: Rethinking German Labour History," in Eley, *Society, Culture, and the State in Germany*, 130f.
50. See Daniel A. McMillan, "Energy, Willpower and Harmony: On the Problematic Relationship between State and Civil Society in Nineteenth-Century Germany," ch. 7 in this volume.
51. Walzer, "Concept of Civil Society," 16. Walzer since has emphasized that many people join associations that reinforce, rather than transcend, the identities inherited through "involuntary associations," such as nation, family, or religion, see his essay in Gutmann, *Freedom of Association*. My argument here, however, is about the ways in which associations can coalesce to create patterns of domination across groups, rather than the way in which individual associations tend to exclude members from their own group.
52. Dahrendorf, *After 1989*, 51, 56.
53. Brian Harrison, *Peaceable Kingdom: Stability and Change in Modern Britain* (Oxford, 1982).
54. See Christopher G. A. Bryant, "Civic Nation, Civil Society, Civil Religion," in Hall, *Civil Society*, 145.
55. Walzer, "Concept of Civil Society," 26.
56. "Deutschland, heil'ges Land der Liebe, dir gilt unser heisses Mueh'n. Moeg aus deiner Soehne Triebe gluecklich neues Leben bluehn," cited in Freudenthal, *Vereine*, 539 (my translation).
57. There is little historical evidence to support the neo-Tocquevillian argument for a correlation between the degree of face-to-face contact in clubs and civic-mindedness. As Daniel A. Bell has shown, the most prevalent type of intimate association in America today is that of the 150,000 Residential Community Associations which tend to erode a commitment to common goods; see Bell, "Civil Society versus Civil Virtue," in Gutmann, *Freedom of Association*, 239–72.
58. Mrs. Layton, "Memories of Seventy Years," in *Life as We Have Known It by Co-operative Working Women*, ed. M. Llewelyn Davies (London 1931), 40.
59. See Julia Roos, "Prostitutes, Civil Society, and the State in Weimar Germany," ch. 11 in this volume.
60. Keane, *Civil Society*, 60ff.
61. Jürgen Habermas, *Faktizität und Geltung: Beiträge zur Diskurstheorie des Rechts und des demokratischen Rechtsstaats* (Frankfurt a.M.,1992), ch. 8; Habermas, *The Structural Transformation of the Public Sphere* (1962, English 1989).

62. Craig Calhoun, ed., *Habermas and the Public Sphere* (Cambridge, MA, 1992); Keane, *Civil Society*; Belinda Davis, "Reconsidering Habermas, Gender, and the Public Sphere: The Case of Wilhelmine Germany," in Eley, *Society, Culture, and the State in Germany*, 397–426.

63. Habermas, *Faktizität und Geltung*, 435; English: *Between Facts and Norms* (1996).

64. Habermas, *Faktizität und Geltung*, 443ff; Cohen and Arato, *Civil Society and Political Theory*, part III.

65. Klaus Eder "Contradictions and Social Evolution," in *Social Change and Modernity*, eds. Hans Haferkamp and Neil J. Smelser (Berkeley, 1992), 320–49.

66. Clark, *Sociability and Urbanity*, 20f.; Brewer, *Pleasures of the Imagination*, 34ff.

67. See Ian McNeely, "The Intelligence Gazette (*Intelligenzblatt*) as a Road Map to Civil Society: Information Networks and Local Dynamism in Germany, 1770s–1840s," ch. 5 in this volume.

68. See John Abbot, "The Village Goes Public: Peasants and Press in Nineteenth-Century Altbayern," ch. 9 in this volume.

69. See Elisabeth Ellis, "Immanuel Kant's Two Theories of Civil Society," ch. 4 in this volume.

70. John Dwyer and Richard B. Sher, eds., *Sociability and Society in Eighteenth-Century Scotland* (Edinburgh, 1993).

71. For this shift in the Scottish Enlightenment, see Hont and Ignatieff, *Wealth and Virtue*.

72. Norbert Elias, *The Civilizing Process: The History of Manners and State Formation and Civilization* (Oxford, 1994).

73. Cited in Morris, *Class, Sect, and Party*, 164, 251.

74. Hall, *Civil Society*; R. Fine and S. Rai, eds., *Civil Society: Democratic Perspectives* (London, 1997).

75. Havel, "Power of the Powerless."

76. Habermas, *Faktizität und Geltung*; Cohen and Arato, *Civil Society*.

77. See Rupert H. Gordon, "Kant, Smith, and Hegel: The Market and the Categorical Imperative," ch. 3 in this volume.

78. As Hegel noted in a comparative observation, a sense of self-respect and rights distinguished material from social deprivation: "In England, even the poorest man believes he has his rights; this differs from what the poor are content with in other countries. Poverty in itself does not reduce people to a rabble; a rabble is created only by the disposition associated with poverty, by inward rebellion against the rich, against society, the government, etc." G. W. F. Hegel, *Elements of the Philosophy of Right* [1821], ed. Allen W. Wood (Cambridge, 1991), §244, p. 266.

79. Adam Smith's use of numbers, as Mary Poovey has recently elaborated, articulated a "double understanding of nature": the "numbers he wanted the legislator to use in the *Wealth of Nations* … described what the market *could* be if legislators left it alone. The numbers actually available to Smith, however, described an *unnatural* state of affairs, in which the true nature of the market had not been allowed to realize itself." Poovey, *A History of the Modern Fact: Problems of Knowledge in the Sciences of Wealth and Society* (Chicago, 1998), 246f.

80. Patrick Colquhoun, a writer on police and agent of West Indian planters, and Elliott, cited in Peter Linebaugh, *The London Hanged: Crime and Civil Society in the Eighteenth Century* (Cambridge, 1997), 428, 432. For applied political economy, see also William M. Reddy, *The Rise of Market Culture: The Textile Trade and French Society, 1750–1900* (Cambridge, 1984).

81. See Madeleine Hurd, "Oligarchs, Liberals, and *Mittelstand*: Defining Civil Society in Hamburg, 1858–1862," ch. 12 in this volume. For a different approach, see Christiane Eisenberg, "Working Class and Middle-Class Associations: an Anglo-German Comparison, 1820–1870," in Kocka and Mitchell, *Bourgeois Society*, 151–78.

82. See Frank Trentmann, "Civil Society, Commerce, and the 'Citizen-Consumer': Popular Meanings of Free Trade in Modern Britain," ch. 13 in this volume.

83. See Mark Bevir, "Socialism, Civil Society, and the State in Modern Britain," ch. 14 in this volume.

84. See George Steinmetz, "The Myth of an Autonomous State: Industrialists, Junkers, and Social Policy in Imperial Germany," in Eley, *Society, Culture, and the State in Germany*, 257–318; Jürgen Kocka, "Capitalism and Bureaucracy in German Industrialisation before 1914," *Economic History Review* 33 (1981): 453–68.

85. See Deborah Cohen, "Civil Society in the Aftermath of the Great War: The Care of Disabled Veterans in Britain and Germany," ch. 15 in this volume.

86. Philip Snowden, *The Faith of a Democrat* (London, 1928), 13. See also Jose Harris, "Political Thought and the Welfare State 1870–1914," *Past and Present* 135 (1992): 116–41.

87. S. Yeo, *Religion and Voluntary Organisations in Crisis* (London, 1976).

88. Jose Harris, "State and Society in the Twentieth Century," in *Cambridge Social History of Britain*, ed. Thompson, III, 114.

89. Taylor, "Invoking Civil Society," 211.

90. For the following, see O. Grell, J. Israel, and N. Tyacke, eds., *From Persecution to Toleration* (Oxford 1991).

91. Jonathan Israel in *From Persecution to Toleration*, eds. Grell, Israel, and Tyacke (Oxford 1991), 130.

92. See Róisín Healy, "Religion and Civil Society: Catholics, Jesuits, and Protestants in Imperial Germany," ch. 10 in this volume.

93. John Dwyer, "Introduction," in Dwyer and Sher, *Sociability*, 11 f.

94. See Harrison, *Peaceable Kingdom*, 252.

95. Dominique Colas, *Civil Society and Fanaticism: Conjoined Histories* (Stanford, 1997). For John Locke, see his *A Letter Concerning Toleration* (London, 1689), 45–48.

96. Dahrendorf, *After 1989*, 29.

97. See John A. Hall, "Reflections on the Making of Civility in Society," ch. 1 in this volume.

98. See Frank Trentmann, "The Erosion of Free Trade: Political Culture and Political Economy in Great Britain, c. 1897–1932" (Ph.D. thesis, Harvard University, 1999), chs. 5, 6. See also Keane, *Civil Society*, 102ff.

99. Van Dülmen, *Gesellschaft der Aufklärer*, 44.

100. Dwyer, "Introduction," 6.

101. Adam Ferguson, *An Essay on the History of Civil Society* [1767], ed. F. Oz-Salzberger (Cambridge, 1995), 28.

102. Clark, *Sociability and Urbanity*, 20; Hertz, *Jewish High Society in Berlin*, 268ff.

103. See Steven S. Maughan, "Civic Culture, Women's Foreign Missions, and the British Imperial Imagination, 1860–1914," ch. 8 in this volume.

104. Lora Wildenthal, "'She is the Victor': Bourgeois Women, Nationalist Identities, and the Ideal of the Independent Woman Farmer in German Southwest Africa," in Eley, *Society, Culture, and the State in Germany*, 371–96.

105. Cited in Antoinette Burton, *Burdens of History: British Feminists, Indian Women, and Imperial Culture, 1865–1915* (Chapel Hill, 1994), 153.

1

REFLECTIONS ON THE MAKING
OF CIVILITY IN SOCIETY

John A. Hall

THE MOST FREQUENT CRITICISM directed against the concept of civil society so much in use in recent years is that it lacks precision.[1] There is a good deal of truth to this charge. One indication is the fact that the works of Jürgen Habermas and Robert Putnam have come to be invoked in discussions of civil society.[2] This is dangerous in the case of the German thinker, given the very particular concerns of his philosophy; it is entirely licentious in the latter case, since the tradition of civic virtue to which the American political scientist appeals stands in direct opposition to the basic ethic of such classical theorists of civil society as Montesquieu and Spinoza. More importantly, there has been much confusion on the issue of whether civil society is an aspiration or a sociological condition. While the notion has both a normative appeal and a characteristic—albeit weak—set of sociological foundations, it is indeed troubling that hope has tended to replace analysis. It is perhaps useful for the reader to bear this crucial point in mind while considering the use of the term in the impressive essays by young historians and theorists assembled here. Is a concept being applied, or perhaps misapplied, to the past as the result of current political fashion? Or is the term merely neutral, an aseptic tool that lets the historical record speak for itself?

Given this lack of precision in the recent debate about civil society, there is a great deal to be said for offering a straightforward theory of civil society as an alternative to tracing the twists and turns of an intellectual debate that has often been misguided.[3] I make no claim that alternative views of civil society cannot be created; my hope rather is that boldness will encourage thought. In this spirit, let it bluntly be said that civil society should be seen not merely as the presence of strong and autonomous social groups able to balance the state but also as a high degree of civility in social relations. As it happens, this is a view that I have held for some time—though whether this should be seen as commendable consistency or a dreadful lack of intellectual development is an open question.[4] In one sense, the maintenance of position is helpful, because some of the chapters that follow have reacted in one way or another to the definition in question. Still, some new points can be made, support discovered, and a worry expressed in relation to nationalism, a topic that deserves more attention in the historical and theoretical literature on civil society.

Reaction to Revolution

Twentieth-century Europe has been the site of two great revolutionary forces, bolshevism and nazism, both of which sought to fundamentally restructure social life. Understanding something of what they sought to achieve will help us explain the surge of interest in, and the particular characterization given to, civil society in recent years.

The essential backdrop to modern history is the desire of the weak to imitate the strong. A sea change in human affairs took place with the industrialization of capitalism in the nineteenth century, and so it is scarcely surprising that our world has been structured in response to this protean shift. No sense can be made of the revolutionary forces noted without realising that they were, although they did not, perhaps could not, admit the fact, strategies of development.[5]

Despite great effort, not nearly enough work has been done on what is involved in imitative development. One general point that needs to be made concerns the precise identification of what a developing society seeks to copy in order to catch up with the leading edge of power. Some early attempts at development assumed that the secret to the modern industrial world lay in parliamentarism, a view famously maintained by Montesquieu. A second stage held it could ignore this on the ground that forced investment and mass education were the real keys to social progress.

The crucial historical exemplar of this approach is, of course, "the Soviet model," although it should be remembered that this was based in part on Lenin's admiration for the way in which Wilhelmine Germany planned its economy during the First World War. But much more important than matters political and economic was the felt need to engineer human souls. State elites seeking to develop their societies often insisted that greater social homogeneity was a prerequisite to success. This sentiment was seen in the political cleansing so characteristic of the first decades of Soviet history. The more celebrated exemplar of the desire for homogeneity is, of course, nationalism. If the extent to which civic nationalism led to brutality often has been forgotten, general attention is now given to the ways to which ethnic nationalism has led not just to expulsions and transfers of populations but to genocide.[6] Political practice saw endless combinations of all these factors: ethnic cleansing often has been justified on the political ground that those not co-cultural with the majority are a fifth column and so politically dangerous; and the history of the Soviet Union witnessed some of the most brutal ethnic policies, particularly of small minorities in contrast to the large titular nationalities whose position, ironically, became stronger under the Bolsheviks than it had been under the tsars.[7] All of this ensured that Europe's twentieth century was going to be fantastically vicious.

Matters were made still worse by what is best termed the urge for moral unity—that is, the desire of semitraditional societies to "catch-all" in their philosophies, to be at once modern and morally complete.[8] There is subtle humiliation involved in the process of modernization: as critics are keen to point out, adaptation is very often to standards other than one's own—and standards, moreover, that tend to a measure of moral emptiness compared to the altogether more complete and warmer moral worlds of traditional society. Accordingly, modernising societies always have on offer ideologists prepared to combine elements of modernity with renewed or eclectic philosophies promising moral warmth in the industrial era. It may be, furthermore, that the desire for moral unity is particularly deeply encoded in the Western intellectual tradition.[9] What is clear is that breakdowns in the process of modernization, that is, the removal of the carrot of affluence so that the huge coercion involved in structural social change comes to the fore, led to the adoption of such totalizing ideologies. Ideologies of this sort have tended to draw heavily on the tradition of civic virtue so prominent in European thought.

Perhaps the best way of summing up these structural and ideological conditions is to say that in much of the twentieth century
the state has been taken as a moral project, with virtue accordingly
seen as a proper object of political action.[10] The state was believed
to possess the capacity to bring human beings a decent life, and it
was adulated accordingly. Such adulation is the absolute opposition of civil society. For one thing, the engineering of human souls
destroyed any conception of a private realm free from political
interference. For another, massive social engineering meant by-
passing established institutions so as to create new conduits of
power. The end result has been that Europe has been the twentieth
century's dark continent, the core of civilization in which tens of
millions have been murdered.[11]

Civil society became a slogan in reaction to the brutal costs of
social revolution. The iterations on the theme have been many. The
democratization movements of Southern Europe first popularized
the term in the 1970s, seeking at that time to replace the politics of
virtue with an appreciation of moral ambiguity and hoping that
strong, autonomous groups would balance state power. Intellectual opposition in Eastern and Central Europe took matters somewhat further, not surprisingly given the greater viciousness and
penetration of state power, in dreams of a societal self-organization so complete that politics would not be necessary. At
times this led to tensions, notably between thinkers in Central
Europe who endorsed capitalism as the prime ingredient of
societal self-organization and ex-Marxists in the West who admired new social movements that were opposed to capitalism.
The contemporary surge in popularity of the term in the Middle
East, Indonesia, China, and Latin America has not led to any
general agreement on terms. While agreement may not be possible, clarification is possible—and it is to that task that attention now turns.

The State and Civility

The most striking characteristic of the recent discourse about civil
society has been its antistatism. At best, the state is allowed to be
present just so long as it is controlled or balanced. This emphasis
on societal self-organization is entirely comprehensible given the
horrors of the historical record, and it is by no means without analytic sense. But antistatism will not do as a general characterization of civil society, either in the abstract and as a description of

the ways in which the term has been used in the past. An alternative case can be made by considering these issues in turn.

One obvious way in which antistatism has been found inadequate is evident in the countries of the erstwhile socialist bloc in the years since 1989. The result of an historical experience is now evident: the removal of a large and predatory state did not and does not, in and of itself, ensure decency in social life. This can be seen in economic affairs. In the absence of a state able to ensure some rules to the game, the attempt to privatize lapsed into sheer piratization—that is, the seizure of profitable assets by the politically connected, which most certainly has not led to the flourishing of economic life. More generally, the absence of public order sees the emergence of a modern feudalism, in which Mafia-style groups at once protect their own and prey on others. These circumstances have led to important changes in the arguments made by key theorists turned practitioners. Václav Havel's long-standing interest in "anti-politics" has now been replaced by an appreciation of politics and a desire to create a responsive state. This is, of course, exactly right. Socialist states were at once despotic and—because they were distrusted—weak; what is needed is both a curtailment of despotism and a re-creation of trust so as to allow functional tasks to be performed more effectively by the state.[12] Differently put, a civil society is one in which there is cooperation, rather than mere balance, with the state. What is needed is a politics of reciprocal consent.[13]

A second analytic weakness of the recent antistatist view of civil society has been the uncritical adulation of social groups. It takes only a moment to see how misleading this can be. On the one hand, not every group deserves moral approbation. Many groupings in human history have been but sealed cages: castes, tight kinship links, sects and political societies have at times sought to contain their members, to deprive them of any possibility of exit.[14] On the other hand, a social world in which militantly organized groups, perhaps of this caged variety, are in a constant state of war with each other is equally unattractive. Powerful societal self-organization does not necessary make a *civil* society. The proper definition of civil society must accordingly concentrate on the individual's right to choose a pattern of development within a world populated with open groups in agreement on the need to respect a measure of diversity in social life.

The most important book yet published on civil society, Dominique Colas's *Le Glaive et le fléau*, has these analytic points at its core, thereby providing very welcome support.[15] Colas has discovered that civil society has a long genealogy, and he is able to demonstrate it is not one structured in terms of an opposition between state and society. To the contrary, the state was seen by Aristotle as a realm free from kinship links and thus a necessary protector of civil relations. This is not to say that despotic power has not been the enemy of civil society in recent years, but it does suggest that civility is not necessarily grounded in the absence of the state. For the opposition at the heart of Western intellectual history is that between civil society and fanaticism, the terms sensibly used to provide the title for the English translation of Colas' book.[16] Fanaticism and enthusiasm can come in many forms, most obviously in religious and political versions; this realization allows Colas to add to the pantheon of theorists of civil society, making Leibniz and Spinoza as important to its history as Montesquieu, Smith, Ferguson, or Hegel.

There is one question that Colas does not theorize; an attempt to do so allows for general highlighting of the argument. Nothing can be more important than to ask about the origins of civility in society. One reason for this is that the account of the origins of civil society that has dominated the field is clearly flawed.[17] According to that account, civil society will go hand-in-hand with the spread of capitalism: increasing structural differentiation of society will create diverse groups sure to press for a looser and more liberal society. This view has been falsified historically by the fact that many cases of development under the auspices of capitalism have been planned by, and continue to function effectively under, authoritarian rule. It may perhaps be the case that capitalists themselves, when all other things are equal, lean toward more liberal regimes. However, in the face of social protest that causes disruptions to business and profit, capitalists and middle classes more generally tend to revert to supporting the party of order.[18] In a nutshell, this social segment is highly opportunistic and thus not a reliable base on which to build a civil society.

None of this is to say that there is no link between capitalism and civil society. The presence of an alternative source of advantage has sometimes made it easier for members of old regimes to exit from positions of power, assured that their fall will not be absolute: this is as true of the members of warring factions in the United States at the end of the eighteenth century as it is of members of the Hungarian communist party in the 1980s.[19] Moreover, social diversity is a necessary condition for civil society. Transitions from authoritarian capitalism to consolidated democracy have proven relatively easy to achieve; this stands in striking contrast to the fragile situation of societies of the former socialist bloc. The social atomism created by revolutionary rule in the latter was so great that now there often are no groups able to represent interests, thereby ruling out of bounds the very notion of social bargaining upon which the consolidation of democracy depends.[20] Finally, there may be some truth to the idea that as capitalism becomes more diverse, that is, as huge planned-from-above industrial giants are revealed to be inefficient, pressure for a civil society mounts: in countries such as Brazil and South Korea, the highly educated labor of small and middle-sized concerns certainly seems to align itself more with the left than the owners of the great conglomerates.[21] Still, a condition of existence is not the same thing as a causal origin, the mere presence of strong, autonomous groups being no guarantee of a decent social order. Differently put, a distinction should be drawn by making use of familiar Marxist notation so as to distinguish between civil society-in-itself and civil society-for-itself.

The most promising line of argument about the creation of civility in society, that is, the shared valuation of non-fanatical, non-enthusiastic politics as something positive, is one that depends less upon social structure than upon historical conjuncture—making the creation of civil society an achievement of social learning and political skill rather than the result of some absolute fate determined by benign social evolution. The general point was captured with characteristic brilliance by the late Ernest Gellner, who loved to tell his friends in the Soviet Union that the secret to civil society in Europe lay in the seventeenth century.[22] Gellner had in mind the birth of the practice and theory of toleration as the result of the long religious wars of post-Reformation Europe. Both sides had suffered massively and hideously as the result of this conflict, without ever being able to wipe out their opponents. Once again the mere presence of strong and autonomous groups, of civil society in-itself, did not guarantee social decency. That condition depends upon a sort of *gestalt* switch whereby the desire to convert and conquer is slowly abandoned, first with reluctance but eventually in a positive spirit when the recognition of a measure of difference comes to be seen as desirable. The peace settlements of 1648 formally took religion out of public affairs, although it remained a key matter for private lives, thereby removing one of the causes for intense geopolitical conflict in Europe. It is worth noting that there was nothing inevitable about the triumph of the idea of toleration, no structural process ensuring that stalemate would be put to positive purpose. The same point can be made about other occasions when stalemate between warring groups led to civil settlement, from the creation of political stability in England at the turn of the seventeenth century to the destruction of apartheid in the very recent past; in both cases, politics ceased to be a zero-sum affair—indeed, it became possible to see opposition as something respectable, even "loyal."[23] It is not easy to explain why settlements were reached at this rather than that occasion, and it may well be that an element of mystery is necessarily attached to a matter that rests so much on changes in political psychology.

A final clarification should be offered about the notion of living with difference. It is crucial to realize that there are two sides to this equation. Certainly, one element at work is an opposition to the fanatical insistence that there is only one way to the truth. In this sense, civil society has about it a measure of relativism, for it asserts that difference is unavoidable, indeed desirable for those who insist that the ends of life are diverse. But the other side of the picture, stressing the sharing of the belief that diversity is acceptable, is quite as important. Relativism is at a discount here, for some differences—most obvious among them, of course, fanaticism and the caging of individuals within social groups—are unacceptable to a civil society. That there is no contradiction here can easily be demonstrated. Montesquieu accepted relativism in matters of religious belief but condemned slavery on universal grounds. Similarly, Mill endorsed diversity *within* the settled world of the seminar-addicted. Civil society is thus a way of life rather than a blanket admission that anything goes.

Nationalism and Civil Society

It may be useful to conclude by highlighting the importance and relevance of discussions of the German and English cases to the theory proposed.[24] For surely more is at issue than differential styles and timing of societal self-organization, important though this is and excellent though several of the following contributions on this topic may be.

A staple of postwar scholarship, represented best in major works by Barrington Moore and Ralf Dahrendorf, was the insistence that German development was pathological in comparison to that of England in being illiberal, statist, and overcentralized—thereby becoming a danger to modernity.[25] The revisionist work of David Blackbourn and Geoff Eley, *The Peculiarities of German History,* rightly became celebrated for the brilliance of its assault on this view.[26] It is indeed true that capitalists concern themselves with the rule of law rather than with liberty, as noted, while forced development is always likely to be illiberal: both of these considerations lend support to Blackbourn and Eley's insistence that German development was thoroughly normal. Furthermore, the realization that capitalist development was not necessarily all sweetness and light made it possible to reconsider the nature of British development: the essays assembled here reflect this development in spelling out the various exclusions that have characterized a putatively civil society. Nonetheless, there may be a case for revising the revisionists. For one thing, intellectual attention quite properly has started to pay attention to non-economic variables: feminists have done most to highlight exclusions from civil society, while my own argument has concerned the importance of political settlement. Still more importantly, the initial contrast drawn by Moore and Dahrendorf, between a liberal (but admittedly imperfect) English and an illiberal German pattern of development, contained fundamental truth. This contrast certainly receives support from some of the discussion in this volume of the German inability to create the concept of a loyal opposition—that is, to create civility in political life.

It should be emphasized firmly that civility is not somehow inherent in the English situation. Self-congratulation of this sort can easily be avoided by recalling the viciousness surrounding the English civil war. Still, civility was established among the political elite at the turn of the seventeenth century. The entry of the people onto the political stage did not disturb this pattern, in large part for two reasons. On one hand, working class radicalism was domesticated by the retention of basic liberalism in the political structure—something made possible, the most recent scholarship tells us, by the variable stressed by Moore: namely the commitment of the English aristocracy to commerce.[27] On the other hand, civil society was not disturbed by the incursion of the people in their second form, as members of national movements. England had been a unitary state since the creation of centralized feudalism at the time of the Conquest, and this allowed the slow creation of a relatively homogenous national culture. The German case was very different on both counts, with national questions, in particular, being able to override civil politics both in Wilhelmine Germany and still more so in the interwar period.

This bring us to a final troubling general reflection best highlighted by considering an element of the work of Ernest Gellner, the most brilliant of all recent theorists of nationalism and the author of a significant book on civil society. The connection in his work between these two factors is not always appreciated.[28] Gellner himself made many detailed points when discussing whether nationalism should be seen as a friend or a foe of civil society. In the final analysis, however, his view is that the national question must be solved before civil society becomes a real possibility. Civilized disputation depends, in this view, upon having a very great deal in common so that matters never get out of hand. There is a great deal of truth to this view, with the chances for civil society being strong today in Poland, Hungary, and the Czech Republic thanks to the ethnic cleansing of Hitler and Stalin. Still, there is a little evidence—the maintenance of the Indian state, the failure of genuine secessionist movements in post-Franco Spain—that goes the other way. Solving the national question may be a condition for civil society, but civility can sometimes help deal with nationalist conflict.[29]

Notes

1. Krishan Kumar, "Civil Society: An Inquiry into the Usefulness of an Historical Term," *British Journal of Sociology* 44 (1993): 375–95.
2. Jürgen Habermas, *The Structural Transformation of the Public Sphere*, trans. T. Burger and F. Lawrence (Cambridge, MA, 1989); Robert Putnam, *Making Democracy Work* (Princeton, 1993). See the critical discussion of these two approaches in Frank Trentmann, "Paradoxes of Civil Society," in this volume.
3. This task has now been more than adequately carried out by Dominique Colas, *Civil Society and Fanaticism*, trans. A. Jacobs (Stanford, 1997).
4. John A. Hall, "In Search of Civil Society," in *Civil Society*, ed. John A. Hall (Cambridge, 1995), 1–31; and Hall, "Genealogies of Civility," in *Democratic Civility*, ed. Robert W. Hefner (Brunswick, NJ, 1998), 53–77.
5. For a brilliant interpretation of Marxism in this light, see Roman Szporluk, *Communism and Nationalism* (Oxford, 1988).
6. Michael Mann, "The Dark Side of Democracy: The Modern Tradition of Ethnic and Political Cleansing," *New Left Review* 235 (1999): 18–45.
7. Anatoly Khazanov, *After the USSR* (Madison, 1996); Rogers Brubaker, *Nationalism Reframed* (Cambridge, 1997).
8. The concept of "catch-all" social theories was developed by Otto Kirchheimer. Analyses of the desire for moral unity in communism and Nazism can be found in Leszek Kolakowski, "The Myth of Human Self-identity," in *The Socialist Idea*, ed. Stuart Hampshire and Leszek Kolakowski (London, 1974); and Jeffrey Herf, *Reactionary Modernism* (Cambridge, 1984).
9. John A. Hall, "A View of a Death," *Theory and Society* 27 (1998): 509–34.

10. The notion of taking the state as a moral project is that of Victor Pérez-Díaz, *The Return of Civil Society* (Cambridge, 1993); Adam Ferguson noted that virtue was the business of the state in classical Greece in his *An Essay on the History of Civil Society* [1767] (Edinburgh, 1966).

11. Mark Mazower, *Dark Continent* (London, 1997).

12. John A. Hall, "Understanding States," in *The State*, ed. John A. Hall (London, 1993), vol. 1.

13. "The politics of reciprocal consent" is a phrase used by Richard J. Samuels, *The Business of the Japanese State* (Ithaca, 1987).

14. Ernest Gellner, *Conditions of Liberty* (London, 1994).

15. D. Colas, *Le Glaive et le fléau* (Paris, 1992).

16. Colas, *Civil Society and Fanaticism*.

17. I have in mind here the hugely influential work of Seymour M. Lipset, even though this has been concerned more with democracy than with civil society. An important recent summary of his position can be found in "Social Requisites of Democracy Revisited," *American Sociological Review* 59 (1994).

18. Misagh Parsa, "Entrepreneurs and Democratization: Iran and the Philippines," *Comparative Studies in Society and History* 37 (1995).

19. On these two cases, see Richard Hofstadter, *The Idea of a Party System* (Berkeley, 1969); and Agnes Horvath and Arpad Szakolczai, *The Dissolution of Communist Power: The Case of Hungary* (London, 1992).

20. Russell Bova, "Political Dynamics of the Post-Communist Transition," *World Politics* 44 (1991).

21. John A. Hall, "States and Economic Development," in *States in History*, ed. Hall (Oxford, 1986). Cf. Francis Fukuyama, *The End of History and the Last Man* (New York, 1992).

22. Gellner, *Conditions of Liberty*.

23. For the British case, see J. H. Plumb, *The Growth of Political Stability in England, 1675–1725* (London, 1968).

24. I use England rather than Britain deliberately, to indicate awareness, especially in light of the following discussions of nationalism, of the historic problems of a composite monarchy, Irish nationalism in the nineteenth and twentieth centuries, and the possibility of other peripheral nationalisms in the future. The pattern of development in question has been determined in large part by English institutions.

25. Barrington Moore, *Social Origins of Dictatorship and Democracy* (Boston, 1966); Ralf Dahrendorf, *Society and Democracy in Germany* (New York, 1969).

26. David Blackbourn and Geoff Eley, *The Peculiarities of German History* (Oxford, 1984).

27. Dietrich Rueschemeyer, Evelyn Stephens, and John Stephens, *Capitalist Development and Democracy* (Cambridge, 1992).

28. I draw here on Ernest A. Gellner, *Nations and Nationalism* (Oxford, 1983) *and Conditions of Liberty*. For discussions of Gellner's position, see the essays assembled in John A. Hall, ed., *The State of the Nation* (Cambridge, 1998).

29. For more details on this, see John A. Hall, "How Homogeneous Need We Be? Reflections on Nationalism and Liberty," *Sociology* 30 (1996): 163–71; and Michael Hechter, *Containing Nationalism*, forthcoming.

PART II

CONCEPTUAL ORIGINS

2

"THE COMMERCE OF THE SEXES"

Gender and the Social Sphere in Scottish
Enlightenment Accounts of Civil Society

Mary Catherine Moran

R ECENT WORK BY HISTORIANS of Britain, France, and Germany
has complicated our understanding of the concepts of "public" and "private" in eighteenth-century Europe. Inspired in part
by Jürgen Habermas's powerful, if somewhat idealized, evocation
of an "authentic public sphere" made up of "private persons" and
located within a "private realm,"[1] scholars of the eighteenth century have begun to question the descriptive and analytic precision
of a binary opposition between separate and mutually exclusive
spheres. Against the stark public/private dichotomy that is often
supposed to have developed during this period, there is a growing emphasis on the multiple and overlapping meanings through
which the categories of public and private were constituted, and a
heightened awareness that the boundaries between these spheres
were fluid and permeable. The common tendencies of various new
approaches to the subject are nicely summarized by John Brewer
when he highlights the importance "of understanding the processes by which the one is represented in and by the other, and of
paying particular attention not to those spaces at the polar ends of
public and private but to the spaces in between."[2] Since the doctrine of separate spheres is frequently taken as one of the theoretical

foundations of modern civil society, this remapping of public and private has important implications for accounts both of the rise and development of civil society and of the exclusion of women from politics and citizenship.

This chapter focuses on the Scottish Enlightenment discourse of civil society known as conjectural history and is intended as a contribution to the remapping of public and private in eighteenth-century Britain. By calling attention to the importance of "society" in the work of such authors as Adam Ferguson, Lord Kames, John Millar, and William Robertson, I want to propose an alternative to the framework of a public/private dichotomy as a means of understanding the exclusion of women from the domain of politics. The works of the conjectural historians have long held a canonical position within Scottish Enlightenment studies, and more recently have attracted a broader notice. A contemporary revival of civil society discourse has generated new interest in a body of work that is alternately seen to have provided the theoretical underpinnings for the development of modern civil society or to have suggested the outlines that such a development should have followed. Yet despite a long-standing interest in these works on the part of scholars of the Enlightenment and a more recent engagement on the part of political theorists and sociologists, there has been remarkably little discussion of the significance of women for Scottish Enlightenment accounts of civil society.[3]

My discussion explores two distinct but related concepts of "society." First, and most broadly, conjectural history conceives of "society" as the sum total of manners, customs, laws, and institutions that forms the object of historical inquiry and the progress of which can be traced from "savagery" to "civility." The constitution of this historical entity might be interpreted as an instance of what Hannah Arendt described as "the rise of the social," where the private concerns of household and economy "invade" the public world of political action—although such an understanding need not share her evaluation of this new realm.[4] While Arendt's notion of an original stark distinction between public and private is historically suspect, her account of the collapsing of public and private into "society" during the eighteenth century captures an important conceptual shift in terms that might have been recognizable to the conjectural historians themselves. In a second, and more limited, sense, conjectural history draws on the notion of "polite society" as a specific sphere found only in civil society, where conversation is the medium of cultural exchange between men and women who are social, but not political, equals. The presence of women is indeed a defining characteristic of this sphere, which is neither public in a political sense nor private in the sense of household and family.

To examine the position accorded women in Scottish Enlightenment civil society discourse is to unsettle the public/private opposition that often serves as an organizing principle for debate surrounding women and civil society. Feminist historians and political theorists have argued persuasively that the exclusion of women from the realm of politics is a constitutive, rather than merely a contingent, feature of civil society both in its conceptual origins and in its various historical and contemporary reformulations. Less persuasive, however, is the argument that this political exclusion must amount to the relegation of women to a private and domestic sphere.[5] The binary logic of such an equation, I would suggest, misses the importance of what Brewer refers to as the "in between." More specifically, in terms of eighteenth-century conceptions, this public/private opposition overlooks the twofold significance of "society" as that which civil society discourse seeks to explain.

The Progress of Society

> In order to complete the history of the human mind, and attain a perfect knowledge of its nature and operations, we must contemplate man in all those various situations wherein he has been placed. We must follow him in his progress through the different stages of society, as he gradually advances from the infant state of civil life to its maturity and decline.
>
> — William Robertson, *History of the Discovery and Settlement of America*

Conjectural history, so named because of its attempt to reconstruct a distant past in the absence of recorded documents,[6] has long been considered one of the paradigmatic achievements of the Scottish Enlightenment. In a series of works that began to appear at midcentury, writers such as Adam Ferguson, Lord Kames, John Millar, and William Robertson sought to account for the rise of civil society in evolutionary terms, highlighting the establishment of private property and the spread of commerce as key developments in the progress from "savagery" to "civility." These works typically charted the movement of societies through successive stages of material subsistence, often according to a "four-stages theory" of the progress from hunting to pasturage to agriculture to commerce. Their authors relied on a wide range of sources, including biblical texts, pastoral poetry, ancient and modern law codes, and travel accounts to supply details of the manners and customs of diverse peoples. And they elaborated a model of historical change that rests on an analogy between individual and societal development: "not only the individual advances from infancy to manhood," as Ferguson put it in his *Essay on the History of Civil Society* (1767), "but the species itself from rudeness to civilization."[7] Given its materialist emphasis, its ethnographic interests, and its concern to uncover general laws governing human progress, it is not surprising that conjectural history has been viewed in light of the growth of the social sciences and assessed in terms of a Scottish contribution to the rise of sociology, anthropology, and political economy.[8]

A somewhat different perspective has recently been offered by Mark Phillips, who views conjectural history in terms of broad shifts in eighteenth-century historical modes and conceptions. Surveying the historiography of eighteenth-century Britain, Phillips points to various forms of historical writing—new and emergent genres as well as older genres newly reconfigured—that challenged the classical conception of history as a narrative of the public deeds of public men. While the paradigm of classical history still carried enormous prestige in the eighteenth century and remained powerful and authoritative as an ideal, in practice, Phillips argues, its authority was undermined by numerous attempts "to find forms of historical narrative that met the needs of a commercial society and recognized the values and activities of a non-aristocratic audience." Conjectural history, he suggests, can be placed alongside a diverse assortment of genres, including religious history, history of manners, history of sciences and literature, and memoir and biography, all of which "defined themselves in relation to a traditional conception of history" and "ranged themselves against [its] strict identification with public life, with all the assumptions about audience, gender, and intellectual authority that accompanied the public domain." If political narrative continued to enjoy its preeminent position in a hierarchy of historical literatures, these new genres carved out "rival narrative spaces" in which the "*inward* lives of individuals and the *everyday* life of societies" took precedence over the great deeds and remarkable events of classical history.[9]

Phillips reminds us of an important historiographical context that is often neglected precisely because conjectural history departs so significantly from the conventions of classical narrative. Because the works of the Scottish historians can be read as founding treatises in political economy, as early anthropology, and as proto-sociology, it is easy to overlook the point that, whatever else they may attempt or effect, these texts present themselves to the reader in the guise of a new kind of history. Yet this point is crucial for understanding conjectural history's interest in women. Conjectural historians claim to offer a novel mode of historical explanation through a form of historical narrative that is defined, both implicitly and explicitly, in relation to the conventions of classical narrative. And it is only by attending to such claims that we can begin to make sense of what might otherwise seem an accidental or incidental insertion of women into the conjectural narrative. The insertion of women, or rather of "woman," is made possible by a replacement of men by "man" as the historical subject and by a displacement of politics onto "society" as the locus of historical change.

To set conjectural history against the conventions of classical history is to throw its displacement of the political into sharp relief. According to the classical paradigm, the historian finds his subject matter in the sphere of politics and war and discovers his audience in the (male) members of a ruling elite. Its eighteenth-century neoclassical versions involve a similar emphasis on the public world of politics, along with a self-conscious imitation of ancient authors and, as Philip Hicks has shown, an increasingly difficult attempt to maintain the traditional dignity of an elite literature in the face of a rapidly commercializing print culture.[10] Conjectural history, on the other hand, emphasizes, to adopt Arendt's description of the social realm in general, "the progress of mankind rather than the achievements of men."[11] The conjectural historian finds the meaning of human history not in individual actions and remarkable events but in what Millar describes as "the gradual improvement of society."[12] This slow but inexorable process is not consciously willed but is rather the unintended outcome of the combined effects of a range of factors, including sexual and familial relations, modes of subsistence and division of labor, and networks of trade and commerce, many of which are peripheral to, if not entirely absent from, political narrative. And where classical narrative recounts the deeds of historical actors who reveal their thoughts and motives when they perform their parts on an historical stage, conjectural history seeks to disclose the gradual unfolding of the inward operations of the human mind—not the thoughts and motives of particular persons but a kind of aggregate subjectivity of the "mind of man," as "it" develops, in the words of Ferguson, from "the first operations of reason and sentiment" to "the highest refinements of political and moral apprehension."[13]

Millar made this challenge to a classical understanding of history explicit in the Introduction to his *Origin of the Distinction of Ranks* (1779). He defined his work as an account of the "natural progress [of] human society" from "ignorance to knowledge, and from rude to civilized manners." This progress, he insisted, cannot be attributed to the "casual interpositions" of a few "particular persons." There is "scarcely any people, ancient or modern," Millar writes, "who do not boast of some early monarch, or statesman, to whom it is pretended they owe whatever is remarkable in their form of government." But "notwithstanding the concurring testimony of historians," he continues,

> concerning the great political changes introduced by the lawgivers of a remote age, there may be reason to doubt, whether the effect of their interpositions has ever been so extensive as is generally supposed. Before an individual can be invested with so much authority, and possessed of such reflection and foresight as would induce him to act in the capacity of a legislator, he must, probably, have been educated and brought up in the knowledge of those natural manners and customs, which, for ages, perhaps, have prevailed among his countrymen.

Against an historical tradition that celebrates the political achievements of "heroes," "sages" and "patriotic statesmen," Millar argues that the impact of individual endeavor has been "exaggerated, and misrepresented." Before an individual can be in the capacity to act, his manners and sentiments have already been formed in accordance with "the general system of behaviour" that governs the society to which he belongs. In Millar's view, then, the individual actions, or "casual interpositions," of the statesman or legislator are only the most obvious manifestations of the larger, but largely hidden, movements of his society. It is beneath this surface that the historian must delve in order to account for the underlying causes and long-term direction of historical change.

This is not to suggest that conjectural history has no interest in political questions relating to government and polity. To varying degrees and with differing emphases, the works of the Scottish historians are animated by a range of concerns and preoccupations—the tension between liberty and authority; the compatibility of commercial wealth and civic virtue—that would meet even the strictest definition of "political." According to the conjectural scheme of historical development, however, even such political matters can no longer be understood solely in political terms but must be interpreted through the wider framework of the social. As "the most Machiavellian" of the conjectural historians,[14] Ferguson, for example, is palpably preoccupied with the recovery of a republican civic virtue, the rudiments of which he finds in the playful sociability and military valor of the American "savage." Yet given his concern to recuperate an ancient form of political virtue compatible with the expanding commercial empire of eighteenth-century Britain, Ferguson's methods as an historian are instructive. For despite his obvious political interests, what Ferguson renders in his *Essay on the History of Civil Society* is by no means a traditional political narrative.

In an attempt to write the "natural history" of the "species," Ferguson seeks to chart the historical variations of a universal human nature. His *Essay* begins with a lengthy section on "the General Characteristics of Human Nature" that reads more like a discourse in moral psychology than an historical narration. "The history of the individual," Ferguson asserts, "is but a detail of the sentiments and thoughts he has entertained in the view of his species; and every experiment relative to this subject should be made with entire societies, not with single men."[15] Not only does this "experimental" method displace the individual in favor of society, or men in favor of "man," but it also defines the history of this subject in terms of his "sentiments and thoughts." This point is reiterated in Book II of the *Essay*, "Of the History of Rude Nations." Here Ferguson complains that "the early historians of modern Europe" applied themselves to "what they were pleased to denominate facts" but overlooked those "characteristics of the understanding and the heart" which convey a knowledge of "human nature." For Ferguson, history consists not in "the events and successions of princes, that are recorded in the order of time," but in the gradual unfolding of man's powers of reason and sentiment as he advances through the various stages of society.[16]

The "society" that moves through successive stages of development corresponds in sense with what Daniel Gordon has described as the "distinctively new" and "modern" meaning that "*société*" acquired during the French Enlightenment. Over the course of the eighteenth century, Gordon suggests, the term *société*, which had originally referred to "small communities and to the convivial life within them," took on much broader connotations and began to refer to "the total field of human experience."[17] Likewise, the Scottish conjectural historians employ the term "society" to refer to the totality of human customs and institutions, including sexual and familial relations, commerce, manners, language, the arts, religion, law, and political associations. And in tracing the progress of society from "savagery" to "civility," conjectural history invests the term *civil society* with a wide range of meanings that extend far beyond a political frame of reference.

To be sure, conjectural historians often identify civil society with a particular form of political association characterized by "compulsory laws," "civil subordination," and "regular government." At least as frequently, however, they equate civil society as political association with "civilized" society as the stage of progress in which manners, customs, and institutions are in a condition of "improvement," "refinement," and "civility." The key term here is perhaps "civility," which still resonates with legal and political meanings derived from "civil" and associated with citizenship, but which also carries a newer cluster of associations relating to manners and politeness. William Robertson, for example, conflates the two sets of meanings when he variously describes the society of the American Indians as "unpolished," as "uncivilized," and as being "in an infant state of civil life," and when he refers to the societies of eighteenth-century Europe as "polished," as "civilized," and as "civil." To put it another way, Robertson *defines* "civil society" in political terms, as a "political union" that places its members "in subjection to government and order,"[18] but he *describes* the emergence and development of civil society in terms of "manners."[19] This tendency to commingle the two sets of associations effectively broadens the meaning of civil society so that, in addition to its more restricted political definition, it also denotes, to adopt Gordon's phrase, "the total field of human experience" as found in a condition of civilization.

Scottish Enlightenment accounts of the rise of civil society thus break down the distinction between public and private that is one of the founding assumptions of classical historiography. The private concerns of household and economy are merged with the public concerns of government and polity in order to trace the progress of man through the various stages of society. And since society includes such elements as conjugal and familial relations, manners, and customs, it is not surprising that women figure in its progress. Works by Kames, Robertson and Millar devote attention to sexual and familial relations and to the sexual division of labor and assign to women a leading role in the civilization of manners. In so doing, they clearly prescribe a domestic position for women. Yet the demarcation of this domestic sphere cannot be accurately described in terms of a public/private opposition, for it is in the very dissolution of such a distinction that women are brought into the conjectural narrative. In its constitution of "society," this genre of historical writing may be read in part as an insertion of women into history—not as individual historical actors, nor as exemplary subjects of "lives of illustrious women,"[20] but as a force or condition that acts upon the mind of man in much the same way as property and commerce.

"The Commerce of the Sexes"

With the History of Man, I dare say your Lordship has (*con amore*) written the History of Women.

— Elizabeth Montagu to Lord Kames (27 October 1773)

One striking example of this insertion of women into history is that of Lord Kames' enormous and ambitious *Sketches of the History of Man* (1774), which includes a lengthy chapter on "The Progress of the Female Sex." Kames once confessed to a female correspondent that he had "long entertained the ambition to become the historian to the Ladies."[21] And in 1769 he wrote to the Bluestocking Elizabeth Montagu—whose admiration of Ferguson's *Essay* "discovered" in Kames the "cloven foot" of envy[22]—of "one curious chapter viz. Progress of the female sex from their lowest savage state to their highest state among refined nations."[23] Kames's *Sketches* not only includes this chapter on women but also explicitly signals its intention of reaching a female readership: "To the Reader. As one great object of the Editor is to make this a popular work, he has, chiefly with a view to the female sex, subjoined an English translation of the quotations from other languages."[24] Kames himself addresses a female audience when he expresses "gratitude to my female readers, if I should be honoured with any."[25]

Kames' chapter on women ranges across cultures and over time, assembling a wealth of "bizarre facts" and "singular customs" in support of its opening statement that "the progress of the female sex, a capital branch in the history of man, comprehends great variety of matter, curious and interesting."[26] At first glance, Kames seems to do little more than offer "a great variety of matter, curious and interesting" as evidence that his subject "comprehends a great variety of matter, curious and interesting." The chapter is characterized by an abundance of anecdote and by a frequent tendency to wander: in the space of a single paragraph, Kames will roam from ancient Greece to ancient Germany to the Scottish Highlands to the Caribbean, before returning to ancient Greece. Yet this mass of detail has the cumulative impact of supporting what is only ancillary to Kames' opening statement, but what is perhaps a more interesting proposition: namely, that "the progress of the female sex" constitutes "a capital branch in the history of man." Few modern readers would share Elizabeth Montagu's opinion that Kames had written *a* history, much less *the* history, of women; fewer still would agree with Hugh Blair's assessment of "the chapter on Women" as "an excellent one."[27] What is significant, however, is the belief, his own and that of his contemporaries, that Kames had written such a history, and the conviction that this history constituted a vital component of the history of "man."

In Kames's account, "the gradual progress of women" consists not so much in the improvement of their own faculties and sentiments as in an increased valuation of their qualities by men. Paternal affection, for example, is something that men develop with the refinement of their sentiments. Maternal affection, on the other hand, is an historical constant, a natural quality "wisely ordained by Providence." For Kames, the practice of infanticide is proof not only of the "insensibility" of men in "barbarous" nations but of the "low condition" of women, who already possess sensibility: "the exposing [of] an infant therefore shows, that the mother was little regarded: if she had been given a vote, the practice would never have obtained in any country."[28] But if women always display refinement in manners and sentiments, men will recognize this refinement only after their own conceptions have improved:

> [The] female sex have risen in a slow and steady progress, to higher and higher degrees of estimation. Conversation is their talent, and a display of delicate sentiments: the gentleness of their manners and winning behaviour, captivates every sensible heart. Of such refinements, savages have little conception: but when the more delicate senses are unfolded, the peculiar beauties of the female sex, internal as well as external, are brought into full light.[29]

The "female sex," then, is characterized by general and apparently universal qualities and faculties—a talent for conversation, delicate sentiments, and gentle manners—that may or may not be perceived by men, depending on their particular stage of development. And while men's "senses" must develop or "unfold," women's "peculiar beauties" are not "unfolded" but rather are "brought into full light." The change, as Kames describes it, is a shift in perspective on the part of men; the direction is toward their "higher and higher degrees of estimation" of women.

A similar, albeit more systematic, account is found in Millar's *Ranks*, which begins with a lengthy chapter on the "Rank and Condition of Women in Different Ages" and which one historian of the social sciences has credited with "the beginnings of a sociology of gender."[30] Millar's chapter on women opens with a remarkable statement:

> Of all our passions, it should seem, that those which unite the sexes are most easily affected by the peculiar circumstances in which we are placed, and most liable to be influenced by the power of habit and education. Upon this account they exhibit the most wonderful variety of appearances, and, in different ages and countries, have produced the greatest diversity of manners and customs.[31]

Drawing upon an eclectic body of sources that includes the Book of Genesis, Homeric epic, and Lafitau's *Mœurs des sauvages ameriquains* (1724), Millar renders a richly anecdotal and often bizarre account of "wonderful variety" and "the greatest diversity" in sexual manners and mores. Embedded in a mass of detail on the marriage rites of the Tartars, the public prostitution of women among the Babylonians, and the Germanic origins of the English law of dower, is a logic of historical change that assigns a key role to women in the progress of society. Michael Ignatieff has interpreted Millar's historicization of sexual and familial relations as a kind of denaturalization, a "demolition of the 'innateness' of family feeling."[32] Yet notwithstanding Millar's attempt at such a demolition, I would argue that in his *Ranks* a notion of a natural and unchanging womanhood serves as the constant against which to measure the changes in the desires and sentiments of men. Tracing the estimation in which women have been held, from the brute insensibility of the savage to the affectionate esteem of the eighteenth-century Briton, Millar attributes this improvement in the treatment of women to the growth and maturation of male sexual passion, a process which corresponds to the rise and development of private property and of social and political stratification.

According to Millar, savage man has "mere sensual appetites" rather than "passions of sex." The material hardships of savage life deprive him of the leisure for "cultivating a correspondence with the other sex," even as the lack of economic and social stratification allows him free and unmediated access to women. This absence of social control and repression inhibits rather than enables the growth of sexual passion. Because he can immediately satisfy his urges, the savage does not entertain anxieties and anticipations that would "stir his imagination" and "awaken his sensibility." He "arrives at the end of his wishes," Millar explains, "before they have sufficiently occupied his thoughts." It is only to be expected, therefore, that the savage will place a low premium on his exchanges with women, for "he must have little regard for pleasures which he can purchase at so easy a rate."[33] With no incentive to court the favor of woman, he accordingly treats her with indifference and contempt.

It is the "acquisition of property" during the period of pastoral life that marks a turning point in the "commerce of the sexes."[34] The ownership of cattle produces disparities of wealth and status, while the invention of pasturing provides the leisure to cultivate notions of refinement and distinction. Whereas the savage could easily "gratify [his] appetites," the shepherd encounters social barriers which "interrupt the free intercourse of the sexes." More specifically, he meets with the "pride of family" and the "insolence of wealth" that accompany an increasingly hierarchical system of kinship, and that tend "to check all familiarity" between the members of different families and "to render their approaches to an intimacy proportionally slow and gradual."[35] Faced with difficulties and delays in its fulfillment, the shepherd reflects on his own desire and experiences "that long continued solicitude, those alternate fears and hopes, which agitate and torment the lover, and which, by awakening his sensibility ... render his prevailing inclinations more irresistible."[36] Thus the indiscriminate appetite of the savage is gradually refined into the discerning taste of the shepherd, whose sexual inclinations are now fixed on one particular object of whom he desires exclusive possession and to whom he will address himself with "a degree of tenderness and delicacy of sentiment." Having discovered the principle of private property through the taming and ownership of cattle, Millar argues, a pastoral people then "discovers some sort of jealousy with regard to the chastity of their women" and "attains some degree of improvement in their manners and morals."[37] Thus the growth of private property, which is also the growth of a proprietary interest in women, leads to progress and refinement in manners, morals, and sentiments.

In a similar vein, Robertson interprets the private ownership of women as an "attachment" to the female sex, a refinement of the passions that marks a dramatic improvement over the "dispassionate coldness" of the American "savage." "As soon as men have acquired distinct ideas of property," he explains, "or when they are so much attached to their females as to watch them with care and jealousy, families of course divide and settle in separate houses, where they can secure and guard whatever they wish to preserve." The communal living arrangements of the American savages must therefore be considered "not only as the effect of their imperfect notions concerning property, but as a proof of their inattention, and indifference towards their women."[38] Like Millar, Robertson equates a private property in women with progress and refinement: "In countries where refinement has made some progress, women when purchased are excluded from society, shut up in sequestered apartments and kept under the vigilant guard of their masters." As property, women acquire value as the objects of a jealous care, a marked improvement, Robertson insists, over their condition in savage society as inconsequential "beasts of burden" to be neglected and despised.[39]

It is striking that neither Millar nor Robertson entertain the possibility that women might have something to lose by a civilizing process that transforms them into a species of property. The movement from savagery to civility certainly entails some measure of a loss of native liberty for men. Accustomed to act "as if he retains all his natural rights entire and undiminished," savage man must relinquish, Robertson suggests, the "proud" and "sullen" independence that constitutes his sole and solitary virtue in exchange for the benefits—material security, military protection and political stability—of union and association.[40] Yet so absolute and unconditional are the benefits of civilization for women that their position provides Robertson with a decisive rejoinder to those Rousseauean philosophers who "describe the manners of the rude Americans with such rapture"[41] that they would seem to deny the advantages of civil over savage society for men. Although the question of "whether man has been improved by the progress of arts and civilization in society" has been "agitated amongst philosophers" in the "wantonness of disquisition," writes Robertson, "that women are indebted to the refinements of polished manners, for a happy change in their state, is a question that can admit of no doubt."[42] The attempt to reconcile individual liberty with the subordination that accompanies specialization and stratification is a tension that runs throughout Millar's text, and one that argues against an interpretation of his work as an unqualified endorsement of "progress": it is surely significant that he ends his inquiry into the origin of the distinction of ranks with an impassioned plea against American slavery. Yet while women enjoy "an unbounded liberty" in the savage state because "it is thought of little consequence what use they shall make of it," they have only to gain, Millar suggests, by a process that deprives them of this sexual freedom in order to grant them their influence over the passions of men.[43]

On the one hand, the depiction of women as property gives them a passive role in the progress of society. Women inspire and enable the growth and maturation of male sentiments and passions, but there is little in these texts to suggest that they themselves develop in similar fashion. The fact that Kames, Millar, and Robertson treat maternal, but not paternal, affection as natural and unchanging suggests that women invariably possess an instinctive refinement that might always place them somewhere between the savage and the civil, between a state of nature and a state of civilization. While man evolves from savagery to civility, woman has apparently been civilized, or almost civilized, all along: almost civilized, because she naturally possesses an affectionate sensibility that will increase in value in accordance with the refinement of man, but never quite civilized, because she does not acquire, but, rather, becomes a species of property.

Yet in a scheme of history that integrates material and cultural forces to account for a progress in manners and morals, this identification of women and property also represents the female sex as a powerful historical force. As J. G. A. Pocock has argued of this historicization of manners, just as property and commerce were thought to refine and polish the passions and sentiments, so were women thought to act in "the role of cultural entrepreneurs, encouraging the exchange of politeness and refinement in a variety of forms."[44] Women, at once inert and mobile, were depicted as the passive agents of civilization. Moreover, the mobility of property and expansion of commerce that characterize commercial society are attended by the movement of women into a sphere of sociability, an expansion of the commerce of the sexes that gives them, in Millar's words, "a general influence upon the commerce of society."[45]

Civil Society and Polite Society

> One will not be surprised, that women in Greece were treated with no great respect by their husbands. A woman cannot have much attraction who passes all her time in solitude: to be admired, she must receive the polish of society.
>
> — Lord Kames, *Sketches of the History of Man*

The historicization of the male personality in conjectural history clearly involves the naturalization of a domestic character for women. Through the successive stages of hunting, pasturage, agriculture, and commerce that mark the phases of men's development, women's position remains domestic. While men's employments and endeavors alter and expand at each stage of historical progress, women's pursuits do not change so much as men's estimation of their domestic role increases. In savage society, as Millar explains it, where physical strength and military courage are the measure of merit, women's "domestic offices" are "naturally regarded as mean and servile, and unworthy to engage the attention" of those who "are almost continually engaged in war, or in hunting."[46] As men begin to diversify their own pursuits, however, they accordingly come to regard women's "diligence and proficiency in the various branches of domestic economy" in a different light:

> When men begin to disuse their ancient barbarous practices, when their attention is not wholly engrossed by the pursuit of military reputation, when they have made some progress in the arts, and have attained to a proportional degree of refinement, they are necessarily led to set a value upon those female accomplishments and virtues which have so much influence upon every species of improvement, and which contribute in so many ways to multiply the comforts of life.

And as man begins to value her domestic role, woman is elevated to "that rank and station which appears most agreable to reason, being suited to her character and talents."[47] Inasmuch as Millar's account of this development is both descriptive and prescriptive, it can be read as an example of the natural association of women and domesticity which has long been identified as the eighteenth-century's dominant ideology of femininity.

This insistence on the domestic, however, should not be interpreted in terms of a strict public/private opposition. While studies of domesticity tend to equate a "domestic" with a "private" sphere for women, Scottish Enlightenment theorists conceived of the domestic as a "social" sphere. As John Dwyer points out, the favorite term of Scottish moralists for the domestic was "the little society."[48] It was in this sphere, they believed, that social affections were first developed and social habits and virtues first acquired. In his *Elements of Moral Philosophy* (1754), for example, David Fordyce begins his section on "Duties to Society" by examining "connections of parents," "duties to parents," and "duties to brethren and sisters," before moving on to consider "connections with the other sex" and "duties of marriage." Robertson refers to the "domestic union" as "the first institution of social life," while Ferguson sets it down as the first "of the principles of society in human nature" that "families may be considered as the elementary forms of society."[49] This tendency to root the social in the domestic derives in part from a tradition of natural jurisprudence that finds the origins of government and polity in the domain of the household, understood not as a sphere that is separate and distinct from a broader world but as a smaller version of the larger entity of civil society.[50] With a growing interest in the social affections and virtues, women were thought to play an increasingly significant role in an increasingly sentimentalized household that was defined not only as a realm of privacy but also as the primary realm of sociability.

Moreover, the domestic was not the only sphere that women were thought to inhabit. Even as conjectural history demarcated a realm of domesticity, it also placed women at the center of what was variously termed "society," "company," and "polite society." If the discovery of a private property in women signals an improvement over the "promiscuous intercourse" of the savage, it is by no means the final stage in the progress of society. It is a necessary, but an intermediate, step in the development of civility. For conjectural historians, the strict confinement of women to the household denotes the state of barbarism, where men have acquired notions of property but have yet to attain notions of politeness and refinement. The elaboration of a social role for women, on the other hand, is a defining characteristic of civil society. ·

This argument had been made by David Hume in several of a collection of essays first published in 1742. In his essay "Of the Rise and Progress of the Arts and Sciences," for example, Hume argued in favor of modern over ancient manners, and attributed the superiority of modern politeness to the society of women. "What better school for manners," he asks, "than the company of virtuous women; where the mutual endeavour to please must insensibly polish the mind, where the example of female softness and modesty must communicate itself to their admirers, and where the delicacy of that sex puts every one on guard, lest he give offence by any breach of decency?" Since the ancient Greeks and Romans considered "the fair-sex" as "altogether domestic," and not "as part of the polite world or of good company," their manners were accordingly impolite and unrefined.[51] Hume elaborated on this social role in another essay devoted to a defense of modern "luxury," by which he means refinement in both liberal and mechanical arts and not, he insists, "refinement in the gratification of the senses." In a discussion that anticipates or, better, partly initiates the conjectural history of manners, Hume again identifies the society of women as a source of improvement:

> The more these refined arts advance, the more sociable men become: nor is it possible, that, when enriched with science, and possessed of a fund of conversation, they should be contented to remain in solitude, or live in that distant manner, which is peculiar to ignorant and barbarous manners. They flock into cities.... Particular clubs and societies are every where formed: Both sexes meet in an easy and sociable manner; and the tempers of men, as well as their behaviour, refine apace.

In this description of the "effects of refinement both on *private* and *public* life," Hume places his emphasis on a social sphere where "both sexes meet in an easy and sociable manner."[52]

If sociability between the sexes is equivalent to refinement and civility, the relegation of women to the confines of the household is the concomitant of barbarism. Significantly, this criterion means that the ancient Greeks and Romans must be described as rude and barbarous in their manners. Conjectural histories treat any number of barbarous nations, from the ancient Germans and Scythians to the contemporary inhabitants of Asia and Lapland. In the case of what Ferguson calls the "conquering" tribes, where men are "guided by interest" but "not governed by law," their rough manners and harsh treatment of women are thought to correspond to their precarious and rapacious means of material gain and to their rudimentary and irregular form of government.[53] Yet Greece and Rome, those "celebrated nations of antiquity,"[54] developed elaborate systems of trade and commerce, made important advances in the arts and sciences, and established political institutions that earned them immortal glory. This lack of civility in otherwise civil societies is a puzzling—and for Millar even a troubling—phenomenon.

Ferguson, Kames, and Millar all make reference to the condition of women among the ancients. For the republican-minded Ferguson, the ancients' treatment of women and slaves is proof of a fallibility that detracts only slightly from their glory: "In the midst of our encomiums bestowed on the Greeks and Romans, we are, by this circumstance, made to remember that no human institution is perfect."[55] No such encomiums are bestowed by Lord Kames. The manners of the Greeks, he asserts, "were extremely coarse; such as might be expected from a people living among their slaves, without any society with virtuous women." No doubt because of his abhorrence of the "pure democracy" of Athens as "the very worst form of government,"[56] Kames is adamant in his dismissal of this barbarous people who "held all the world except themselves to be barbarians."[57] More vexed in its approach to this subject is the discussion by Millar.

It is because of the position of women that Millar describes the manners of the ancient Greeks as impolite and unrefined. Yet his treatment of this theme evinces more than a trace of anxiety. When the Greeks began to emerge from the heroic age of Homer to the period that is celebrated for its arts and philosophy, Millar writes, "from an inviolable respect to their ancient institutions"—earlier described as their "ancient barbarous manners"[58]—women remained in their "recluse situation." The maintenance of this practice, he surmises, had something to do with their "democratical form of government," which had a tendency "to occupy the people in the management of public affairs, and to engage them in those pursuits of ambition, from which the women were naturally excluded." But while this system of manners "might be conducive to the more solid enjoyments of life," Millar concedes,

> it undoubtedly prevented the sexes from improving the arts of conversation, and from giving a polish to the expression of their thoughts and sentiments. Hence it is, that the Greeks, notwithstanding their learning and good sense, were remarkably deficient in delicacy and politeness, and were so little judges of propriety in wit and humour, as to relish the low ribaldry of an Aristophanes, at a period when they were entertained with the sublime eloquence of a Demosthenes, and with the pathetic compositions of a Euripides and a Sophocles.[59]

In an apparent paradox of historical development, the Greeks attained a high degree of progress in the arts, sciences, and government even as the strict separation of the sexes left their manners and sentiments indelicate and unrefined.

The superior refinement of modern manners, Millar suggests, can be attributed in part to the "lasting impression" of Gothic chivalry. The "great respect and veneration for the ladies" that arose in an earlier feudal age "has still a considerable influence upon our behaviour towards them, and has occasioned their being treated with a degree of politeness, delicacy, and attention, that was unknown to the Greeks and Romans."[60] Once the "disorders" of feudalism had "subsided," Millar explains, the "extravagance" of feudal veneration was modified into a reasonable estimation of the "useful talents and accomplishments" that women employed "in carrying on the business and maintaining the intercourse of society."[61] Yet this improvement in manners is also the result of the material affluence produced by great advances in the arts and manufactures. For as they "multiply" the "conveniencies of life," mankind become "more refined in their taste, and luxurious in their manner of living."

In an advanced commercial society like that of eighteenth-century Britain, therefore, "the pleasures which nature has grafted upon the love between the sexes" become "the source of an elegant correspondence." Women are, in Millar's words,

> encouraged to quit that retirement which was formerly esteemed so suitable to their character, to enlarge the sphere of their acquaintance, and to appear in mixed company, and in public meetings of pleasure. As they are introduced more into public life, they are led to cultivate those talents which are adapted to the intercourse of the world, and to distinguish themselves by polite accomplishments that tend to heighten their personal attractions, and to excite those peculiar sentiments and passions of which they are the natural objects.

As we saw in his treatment of the savage, Millar's account of the progress of society "from ignorance to knowledge, and from rude to civilized manners," is in part a history of the refinement of male passions. Here, women's "polite accomplishments" are closely linked to their "personal attractions" in a manner that "excites" the passions of men. In polite and refined nations, Millar goes on to observe, there is "the same free communication between the sexes" as is found in savage society.[62] But whereas savage society permits this freedom because it has not yet discovered the virtue of chastity, civil society can allow it because norms of chastity have been so thoroughly internalized through the civilizing process.

Millar's approval of this social role for women is not without its reservations. The "love of pleasure," Millar worries,

> when carried to excess, is apt to weaken and destroy those passions which it endeavours to gratify, and to pervert those appetites which nature has bestowed upon mankind for the most beneficial purposes. The natural tendency, therefore, of great luxury and dissipation is to diminish the rank and dignity of women, by preventing all refinements in their connection with the other sex, and rendering them only subservient to a species of animal pleasure.[63]

Invoking the examples of the "voloptuousness of the Eastern nations" and of Rome's infamous decline into sexual "debauchery" and political "despotism," Millar gives voice to what is probably the central anxiety underlying the conjectural theory of progress. The semantic slippage that is possible from "refinement" to "luxury" suggests the direction of this concern. If both commerce and the commerce of the sexes occasion the progress of society to politeness and refinement, so might they occasion its devolution into corruption and luxury. Just as increased wealth and commerce can lead to indulgence and luxury, so might women polish the manners of men into effeminacy and voluptuousness. Commerce and women, the passive agents of civilization, might also serve as the passive, or perhaps not so passive, agents of decline.

Yet despite his anxiety over women's social role, Millar views the realm of sociability as a fundamental characteristic of civil society. As Millar describes it, the decline of civilization would be a descent into a "voluptuous" barbarism, where women are "reduced into slavery and confinement" even as men are degraded into political subjection and isolation. He thus draws upon the well-worn eighteenth-century discourse of "Oriental despotism," which held that the private enslavement of women ensured the political enslavement of men. "Polygamy," as Adam Smith had explained it in the lectures on jurisprudence that Millar attended as a student, "is prejudiciall to the liberty of the [male] subject."[64] Because their "extreme jealousy" over their women "hinders them altogether from receiving one another into their houses," the men of "Eastern nations" are "incapacitated to enter into any associations or alliances to revenge themselves on their oppressors, and curb the extravagant powers of the government and support their liberties."[65] A strictly private position for women, in other words, eliminates the possibility of a public sphere for men. Thus in the end Millar comes down on the side of the progress of civility with a qualified endorsement of women's role in "carrying on the business and maintaining the intercourse of society."[66] In so doing, he contributes to an eighteenth-century narrative in which the "rank and condition of women" are central criteria for judging the merits of what Arendt called "the rise of the social." While this Scottish Enlightenment account of the rise of civil society could still pay homage to the political achievements of the ancients, its ultimate tendency was to reject the classical public/private dichotomy in favor of an intermediary sphere that was thought to guarantee both civic and domestic virtue.

Notes

For criticism and encouragement, I would like to thank Toby Ditz, Jeffrey Lomonaco, J. G. A. Pocock, Judith Walkowitz, and Paul Winke. I am grateful for the support of the Social Sciences and Humanities Research Council of Canada.

1. Jürgen Habermas, *The Structural Transformation of the Public Sphere: An Inquiry into a Category of Bourgeois Society* [1962], trans. Thomas Burger (Cambridge, MA, 1989), 30.

2. John Brewer, "This, That and the Other: Public, Social and Private in the Seventeenth and Eighteenth Centuries," in *Shifting the Boundaries: Transformations of the Languages of Public and Private in the Eighteenth Century*, ed. Dario Castiglione and Lesley Sharpe (Exeter, 1995), 10. Other recent challenges to the public/private dichotomy include Dena Goodman, "Public Sphere and Private Life: Toward a Synthesis of Current Historiographical Approaches to the Old Regime, *History and Theory* 31, no. 1 (1992): 1–20; and Lawrence Klein, "Gender and the Public/Private Distinction in the Eighteenth Century: Some Questions about Evidence and Analytic Procedure," *Eighteenth-Century Studies* 29, no. 1 (Fall 1995): 97–109.

3. On women and the Scottish Enlightenment, see Jane Rendall, *The Origins of Modern Feminism in Britain, France, and the United States, 1780–1860* (New York, 1984); Rendall, "Virtue and Commerce: Women in the Making of Adam Smith's Political Economy," in *Women in Western Political Philosophy*, ed. Ellen Kennedy and Susan Mendus (Brighton, 1987), 44–77; and Sylvana Tomaselli, "The Enlightenment Debate on Women," *History Workshop Journal* 20 (1985): 101–24.

4. Hannah Arendt, *The Human Condition* (Chicago, 1958), 38–49.

5. The most influential work of feminist political theory on civil society is Carole Pateman, *The Sexual Contract* (Stanford, 1988). But also see the work of Daniela Gobetti, whose notion of an "informal public" corresponds to what I am calling the "social" (*Private and Public: Individuals, Households, and Body Politic in Locke and Hutcheson* [New York, 1992]). Of the many historians of women who emphasize a strict public/private distinction, see Leonore Davidoff and Catherine Hall, *Family Fortunes: Men and Women of the English Middle Class, 1780–1850* (Chicago, 1987); and Joan Landes, *Women and the Public Sphere in the Age of the French Revolution* (Ithaca, 1988). The significance of the social has, in fact, begun to attract the attention of scholars working in the history of women in eighteenth- and nineteenth-century America. See Rosemarie Zagarri, "Morals, Manners, and the Republican Mother," *American Quarterly* 44, no. 2 (June 1992): 192–215; and Karen V. Hansen, "Rediscovering the Social: Visiting Practices in Antebellum New England and the Limits of the Public/Private Dichotomy," in *Public and Private in Thought and Practice: Perspectives on a Grand Dichotomy*, ed. Jeff Weintraub and Krishan Kumar (Chicago, 1997): 268–302.

6. The term was first used by the Scottish moral philosopher Dugald Stewart, who referred to the work of the Scottish historians as "*Theoretical* or *Conjectural History*, an expression which coincides pretty nearly in its meaning with that of *Natural History*, as employed by Mr. Hume." Stewart, "Account of the Life and Writings of Adam Smith, LL.D." (1794; reprinted in Adam Smith, *Essays on Philosophical Subjects*, ed. W.P.D. Wightman [Indianapolis, 1982], 293).

7. Adam Ferguson, *An Essay on the History of Civil Society* (1767; reprint, ed. Fania Oz-Salzberger, [Cambridge, 1995]), 7.

8. See, e.g., Ronald Meek, *Social Science and the Ignoble Savage* (Cambridge, 1967); and Richard Olson, *The Emergence of the Social Sciences, 1642–1792* (New York, 1993). For a critique of this tendency to "look forward rather than backward" for the context in which to place Scottish conjectural history, see Roger L. Emerson, "Conjectural History and Scottish Philosophers," *Historical Papers/Communications Historiques* [of the Canadian Historical Association] (1984): 63–90.

9. Mark Salber Phillips, "Reconsiderations on History and Antiquarianism: Arnoldo Momigliano and the Historiography of Eighteenth-Century Britain," *Journal of the History of Ideas* 57, no. 2 (April 1996), 299. Also see his "'If Mrs. Mure Be Not Sorry for Poor King Charles': History, the Novel, and the Sentimental Reader," *History Workshop Journal* 43 (Spring 1997): 111–131, and "Adam Smith and the History of Private Life: Social and Sentimental Narratives in Eighteenth-Century historiography," in *The Historical Imagination in Early Modern Britain: History, Rhetoric, and Fiction, 1500–1800*, ed. Donald Kelley and David Sacks (Cambridge, 1997), 318–42.

10. Philip Hicks, *Neoclassical History and English Culture, from Clarendon to Hume* (New York, 1996).

11. Arendt, *The Human Condition*, 49.

12. John Millar, *The Origin of the Distinction of Ranks: Or, an Inquiry into the Circumstances Which Give Rise to Influence and Authority, in the Different Members of Society* (4th ed., 1806; reprint, ed. John Valdimir Price, Bristol, 1990), 8.

13. Ferguson, *Essay on the History of Civil Society*, 14.

14. J. G. A. Pocock, *The Machiavellian Moment: Florentine Political Thought and the Atlantic Republican Tradition* (Princeton, 1975), 499.

15. Ferguson, *An Essay on the History of Civil Society*, 10.

16. Ibid., 77–8.

17. Daniel Gordon, *Citizens without Sovereignty: Equality and Sociability in French Thought, 1670–1789* (Princeton, 1994), 51–52.

18. William Robertson, *The History of the Discovery and Settlement of America* (1777; reprint, London, 1826), 110.

19. "I shall conduct my researches concerning the *manners* of the Americans in this natural order," writes Robertson (*History of America*, 93, emphasis mine), placing under the rubric of "manners" such topics as bodily constitution, qualities of mind, domestic state, political state and institutions, war and public security, arts, and religious ideas and institutions.

20. On the Plutarchan genre of "lives of illustrious women" as "the oldest form of women's history with the Western historiographical tradition," see Gianna Pomata, "History, Particular and Universal: On Reading Some Recent Women's History Textbooks," *Feminist Studies* 19 no. 1 (Spring 1993): 7–50.

21. Letter of Kames to an unnamed correspondent, n.d., quoted in William C. Lehmann, *Henry Home, Lord Kames, and the Scottish Enlightenment* (The Hague, 1971), 249–50.

22. "The Professor [i.e., Adam Ferguson] is the only subject," Kames complained on receiving a letter from Mrs. Montagu full of praise for Ferguson's *Essay*, "not a word of my concerns … you have discovered the cloven foot, a rivalship between the two authors." Kames to Elizabeth Montagu, 16 April 1767, reprinted in Alexander Tytler, *Memoirs of the Life and Writings of the Honourable Henry Home of Kames*, 2 vols. (1807; reprint, Bristol, 1993), 2:52.

23. Kames to Elizabeth Montagu, 9 December 1769, reprinted in Helen Whitcomb Randall, *The Critical Theory of Lord Kames* (Northampton, 1944), 110.

24. Henry Home (Lord Kames), *Sketches of the History of Man* (4th ed. 1778; reprint, ed. John Vladimir Price, Bristol, 1993), 1: 1.
25. Kames, *Sketches*, 2:90. The "editor" was either the Edinburgh bookseller William Creech or the Edinburgh printer William Smellie. Creech was the Edinburgh publisher of the *Sketches*. Smellie, printer for Creech, compiler of the first *Encyclopaedia Britannica*, and author of *Literary and Characteristical Lives of J. Gregory, M.D., Henry Home, Lord Kames, David Hume, and Adam Smith, LL.D.* (Bristol, 1997), corresponded with Kames concerning the *Sketches* and may have played some role in editing the work.
26. Kames, *Sketches*, 2:1–2.
27. Hugh Blair to Kames, 2 April 1774, reprinted in Tytler, *Life of Kames*, 2:149.
28. Kames, *Sketches*, 2:47.
29. Ibid., 2:41.
30. Olson, *Emergence of the Social Sciences*, 178.
31. Millar, *Ranks*, 14.
32. Michael Ignatieff, "John Millar and individualism," in *Wealth and Virtue: The Shaping of Political Economy in the Scottish Enlightenment*, ed. Istvan Hont and Michael Ignatieff (Cambridge, 1983), 319–20.
33. Millar, *Ranks*, 21.
34. Ibid., 59.
35. Ibid., 60–61.
36. Ibid., 15–16.
37. Ibid., 62.
38. Robertson, *History of America*, 120.
39. Ibid., 103.
40. Ibid., 131.
41. Ibid., 93.
42. Ibid., 103.
43. Millar, *Ranks*, 101.
44. J. G. A. Pocock, "The Mobility of Property and the Rise of Eighteenth-Century Sociology," in Pocock, *Virtue, Commerce and History* (Cambridge, 1985), 117–18.
45. Millar, *Ranks*, 100.
46. Ibid., 32–34.
47. Ibid., 89–90.
48. John Dwyer, *Virtuous Discourse: Sensibility and Community in Late Eighteenth-Century Scotland* (Edinburgh, 1987), 104–5.
49. David Fordyce, *The Elements of Moral Philosophy* (1754; reprint, ed. John Valdimir Price, Bristol, 1990), 147–169; Robertson, *History of America*, 103; Adam Ferguson, *Principles of Moral and Political Science*, 2 vols. (1792; reprint, New York, 1978), 1:27.
50. On the significance of natural jurisprudence for Scottish Enlightenment theory, see Knud Haakonssen, *Natural Law and Moral Philosophy: From Grotius to the Scottish Enlightenment* (Cambridge, 1996); Istvan Hont, "The Language of Sociability and Commerce: Samuel Pufendorf and the Theoretical Foundations of the 'Four-Stages Theory'" in *The Languages of Political Theory in Early Modern Europe*, ed. Anthony Pagden (Cambridge, 1987): 253–276; and James Moore and Michael Silverthorne, "Gershom Carmichael and the Natural Jurisprudence Tradition in Eighteenth-Century Scotland," in *Virtue and Commerce*, 73–87.
51. David Hume, "Of the Rise and Progress of the Arts and Sciences" [1742], in *Essays Moral, Political, and Literary*, ed. Eugene F. Miller (Indianapolis, 1985),

134. While Hume first published fifteen essays under the title *Essays Moral and Political* in 1741, "Of the Rise and Progress of the Arts and Sciences" did not appear until the second edition in 1742.

52. David Hume, "Of Refinement in the Arts," in *Essays*, 271. This essay first appeared in the third edition of Hume's *Essays* (1752) under the title "Of Luxury."

53. Ibid., 101.

54. Ibid., 217.

55. Ferguson, *An Essay on the History of Civil Society*, 176.

56. Kames, *Sketches*, 2:227.

57. Ibid., 1:373.

58. Millar, *Ranks*, 69.

59. Ibid., 96.

60. Ibid., 86. In a similar vein, Ferguson writes that while feudal notions were often "lofty" and "ridiculous," there is not doubt of "their lasting effects on our manners." And if, he adds, "our rule in measuring degrees of politeness and civilization is to be taken from hence,… we shall be found to have greatly excelled any of the celebrated nations of antiquity" (*Essay*, 193).

61. Millar, *Ranks*, 97–98.

62. Ibid., 100–101.

63. Ibid., 102.

64. Adam Smith, *Lectures on Jurisprudence*, ed. R.L. Meek, D.D. Raphael, and P.G. Stein (Indianapolis, 1978), 157.

65. Ibid., 153–4. A similar argument can be found in Hume's "Of Polygamy and Divorces," *Essays*, 184–5.

66. Millar, *Ranks*, 98.

3

KANT, SMITH, AND HEGEL

The Market and the Categorical Imperative

Rupert H. Gordon

Introduction

THE STABILITY OF THE INSTITUTIONS and opportunities of civil society are a product of social and political mechanisms that check
its selfish dimensions and destructive potential by recognizing,
preserving, and protecting the rights and dignity of individuals.
At the same time, a practical commitment by individuals to the
dignity of "others," a learned, subjective disposition of mutual
respect and civility, grounds and supports the formal "policing"
institutions of the state, and gives rights claims an important cultural foundation. The social institutions that foster elements of a
liberal culture to support a liberal polity represent an important
connection between the spheres of "civil society" and the "state."
This connection is the focus of this chapter.

G. W. F. Hegel (1770–1831) has been called "revolutionary" for
his conceptual separation of "civil society" from the "state."[1]
Indeed Hegel does make such a conceptual division and does
break new ground in comparison to other German thinkers of the
late eighteenth and early nineteenth centuries by bringing a "foreign" political economic framework derived from British experience to bear on a nascent bourgeois economy of the German states.[2]

Still, Hegel also places political economic institutions fully within the framework of social ethics, and in this respect, he continues an intellectual tradition that stretches at least from Montesquieu in France to the Scots of the 1700s.

This chapter will examine a key continuity between "civil society" and the "state" in Hegel's political thought. Like the Scots Adam Smith and James Steuart, Hegel sees the market as a crucial institution of social education (*Bildung*)[3] for teaching modern subjects about human dignity. For Hegel, the market teaches the essence of Kant's categorical imperative as a component of practical, ethical life (*Sittlichkeit*) rather than demanding adherence to it as a matter of principled, but abstract, morality (*Moralität*). For Hegel, Smith, and Steuart, the persuasive and dialogical relationships of market exchange foster mutual respect and counter human impulses to dominate others.[4] Thus the market is a source of dignity, in more than a simple material sense. Indeed, in Hegel's system these dispositions of "civility" fostered in civil society provide crucial cultural and foundational support to formal state institutions designed to protect individuals and preserve social peace. A detailed examination of Hegel's writing on poverty and civil society gives this claim interpretive strength and yet simultaneously expresses reservations about the practical success of the educative market mechanism. Finally, Hegel's insights are used to sketch ways in which the institutions of the contemporary marketplace might be developed and structured to serve better the task of ethical education. Hegel's thought, then, shows us the value of a political economic approach that integrates the market into a continuity of social and ethical concerns, rather than constraining and containing it as a necessary evil.

Kant and the Categorical Imperative

For Kant, individual action is subject to universal laws of morality—laws that hold for "all *rational beings as such*—not merely subject to contingent conditions and exceptions, but *with absolute necessity.*"[5] Without exception and regardless of particular circumstances or differences, individuals are to be accorded the same respect by others. While Hegel shares this commitment to universal respect for persons, his formulation diverges from the Kantian in important ways.[6]

The principal difference between Hegel and Kant on this issue relates to the form this commitment takes. For Kant, this prescription must be understood as "a categorical imperative"—"one which represented an action as objectively necessary in itself apart from its relation to a further end."[7] For Kant, a will is only good when it is good in itself, rather than as a product of other inducements. Kant's vision of moral action is action in accord with duty. And duty is action in accord with certain edicts, that is, *"out of reverence for the law."* The law that ultimately governs our interactions with others is: *"Act in such a way that you always treat humanity, whether in your own person or in the person of any other, never simply as a means, but always at the same time as an end."*[8]

A key interpretive controversy here concerns what constitutes faithful institutionalization of the categorical imperative's core concept—the idea of "respect for persons."[9] In Kant's political writings, rights, law, and the consent central to a republican contract concretize this concept.[10] In the abstract, however, this commitment demands a universal valuation of human beings regardless of, and in spite of, their differences. Here we have a vision that embodies the old "golden rule," the idea that we ought to "do unto others as we would be done unto." Hegel rejects this Kantian edict as too abstract, and favors a lived, practical commitment that is the product of institutional learning or "Bildung." Hegel takes up the essence of the Kantian vision with his famous philosophical discussion of "recognition" and then connects it to the mechanisms of a market economy. For Hegel, by treating individuals as "means" to our own satisfaction in a market economy, we come to respect them as persons—an approach that departs radically from the Kantian vision of an ethics of "ends in themselves."

Hegel, Kant, and the Philosophical Idea of "Recognition"

Hegel's commitment to a form of the categorical imperative is easily discerned from the "theory of recognition" presented in the famous "Lordship and Bondage" dialectic of *The Phenomenology of Mind.* In this passage, self-consciousness comes to exist not only "for itself" but also "for another." By surrendering its connection to natural desire (*Begierde*), consciousness is liberated: it becomes free to choose rather than remaining enslaved to follow natural instincts. Only in the mutual recognition of free consciousnesses can the deepest impulses of natural instinct and the accompanying desire to dominate the other be overcome.

In Hegel's account of the trial by death of the Lord and Bonds-man, one consciousness demonstrates "by risking life"[11] that "the essential nature of self-consciousness is not bare existence"[12] and obtains a form of freedom. But by failing to recognize the "other" who is made subject, the master consciousness still relates to the world in the mode of desire, demanding and consuming objects "for itself."[13] At the same time, however, the bondsman moves beyond the mode of desire, holding it in check through work, and developing freedom from desire in his explicit existence for the "other," who is his lord and master.[14] Existing for the other, rather than dominating the other, is the true route to freedom. Finally, in strikingly Kantian language, Hegel declares: "But for recognition proper there is needed the moment that what the master does to the other he should also do to himself, and what the bondsman does to himself, he should do to the other also."[15] This statement indicates Hegel's commitment to the "golden rule," civility, non-domination, and the idea of mutual "respect for persons."

Although the "recognition-as-categorical-imperative" idea may detail a philosophical foundation of Hegel's system, it is not a prac-tical, ethical principle as such: this commitment is simply too ab-stract on its own. In Hegel's view, "respect for persons" must be learned and understood by individuals in real-world interactions with others. In these interactions a person comes to understand *why* she or he should adhere to this doctrine and what its practical foundations are. This process requires a concrete manifestation that makes the abstract essence of the categorical imperative appear as part of human life. The key to Hegel's thinking on this matter, and to his idea of the market, is the way that it challenges the abstract formalism of Kant's commitment to respect for persons.

Hegel, the Market, and Dignity

In contrast to Kant's dualistic vision of ethical life, in which moral-ity and personal inclinations are at odds, Hegel takes up a position more like that of his civic humanist progenitors: personal inclina-tions are transformed or "educated" by institutional structures and interactions to yield higher behaviors. Hegel's civil society begins with "*private persons* [who] ... have their own interest as their end."[16] Here individuals, engaged in bourgeois economic activity pursue ends dictated by a mixture of "natural necessity and arbitrariness"[17] satisfying "subjective needs," working and possessing and protecting their property.[18] Still, Hegel holds that in a modern political economy an "individual cannot accomplish the full extent of his ends without reference to others; these others are therefore means to the end of the particular [person]."[19] Hegel's apparent instrumentalism represents a stark departure from the Kantian position in which we are enjoined to "*treat humanity ... never simply as a means, but always at the same time as an end.*"[20] For Hegel "others" are seen to be "human resources," with a function or role to play in the fulfillment of the self. Paradoxically, this "means-end" construction of the market turns in on itself and yields, instead, a universal respect for the other, which is consistent with the essence of Kant's edict. So Hegel's system of needs turns the instrumental treatment of others for self-interested purposes into an awareness of the respect due to persons as persons.

Hegel describes this transformation through marketplace education and the "reciprocal relation between needs and work": "this very sphere of relativity—as that of *education*—which gives right an *existence* in which it is *universally recognized, known* and *willed*, and ... has validity and objective actuality."[21] He continues: "It is part of education [Bildung]..., that I am apprehended as a *universal* person in which [respect] *all* are identical."[22] In this sphere of life, human beings recognize each other as fundamentally the same, as people who must all work and satisfy universal needs in a market economy—*homines economici*. In light of this universality, Hegel contends: "A *human being counts as such because he is a human being*, not because he is a Jew, Catholic, Protestant, German, Italian, etc."[23]

By relating the "metaphysic of lord and bondsman" to Hegel's civil society and the market, this "mechanism of recognition" can be understood more concretely. First, the prohibition against the domination of the other implicit in the outcome of the "Lordship and Bondage" dialectic helps us better understand the relationship between "self-interested" individuals in Hegel's civil society: others are not valueless means or instruments for domination and manipulation for purely selfish purposes. Instead, others are resources of value that must be respected—beings that have dignity. Second, we can understand the deeply complex character of the economic individual's relationship to other beings. Hegel says:

> Needs and means ... become a *being* for *others* by whose needs and work their satisfaction is mutually conditioned. That abstraction which becomes a quality of both needs and means ... also becomes a determination of the mutual relations between individuals. This universality, as the *quality of being recognized,* is the moment which makes isolated and abstract needs,... into *concrete*, i.e. *social* ones.[24]

Thus mechanisms of the system of needs spill over into personal relations. Recognition transforms the abstract legalism of "respect for persons" into real and concrete modes of social interaction and experience, and the activities of civil society produce a culture of nondomination and mutual respect.

A fuller appreciation for this mechanism of "realization" or "concretization" emerges from a deeper exploration of Hegel's "system of needs." In a modern political economy with a division of labor individuals work to gain monetary resources to pursue their own ends and needs. In so doing, however, they produce products that are—exchanged with others, to satisfy these others' needs. Thus the "system of needs" as an institution of modern political economy ensures, that in the pursuit of his or her own subjective satisfaction, each also satisfies the "other."[25] In seeing this "other" as a player in the market, one party appreciates the other not as a "particular" person but as he or she sees all persons, as an economic actor with whom one must interact. In the course of satisfying particular needs, each person sees the other as one who she or he must respect in the same way each sees himself or herself as being respected. In the free market, all come to understand that domination and manipulation fail as modes of satisfaction. Instead, a merchant must respect the dignity of his or her customers, or they will turn elsewhere. Consumers must respect the dignity of the merchants from whom they purchase, or the merchants will not sell to them. Without a system of mutual recognition in a market economy, the subjective satisfaction of each and all shall fail. Here, then, is an Hegelian, commercialized, bourgeois[26] version of the Kantian categorical imperative—brought about and learned as a principle of practical life and wisdom by the individual's activity in the market of civil society.

Clearly this view of the market and its role in ethical education is an "ideal type." Under varied, real world conditions, the system would not function as Hegel suggests it should. First, Hegel's model presupposes some form of direct interaction between merchant and consumer. Indeed, it is the relationship of dialogue and persuasion underlying direct interaction between parties to a commercial transaction—the "higgling and bargaining," to use Adam Smith's phrase—that gives Hegel's educative market mechanism its greatest force.[27] Further, if market power were centralized in monopoly enterprises, or if individuals were unable to guarantee basic material sustenance, or if market relations were substantially closed off to entry because of barriers involving education, training, and the like, the market's "dignity potential" obviously would be undermined: it is not just *any* market, and not an entirely "free market," that can realize this potential. A discussion below will show that Hegel is aware of, and concerned with, exactly these kinds of problems seemingly endemic to modern political economic systems.

A second dimension of the system of needs brings about an important element of "equal recognition" central to the Hegelian version of the categorical imperative. For Hegel the key here is the "imitative drive, which affords the stimulus to obtain the same unknown enjoyment for oneself or in general to acquire what the other has."[28] In great contrast to Rousseau and Kant, who saw ethical degradation in imitation, Hegel declares: "By dint of representation the enjoyment becomes something subjectively universal, a habit and need. It is then no less necessary to give this equality determinate existence for the other, and to make oneself aware of being regarded and *recognized* by the other as his equal."[29] Further he declares: "One is faced with the consciousness of one's *identity* with the other and at the same time the consciousness of inequality [i.e., difference]. The imitative drive comes into play, coupled with confidence that what the other has, must be pleasing to one's self too."[30] Hegel is giving systematic and philosophical treatment to the bourgeois practice of "keeping up with the Joneses." This is a genuine celebration of a genuinely bourgeois ethic.

Indeed, it is truly remarkable that for Hegel the formal protections of "right" under the "administration of justice"[31] are a product of the educative process of market interactions and imitations. In his 1817–18 lectures on the *Philosophy of Right*, Hegel says:

> By means of education [Bildung],... through the mediation of the universal interchange of work and means ..., individuals *become* ... a subjectivity that is ... inwardly universal. *Formal right* makes its appearance, and, however intimately it is implicated and has its essential content in the aim of [satisfying] needs, it must ..., as the substantive element underlying this aim, be embodied in something independent ...[:] the *administration of justice*.[32]

Even the formal protections of right, law and justice, and state institutions, then—structures that Kant sees as "institutional" manifestations of his categorical imperative[33]—are possible only because of the "prior" subjective education undergone in the market sphere.

The "priority" of the market's subjective education to institutions of formal right and justice can be understood in three ways.

First, the evolutionary character of Hegel's writing could suggest that the development of a liberal "culture" is *temporally or causally* prior to formal right. More productive, however, is to consider subjective education about the value of persons as philosophically foundational to the institutions of justice and rights claims, and as representative of Bildung. The latter point means that, while we may live under the rule of law and within the constraints of state institutions that help "teach" us the value of others by inculcating habits of order and respect, it is only when we become conscious of the rationale for these habitual practices that we are "*gebildete Menschen*," developed persons. Thus, from the point of view of Bildung, the market process is important for its "consciousness raising function."

From the point of view of "foundational priority," the relationship between the market's educative function and the philosophical foundation of rights claims presents a genuinely complex problem: to what degree do rights claims and liberal systems of justice always depend on some prior disposition of respect? For example, John Charvet has shown that Brian Barry's argument for "justice as impartiality" cannot reject justice as mutual advantage as a viable system of justice without the constraints of a strong commitment to equal respect for persons.[34] Similarly, the Rawlsian split between "political" and "comprehensive doctrines"[35] might be said to be successful only because of a precontractual agreement that persons have an inherent, equal value that then grounds society's respect for their right to hold differing comprehensive doctrines post-contract. While Rawls defends himself by arguing that his well-ordered society depends on an "overlapping consensus"[36] on such issues, he does not tell us how this consensus is developed or sustained. Hegel, in contrast, takes this "overlapping consensus" behind formal institutions of justice to be important business and attends directly to how it is developed through market interactions. Here Hegel's emphasis on the continuity between civil society and the state is especially instructive. The formal liberal institutions and practices of the Hegelian state demand the support of a liberal culture. This liberal culture emerges from interactions that occur between individuals, outside the state, in Hegelian civil society.

Interestingly, Hegel is not alone in arguing for the educative role of market institutions and commercial relations. The *doux commerce* thesis—the view that capitalism produces civilization and gentle manners among commercial peoples—has a long history in eighteenth and nineteenth century European thought stretching from Montesquieu through the figures of the Scottish Enlightenment to the American revolutionary Thomas Paine.[37] In the next section I take up the work of two prominent Scottish political economists—Adam Smith and Sir James Steuart. These thinkers are of interest here for two reasons: first, because of their intellectual importance to Hegel and his understanding of modern political economy;[38] and second, because they share the particular version of the doux commerce thesis that the account here attributes to Hegel. Not only do they see commercial relations as "civilizing," but they see the modern market as an important sphere for intersubjective understanding, as a crucial locus for teaching and learning "respect for persons." This Scottish political economy will deepen the overall account of the market's role in ethical education.

Scottish Political Economy and Ethical Education

Unlike Kant, and much more like Hegel, both Steuart and Smith have a genuine interest in educating and developing subjective inclinations. For each, "self-interest"[39] is transformed and educated in important ways when subject to the forces of a modern political economy. Steuart places his discussion of economic concepts like "competition," "supply and demand," and "international trade" squarely under the rubric of "the spirit of a people."[40] He explains this fundamental concept at the start of his *Inquiry* as "the customs of a country."[41] For Steuart, one of the chief duties of the "statesman" or governor is to manage this spirit, to both respect it—"the political oeconomy in each [nation] must necessarily be different"[42]—and transform it with political and economic institutions. Steuart declares:

> It is the business of a statesman to judge of the expediency of different schemes of oeconomy, and by degrees to model the minds of his subjects so as to induce them, from the allurement of private interest, to concur in the execution of his plan.... The great art of political oeconomy is, first to adapt the different operations of it to the spirit, manners, habits, and customs of the people; and afterwards to model these circumstances so as to be able to introduce a set of new and more useful institutions.[43]

Ultimately, then, Steuart is concerned with the formation of habits, attitudes, and mores and with the use of institutions—especially economic ones—to change and develop them.

Steuart's approach resonates with Hegel's concern for the key civil societal values of nondomination and mutual respect in the marketplace. Explaining "double competition," Steuart says:

> The competition between sellers does not appear so striking, as that between buyers; because he who offers to sale, appears passive only in the first operation; whereas buyers present themselves one after another; they make a demand, and when the merchandise is refused to one at a certain price, a second either offers more, or does not offer at all: but soon as another seller finds his account in accepting the price the first had refused, then the first enters into competition, provided his profits will admit his lowering the first price; and thus competition takes place among the sellers, until the profits upon their trade prevent prices from falling lower.[44]

Here the incessant action of "double competition"—a condition in which multiple operators on both supply and demand sides compete and are affected in competition by actions on the other side—prevents any kind of marketplace coercion or domination.

For Steuart, the state must take an active role to preserve the relations of nondomination in double competition. "This happy state [of double competition] cannot be supported but by the care of the statesman...."[45] While the purpose of Steuart's concern with both the "spirit of a people" and "double competition" relate closely to the implementation and maintenance of efficient economies, they also imply a concern with ethical education. For Smith, though, the relationship is much more explicit. Indeed, in his *Theory of Moral Sentiments*, Smith focuses—with striking similarity to Hegel's position—on the intersubjective development of morality, as the product of a process of "recognition."[46] In this process, a moral "actor" attempts to garner the "sympathy" of a moral "spectator," who, in turn, attempts to "enter into the sentiments" of the actor.[47] This process develops in us a "moral sense," "propriety" and "virtue,"[48] and fosters respect for the other as "the great precept of nature to love ourselves only as we love our neighbour...."[49]

How did Smith relate this early understanding of intersubjective identification to the market as an institution? Like Steuart and Hegel, Smith sees a dimension of market relations that curtails domination and builds respect for "the other."[50] In market relations, the essence of exchange activity is not deception or domination but persuasion. In his *Lectures on Jurisprudence*, Smith describes exchange: "The offering of a shilling, which to us appears to have so plain and simple a meaning, is in reality offering an argument to persuade one to [exchange] as it is for his interest."[51] Exchange demands that each person understand the needs of the "other" and then determine how he or she can best meet or serve those needs. Then, in the offering of an exchange, one person attempts to demonstrate his or her successful recognition of this other's position. Inherently, however, one demonstrates respect for the "personhood" of the other by participating in an exchange rather than, for example, in robbery or war. One does not demand a trade by force but accepts the free will of the other, and attempts to sway it by understanding the other's wishes.[52]

This represents a radical reformation of what Smith describes in his *Lectures on Jurisprudence*, as "natural to mankind": "the love of domination and authority over others."[53] Like Hegel, Smith knows that the easiest form of recognition to gain and maintain, and the easiest form of satisfaction of needs, is that which a master enjoys from his slaves; indeed he contends that the "love of domination" makes mine owners pay Scottish colliers higher wages than if they employed free labor.[54] To seek recognition in the free marketplace, in the realm of exchange is much more difficult. The dynamic of the modern marketplace compels us to surrender our impulses to dominate others in favor of respect and recognition.

This dynamic, of course, depends on a crucial structural characteristic of the modern marketplace: its decentralization. The chief assumption for Smith, as for Hegel and Steuart, is that the market is open enough to prevent structural coercion and allow both "unpersuaded" merchants and "unpersuaded" consumers the choice to seek satisfaction from a more "understanding" or respectful party. In addition, the decentralized character of the market helps prevent exorbitant returns under mercantile monopolies that encourage the indulgence of impulses of domination. Indeed, this is what compels Smith, like Steuart, to call for certain state interventions in the economy. Like Steuart's statesman, who is to protect the dynamic of "double competition," Smith demands that governments protect the competitive character of the market by preventing monopolies from developing.[55]

For Smith, then, as for Hegel, the market is a special locus of intersubjective activity, of mutual identification and respect; it is an institution that educates human impulses and inclinations to develop beyond primitive modes of satisfaction through domination into those of mutual recognition and valuation. Further, the liberating capacity of market institutions grounds the Scots' commitment to state intervention in the economy to preserve its nondominating character. This position on state-market relations—something less than a strict private/public separation—will help us to think about ways to maintain the ethical function of the market in light of the problems of poverty and the criticisms of skeptical Marxists.

Market Failure: Hegel, Marx, and the Problem of Poverty

Hegel's writings on poverty reveal that he does not have an unblemished faith in modern market institutions. Indeed, they suggest an ambivalence on Hegel's part about the genuine material and ethical "civility" of the political economic institutions of civil society. Yet in doing so, these writings further support the interpretive arguments made here about the connection, in Hegel's thought, between the market and ethical education. While Hegel is concerned with combating the material effects of poverty,[56] his writings also reveal a fundamental concern with the market's failure to universally instill "respect for persons" in all who participate in its relations. Thus while Hegel is aware of the material effects of market relations and the grinding poverty they can produce,[57] his real focus moves beyond these material concerns to poverty's ethical effects.

When we speak of "market failure," what do we mean? Certainly we speak of the capacity of capitalist institutions to strip a segment of society of its dignity, denying workers opportunities for self-development, basic material sustenance, and freedom of choice—the capacity of capitalist institutions to create "an underclass." These arguments have been well made by Marx[58] and present a challenge to the Hegelian market vision. How can we answer them?

First, Hegel's writings show an awareness of these "market failures" and the problem of poverty as central to a paradoxical condition of civil society. Indeed, in his 1819–20 Berlin lectures on civil society, Hegel says: "The emergence of poverty is generally a consequence of civil society and grows necessarily out of it."[59] This state of poverty is a product of the development of efficiencies in the capitalist system—because of mechanization and the amassing of wealth and capital in few hands.[60] Hegel also demonstrates an awareness of the material and social effects of poverty when he claims that the "*limitation* ... dependence and *want*" it produces "leads to an inability to feel and enjoy the wider freedoms and particularly the spiritual advantages, of civil society."[61]

More than this, however, Hegel expresses serious concern about another dimension of this "all-encompassing misery and deprivation"—its "moral degradation."[62] More than just a poor class, this moral degradation creates what Hegel calls a "rabble."[63] Key to the character of a rabble is a loss of self-respect, and of the respect and recognition of others. Hegel says:

> the poor person feels himself excluded and despised,… an inner revulsion and revolt arises within him…. Within civil society it is not only natural need which the poor person has to combat;… [also] self-consciousness is pushed to [an] extreme where it does not possess any rights, where freedom has no existence… [O]ut of this situation … arises this kind of shamelessness which we discern among the rabble.[64]

Hegel's concern in this regard extends to the wealthy, too. In the Berlin Lectures, Hegel says: "Just as poverty appears … as the basis of the descent into the rabble,… so similar a descent into ruffian-like behavior appears on the side of the rich. The rich person regards everything as something which can be bought by him … Wealth can thus lead to the same disrespect and shamelessness to which the poor rabble has recourse."[65] Market failure is ethically damaging not only for the impoverished, then, but also for the wealthy. As they accumulate money and power and can withdraw from the interactions of a commercial market the wealthy grow corrupt and regress into a "master mentality," in which domination and pure, immediate self-satisfaction are governing modes of life. "These two sides, poverty and wealth, thus constitute the corruption of civil society."[66] Ultimately, for the success of his ethical market mechanism of practical education, Hegel recognizes that everyone must be a *Bürger*, a *bourgeois*.

This discussion has revealed two important points. First, Hegel's concern with the problem of poverty acknowledges, but transcends, the materialist concerns of some critics. While he recognizes the effects of "market failure" on the societal activity of the impoverished, Hegel's chief concern relates to the market's failure as an institution of ethical education—its capacity to corrupt both the poor and the wealthy. While this helps to substantiate my interpretive claim about the role of market relations in Hegel's political philosophy, it also appears to strike a serious blow to the market's efficacy in that capacity. Second, Hegel's contention that poverty and wealth constitute "the corruption" of civil society suggests that some form of intervention to prevent such corruption would be consistent with his aims. In fact, he presents certain clues about what kind of intervention is worthy of consideration.

Hegelian Insights and Contemporary Markets: Rethinking Hegel's Approach

Both Hegel's comments in the Berlin lectures and his interest in Steuart and his statesman suggest that some form of state intervention in the economy to preserve its "dignity" function is justifiable. Hegel's own solutions to the problem seem insufficient, however. While Hegel does speak of the need to provide basic subsistence to all, he expresses reservations about "charity" undermining the poor's "self-respect."[67] Hegel recommends work opportunities—a kind of "full employment" program—to remedy the material problems of the indigent while maintaining their self-respect. But he contends this would only lead to overproduction and, ultimately, more unemployment and poverty.[68] Finally, in the *Philosophy of Right*, Hegel settles on colonization as the only solution to the problem.[69] In new colonies, persons who are "surplus" in the homeland's system of needs can participate fully in a new one.

These solutions are unsatisfactory, especially in contemporary post-Keynesian, postcolonial circumstances. But, Hegel's suggestion that all are entitled to a share in the "*universal and permanent resources*" of civil society is more fruitful. His comments on the corrupt nature of both wealth and poverty suggest a need to "moderate" extremes of wealth in a given society. This could be done with a redistributive income tax, but one that redistributed capital rather than "charitable sustenance." For example, a system of venture capital distribution, made available to assist the unemployed to open or participate in small business enterprises— or even the direct distribution of corporate shares to individuals to both curtail the "mastery" of corporate owners and introduce the indigent into the economic system—might be of use here. A new "Hegelian" socialism of sorts might offer real opportunities for everyone to "be a bourgeois."[70] Certainly the British New Labour "stakeholder society" embodies this approach. Prime Minister Tony Blair has said: "Let us talk of rising living-standards, and let's make that mean cash in the pocket. But let's make it mean more than cash too. Let's make it mean rising standards of behavior,... rising standards of mutual respect."[71] Blair, too, sees the market as an institution that generates both material dignity and intersubjective respect.

The "stakeholder approach" also welcomes the opportunities presented by new electronic technologies that may bring a radical wave of decentralization to contemporary capitalism. On the one hand, the development of "market-directed" technologies and a greater degree of niche marketing may help achieve structural changes in mass markets that create different consumer patterns. For example, such "localism" could help realize the vision of small-scale, decentralized production and distribution, even in capital-intensive industries, presented in E. F. Schumacher's book *Small is Beautiful*. Here a general skepticism about Taylorite models of production is synthesized with an appreciation of the ethical potential of a decentralized market system.[72] Similarly, niche marketing could help produce the small, decentralized network of workshops and firms that was central to Hobson's apparently utopian construct of "qualitative consumption" and the "citizen-consumer."[73] The radical fragmentation of media markets into "specialty channels" and "niche publications" suggests such a process of decentralization is underway. Moreover, the "virtual" world of commercial exchange could fuse this pluralistic model with the classical vision of interpersonal market interaction. Thousands of individuals running home businesses on the internet—"stakeholders in a modern economy"—for niche national, and even global, markets may produce the truest representation ever of the eighteenth-century market so central to Smith, Steuart, and Hegel.[74]

The argument can even be made that recent attempts to improve consumer confidence and competition in mass consumer markets may embody the Hegelian market ethic. Marketers in competition for sales treat individuals as instruments in the construction of markets; but in so doing, marketers must come to know and recognize these individuals and "attend to their wills" with persuasive messages, product design, and consumer service. Thus, even mass consumerism has the potential to be a source of this practical learning, and dignity.[75]

Conclusion

George Bernard Shaw was being caustically sarcastic when he had the shopkeeper in his 1933 play *Village Wooing* say: "Manners will never be universally good until every person is every other person's customer."[76] Nonetheless, the object here has been to reveal how this might be understood as correct. First, this has been shown to be true for Hegel, by associating his philosophical concept of recognition both with Kant's categorical imperative, and the market as an institution of Bildung. A reading of Hegel's discussion of the system of needs and an analysis of his concerns have substantiated this interpretive point. Second this conceptual relationship has been substantiated, and important dimensions of Hegel's intellectual roots illustrated, in a discussion of the work of Adam Smith and James Steuart. In both these thinkers, there is a visible concern with the "educative" capacity of market relations. Finally, a response to objections that might be offered to the market educational model has been canvassed, and efforts have been made to develop Hegel's insights into more effective solutions to "market failures" than those he offers.

The contemporary market is the most influential of all civil institutions in the world today. It continues to be an institution that, despite the opportunities it offers, and its apparently necessary relationship to liberal democracy, also continues to challenge notions central to liberal democracy, such as, dignity and respect for persons. In this light it is important to begin to look not only for new ways to consider "regulating" or structuring the market but also for ways in which these regulations and structures might help develop a new conception of the market and its function. Despite his conceptual separation of "state" and "civil society," Hegel's emphasis on the interrelationship of these spheres opens the door to a reappraisal of the market's function. Like the Scots who preceded him and thinkers who followed him—Mill, Hobson, Hobhouse, Keynes—Hegel chose to see the market as more than an efficient mechanism of allocation.[77] Instead, he situates the market within a broader ethical theory. For Hegel, the market provides support to social values like "respect for persons" and to state institutions like rights and the administration of justice. It does so both as a theoretical foundation and as a practical mechanism of acculturation. The market appears to be here to stay, and we need to think not about how to live with the market as a necessary evil but, rather, how to integrate it into broader social concerns. As Hegel helps to reveal, the nexus between the abstract principles of a liberal society and the practical, intersubjective potential of market relations is exactly where this process can take place.

Notes

The author gratefully acknowledges the support of the Social Sciences and Humanities Research Council of Canada and the Institute for Humane Studies. Thanks to Steven B. Smith, Shelley Burtt, Allen Wood, Steven Young, Frank Trentmann, Jane Gordon, and Rebecca M. Tuff for helpful comments on earlier drafts. An earlier version of this essay was presented at the 1997 Canadian Political Science Association Annual General Meeting.

1. See Manfred Riedel, *Between Tradition and Revolution*, trans. Walter Wright (Cambridge, 1984), esp. ch. 5.
2. On the economy of the German states in Hegel's time, see Reinhart Koselleck, *Preussen zwischen Reform und Revolution* (Stuttgart, 1967). For more historically specific Hegelian reflections on the German states and civil society, see G. W. F. Hegel, "The German Constitution" [c. 1800] in *Hegel's Political Writings*, trans. T. M. Knox (Oxford, 1964), 143–242. As a social-historical complement to this Hegelian text, see Mack Walker, *German Home Towns* (Ithaca, 1971).
3. For a historical examination of a concrete institution of Bildung, see Daniel A. McMillan, "Energy, Willpower, and Harmony," in this volume.
4. On the centrality of these values to civil society, see John A. Hall, "Reflections on the Making of Civility in Society," in this volume.
5. Immanuel Kant, *Groundwork of the Metaphysic of Morals* (1785; reprint, New York, 1964), 76. All emphasis in citations is original.
6. The interpretation of Kant offered here follows Hegel's critique, which some may argue is unfair. For another approach to Kant, see Elisabeth Ellis, "Immanuel Kant's Two Theories of Civil Society," in this volume.
7. Kant, *Groundwork*, 82.
8. Ibid., 68, 96.
9. See Roger Scruton. "Contract, Consent and Exploitation," in *Essays on Kant's Political Philosophy*, ed. Howard Williams (Chicago, 1992), 220.
10. See Immanuel Kant, "Idea for a Universal History with a Cosmopolitan Purpose" [1784], in *Political Writings*, ed. Hans Reiss, trans. H. B. Nisbett (Cambridge, 1976), 41–60.
11. G. W. F. Hegel, *The Phenomenology of Mind* [1807], trans. J. B. Baillie (New York, 1967), 233.—For the German see G. W. F. Hegel, *Werke* (Frankfurt, 1970), 3: 149.
12. Ibid.
13. Ibid., 234; Hegel, *Werke*, 3: 150.
14. Ibid., 239–40; Hegel, *Werke*, 3: 152–155.
15. Ibid., 236; Hegel, *Werke*, 3: 152.
16. G. W. F. Hegel, *Elements of the Philosophy of Right* [1821], ed. Allen Wood, trans. H.B. Nisbett (Cambridge, 1991), 187. This text is cited by section number, with an "R" for the remark and an "A" for the addition. For the German see Hegel, *Werke*, 7.—Section notations are the same in the German and English editions.
17. Ibid., 182.
18. Ibid., 189, 218.
19. Ibid., 182A.
20. Kant, *Groundwork*, 96.
21. Hegel, *Elements*, 209.
22. Ibid., 209R.
23. Ibid.
24. Hegel, *Elements*, 192.

25. Ibid., 189–208.
26. The word "bourgeois" is used here deliberately. First, the German term *bürgerliche Gesellschaft* has dual connotations as both "civil" and "bourgeois" society. Second, this is a word Hegel himself uses to define the modern person as the "burgher or *bourgeois*" (Hegel, *Elements*, 190R; see also G. W. F. Hegel, *Lectures on the History of Philosophy* [1825], trans. E. S. Haldane and Frances H. Simson (Lincoln, 1995), 2: 209). Finally, for Hegel, "the bourgeois" is a hero, in ways that he or she simply is not for Rousseau and Kant (see below) and in others that are radically different from Marx's rationale for lionizing the bourgeoisie. For an excellent account of Hegel's relationship to the bourgeois world and "the bourgeois" as a symbol in modern political thought, see Steven B. Smith, "At the Crossroads: Hegel and the Ethics of *Bürgerliche Gesellschaft,*" *Laval théologique et philosophique* 51, no. 2 (June 1995): 345–62.
27. For more on the mechanics of this "higgling and bargaining model," see the discussion of Smith below.
28. G. W. F. Hegel, *Lectures on Natural Right and Political Science: The First Philosophy of Right*, ed. Otto Pöggeler et al., trans. J. Michael Stewart and Peter C. Hodgson (Berkeley, 1995), 95. This text is cited by section with an "R" for the remark.—For the German see G. W. F. Hegel, *Naturrecht und Staatswissenschaft*, ed. Otto Pöggeler et al. (Hamburg, 1983).—Section notations are the same in the English and German editions. See also Hegel, *Elements*, 193.
29. Hegel, *Lectures*, 95; also see Hegel, *Elements*, 192–93. Cf. Jean-Jacques Rousseau, "Discourse on the Origins of Inequality," in *The Basic Political Writings*, trans. Donald A. Cress (Indianapolis, 1987), 67–68; and Kant, "Idea for a Universal History," in *Political Writings*, 49
30. Hegel, *Lectures*, 95R.
31. Hegel, *Elements*, 209–29.
32. Hegel, *Lectures*, 108; see also Hegel, *Elements*, 207–9.
33. Immanuel Kant, "Perpetual Peace: A Philosophical Sketch" [1795], in *Political Writings*, 93–130.
34. John Charvet, "Impartial Justice and the Good," MS. See also Matt Matravers, "What's 'Wrong' in Contractualism," *Utilitas* 8, no. 3 (November 1996): 329–40.
35. See John Rawls, *Political Liberalism* (New York, 1996), 47–131.
36. Ibid., 133–72.
37. See Albert O. Hirschman, "Rival Views of Market Society," in *Rival Views of Market Society* (New York, 1986), 106–9. For a more detailed discussion of the doux commerce thesis, see Albert O. Hirschman, *The Passions and the Interests* (Princeton, 1977).
38. On this relationship, see Paul Chamley, "Les origines de la pensée économique de Hegel," in *Hegel Studien* 3 (1965): 225–61; Raymond Plant, "Economic and Social Integration in Hegel's Political Philosophy," in *Selected Essays on G. W. F. Hegel*, ed. Lawrence S. Stepelvich (Atlantic Highlands, 1993), 76–103; Smith, "At the Crossroads"; Georg Lukacs, *The Young Hegel*, trans. Rodney Livingstone (London, 1975), 168–78; Norbert Waszek, *The Scottish Enlightenment and Hegel's Account of Civil Society* (Dordrecht, 1988).
39. See Sir James Steuart, *An Inquiry into the Principles of Political Oeconomy*, ed. Andrew S. Skinner (Edinburgh, 1966), vol. 1, bk. 2, intro., 142; and Adam Smith, *An Inquiry into the Nature and Causes of the Wealth of Nations* (Indianapolis, 1981), bk. 1, ch. 2, 25.
40. Steuart, *An Inquiry*, bk. 1, intro., 17; and bk. I, ch. 2, 22–29.
41. Ibid., bk. 1, ch. 2, 22.

42. Ibid., bk. 1, intro, 17.
43. Ibid., bk. 1, intro, 16.
44. Ibid., bk. 2, ch. 7, 174.
45. Ibid., bk. 2, ch. 10, 195.
46. No definitive historical evidence exists that Hegel read Smith's *Theory of Moral Sentiments*, although two German translations of the work were produced before 1800. See Waszek, *Scottish Enlightenment*, 266. An English copy of *The Wealth of Nations* was found in Hegel's library at his death; see Waszek, "Appendix IV," in *Scottish Enlightenment*, 283.
47. Adam Smith, *The Theory of Moral Sentiments* (Indianapolis, 1982), part 1, sec. 1, ch. 5, 23.
48. Ibid., part 1, sec. 1, ch. 5, 25.
49. Ibid.
50. My argument in this section owes a great deal to Thomas Lewis, "Between Political Theory and Political Economy: Adam Smith on Establishing Individual Liberty," MS, presented at the Canadian Political Science Association Annual General Meeting, Brock University, St. Catherines, ON, 4 June 1996.
51. Adam Smith, *Lectures on Jurisprudence* (1763; reprint, Indianapolis, 1982), 352; see also Part 2, 493–4. See also Smith, *Wealth of Nations*, bk. 1, ch. 2, 26.
52. On the moral import of "higgling and bargaining" for Smith, see Nicholas Phillipson, "Adam Smith as Civic Moralist," in *Wealth and Virtue*, eds. Istvan Hont and Michael Ignatieff (Cambridge, 1983), 191–98; Peter Minowitz, *Profits, Priests, and Princes* (Stanford, 1993), 67–81; and Donald Winch, *Adam Smith's Politics* (Cambridge, 1978), 70–102.
53. Smith, *Lectures on Jurisprudence*, 16 February 1763, 192. See also *Lectures on Jurisprudence*, 16 February 1763, 187; and Report Dated 1766, Domestic Law, 452.
54. Smith, *Lectures on Jurisprudence*, 16 February 1763, 19–93.
55. Smith, *Wealth of Nations*, bk. 4, sec. 3, 630–1. See also Smith's extensive discussion of the "police" powers of the state in *Lectures on Jurisprudence*, 24 December 1762, 5–14; and 17 January 1763, 71–86.
56. Hegel, *Elements*, 252–6.
57. On Hegel's writing on poverty, see Raymond Plant, "Economic and Social Integration;" and Shlomo Avineri, *Hegel's Theory of the Modern State* (Cambridge, 1971), ch. 7.
58. Karl Marx, *The Manifesto of the Communist Party* (London, 1988), 82; and Karl Marx, *Capital*, trans. Ben Fowkes (New York, 1976), vol. 1, ch. 10, sec. 2–4, 353–74.
59. Shlomo Avineri, Appendix to "Feature Book Review: The Discovery of Hegel's Early Lectures on the Philosophy of Right," *The Owl of Minerva* 16, no. 2 (1985): 206. See also Hegel, *Elements*, 244.
60. Avineri, Appendix, 206; see also Hegel, *Elements*, 244.
61. Hegel, *Elements*, 243.
62. Avineri, Appendix, 206.
63. Hegel, *Elements*, 244.
64. Avineri, Appendix, 206–7.
65. Ibid., 207. This discourse of vice echoes themes in both Calvinist and republican thought.
66. Ibid.
67. See Hegel, *Elements*, 245. See also Hegel, *Lectures*, 118R; and Avineri, Appendix, 207.
68. See Hegel, *Elements*, 245; and Hegel, *Lectures*, 118R.

69. See Hegel, *Elements*, 248.
70. For a different application of Hegelian principles to contemporary conditions, see Jay Drydyk, "Capitalism, Socialism and Civil Society," *Monist* 74, no. 3 (1991): 457–77. For a contemporary argument with affinities to this "Hegelian socialism," see Jeremy Rifkin, *The End of Work* (New York, 1995), esp. 228.
71. Tony Blair, *New Britain: My Vision of a Young Country* (London, 1996), 308. On the "stakeholder society" in general, see part 4, chs. 34–36, 291–321.
72. E. F. Schumacher, *Small is Beautiful: Economics as if People Mattered* (London, 1973).
73. See Frank Trentmann, "Civil Society, Commerce, and the 'Citizen-Consumer,'" in this volume.
74. Blair, *New Britain*, 295. See also 296.
75. For an especially interesting indictment of this general view on the grounds that modern consumer markets do not produce any kind of meaningful choice, see Ronald Beiner, *What's the Matter with Liberalism?* (Berkeley, 1992).
76. George Bernard Shaw, *Too Good to Be True, Village Wooing and On the Rocks* (London, 1934), 131.
77. See Trentmann, "Civil Society, Commerce, and the 'Citizen-Consumer,'" in this volume. As an example of the latter position, see Armen A. Alchain, *Economic Forces at Work* (Indianapolis, 1977).

4

IMMANUEL KANT'S TWO
THEORIES OF CIVIL SOCIETY

Elisabeth Ellis

> Here, 'tis like, the common question will be made, who
> shall be judge whether the prince or legislative act contrary
> to their trust?...
>
> But further, this question (who shall be judge?) cannot
> mean, that there is no judge at all. For where there is no judi-
> cature on earth, to decide controversies amongst men, God
> in heaven is judge: he alone, 'tis true, is judge of the right.
>
> — Locke, *Second Treatise of Government* (1690)

KANT'S THINKING ON CIVIL SOCIETY bridges a gap between old
and new conceptions of the term. Up to the 1780s, writers in
the social contract tradition used the term "civil society" (*societas
civilis*) to designate the opposite of the state of nature: *societas
civilis* was what human beings entered upon giving up their natural liberty in exchange for security.[1] Toward the end of the eighteenth century, however, "civil society" came to mean something
quite different. Rather than encompassing the entirety of a governed group, ruler and ruled alike, "civil society" began to stand
for organized society outside the state. The question of the proper
relationship between the state and civil society, which could not
have been raised under the old conception of the term, became
important: civil society was seen variously as being controlled by
the state, using the state to represent its interests, criticizing the
state, or legitimizing the state.

Kant's political thought contains elements of both the old and new concepts of civil society. On the one hand, Kant's version of social contract theory offers a principled defense of political power. This account of the legitimacy of the state's coercive apparatus is bolstered by a complementary account of individual political obligation. To the theory of the *societas civilis*, then, Kant contributes a justification of the state's dominion based on every person's obligation to secure his neighbors' freedom by submitting to a common authority, that is, by entering the *societas civilis*. On the other hand, Kant's concept of publicity, present in his writings on *societas civilis* and worked out more fully in his political essays, constitutes an alternative theory of civil society, one that conceives of civil society in the new sense of the term, as organized society outside the state. Kant was writing at the historical moment between the decline of the old sense and the rise of the new meaning of "civil society." Reinhart Koselleck has described this period (1750–1850) as "*Sattelzeit*," a time of tremendous conceptual flux during which the modern constellations of meaning for many social and political concepts were worked out.[2] Rather than merely reflecting these two currents of meaning, Kant's work represents an attempt to solve the problems inherent in the first concept of civil society via innovations introduced in the second. Theorists of civil society after Kant moved beyond early attempts to embody universally authoritative principles in the *societas civilis*, identifying the new civil society, or elements within it, as the bearer of merely particular interests and opinions. Kant, by contrast, attempted to resolve the problem of the early social contract theorists by using civil society—newly conceived as a public sphere—to achieve the most true and authoritative political judgment possible in this world.

Early theories of *societas civilis* tried to solve a critical problem of government: who shall be judge on earth? Social contract theorists like Hobbes and Locke agreed that human nature, while making human beings partly rational and capable of improvement by instruction, also precludes them from being fit judges in their own cases. Irrational passions, such as revenge, and more rational interests, such as greed, inevitably lead individuals astray in judging the rightness of public acts. The search for authoritative political judgment on earth led Hobbes to propose the artificial person of the sovereign, and Locke to counter with the legislative will of the people (neither writer was willing to abandon the hope of worldly peace for the meager comfort of heavenly justice).[3] *Societas civilis*, according to the early social contract theorists, solves the problem of authoritative political judgment on earth by investing certain human actors with that responsibility: the Hobbesian sovereign's judgment may be iniquitous, but it is never unjust; Locke's members of *societas civilis* entrust all disputes to their representative, though ultimately "the people shall be judge."[4]

Kant, like his predecessors in social contract theory, provided an account of individuals' obligation to enter into the *societas civilis*; like them, he recognized that natural human failings will cause both powerful sovereign and obedient subjects to perform their duties less reliably than they ought. The problems that Hobbes and Locke faced as they tried to construct a reliable secular substitute for perfect, but unavailable, divine justice were even worse for Kant. Unlike Hobbes, Kant was unwilling to rely on the rational interest of a human sovereign in the well-being of the commonwealth to counterbalance the factors working against that sovereign's judgment (the corruption of power, the temptations of passion, even a simple lack of understanding). Unlike Locke, Kant began with a moral theory that prohibits citizens from endangering the civil order, just or unjust. Kant would have to find the source of reliable political judgment on earth in the very theoretical innovations that kept him from accepting classical social contract theory.

Kant's own epistemological commitments make what Hobbes called "inconveniences" into thorny contradictions. In the first place, Kant applies his distinction between phenomena and noumena to the sphere of politics, breaking political life into actual (phenomenal) and ideal (noumenal) spheres. Manfred Riedel has translated this distinction into modern terms as a break between facts and norms.[5] Different standards of inquiry apply to possible knowledge of each of these spheres: while knowledge of phenomena relies on useful but ultimately uncertain inductive reasoning, knowledge of noumena—of unchanging, "categorically true" things—is reached via deductive reasoning from the conditions of understanding. Accordingly, Kant's ideal *respublica noumenon*[6] serves as a sort of model for the actual *respublica phenomenon*. Such a theory necessitates a mechanism whereby this ideal model (*respublica noumenon*) would be applied to practical politics.[7] Hobbes and Locke both offer relatively simple mechanisms for the application of judgment to the political sphere (for Hobbes, once the state is in place, the sovereign retains a monopoly on public judgment; for Locke, in times of serious disjuncture, the right to judge reverts to society). Neither theorist expects that the judgment thus achieved will be perfect, but each hopes to have provided the closest possible human approximation of perfect political judgment. Kant's mechanism for applying ideal political judgments to practical politics is more ambitious and less direct than those of his predecessors; he aims for more nearly perfect political judgment, but is willing to wait quite a while to achieve it (as I shall explain in what follows).

Further complicating Kant's political thought is a distinction, from his practical philosophy, between inner and outer freedom. Inner freedom has to do with ethics; a person is inwardly free insofar as that person subjects himself or herself to the moral law. Outer freedom, on the other hand, means much the same thing for Kant as it did for Hobbes (the absence of impediments to motion), and has to do not with the moral but the civil law.[8] Kant does not limit his political considerations to those related to outward freedom, though he concentrates on legalistic considerations in his "Doctrine of Right," the *Rechtslehre*.[9] Instead, Kant seeks to bridge politics and ethics via the practical political *effects* of commonly recognized moral truths.[10]

Publicity is the mechanism Kant chooses to connect politics and ethics. Over the course of several decades of work, Kant develops, rejects, and modifies a number of versions of a theory of publicity that would allow flawed human beings to apply their closest approximations of ideal judgment to practical political life. Kant's views on the mechanism by which people might apply timeless ethical truths to particular political situations change as his theory of publicity develops. However, the old question raised by early theorists of civil society as a *societas civilis* remains at the center of his inquiry: who shall be judge of right on earth? Kant responds to this old question of the social contract theorists with his new conception of organized society in relation to the state: his theory of publicity constitutes an early version of our modern sense of civil society.

I

In the *Rechtslehre*, Kant draws on social contract theory and his own moral philosophy to produce an image of the just state (and system of states) grounded in reason: the perfect *societas civilis*. As in his major works of critical philosophy, Kant argues in the *Rechtslehre* in the ideal style, drawing conclusions intended to be valid for "every rational being as such."[11] The formal principles set out in the *Rechtslehre* are based on the moral law, which in turn is supposed to express ordinary moral reason. For example, Kant argues that "morally practical reason pronounces in us its irresistible *veto*: *there is to be no war*."[12] He recognizes that the actual world is not in harmony with these moral precepts, but insists on their reality as ideals held in common. Even though Kant's formal political philosophy is ideal (that is, present nowhere on earth except as a model in the minds of rational people), it is binding nonetheless, as it expresses necessary conclusions from "the moral law within us."[13]

The same holds true for more mundane ideals, such as constitutionalism. As Kant puts it in "The Contest of Faculties," "If we think ... of the commonwealth in terms of concepts of pure reason, it may be called a Platonic *ideal* (*respublica noumenon*), which is not an empty figment of the imagination, but the eternal norm for all civil constitutions whatsoever ..."[14] The principles of constitutional government Kant outlines in the *Rechtslehre* are not products of experience, of historical trial and error, and thus do not vary over time or place. As norms, they must be "derived *a priori* by reason from the ideal of a rightful association ..."[15] Kant argues that the very universality of the norm of constitutional government promotes its eventual realization, though he realizes that the actual world fails to approach the standards set by moral reason. Despite their ideal status, therefore, Kant expects the formal principles of the *Rechtslehre* to have practical political effects. For Kant, the doctrine of right, based on the moral law, is the fundamental basis of all politics, since it provides the only possibly universal standards of political legitimacy.

The most important standard provided for political life by universal reason is that of the just state (*societas civilis*). People have an obligation, Kant claims, to enter the *societas civilis* and to give up their "wild" freedom. This is so because in order to develop his or her capacities, each individual requires that the freedoms of others be restricted: all must submit to a common authority, whose impartial judgment will stand for all parties.[16] Given that human beings are not perfectly rational, but governed by both reason and by "pathological" desires, they experience the ideal of the just state as a moral obligation to enter into civil union. (Consider the impossible case of perfectly rational human beings. Such beings would experience the just state not as an obligation but as a law as natural as gravity; no obligation or coercion would be required to get them to obey just laws.)[17] Since each individual recognizes the validity of the civil order, but at the same time would except himself or herself from its restrictions, Kant argues, the "just civil constitution" is one in which "*freedom under external laws* would be combined to the greatest possible extent with irresistible force."[18]

The perfect *societas civilis*, in which there are no exceptions to the rule of law, cannot be achieved on earth. It exists, for Kant, as an ideal to which actual societies may be compared. Comparisons between commonly recognized ideals and actual political situations have a sort of moral force in their own right. For example, Kant observes that after the Glorious Revolution (1688) the British Government suffered from a disjuncture between its publicly acclaimed ideal of constitutional monarchy and the actual state of absolute rule. "This corrupt system, however, must naturally be given no publicity if it is to succeed. It therefore remains under a very transparent veil of secrecy."[19] Here Kant applies his theory of publicity's moral force to a concrete political example: a government can subvert its publicly legitimating ideal only under conditions of secrecy.

Real-world *societates civiles* are subject to faulty outcomes caused by flawed human nature, contained in institutions that can only partly mitigate those failings (this is Kant's view as well as those of his predecessors). Locke's solution to the problem of corruption among the people's representatives was to retain the people's right to judge whether the state is legitimate, and to back that right of judgment with the use of force, if necessary. Thus for Locke, the right of revolution was one mechanism for closing the gap between the just and the actual state.[20]

This option was not available to Kant. For him, such a right to revolution is incoherent on several grounds. First, it violates our primary duty to protect our neighbors' rights by submitting to a common authority (the entrance to the *societas civilis*).[21] Second, it violates the concept of sovereignty by withdrawing real authority from the representative and placing it back in the hands of the people.[22] Finally, and more practically, revolution is unlikely to replace corruption with justice.[23] Kant agrees with his predecessors in social contract theory that human judges of political right will never be perfectly just. Instead of responding to this problem by relaxing the rights and duties outlined in his ideal conception of the just state, however, Kant introduces a new institution to mediate between the *respublica noumenon* and the *respublica phenomenon*: publicity.

II

Kant's formal political theory of the *Rechtslehre* set forth timeless, universal principles of right. To become practical, these ideals would have to be supplemented by a theory that could mediate between formal standards and historical conditions. In his theory of publicity, Kant took fundamental principles of political right as given and asked how "historical" human beings could put them into practice.[24] In other words, Kant supplements his image of the ideal state with an account of the transition toward perfect justice.

To put it simply, the theory of the just state tells us what the goals of human progress must be, but nothing about how we might reach them. As in the case of the right of revolution, there is a wide gulf between an end recognized by all (the just state, say) and the means available to an individual to pursue it—since any action to overturn the existing civil order puts the actor in contradiction to the moral law.[25] Kant attempts to bridge this gulf by examining human endeavors from a perspective that combines morality (ordinarily applied to individuals) and empirical history (applied to humankind as a species).

In his early essay on enlightenment, Kant considers the question that prompts much of his historical work: how can humankind make progress toward perfection? Reason, he argues, provides a universally applicable image of this perfection; unfortunately, we cannot be confident that we have the means to achieve it. Kant begins with the claim that any such progress cannot be made individually. "There is more chance," Kant writes, "of an entire public [*ein Publikum*] enlightening itself. This is indeed almost inevitable, if only the public concerned is left in freedom."[26]

The need for a mediating institution between universal standards and practical politics was clear already in Kant's ideal-philosophical works. The formal *Rechtslehre* lacks an account of a mediator between the timeless "form" and the historical "material" of politics: an authoritative, disinterested, and yet also worldly judge of political and social institutions would occupy the theoretical white space left in Kant's doctrine of law. Yet Kant did not arrive at his image of the public sphere via deductions from the necessary conditions of understanding. Rather than restricting himself to theoretically or practically necessary truths, Kant combines rational and empirical principles of inquiry to sketch an account of the "public." The image of the public sphere found in Kant's political essays reflects more than the strictly formal and ahistorical conclusions of his practical philosophy. Rather, Kant's historical account of the public sphere takes many of its characteristics from the peculiar qualities of the nascent public sphere to which he himself belonged.

Over the course of the eighteenth century, the literary "world of letters" was transforming itself into a critical public sphere in the modern sense, addressing matters of common interest, including controversial political and social issues.[27] Kant's writings on publicity are representative of a brief moment in this process. For the early part of the century, the public sphere was dominated by moral weeklies and literary journals that sought to lead public tastes while avoiding political entanglements. By the mid-nineteenth century, the advent of mass institutions that sought and formed the new political force of public opinion made Kant's and his contemporaries' Enlightenment ideal of a sphere representing a single public will based on rational truths seem quaint indeed. For a few brief moments in the history of modern political discourse, however, the enlightenment ideal of the public sphere as a scholarly republic of letters ruled the field. [28]

Rather than inventing the concept of the public sphere as a solution to purely philosophical problems, Kant approvingly observed and borrowed from the developing world of letters around him. Kant himself participated in an ongoing series of controversies published in the *Berlinischer Monatsschrift*. Founded in 1783 by Johann Erich Biester and Friedrich Gedike, the *Berlinischer Monatsschrift* (*BMS*) became "the most important forum that the German Enlightenment possessed during its last and highest phase."[29] The journal was at once intellectually daring and politically pro-establishment, characteristics that led to its longevity (it lasted thirteen years), its popularity, and, after a change of government, to its eventual dissolution in 1796.[30] The contents of the *BMS* included polemics, scholarly articles, both satirical and more serious poetry, travel reports, proposals for civic improvements, and sermons; such a mix was typical of cutting-edge magazines of the time. The *BMS* was one of a group of new German-language journals that in the late eighteenth century moved beyond the standard format of moral homily, instruction in matters of taste, and literary discussion.

The debate that prompted Kant's essay, "An Answer to the Question: What Is Enlightenment?" illustrates just the kind of intellectual exchange on politically relevant topics that Kant took as a model for his theory of publicity. In 1783, the *BMS* published a particularly tendentious anonymous piece: "Suggestion, that the Clergy Cease to Trouble Themselves with Performing Marriage Ceremonies."[31] "Suggestion" argues in favor of civil marriage on the grounds that marriage is a contract like all other contracts; while some official support of contracts is necessary, no case can be made for making the marriage contract alone the object of religious rather than civil authority.[32] The author argues further that not only was the religious sanctioning of marriage unnecessary, since enlightened people do not need ceremonies to mark their contracts, but that the separation of the marriage contract from other contracts might lead to the denigration of all other civil contracts. The author imagines an ordinary person reasoning thus: "God himself wills that I do not break certain contracts or laws; the others, however, are only made by men, and thus do not mean very much."[33] A reader today might expect such an article to proceed to argue for the separation of church and state. Instead, our radical author argues for the total subsumption of the church into the state. "Let politics and religion, laws and catechisms be one!"[34] The author ultimately argues for civil *religion* in what would later, if briefly, become the French style: the rational union of church and state in the interest of the people's happiness.

"Suggestion" received a number of replies, several of which favorably compared the practices of other countries to those of Prussia.[35] The reply that inspired Kant's essay, however, took the opposite view, invoking foreign customs such as French decadence as negative examples while praising ordinary German morality. When the Protestant clergyman Johann Friedrich Zöllner, author of enlightened moral advice books, and a member of the Berliner Mittwochgesellschaft (Wednesday Society),[36] replied to "Suggestion," he defended the special status of the marriage contract as the basis for its remaining outside state control. Like the author of "Suggestion," Zöllner defends a position different than a present-day reader might have predicted, especially from a powerful civil servant and member of the established church hierarchy. Rather than simply defending the current system, Zöllner argues that the intimacy of marriage puts it beyond the state's reach. He treads a very narrow path, not directly critical of the state's role in regulating religion (and not arguing for a separation of church and state), but also stressing that the church possessed legitimate spheres of authority independent of the state.[37]

Running through Biester's and Zöllner's arguments about civil marriage is a more fundamental debate of interest to *Aufklärer*: could the process of *Aufklärung* itself become dangerous to public morality?[38] Underlying the whole exchange is the common worry that the progress of reason, while good for debunking superstition and eliminating barriers to social and economic change, might go too far, and eliminate the bases of social stability.[39] As Zöllner puts it, the useful work of preachers in assisting human happiness and in teaching the young would become endangered by the measures suggested by Biester: they would "destabilize the first principles of morality, bring down the worth of religion, and confuse the heads and hearts of people in the name of *Aufklärung*."[40]

In a subsequent note expressing this anxiety, Zöllner asked the question that inspired Kant's essay: "What is enlightenment? This question, which is nearly as important as: What is truth? ought really to be answered, before one begins enlightening! And I have yet to find it answered anywhere!"[41]

This argumentative style that evaluates practical questions of governance on the basis of universalistic ideals available to all rational persons must have appealed to Kant, who incorporated such a style into his image of the reasoning public. In addition to the model provided by the actual public sphere of which Kant was both a sympathetic observer and an active member, Kant had access to new ideas about the role of publicity that were published in that arena. As Lucien Hölscher has observed, by this time the concept of *Publizität* (from the French, *publicité*) brought with it a "new, mostly positive assessment of freedom of expression, one that had established itself in republican and enlightenment circles since the seventies."[42] Late seventeenth- and early eighteenth-century celebrations of the musical and theater-going "publics" paved the way for the more egalitarian conception of the reading public.[43] The participants in the new literary and political public sphere were all fortunate enough to be educated, and thus belonged mainly to the middle and upper classes. However, members of the "republic of scholars" defined their group without reference to class distinctions, as open to all persons willing to exercise their own reason in public, in a new sphere "beyond the political order."[44] Kant was writing in an environment that combined political absolutism with an unprecedented ease of scholarly and literary publication. University teachers in Frederick the Great's Prussia were still required to adhere to government-approved textbooks; new books needed the imprimature of a censor or designated university official. Even so, the last decades of the eighteenth century saw the institutions of the bourgeois public sphere flourish along with their social bases in the educated middle classes.[45]

Kant, then, had ample opportunity to model his image of the public sphere on the rich intellectual exchange going on around him. Part of the appeal of this "world of readers," in fact, was its cosmopolitan nature. Writers addressed each others' arguments according to their persuasiveness, without regard for social distinction, geographic location, or any other particular personal quality. By the time Kant published "An Answer to the Question, What Is Enlightenment?" (1784), he had incorporated a number of the qualities of the actual public sphere into an early version of his concept of the ideal "public."

III

Kant's reply to Zöllner's question does define enlightenment, but it also engages a number of other topics. The essay was not intended to be a comprehensive political treatise. Rather, "What Is Enlightenment?" is partly a republican polemic, partly a plea for royal enlightenment, and partly speculative social history. Through all this, it becomes a provocative, if incomplete, theory of the public sphere. Much of the essay is devoted to establishing the proper relationship between the public sphere and the ruling government. "What Is Enlightenment?" is thus a contribution to the theory of civil society in the new sense of the word, even as it seeks to constitute an authoritative source of political judgment along older lines of social contract theory.

Kant begins his essay with a now-famous definition of *Aufklärung*: "Enlightenment is man's emergence from his self-incurred immaturity. Immaturity is the inability to use one's own understanding without the guidance of another."[46] Kant defines *Aufklärung* against a common condition of immaturity or dependence. In an examination of the causes of this unenlightened state, Kant initially points to the individual shortcomings of "laziness and cowardice." Almost immediately, however, he reveals their origins in social history. Kant concludes that the problem of enlightenment should be addressed at the level of a "public," rather than simply by exhorting individuals to think for themselves. Instead of the "man" of his initial definition of enlightenment, Kant becomes concerned with particular "men" organized as a "public." Kant assumes throughout the essay that the experience of dependence has enduring negative consequences for a person's ability to reason for himself or herself. A long-dependent public suddenly freed of "personal despotism" or "greedy or power-hungry oppression" will likely replace its old, unfree modes with new, equally unfree ones. Revolutionary change cannot further the cause of enlightenment. A public may make only slow progress toward that goal. Having ruled out revolution as the motor of public enlightenment, Kant identifies his preferred alternative: the freedom, granted by a ruler to his subjects, to make public use of their reason.

Like other writers of the late Enlightenment, including Biester and Zöllner, Kant makes a considerable effort to address worries that increased civil freedoms, and especially freedom of expression, will lead to disorder rather than to peaceful reform. Freedom of speech, he argues, should not be absolute: acceptable limits on freedom place boundaries on its "private" use, while unacceptable limits on freedom would limit its "public" use. The public use of reason is exercised "*as a man of learning [Gelehrter]* addressing the entire *reading public.*"[47]

In demarcating the public realm, Kant excludes every arena of life except that in which members, free of any of the claims of necessity or of arbitrary differences, express their points of view as equals. Kant's "private" realm encompasses most of life. It includes not only what we would today understand as private life (the family household, the business world, religious institutions, and most social organizations), but also much of what we would call public (political life, military life, economic life). Kant refers to three types of people in their "private" roles: officers (who may not reason with their superiors over every order), taxpayers (who must pay even when they do not agree with a levy), and clergymen (who ought to preach the doctrine of their church). Each of these activities is associated with necessity: individuals acting according to motives not completely their own are pursuing what Kant calls "domestic" (*häuslich*) activity. Such cases are relegated to the private sphere, in which an individual's use of reason "may quite often be very narrowly restricted without undue hindrance to the progress of enlightenment."[48]

Kant's distinction between "public" and "private" has struck a number of commentators as counter-intuitive or at odds with ordinary usage. For Kant, one speaks publicly as a scholar to the cosmopolitan reading public only according to one's own lights, independent of any pecuniary, political, or social considerations. One speaks privately in a particular role: not freely, but in the name of some other authority. While acting in some civil or otherwise appointed office, a person makes only private—that is, not free—use of his reason. However, even persons who sometimes speak "privately," in the name of particular institutions retain their "world citizenship," and with it their right to public expression, if only "in writing" and "in the manner of a scholar." Kant's public/private distinction is confusing at first because he excludes the government from the public sphere (ignoring the sense of *öffentlich* [public] as *staatlich* [of the state, or official]).[49] However, such a distinction was not without precedent, even among Kant's fellow contributors to the *BMS*. Kant could not have known that his essay was being discussed at the meetings of the Berliner Mittwochgesellschaft, but he would, I think, have been pleased by Moses Mendelssohn's characterization of his public/private distinction to that group as "merely a bit strange in its expression."[50]

A number of authors from the *BMS* circle made similar distinctions, including the anonymous author of "On Freedom of Thought and Publication," who distinguished between "subordination" and "freedom to think aloud."[51]

Rather than distinguishing between public and private speech on the basis of individual motivation, as Kant does in his ethical works with the distinction between autonomous and heteronomous motives, in "What Is Enlightenment?" he specifies particular realms in which speech is considered public or private. In the public (*öffentlich*) arena for the free use of reason, arguments and evidence in written form are exchanged among participants in public discourse. The same officer, taxpayer, and clergyman, whom Kant has described in their private capacity as parts of the civil machines in which they find themselves, are now allowed, in their public capacity, to express themselves freely, even on matters concerning their private roles. Unlike the private use of reason, "*public* use of man's reason must always be free, and it alone can bring about enlightenment among men."[52]

The question of how such a sphere of public reason would in fact promote general enlightenment arises immediately (especially given Kant's many hints that freedom from self-incurred tutelage is freedom not only to reason but also to rule oneself). In "What Is Enlightenment?" Kant does not provide an abstract account of how the freedom to reason publicly brings about societal improvements. Instead, after distinguishing between the free, protected, public realm and the necessity-governed, legitimately regulated, private one, Kant launches into an extended discussion of the roles of the state, the cleric, and the "world citizen" with regard to official religious doctrines. He makes clear throughout the essay that what applies to the sphere of religion may eventually apply to other spheres as well, including other areas of government.[53] By proposing a mechanism for mediating between the views of the public on religious freedom and views of state regulators of religious affairs, Kant has formulated an early version of a modern theory of civil society–state relations, in which organized society indirectly and non-coercively (that is, not via any scheme of direct representation) influences government policy.

As Kant introduces his example of the individual clergyman's duty to preach official doctrine, he initially is able to apply his public/private distinction without qualification. When teaching in the name of the church, the clergyman must act as a "*Geschäfts-träger*" (man of business) of the establishment, since every organization requires "*Glieder*" (limbs, members), who will act for the organization and not by their own lights. The clergyman need not worry, on this first account, about hypocrisy, because he is explicitly acting in the name of another. "He will say: our church teaches this or that, and here are the arguments it uses."[54] As an independent scholar, outside his clerical duties, the clergyman can and ought to make public his conclusions about the rightness of church orthodoxies and suggest possible improvements.

This neat division between a civil servant's public and private roles begins to unravel almost immediately, however. First Kant says that the cleric may in good conscience preach doctrines with which he does not fully agree, since they may be true in a way he does not understand. But then Kant adds the requirement that official doctrine may not contradict "*der innern Religion*"; if it did, the clergyman would have to resign his post.[55] For the first half of this thought, the clergyman easily negotiates the private/public boundary by subordinating his own religious thoughts to his role as speaker in the name of the church. Kant shows us the clergyman saying to himself modestly that there may be truth hidden in these doctrines that he has been unable to see. But in the last instance, the clergyman's "inner religion" is the test of whether church doctrine may be preached without endangering his conscience. Using his own reason, the clergyman has access to a source of authority greater than that of the (by implication, temporal, material, worldly) power of the church. Kant does not assume that each individual clergyman will necessarily be correct in his assessment, but that to live with an easy conscience, he may not preach anything that his reason tells him is false.

Kant passes over the difficulties into which he has placed his exemplary clergyman at this point. The claim that the clergyman is ultimately beholden to his own reason is followed by a simple reassertion of Kant's distinction between public and private:

> Thus the use which someone employed as a teacher makes of his reason in the presence of his congregation is purely *private*, since a congregation, however large it is, is never any more than a domestic [*häuslich*] gathering. In view of this, he is not, and cannot be free as a priest, since he is acting on a commission imposed from outside [*im fremden Auftrag*].[56]

Kant contrasts this private role of the clergyman with the freedom he enjoys as a scholar in public: "the unlimited freedom to make use of his own reason and to speak in his own person."[57] Though Kant has been speaking of the clergyman's individual

conscience, he makes clear that what matters about clerical con-
sciences is their role as spiritual guardians, or speakers for society.
In the first place, Kant states, it would be ludicrous to have unenlightened guardians. But second, even the most enlightened
guardians could not rightly establish a permanently authoritative
religious doctrine that excludes the possibility of future improvements. This, Kant flatly declares, would "be a crime against
human nature, whose original destiny lies precisely in such
progress."[58] To this Kant adds a premise from his theory of the
societas civilis: "To test whether any particular measure can be
agreed upon as a law for a people, we need only ask whether a
people could well impose such a law on itself."[59] For Kant, the
example of the clergyman's relation to the church stands for the
relations between individuals and authoritative institutions more
generally, and especially for the relation between the subject and
the state. His formula for enlightened legislation echoes the formula just given for the conscience-stricken clergyman: preach a
doctrine if it is possible that it is the true doctrine (and enact a law
if it is possible that it reflects the true will of the people).

The explicit object of Kant's inquiry here is not general governmental reform, but how official church doctrine might rightly
be instituted (a religious free-for-all is a possibility not even acknowledged in the essay). Kant proposes more radically enlightened institutional reform for the spiritual arena than for the
temporal one. While he proposes concrete institutions for regular
consultation with actual members of the public on religious matters, Kant requires only that the people "could have" backed a
proposed change in general legislation. In both spheres, the people must be allowed actually to express themselves in public (in
the manner of scholars). Only in the case of religious observance,
however, does Kant outline an actual procedure for public consultation. This procedure, admittedly, is a feeble one by modern
standards (if leading clerics propose a change, the public ought to
be allowed to discuss it; once a general sentiment is reached, they
ought to be allowed to bring a proposal before the throne[60]). This
is as close as Kant comes in this essay to suggesting that publicity
might play a representative role (say, representing the will of the
people to the sovereign). Kant's argument here for protected public discussion of matters of common interest stops short of insisting that such discussion represents the will of the people, a point
of view which would have undermined the legitimacy of the sovereign. Rather, in "What Is Enlightenment?" public discussion of
matters of common interest serves to develop ideas about im-

provements, to bring these improvements to the sovereign's attention, and, along the way, to enlighten the members of the public themselves.

Kant does not explicitly propose the creation of institutions for public enlightenment with regard to legislative matters, as he does for spiritual ones. He identifies religious dependence as the most dangerous kind of immaturity, from which it follows that freedom of discussion about matters of conscience matters more than other types of free speech. However, he also mentions more than once that the sovereign would do well to allow public discussion on political topics. The comparison between a free realm for discussion of religion and one for discussion of politics becomes more explicit as the essay progresses. The institutions for carrying on this public discussion, though only illustrated with regard to religion, are clearly meant to facilitate broader topics.

The remainder of the essay is devoted to a series of arguments aimed directly at would-be enlightened rulers. Kant advises them to keep aloof from religious matters, as such interference degrades their majesty, while he supports secular rulers' (and not the church's) ultimate authority over established religious practices. Allowing free discussion of these, and even of political matters, will not only not harm civil order, Kant argues, but actually help both their current rule and their posthumous reputation. For the would-be enlightened ruler, Kant draws a flattering picture of the course of history, with enlightened freedom of public discussion as the result of a glorious ruler's liberation of his people from the primitive bonds of tutelage.

Kant's own protests notwithstanding, in his example of the clergyman-intellectual's dual roles, the scholar's (public) reason ultimately trumps the clergyman's official (private) duty. Similarly, Kant's attempts to persuade the ruler to allow enlightenment to flourish fail to disguise his conviction that the ruler's absolute sovereignty must eventually bow to an enlightened people's readiness for self-rule. Just before Kant equates "the age of enlightenment" with "the century of *Frederick*," for example, he expresses the hope that "men as a whole" will reach a state in which "the guidance of others" is no longer needed in religious matters.[61] Each time Kant stresses that rulers may remove "outward" obstacles to humankind's spiritual enlightenment, and each time he claims that freedom of conscience is harmless to the ruler, Kant reinforces the implication that "inner" religious life is beyond the ruler's power. Rulers' attempts to regulate religious life have only set up blunt, "outer" obstacles to enlightenment.

These may hinder a people's rapid progress but cannot prevent progress altogether. Another comment on the effectiveness of a ruler's interference in realms Kant claims should be left to public discourse comes in his explanation of why he has focused on religious regulation in an essay on enlightenment: because, he says, rulers are not interested in regulating the arts and sciences (!).[62]

Kant is exhorting would-be enlightened rulers to follow a path that, on the one hand, should ensure their present power and glorious reputation, while, on the other hand, would over the long run spell their obsolescence. In this and subsequent remarks, including the famous praise for Frederick II's policy of "argue as much as you like, but obey," Kant seems to be withdrawing the slight suggestion made earlier in the essay that publicity might actually represent the people's will, and thus provide an alternative source of coercive political authority to the monarchical ruler.[63] Instead, he suggests here that intellectual life, to be fully free, must be walled off from the practice of politics. Such a point of view resonates with the earlier distinction between free public and dependent private reason: public reason functions as such only in an arena designed to protect it from outside influences, in which the only standards are those governing ideal scholarly debate. Only "public" life, independent of financial and social considerations, is free to subject itself to the rule of reason alone. This public sphere exists in the world of letters (*Lesewelt*), in which everybody, no matter what his worldly position, functions "as a scholar." Such a position contributes to our understanding of Kant's role as an early theorist of the new sense of civil society. For he insists that the source of authoritative judgment (the public) must remain separate from the corrupting, "private," and particular influence of real coercive power.

Kant has made a case for the continued political power of an enlightened ruler who would protect a public arena for discussion while monopolizing the use of coercive force to maintain civil order. By protecting such a public sphere, however, the enlightened ruler seems to be recognizing it as a source of authoritative judgment.[64] Kant's only explicit illustration of this point, it is true, is his weak-sounding proposal that before religious regulations are promulgated, the public be allowed to discuss them, and to bring the results of such a discussion "before the throne." However, even without a politically representative function for the public sphere, the institutions Kant proposes for an enlightened state ensure that the free arena for public discussion is treated, not as directly authorizing the sovereign, but as the authoritative source of judgment on matters of public concern. The public sphere is the protected realm in which matters of common concern may be discussed by free and equal participants in the manner of scholars. As such, speakers in public can judge each others' arguments only by standards available in principle to all: universal principles of reason. Representatives of the state are in principle excluded from the public sphere, Kant argues, because they take as their standard not universal reason but the particular needs of the sovereign.[65]

In "What Is Enlightenment?" therefore, intellectual freedom has a two-fold relationship to political life. First, the enlightened ruler, as enlightened ruler, treats the free public sphere as an authoritative source of political judgment. Second, and somewhat paradoxically, this authoritative status is guaranteed by the public sphere's very separation from the practice of politics. No direct, potentially coercive, representative role is imagined for the public sphere in matters of political business. Instead, members of the public sphere are free both of political interference and of direct political responsibility; these freedoms, Kant argues, allow them to judge according to (public) standards of truth rather than (private) needs or political expediency. At the end of the essay, Kant predicts that, once people grow more accustomed to thinking for themselves, "even governments" will respond to "man's inclination and vocation to *think freely*."[66] This point raises a problem for the view Kant expresses in "What Is Enlightenment?" If the legitimacy of the public sphere is guaranteed by its purity (including its separation from the "domestic" affairs of practical politics), then how can Kant expect the people eventually to rule themselves? This he evidently does, flattery to princes and references to paradox notwithstanding. Kant's several references to the people's vocation eventually to rule themselves make his view clear.

The questions that Kant leaves unanswered have mainly to do with the relationship between the public sphere and the state: if a person's natural vocation as a reasoner ultimately trumps obligations on that same person as a part of a civil machine (as it did in the case of the clergyman), how can order be legitimately maintained? If the answer to this question has to do with restricting the function of the public sphere to "harmless" expressive speech, then how does Kant expect progress to come from the "free public use of reason"? What does Kant think is the proper relationship between the ruling state and the realm of free public discussion of matters of common interest? Does this change over time? Does publicity, as source of authoritative political judgment, eventually become politically authoritative itself? If so, how does it retain its intellectual authority?

Kant wrote "What Is Enlightenment?" as an answer to a question posed by another writer in the *Berliner Monatsschrift*. In such an occasional essay, however profound and influential, a reader cannot expect to find a complete set of answers to questions such as those raised above. Nevertheless, Kant's essay offers an important new conception of the role of civil society and its relationship to the state. First, the essay outlines the problem of locating the worldly source of authoritative political judgment in terms that would be familiar to the early social contract theorists. Second, it hints that the solution of the *societas civilis* will not succeed, mainly because representatives of the state make decisions based not on ethical truth, but on particular interests. Finally, the essay proposes a preliminary solution to the old problem via a new conception of the civil society–state relationship, in which authoritative political judgment is located in the public sphere.

IV

Kant's early defense of free public expression did not develop into a full-fledged theory of the role of the public sphere for more than a decade. Between 1784 ("What Is Enlightenment?") and 1798 ("The Contest of Faculties"),[67] the public debate sparked by the French Revolution provided Kant with a renewed empirical model for his mature account of the public as agent of progress, just as the nascent political world of letters had provided an image of the public sphere for his earlier version.

Kant was especially moved by the willingness of writers to speak out on political topics even when such speech endangered them. In "The Contest of Faculties," Kant writes:

> We are here concerned only with the attitude of the onlookers as it reveals itself in *public* while the drama of great political changes is taking place: for they openly express universal yet disinterested sympathy for one set of protagonists against their adversaries, even at the risk that their partiality could be of great disadvantage to themselves. Their reaction (because of its universality) proves that mankind as a whole shares a certain character in common, and it also proves (because of its disinterestedness) that man has a moral character, or at least the makings of one.[68]

Kant was not, of course, sympathetic the more violent aspects of the French Revolution; his denunciation of the treatment of Louis XVI is particularly famous.[69] Nevertheless, Kant was fascinated with political action that seemed to be motivated by general conclusions about political right. He was especially interested in the sometimes dangerous public discussion in Prussia on French revolutionary affairs.

The central question of the second section of "Contest" is whether humankind is making progress toward perfection. Kant looks for a "sign" that might indicate such progress. A little too fortunately for his argument, Kant is able to say that there *has* been a historical sign of the tendency toward self-betterment that reason tells us should be evident in human history. The French Revolution has inspired enthusiastic, selfless expressions of sympathy for the cause of national self-determination and for the reduction in wars of aggression that, Kant argues, naturally follows the establishment of a republican constitution. Like the public of "What Is Enlightenment?" these sympathetic public partisans of the republican cause judge political institutions and events disinterestedly, according to universal standards of right. Significantly, the public observing the revolutionary action across the Rhine is represented by Kant to the civil authorities as harmless; their talk should be considered "innocuous political gossip."[70] These judges in the public sphere are described as witnesses to events that are beyond their control and in which they have no material interest. Their accounts are therefore especially reliable.

If the judgment of the public is powerless, however, it is hard to see how this public can fulfill its role as the mechanism of human progress toward perfection. Kant's protests to those who would limit freedom of expression—that public deliberation on political matters cannot have any concrete effect—are not exactly disingenuous. After all, as he writes in "What Is Enlightenment?" a ruler with a large, well-disciplined army can afford to tolerate public political discussion. But while Kant argues that local enlightened absolutist rulers have nothing to fear from "innocuous political gossip," he also identifies the public sphere as the force, however non-coercive, behind human progress. Furthermore, as Kant argues in the *Rechtslehre*, such progress necessarily leads to cosmopolitan republican governance (progress as such would bring the actual world closer to the ideal image generated by the moral principles shared by all; these principles demand respect for human rights, among other republican ideals). Beside his claims about the harmlessness of public deliberation in the near term, then, Kant must make equally strong claims about the effects of public judgment in the long term.

At this point, the problems established by Kant's predecessors in social contract theory—of finding an authoritative judge of public right on earth, and of retaining that judge's authority while allowing the judgments to have some effect—are as yet unresolved. In "Contest," however, he does propose a solution to these questions. Judges in the public sphere derive their authority from the special qualifications Kant outlines in "What Is Enlightenment?" and elsewhere; these ensure that such judges take their standard of right from universal reason alone. Public judgment may be conditioned by no contingent factor (only the object of judgment and the partisan's own sympathy are provided by experience). Once given, however, this judgment becomes a force in the world.

Kant offered an early, very moderate account of the power of public judgment in "What Is Enlightenment?" In 1784 he imagined a situation in which the people object to a change in religious regulations: they should be allowed to discuss the matter freely; if, after a while, no relief is given, then the public may bring its suggestion before the throne.[71] By the time Kant has witnessed the outpouring of public sympathy for the republican cause in France, however, he is willing to make stronger suggestions about the force of public judgment. In a note to "Contest," Kant asks:

> Why has no ruler ever dared to say openly that he does not recognize any *rights* of the people against himself?... The reason is that any such public declaration would rouse up all the subjects against the ruler, even although they had been like docile sheep, well fed, powerfully protected and led by a kind and understanding master.... For beings endowed with freedom cannot be content merely to enjoy the comforts of existence.[72]

Kant's claim, then, that the disputes of scholars should be tolerated by the state as harmless sounds somewhat disingenuous. Their disinterested inquiry according to standards of reason allows members of the public sphere to claim "right" in the sense of correctness; however, they also acquire "right" in the sense of moral authority. Moral authority, Kant insists here and throughout his political work, is a motive force in the "historical" world. The mechanism for this effect is the institution of publicity. Thus for Kant the public sphere, merely through its judging function, and without any coercive apparatus, constitutes a powerful agent of historical progress.

V

Kant's theory of publicity in "Contest" is both more radical and more conservative than its predecessor in "What Is Enlightenment?"

On the one hand, "Contest" provides an example of judges in the public sphere directly addressing political issues, including even such dangerous ones as revolution. Unlike their milder counterparts in "What Is Enlightenment?" the fiery public partisans in "Contest" openly compare current political conditions to absolute standards of moral right, even when those comparisons threaten the ruling regime. On the other hand, in clarifying some of the questions left open in the earlier essay, Kant further restricts any immediate practical effects the public sphere might have. In "What Is Enlightenment?" Kant recognizes the state's interest in stability by restricting "private" speech, while protecting "public" discussion in the interest of progress. In "Contest," however, he makes explicit what was only implied in "What Is Enlightenment?" namely, that political action of any sort other than speech is reserved to the state. The state, though goaded forward by the stimulus of ethical truth made public by partisans of right, retains its monopoly on action to the last: progress proceeds not *"from the bottom upwards,* but *from the top downwards."*[73] The task of bringing the actual state in line with the precepts of moral right is "the *duty* of the head of state (not of the citizens)."[74]

Such a conservative move, disheartening as it must have been to Kant's more revolutionary contemporaries, answers the questions about the relation between the public sphere and the state that "What Is Enlightenment?" left open. First, the authority of Kant's judges in the public sphere is now safe from corruption by contact with the coercive power of government, for all such force is reserved to the state. Along the same lines, Kant adheres to the precept of moral right that forbids citizens from endangering the state, even if it is unjust, as long as it preserves civil order. Second, Kant reveals the mechanism whereby the public sphere is supposed to have a practical effect on political life: comparisons between ideal and actual political life made in the public sphere will, slowly, influence the people and with them those in charge of the state. These leaders, Kant is confident, will make progressive reforms: "the state … will reform itself from time to time, pursuing evolution instead of revolution, and will thus make continuous progress."[75] What insulates the authority of the public sphere from the potentially corrupting influence of its practical effects is that, given the slow pace of reform, participants in the public sphere will be unable to observe any direct results of their suggestions. Their sole motivating interest, Kant is hopeful, will remain the universalistic interest that invested the public sphere with its moral authority in the first place: the interest shared by all "rational beings as such" in moral right.

From the point of view of everyday practical politics, Kant has taken a circuitous route back to the same "inconveniences" suffered by the early social contract theories of Hobbes and Locke. Kant has ruled out the state as a possibly authoritative judge of public right, but he has also eliminated civil society, constituted as a public sphere, from consideration as a legitimate wielder of coercive political power. From the perspective of day-to-day governance, the Kantian political system subjects citizens to the arbitrary rule of an unpredictable human sovereign, without even the redress offered by Locke in the form of a right of revolution. In this light, the innovation of a modern sense of civil society, seen as a source of authority separate from the state, appears stillborn: the public sphere is the pure, but impotent, source of political judgment.

Fortunately for Kant's theory, the long view presents a more optimistic picture. Kant's theory of the public sphere resolves the old problem of the social contract theorists by locating an authoritative source of political judgment in the world. While retaining the old ideal of a *societas civilis* legitimated by conformity with the general interest, Kant's account of the source of this interest provides a theory of civil society in the newer sense of the term, as organized society outside the state. Moreover, Kant's public sphere constitutes a potentially workable, if extremely slow, mechanism for the application of ethical precepts to political practice. "All politics must bend the knee before right," Kant concludes, "although politics may hope in return to arrive, however slowly, at a stage of lasting brilliance."[76]

Notes

The author would like to thank the Henry Robert Braden Fund and the Andrew W. Mellon Fellowships for their support of research for this chapter. She is also grateful to the participants in the November 1996 conference on civil society, at the Center for European Studies, Harvard University, and especially to Frank Trentmann, for valuable comments on earlier versions of this work.

1. For the sake of convenience, I shall use the Latin term *"societas civilis"* for the older sense of a governed body of people, leaving "civil society" to stand for the newer sense of the term. I am indebted to John Keane for the distinction between the old and new senses of "civil society": John Keane, "Despotism and Democracy: The Origins and Development of the Distinction Between Civil Society and the State, 1750–1850," in *Civil Society and the State: New*

European Perspectives, ed. John Keane (London, 1988), 35–71. See also Manfred Riedel, "Gesellschaft, bürgerliche," in *Geschichtliche Grundbegriffe: Historisches Lexikon zur politisch-sozialen Sprache in Deutschland*, ed. Otto Brunner, Werner Conze, and Reinhart Koselleck (Stuttgart, 1972–84), 2:719–800; 739, 741, 746–747.

2. Koselleck himself used the term only casually. However, as his translator Keith Tribe has observed, *Sattelzeit* "has since become a concept in its own right." Keith Tribe, "Translator's Introduction," in Reinhart Koselleck, *Futures Past* (Cambridge, Mass., 1985 [1979]), x. Also cited in Melvin Richter, *The History of Political and Social Concepts: A Critical Introduction* (New York, 1995), 17–18.

3. In fact, when Locke speaks of a reversion to divine judgment on earth, he is referring to the resort to violent conflict among men, whose outcome can be assumed to be determined by God. John Locke, *Second Treatise of Government*, ed. Mark Goldie (London, 1993 [1690]), secs. 222, 241; 227, 239–240.

4. Thomas Hobbes, *Leviathan*, ed. Edwin Curley (Indianapolis, 1994 [1651]), II:xviii, 113; Locke, *Second Treatise*, sec. 240, 239.

5. Manfred Riedel, "Transcendental Politics? Political Legitimacy and the Concept of Civil Society in Kant," *Social Research*, Autumn 1981: 588–613; 601–602.

6. Kant's spelling of the Latin term for "ideal state." In this and all subsequent quotations, emphases are in the original.

7. Kant, "The Contest of Faculties," in *Kant's Political Writings*, ed. Hans Reiss, trans. H.B. Nisbet (Cambridge, 1991), 187.

8. Kant, *The Metaphysics of Morals*, ed. Mary Gregor (Cambridge, 1996 [1797]), 14.

9. The *Rechtslehre* comprises the first part of Kant's *Metaphysics of Morals*. Its formal title is *The Metaphysical First Principles of the Doctrine of Right*.

10. Kant's ethical theory is based on the premise that all human beings (indeed, all limited rational beings of any kind) share a faculty of practical reason that allows them to discover moral truths and apply them to everyday situations. As is well known, he argues that the formal test for whether a principle is a "moral truth" is whether it may hold as a universal law without coming into contradiction with itself. But Kant does not suppose that ordinary people consciously apply the categorical imperative to their lives. Instead, most people simply recognize a few common moral precepts (such as honest dealing, or doing no harm) as the basis for ethical interaction. In his ethical work, Kant tries to set these commonly recognized moral truths on a solid foundation in reason. Kant, *Foundations of the Metaphysics of Morals*, ed. Lewis White Beck (New York, 1985 [1785]), 20 and *passim*.

11. Kant, *Foundations*, 28.

12. Kant, *The Metaphysics of Morals*, 123.

13. Ibid.

14. Kant, "Contest," 187.

15. Kant, *The Metaphysics of Morals*, 124.

16. Ibid., 90.

17. Ibid., 14.

18. Kant, "Idea for a Universal History with a Cosmopolitan Purpose," in Reiss, ed., 45.

19. Kant, "Contest," 187.

20. In fact, Locke's separation of society and government with regard to the right of revolution might be seen as an early sign of the emerging new sense of "civil society," with the unitary commonwealth (*societas civilis*) breaking up into society and state.

21. Kant, *The Metaphysics of Morals*, 124.
22. Ibid., 96–98.
23. Kant, "An Answer to the Question: What Is Enlightenment?" in Reiss, ed., 55.
24. Of course, Kant's formal political work was not published until 1797, more than ten years after his early speculations on publicity. However, by 1781 at the latest, Kant had set out the basic moral precepts on which the principles of political right are based. Kant, *Critique of Pure Reason*, ed. Norman Kemp Smith (New York: St. Martin's Press, 1929 [1781]).
25. Kant, "On the Common Saying: 'This May be True in Theory, but it does not Apply in Practice,'" in Reiss, ed., 81.
26. Kant, "What Is Enlightenment?" 55.
27. Hans Erich Bödeker, "Prozesse und Strukturen politischer Bewußtseinsbildung der deutschen Aufklärung," in *Aufklärung der Politisierung-Politisierung der Aufklärung*, ed. Hans Erich Bödeker (Hamburg, 1987), 10.
28. What is remarkable, in retrospect, is the staying power of such an ideal image of the role of publicity in political life, despite political and social changes that eventually undermined its historical basis. Sec Lucien Hölscher, "Öffentlichkeit," in *Geschichtliche Grundbegriffe*, ed. Otto Brunner, et al., 413–467.
29. Werner Kraus, quoted in Norbert Hinske, *Was Ist Aufklärung? Beiträge aus der Berlinischen Monatsschrift*, 2nd ed. (Darmstadt, 1977), xx.
30. The BMS was second only to the Jena-based *Allgemeinen Literaturzeitung* in subscriptions. Ilonka Egert, "Die 'Berlinische Monatsschrift' (1783–1796) in der deutschen Spätaufklärung," *Zeitschrift für Geschichtswissenschaft*, vol. 39, no. 2 (1991): 130–52;131.
31. E. v. K., "Vorschlag, die Geistlichen nicht mehr bei Vollziehung der Ehen zu bemühen," BMS II, 1783, 265–276; reproduced in Hinske, *Was Ist Aufklärung?* 95–106. The author was probably Biester, who used the pseudonym "E. v. K." more than once. Hinske, *Was Ist Aufklärung?* xxxvii.
32. E. v. K., "Suggestion," 95 f.
33. Ibid., 98.
34. Ibid., 102.
35. Hinske, *Was Ist Aufklärung?* 107–133.
36. The Berliner Mittwochgesellschaft was a private group of scholars, men of letters, bureaucrats, and others who met on a regular basis to discuss social, political, and scientific policy from an enlightened point of view. James Schmidt, "The Question of Enlightenment: Kant, Mendelssohn, and the *Mittwochgesellschaft*," *Journal of the History of Ideas*, vol. 50, no. 2 (1989): 269–91; 272.
37. Friedrich Zöllner, "Ist es rathsam, das Ehebündniß nicht ferner durch die Religion zu sanciren?" reproduced in Hinske, *Was Ist Aufklärung?* 107–116.
38. This topic was frequently discussed, for example, at the meetings of the Berliner Mittwochgesellschaft. Schmidt, "The Question of Enlightenment," 273, 278–80.
39. See Hinske, *Was Ist Aufklärung?* xli.
40. Zöllner, "Ist es rathsam," 115.
41. Ibid.
42. Hölscher, "Öffentlichkeit," 446–47.
43. Ibid., 432–36. See also Otto Dann, ed., *Lesegesellschaften und bürgerliche Emanzipation: ein europäischer Vergleich* (Munich, 1981).
44. Hölscher, "Öffentlichkeit," 436.
45. Jürgen Habermas, *The Structural Transformation of the Public Sphere: An Inquiry into a Category of Bourgeois Society*, trans. by Thomas Burger, with Frederick

Lawrence (Cambridge, Mass., 1989 [1962]). For a critical introduction to the huge literature inspired by Habermas's study, see Craig Calhoun, ed., *Habermas and the Public Sphere* (Cambridge, Mass., 1992).

46. Kant, "What Is Enlightenment?" 54 (emphases removed).

47. Ibid., 55.

48. Ibid. Habermas interprets "What Is Enlightenment?" and its public/private distinction somewhat differently, asserting that what Kant called "publicity" is the same thing that Hegel later called "public opinion" ("[the concept of publicity] in Kant lacked only the name of 'public opinion'"[Habermas, 108]). Such a reading serves to keep the structure of Habermas's book coherent, since it moves from an account of the origins of publicity, through the representational aspirations of nineteenth-century democratic theory, to a critique of capitalist misuse of the institutions of publicity. However, for Kant, publicity is not at all the same as public opinion. Public opinion, as understood by the turn of the century, *represents* people's will on a topic [Hölscher, 466–467]. In "What Is Enlightenment?" Kant rejects this view of publicity, preferring to see it as a means to disinterested, universally applicable points of view. Public opinion is necessarily interested, and often changes according to arbitrary or even no visible standards. Publicity for Kant, on the other hand, is supposed to approximate ideal judgment on earth.

49. Hölscher, "Öffentlichkeit," 413 and passim.

50. Cited in Hinske, *Was Ist Aufklärung?* l.

51. Cited in Hinske, *Was Ist Aufklärung?* li. The author was Ernst Ferdinand Klein.

52. Kant, "What Is Enlightenment?" 55.

53. Ibid., 59. For a different view, see John Christian Laursen, "The Subversive Kant: The Vocabulary of 'Public' and 'Publicity,'" *Political Theory*, vol. 14, no. 4 (1986): 584–603. See also Laursen, *The Politics of Skepticism in the Ancients, Montaigne, Hume, and Kant* (Brill, 1992).

54. Kant, "What Is Enlightenment?" 56.

55. Ibid. Nisbet translates this as "the essence of religion," which is correct, but which loses the sense, present in the German, that this essence is present *in the mind of the cleric.*

56. Ibid., 57.

57. Ibid.

58. Ibid.

59. Ibid.

60. Ibid.

61. Ibid., 58.

62. Ibid., 59.

63. Ibid.

64. He admits that this position appears paradoxical from the ruler's point of view. Kant, "What Is Enlightenment?" 59.

65. Kant elaborates on this position in his introduction to "Contest of Faculties."

66. Kant, "What Is Enlightenment?" 59–60.

67. This chapter addresses only the second section of "Contest" (the other two are concerned with theological issues and with the field of medicine). This second section was written three or four years before its publication as part of "Contest" in 1798. Hermann Klenner, notes to Immanuel Kant, *Rechtslehre: Schriften zu Rechtsphilosophie*, Klenner, ed. (Berlin, 1988), 530.

68. Kant, "Contest," 182.

69. Ferenc Fehér, "Practical Reason in the Revolution: Kant's Dialogue with the French Revolution," *Social Research*, vol. 56, no. 1 (1989): 161–185, 167–168.
70. Kant, "Contest," 183.
71. Kant, "What Is Enlightenment?" 57.
72. Kant, "Contest," 183.
73. Ibid., 188.
74. Ibid. Kant draws a similar conclusion in the *Rechtslehre*: "The attempt to realize this idea [of constitutional government] should not be made by way of revolution…. But if it is attempted and carried out by gradual reform in accordance with firm principles, it can lead to continual approximation of the highest political good …" (Kant, *The Metaphysics of Morals*, 124).
75. Kant, "Contest," 189. There are clear similarities between Kant's view and later accounts of the political system of "enlightened absolutism" and its internal contradictions. As Gianfranco Poggi has observed, the policies of enlightened absolutism "revealed and often unwittingly fostered the start of a remarkable change in the internal configuration and political significance of civil society. In the long run, such change would transform the system of rule by realizing the civil society's demand for an active, decisive role in the political process." Gianfranco Poggi, *The Development of the Modern State: A Sociological Introduction* (Stanford, 1978), 79. However, although Kant shares a concern for gradual rather than revolutionary progress with theorists of enlightened absolutism, his categorical rejection of paternalism and eudaemonism exclude him from such company. See *Der Aufgeklärte Absolutismus*, ed. Karl Otmar Freiherr von Aretin (Cologne, 1974), especially the contributions of Hartung and Lefèbvre.
76. Kant, "Perpetual Peace, a Philosophical Sketch," in Reiss, ed., 125.

Part III

Associational Life and the Education of Citizens

5

The Intelligence Gazette (*Intelligenzblatt*) as a Road Map to Civil Society

Information Networks and Local Dynamism
in Germany, 1770s–1840s

Ian F. McNeely

A SURPRISINGLY VIGOROUS PRINT MEDIUM flourished in provincial Germany in the early nineteenth century, one bringing local notables together with state officials under the banner of Enlightenment.[1] The intelligence gazettes (*Intelligenzblätter*) depict a small-town world pulsating with ideas and entrepreneurship and committed to disseminating information for the purposes of local, civic improvement. As local announcement bulletins, the gazettes abstained from the cosmopolitan, critical, uncensored, rational discourse that Jürgen Habermas and others have made central to the public sphere's history.[2] This, together with their status as semi-official organs dependent on state and local governments, has contributed to their neglect by scholars and a belief that they lacked progressive potential. Yet precisely in their mundane practicality, the gazettes traced out networks of social communication ushering both their readers and producers into civil society. At a level of everyday practice often untapped by the historical literature, the gazettes reveal how civil society in Germany emerged not so much under the state's guidance as in a sphere of dynamism, partnership, and conflict at the interface between state and local society.[3]

Typically, intelligence gazettes consisted of three to six double-sided leaves and resembled miniature newspapers. By 1800, there were 160 Intelligenzblätter in towns and cities all over Central Europe, with a combined circulation of more than 100,000 copies. If one reckons ten users per copy, a standard press historians' method, these publications collectively reached over one million readers.[4] In their original, eighteenth-century incarnation, gazettes embodied the paternalistic desire to bring practical knowledge to the people. Though their content varied over time, they included government decrees, public legal and property notices, private advertisements, statistical and price tables, anecdotes, and didactic essays on agriculture, economics, science, natural history, and other subjects. Such information was thought to further social development and economic progress. In the hands of publicists like Justus Möser, gazettes promoted the dissemination of reason and utility, stressing the governance of personal conduct and the creation of productive citizens for modern economies. Most enjoyed state sponsorship and supported the mercantilist and pedagogical aims of the so-called popular Enlightenment (*Volksaufklärung*).[5]

The utility and popularity of the new medium ensured that its usages would eventually outstrip the paternalistic intentions of state promoters and become subject to local appropriations. But the mold, once cast and then held in place by censors' categories, only gradually outgrew its original shape. Censors constrained intelligence gazettes to develop in a circumscribed, ostensibly depoliticized space by distinguishing them from political and deliberative—*räsonnierende*—newspapers in the classic Habermasian mold. Papers offering *Intelligenz* were subjected to much less surveillance and fewer taxes than those engaging in *Räsonnement*. Intelligenz[6] was practical, useful, and earthbound, conveying only the information and habits of mind the productive citizen should have. Räsonnement was abstract, reflective, and critical, with an irresponsible tendency to frivolity and, ultimately, politics. Intelligenz was just the form of deliberation state reformers with a taste for popular Enlightenment wished to cultivate. Räsonnement was, at best, a potent instrument to be kept in the hands of a responsible educated elite, and at worst, a weapon that could be used to attack the state and its policies. Räsonnement was at home in the intimate society of the salons and the cosmopolitan discourse of the literary journal. Intelligenz belonged on the trader's ledger, near the craftsman's workbench, and in the bureaucrat's chambers.

Between the 1770s and the 1840s, the intelligence gazettes facilitated a long apprenticeship in public involvement for a large segment of the German population. With an immediate connection to the world of practical interests, Intelligenz, more than Räsonnement, approximated the habits and forms of reasoning appropriate to the middle ground of civil society. The medium's growth toward autonomy and, ultimately, political critique illustrates that its resonance in society extended far beyond the theoretical project concocted by supporters of popular Enlightenment. In the kingdom of Württemberg, the focus of this study, the gazettes' evolution followed a general shift in power from state to civil society, responding to market forces, liberalizing trends in administration, changing reading practices, and the increasing sophistication of their local supporters. Asserting their independence, more than fifty counties (*Oberämter*) in the kingdom founded their own gazettes in the 1820s–30s, each spontaneously and without state coordination. These enterprises brought together a diverse, activist class of local civic leaders and organized a heretofore diffuse set of needs for information among a broad reading public. Especially in this final, nineteenth-century incarnation, the intelligence gazettes furnished the raw material for civil society's knowledge of itself. By imparting cognitive coherence to a nascent social formation, they acted as a "road map" to civil society and helped pave the way for its emancipation from state tutelage. To show how this road map changed, however, we must begin by asking how it was originally intended to be used.

* * * *

THE CATEGORY OF "INTELLIGENCE" originated not in the censors' imaginations but as a real form of communicative practice that had spread from England and France to Germany in the early eighteenth century. The term Intelligenz initially referred to services offered by semi-private information clearinghouses often managed by moonlighting bureaucrats. So-called "address counters" (*Adreß-Comtoirs*) or "intelligence offices" (*Intelligenzbüros*) in large trading centers like Hamburg and Leipzig customarily dealt in goods and services for which demand could not be met by local commercial establishments. These included books, luxury items, medicines, and used housewares, all having a limited, irregular, or dispersed customer base, as well as lost and found, credit, and other commercial services.[7] Intelligence gazettes began as outgrowths of these enterprises, and thus, from the very beginning, concrete affiliations with the marketplace stamped the gazettes' history in the Germany states. Unlike the classic literary-political newspaper, which also had a business side, commercialism was the transparent purpose and practicality the ideological underpinning of what was called *Intelligenzwesen*. This term, the umbrella category for both the print medium and its affiliated institutions, points to the semantic overlap between "intelligence" as a mental construct and as a marketable commodity. *Intelligenzien* were the quanta of information which brought usefulness to the common reader whether they were plucked from the printed page or obtained at an actual business establishment.

It was this immediate connection to the world of things that made the Intelligenzblatt such a unique and potent medium.[8] Intelligence gazettes excited reformers' imaginations precisely because their scope was mundane and practical. Justus Möser, the eighteenth-century publicist and administrator, pioneered a straightforward, pared-down aesthetic for his *Osnabrückische Intelligenzblätter*. He tailored scientific and instructive essays to local conditions, practical purposes, and unpretentious reading tastes. Frivolous, "satirical" articles he excised as irrelevant. And lest his format be perceived as dry or starkly utilitarian, Möser proposed layout innovations inspired by the example of German-American "Intelligencers."[9] These featured easy-to-read, "immediately graspable" rubrics and formatting tricks, including large blocked letters and the placement of icons beside advertisements. Such icons included saddled horses for those providing services, or filled purses for those offering credit. These techniques, besides targeting the semi-literate, enhanced the accessibility of information. Intelligence gazettes' novelty as a print medium was to render their individual components easy to abstract, collect, and peruse, gathering together the objects of civil society. As part of a general move from "intensive" (mainly religious) to "extensive" practices of reading, the gazettes helped call forth what Roger Chartier terms a "freer, more casual, and more critical" way of reading, ideally suited to the processing of practical knowledge.[10]

Only relatively late in the eighteenth century did the gazettes' semi-official character achieve predominance. From the 1770s, German states increasingly provided them with financial support, and official decrees and announcements began taking up an ever-larger column share.[11] Acting as the medium's midwives, state officials loosened the gazettes' dependence on market forces and thus facilitated a much wider territorial coverage. To be sure, this delivered an artificial impulse to their development. The policy of *Intelligenzzwang* or "compulsory intelligence" was among the crudest methods of state interference, by and large limited to Prussia.[12] This policy established regional monopolies on the publishing of both official and private announcements and compelled certain public authorities to subscribe to and locally distribute intelligence gazettes. Whether coercively, in this way, or more spontaneously, gazettes gradually displaced older, more irregular, and less efficient forms of publicity: the posting of ordinances at town halls and public readings by town criers or, for more important decrees, from the pulpit. In bureaucrats' eyes, the new medium promised to bring continual, regular, and covert reinforcement of state authority as a consequence of its form, a printed bulletin of public record.

State reformers' broader vision for the gazettes was essentially cameralist, to harness local development under the aegis and watchful eye of a state institution. "Intelligence" was for them the handmaiden of *Statistik*, the German academic discipline devoted to the systematic and detailed study of statecraft. Statistik encompassed not just the arithmetical tabulations we associate with the term, but all the individual data for the science of state, including laws, ordinances, treaties, and other political information.[13] Like Intelligenzien, statistics only took on a greater meaning when collected and studied. The difference was that while Statistik surveyed the whole, assigning each particularity its proper place from the vantage point of the intellectual, Intelligenz relied on the effects of passive accumulation of knowledge for limited purposes. From this perspective, the policy of promoting intelligence was to enable each citizen, in accordance with his social station (*Stand*), to adapt to the currents of economy and society that were steered and analyzed benevolently from above. Gerhard Petrat has likened this process to the Foucaultian "work of ordering," a dynamic contributing simultaneously to individual initiative and the ultimate internalization of the rules and regularities of the modern economy.[14] In this spirit, an 1802 volume entitled *Intelligence Gazette Help for the Uneducated Private Man* taught readers how to both draft and interpret classified advertisements:

> Simplicity and clarity result ... from order, precision, and brevity or exactness, and therefore require the most practice and care. If your collected observations give you a general, albeit here and there also dark, idea of the whole, a continued attentiveness will clarify the individual

parts little by little…. Their order on the paper will, indeed must, diverge perhaps entirely from the order *in your soul*, since the one is *your* conception and the other should be for others who have other needs, abilities, etc.[15]

Notionally, intelligence gazettes enacted what contemporary German scholars have called the "social disciplining" of their readers. This conceptual paradigm, which one-sidedly dominates the current scholarship on the medium, underscores the subtle, precocious efforts of the early modern state to govern the behavior of individuals and populations. It is also of long provenance, deriving from the ideas of Max Weber, Gerhard Oestreich, and Norbert Elias. In its newer form, the concept of social discipline reflects a Foucaultian sensitivity to the connections between knowledge and power.[16] Here, it is argued, the intelligence gazette employed discursive techniques to ensure obeisance. The whole genre of didactic essays, a popular feature of the late eighteenth century, was an especially rich field for the construction of the productive citizen. These essays concentrated directly on the pedagogy of the common person and greatly widened the scope of Intelligenz from commercial, legal, and statistical matters to all spheres of life bearing on productive capacities: agronomy, medicine and sanitation, householding, diet, natural science, meteorology, and so forth. Articles employed the methods of reason and persuasion; personal, experiential accounts (*Erfahrungsberichte*); mocking, paternalistic warnings against peasant prejudices and superstitions; and the soothing authorial voice of the practical advice-giver—all of which encouraged readers to adopt new innovations and internalize new maxims of conduct.[17]

All these practices were novel techniques reflecting the confluence of rationalist pedagogy with the absolutist state in the period of "popular Enlightenment."[18] But one should not take these innovations at face value. Resistances and unanticipated consequences often resulted when reason was bent to matters of state and economy. For example, while intelligence gazettes offered commentaries on new legal ordinances with reasoned justifications for state reforms, they also implicitly placed state authority in question, especially when, as was common, such commentaries appeared alongside similar legislation drawn from other states. "Experiential accounts" similarly invited the resistance of those whose personal experience simply differed. One local official wrote to the *Lippisches Intelligenzblatt* complaining that he had met up against recalcitrance and obstinate adherence to traditional practices when, following an article he had read in the gazette, he tried to introduce new culinary applications for salt to the local peasantry.[19] Such were the pitfalls in grafting rational practices onto Intelligenz, with its ever-practical referents. Though reformers *envisioned* the medium as instilling rational and obedient conduct and promoting the growth and health of populations and their productive powers, their forays into Räsonnement often had ambiguous, unexpected results.[20]

Only an event as crucial to the testing of the state's power as the Napoleonic conquests could reveal the true inefficacy and practical limits of this disciplinary paradigm. These conquests reorganized the map of Germany and made territorial integration and the conversion of new subjects into state citizens (*Staatsbürger*) pressing necessities. Here we turn to developments in Württemberg, a Napoleonic German state *par excellence*, which doubled its territorial size and population between 1803 and 1806. There, the development of intelligence gazettes reflected the difficulties and potentials the new medium held for the purpose of constructing a new, more integrated state with an active and informed citizenry.

Württemberg was extremely late to develop a network of Intelligenzblätter. There the Cotta family had long held a monopoly on intelligence gazettes, one which the government abolished between 1806 and 1808. After this, the state began to officially recognize and sanction gazettes elsewhere in the kingdom. Of the ten gazettes existing in Württemberg in 1806, nine were published in its post-Napoleonic acquisitions, and all but two of these in former Imperial Free Cities. Authorities wished to promote a greater uniformity among these enterprises and extend their territorial coverage more comprehensively, from the urban centers out over the countryside. They also set guidelines standardizing their content to subjects such as police ordinances, troop quartering, searches for missing persons and deserters, warnings about swindles, lost and found articles, food and commodity prices, weather and epidemic observations, new discoveries, strange natural occurrences, and births and deaths.[21]

The trend in Württemberg was toward an increased reliance on Intelligenzblätter as replacements for oral publishing by town criers. This was accompanied by a halting move to make citizens legally *responsible* for the information—especially laws and ordinances—they made known. While several initiatives failed to give intelligence items a "perfectly binding power" on citizens, and traditional methods of publicizing information continued, the government's reasoning nonetheless inclined to the view that since "every inhabitant will have the opportunity to read [an intelligence gazette's] content himself, ... that person who fails to do so will have only himself to blame for whatever disadvantages that result."[22] Starting in the first two decades of the nineteenth century, government officials relied massively on the new medium to search for creditors in bankruptcy cases; publicize auctions, markets, fairs, and sales of forfeited property; inform subjects of new commercial and mercantile regulations; and make offers of public credit known. All this meant that individuals wishing to participate in property markets and commercial life ignored the latest intelligence at their peril. Alongside other disciplinary institutions and media—the *Hauskalender*, for example, subjected to new regulation at this time[23]—intelligence gazettes cultivated habits among citizens favoring rational market calculation on one hand, and adherence to state directives on the other.

The implicit appeal to citizens' self-interest marked a subtle shift from the more paternalistic aims of the popular Enlightenment by submitting intelligence gazettes to the laws of the market and the structure of economic incentives. By this standard, the state's powers could be quite limited. In particular, efforts to centralize and coordinate the distribution of intelligence foundered for lack of effective marketing and packaging. The government's only real attempt to found a statewide intelligence gazette was the short-lived *General Intelligence Gazette for New Württemberg* (1804–06), which circulated exclusively in the kingdom's post-Napoleonic acquisitions. The gazette's backers intended it mainly for local officials promoting cameralistic goals such as cultivating the commodity markets. Providing "reliable news about the various arrangements, the culture, and the inner structure of the new [lands]" explicitly served the agenda of territorial integration.[24] Substantive articles commended the practical scientific findings of (private) "learned men" to state "economists" in the trenches, touting the advantages of lightning rods, the "Papinian" cooking pot, and Pestalozzi's pedagogical methods, for example.[25] Discursively, the *General Gazette* thus envisioned economic development as a partnership between government and leading inventors and intellectuals—one that yet remained to be realized as an actual social formation, however. Its content still inclined toward the official, the hierarchical. New regulations to be implemented and new duties to be discharged by officials and citizens dominated its pages. Plagued by a failure to engage any public constituency, the paper attracted no more than a few hundred subscribers, among them very few private citizens, and struggled financially as a result.[26]

* * * *

ONLY ON THE LOCAL LEVEL did the growth of Intelligenzblätter finally take off and succeed in promoting the networks of civil society. On this level, the disciplinary paradigm that the state had been unsuccessful in sponsoring finally dissipated amidst rival local interests and conditions. Here, Intelligenz fulfilled social needs for practical information, not just an Enlightenment vision. To be sure, it took nearly two decades after the formal monopoly on intelligence had been abolished before even a partial coverage of Württemberg existed. By the 1820s, however, gazettes had become the dominant print medium, numbering fifty separate enterprises compared with only nineteen political papers and thirty-three of miscellaneous non-political content. On the eve of 1848, fifty-seven of sixty-four counties across the kingdom possessed their own Intelligenzblatt.[27] These local gazettes appeared once or twice weekly with a print run of several hundred copies at a yearly subscription rate of 1–2 Gulden. Once a backwater of uneven development, untouched by the first wave of eighteenth-century gazettes, Württemberg now overtook its neighbors and quickly acquired a uniform information network spanning most of its territory.

This rapid development took hold spontaneously and without coordinated intent. County level intelligence gazettes were the fruits of collaborative effort among middling bureaucrats, town elders, enterprising guild printers, and (sometimes) crusading pastors and local civic or agricultural societies. These civic leaders converged with different purposes in mind: streamlining administrative communication, promoting local markets, turning profits, providing instruction and entertainment, and generally introducing ordinary citizens to dealings outside their home villages. They owed their coming together entirely to the discursive, integrative power of Intelligenz: to a deeply diffused excitement about practical knowledge that struck them as a novel participatory opportunity. At no point did the Württemberg state itself undertake a centralized or systematic program to provision its citizenry with local Intelligenzblätter.[28] Especially after the Karlsbad decrees (1819) cracked down on press freedoms, the interior ministry was content mostly to ignore the medium while it remained preoccupied with regulating, taxing, and censoring overtly political material. It would be mistaken, however, to regard the vacuum thus created for local civic boosters solely as a product of state neglect. Intelligence gazettes instead flourished in a space intentionally carved out by bureaucratic reforms and aimed at emancipating county leaders.

Specifically, the advent of intelligence gazettes followed changes in the technology of information provision in small Württemberg towns, as well as transformations in their culture of publicity and structure of political influence. Bureaucratic reforms of the 1820s dismantled previous communication monopolies existing for hundreds of years in the old Württemberg duchy, and extended to its new acquisitions under Napoleon. Until then the reproduction and dissemination of official announcements called "circulars" had fallen to a powerful class of municipal scribes (Schreiber).[29] The scribes' monopoly helped ensure that valuable information remained hoarded in the county seats, which occupied a special constitutional position as centers of urban notable power in parliament and usually functioned as personal satraps of the scribes. This kept smaller localities in the dark about the goings-on there. A 1725 ordinance pleaded with scribes to keep all outlying villages informed on "points which come into common deliberation" at county council meetings. The state's interest here had been both political, to favor the countryside at the county seats' expense, and cameralistic, to promote even fiscal exploitation of the hinterland and its population.[30] But as long as scribes continued to be the sole providers of regional information, the policy lacked any hope of enforcement. The same held true, incidentally, of repeated government exhortations that the scribes contribute intelligence items to the Stuttgart *Weekly Announcements*.[31]

Under the scribes' tutelage, information had functioned as a resource for an elitist brand of political activism, centered on elaborate exchanges of information among the oligarchic county seats. For example, a network of mundane circulars passed among scribes on the edge of the Black Forest since the seventeenth century became politicized by the 1790s as the forum in which a republican "*Cahier*" was drafted and debated.[32] The document imitated the cahiers of the French Revolution without resting on a truly popular political mobilization. Here, a sense of solidarity and shared grievance had emerged from practices of intra-administrative communication, taking the form of a written, legalistic protest. This was but one instance of an extreme, righteous formalism tied to the hegemony of the scribes and alien to the pragmatic sensibilities associated with Intelligenz. Leaders in county seats were more concerned with defending political privilege than promoting economic growth or administrative rationalization, and the very culture of official writing conformed to these interests.[33] The eighteenth-century situation had indicated less a general backwardness than a robust information economy nonetheless marked by severely restricted publicity and access gradated by proximity to the scribes. This arrangement, at least in the extent of power it granted the scribes, had been a unique hindrance to Württemberg's development of intelligence gazettes. All this changed in the decades after Napoleon. By the 1820s, owing to the state's new power in the wake of its Napoleonic acquisitions, the balance of power had been reversed. Edicts of 1818, 1822, and 1826 both restored local self-government and strengthened the central administration, converting the scribes into mere notaries public.[34] State officials explicitly intended that intelligence gazettes take over the scribes' previous monopoly on official circulars and announcements.[35] Thus ensued the decade of the intelligence gazettes' greatest expansion.

The reforms favored two types of civic leaders who proved central in establishing intelligence gazettes: local officials and guild printers. The first group, consisting of royal county superintendents (*Oberamtmänner*) along with county councils (*Amtsversammlungen*), profited the most, politically, from the elimination of their local rivals, the scribes.[36] As middling state and local officials their concerns were primarily for the economic development and smooth administrative operation of their districts. Intelligence gazettes appealed to them in both respects. Particularly the speed and regularity of the new medium hastened the arrival of news in out-of-the-way places.[37] This fundamentally technological innovation undermined the ability of scribes to hoard information at the county seats. Financing arrangements reinforced the dispersal of power. Sometimes, village offices had their subscription costs covered by local public coffers and their announcements inserted free of charge into the local gazette. In other cases, the county government paid the bill, ensuring full geographic coverage and unburdening localities of a significant expense. The county of Öhringen took this one step further. At the instigation of its councilors, the county contracted with the publisher Erbe to provide a bulk rate for ninety-eight copies of his Intelligenzblatt. This assured at least one copy for every village mayor (*Schultheiß*) in the county and secured the contract's "chief intent ... [of] informing the public of all [official] arrangements."[38]

Such coverage by no means democratized the flow of news, but it did vastly multiply the number of circles within which Intelligenz was communicated. This diffusion reduced the social distance between those who occupied a privileged position in the information economy and those who did not. At a certain point, in the town hall (*Rathaus*) where the village mayor had his office, the lines between local officials (who had historically monopolized intelligence) and the middle-class public (now more able to use and consume information) became blurred. At this site, and at places like the town pub or *Wirtshaus*, where subscriptions to the gazettes were often taken out, intelligence entered the webs of local rumor and competition, becoming a form of symbolic capital with which village and small-town notables jockeyed for position by keeping apprised of the latest news.[39] The shift toward a more negotiated relationship between local officials and their publics was made possible by the move from handwritten circulars to published intelligence accessible to all. The circular system had relied on the sporadic, ad hoc, discrete publication of each "individual item, *in itself uninteresting*"—except to those local notables, like the scribes, whose office had given them such interest and the means to exploit their knowledge. By contrast, a cascade of news items, it was thought, potentially constituted a critical mass of "important interest" to broader segments of the population by promoting a more passively acquired familiarity.[40] In this way, the rapid, periodic, comprehensive, impersonal distribution of information to even the smallest communities greatly increased the likelihood that matters of state and society would regularly be viewed as important matters of local civic concern by the middle-class public.

Publishers, the second group of civic leaders, activated this theoretical potential and gave this public a more concrete shape. Their efforts catalyzed new practices of publicity and actively formed new markets for information. To be sure, seldom did they follow any explicit political agenda. Often they were merely impoverished guild printers looking for a secure, government guaranteed source of income. Leuze, from Urach, was a well-known public drunk. Grözinger, of Reutlingen, was regarded as a "simple, poor printer who may not possess the necessary intellectual qualities [to print] deliberative [*räsonnierende*] articles."[41] Others, though they did preside over larger publishing empires, still looked upon gazettes as sources of easy money to finance their more prestigious literary-intellectual publications. J. G. Ritter, though every inch the businessman who fought for calendar and intelligence privileges in Ellwangen and Gmünd, relied on county superintendent Milz to set up the Jagst region Intelligenzblatt. Evidently Ritter's collaboration with J. G. Pahl on the *Nationalchronik der Teutschen*, a regionally respected critical and political magazine, commanded more of his attention.[42]

None of this should detract from publishers' pivotal role, however. The source of innovation in the medium now lay more in adjusting it to market conditions than in promoting a by now well-established ideology of popular Enlightenment. By acting as ciphers for market demand, publishers were forced to tailor the content of their papers to the general societal fascination with civic utility and practical information. This prompted ad hoc changes of format and content in order to maximize readership. Such permutations in turn forged new paths into civil society, paths illuminated by the discourse of Intelligenz. The Hall guild printer Friedrich Haspel struggled for years to establish a solvent business in the publishing trade and submitted a series of prospectuses to local and regional censorship boards. An unusual concatenation of diverse intelligence items made up his proposed "Civic Polytechnic-Amusing Citizens' Journal for All Estates" of 1828. Besides announcements and advertisements, Haspel intended to include essays from the local Association for the Teaching and Improvement of the Trading and Commercial Estates. Even more interestingly, he further envisioned the establishment of a so-called "commission bureau" as an adjunct office to the gazette. Commission bureaus served the business needs of local merchants with designs on regional markets. They prepared translations and expert opinions, placed help wanted ads in intelligence gazettes, navigated thickets of bureaucratic regulation, and mediated "private contacts that ... customers cannot or do not wish to form." Such services thrived where the traffic in commercial and societal contacts had been emancipated from previous administrative monopolies. After casting about for several years, Haspel concluded a successful contract with the Gaildorf county council to publish his intelligence gazette in a modified form.[43]

What is noteworthy about such activity are the networks of alliances printers had to form in order to sell their product. They solicited contributions and/or financial support from a range of sources, including local agricultural improvement societies, of which the one in Gmünd was the most prolific; county superintendents who shepherded "improving" articles into their pet publications; charitable institutions and religious foundations; or local notables like preachers, factory-owners, and agriculturalists. Publishers included notices and sometimes minutes of private agricultural, reading, social, and charitable associations and county fairs. They also acted as information clearinghouses for private citizens whose advertisements for various products, services, and found items instructed readers to "inquire with the editors." The publisher Stahl offered "each businessman, professional, etc. the opportunity for a few *Kreuzer* to put his articles up for sale, which is of great utility for those who deliver excellent works that suffer from lack of demand because they are not known to the public."[44] In the cases of Rottweil and Esslingen, it appears as well that publishers spearheaded a market penetration of the countryside as a means of extending their audience.[45]

In all these cases, experimentation with new forms of content provision capitalized on the new opportunities for institutional connections available in a rapidly expanding civil society: commission bureaus, agricultural societies, local governments, guilds, and foundations were but a few of their concrete manifestations. Not all these projects were successful, to be sure, but the space they inscribe in their archival traces denotes the range of possibility within which publishers conceived of "intelligence" and offered it to their publics.

Over time this format ceased being coextensive with Intelligenz in its traditional sense. Frenetic market response ultimately ripped the intelligence gazettes from the state-policed confines of their medium. In the 1830s and 1840s their publishers fought increasingly bitterly with paternalistic superintendents who expunged articles they found impious. Regional censors objected to the ever-growing number of "merely entertaining" articles at the expense of practical, didactic essays. And interior ministry officials capriciously withheld permissions and demanded steep stamp taxes to print political news, even when it was simply reprinted out of pre-censored newspapers higher up in the food chain. These conflicts resulted from a more honest reckoning by publishers with their publics, based on the realization that the Enlightenment dream of reaching the *Volk* had been too idealistic. A publisher in Künzelsau who ran an "immoral" article depicting Luther in a bad light ran afoul of a "puritanical and pietistic" censor in the form of the county superintendent, who objected that "civic utility" had taken a back seat to entertainment. The author, a local preacher, had improperly depicted the devil as a "green hunter" in unholy alliance with a knight. This depiction was not judged a suitable representational device for "instructing the people." Dominikus Kistler, the publisher, replied that "the very nice idea that many readers have, that this *Kocher and Jagst Messenger* is an educational paper for these village inhabitants … is impractical.... These inhabitants neither read nor pay for the paper." They did not count among the "subscribers from the middle and educated class at whom the entertaining portion of my paper is directed."[46]

To this middle-class audience, the exclusion of politics, though constitutive of Intelligenz as a form of reason with purely practical referents, had grated from the very beginning. Some publishers complained of subscription cancellations on account of political censorship. Others grudgingly accepted the exclusion of political news upon founding their enterprises, only to sneak in such content later. By 1848–49 this tension flared into outright hostility, leading to at least one reprisal by a Sulz county superintendent infuriated by the local intelligence gazette's stray into "democratic" politics. He called it "one of the dirtiest" newspapers in Germany for indulging "cravings for revolution" and "liberati[ng] all passions" and soon retracted all of its official business. In such cases it was clear that when politics was demanded "already in the first weeks" of a gazette's life, a mature, *bürgerlich* market already existed, ready to engage in Räsonnement.[47] The paradox was that only government support had enabled the medium to thrive, by maintaining full geographic coverage, keeping subscription costs low, ordering sample copies and making them publicly available at town halls, and serving the civic end of providing information of local scope and practical application. Since the gazettes' founding, in other words, only practical knowledge exclusive of politics could embrace the whole condominium of interests necessary to support the new medium.

Nonetheless, in the decades leading up to 1848, the intelligence gazettes had finally acquired a sufficient critical mass of societal contacts at the local level to support themselves financially. Only here did the supply of and demand for information become thick enough to actually be useful. The *local* market in information was concentrated enough to appeal to common peasants and tradesmen taking out advertisements in intelligence gazettes, and, at the same time, broad-based enough to generate economies of scale for the gazettes' owner-publishers. The 1830s and 1840s were marked by a clear privatization of the medium as the proportion of nonofficial content grew. In the *Öhringer Intelligenzblatt* the ratio of private to official nonstatistical column space increased from 1:8 in 1823–24 to 7:8 in 1835; in the same period, the number of insertions originating in the countryside grew from a quarter to over a third of all private ads.[48] Many private advertisements themselves exhibited a distinctly entrepreneurial bent. In columns previously filled with notices from wealthy book shop owners, servant girls offered to clean house. December issues featured recommendations for

Christmas presents. Craftsmen offered "recommendations" for their wares and "guaranteed quick and prompt delivery." Peasants made extra money on the side selling straw and timber.

At the root of the turn toward politics, entertainment, and critical content, then, was a market base secure enough to permit publishers to push up against old, resented limitations. Politics was only one interest among the many that the gazettes cultivated, but one whose potential to increase readership publishers could ill afford to ignore. This turn was not inevitable but a patterned response to market forces. For example, the Raach brothers, having unwittingly acquired an intelligence gazette without its attached official monopoly, found themselves forced to innovate. Their *Rems Valley Messenger* flourished in the 1840s, featuring political news, poetry, "charades," and private advertisements, while its competition, the officially sanctioned and increasingly boring *Amts- und Intelligenzblatt*, careened toward financial ruin.[49] Much as public financing had artificially prolonged the life of the intelligence gazette—and promoted all its associated societal networks—so the increased willingness to found independent ventures now testified to publishers' possession of an alternative to Intelligenz as a road map for their precarious undertakings. This new road map was the classic nineteenth century newspaper, whose time had come in Württemberg by the 1850s.

* * * *

THAT INTELLIGENZ ULTIMATELY ISSUED INTO RÄSONNEMENT is a development with tempting implications. It suggests a deep and historically novel link between evolving reading practices and civil society's autonomy from the state. A potent, independent "imagined community" was prefigured in the very objects of knowledge populating the map of intelligence itself.[50] Private property sales, listed serially in the columns of intelligence gazettes, created an identity among households indefinitely replicated across the countryside. Commodity prices printed weekly showed one's own locality alongside others, gathering villages into regions of a scope intelligible to the common reader. A pair of advertisements for a single tobacco pipe, lost and found the same week by strangers on the road from Oberohrn to Waldenburg, testified to the power of Intelligenzblätter to render anonymous, chance interactions meaningful.[51] Such items inscribed a dense map of contacts and drew in ever widening circles to a community whose participants had material stakes in learning how to read this map. Without such a guide, these material interests remained merely an inchoate "system of needs" (Hegel); without the interests, the notion of Intelligenz became a useless, empty category.

Recent theories of the public sphere almost uniformly see its power and potential as deriving from its *dis*interestedness, its impracticality and distance from social affairs. Jürgen Habermas is perhaps the best exponent of this view. His notion of rational-critical debate sees the "bracketing" of social inequality, political difference, and state power (in the salon, in the newspaper) as the root of the public sphere's legitimacy. For him, the press exists to abstract the objects of Räsonnement from their social settings, to develop and publicize them as critical judgment, and to raise morality out of the intimate sphere and up before a general public. Habermas skims lightly over the transformation by which the subjects of intimate discourse, in the family or in its mirror in literature, acquire relevance to affairs of politics, state, and society. In other thinkers' hands—especially Reinhart Koselleck's—the direct transposition of moral(istic) categories onto politics is in fact dangerously irresponsible, holding public institutions up to an impossibly high standard negotiable only in private and in secret.[52]

Koselleck's own work offers an alternative to Habermas by tracking the emergence of societal interests devoid of inherent moral content but coalescing into criticism of the state. His acount of modernization in Prussia traces societal protest—culminating in the 1848 revolution—to a structural chasm, itself created by the state, between social-economic emancipation and persistent political unfreedom.[53] His is the classic treatment of civil society's origins in, and later rebellion against, state tutelage.[54] The intelligence gazettes bear strong parallels to this story. They, too, navigated a tortuous road from censorious state sponsorship via market capitalism to critical independence between 1770 and 1848. However, they also pioneered new forms of intellectual and representational labor whose importance Koselleck fails to appreciate. Koselleck treats civil society as the outcome of a conceptual determinism, the intellectual force of new ideas about societal emancipation implemented from above by bureaucratic reformers. Here he fails to explain how these ideas actually became woven into the dense webs of interpersonal commerce and contact. My account follows these ideas into the realm of daily reception and appropriation. Originating as a project to develop "civil society," the intelligence gazettes subsequently called forth new institutional networks, social contacts, and readerships, as they were revamped successively by Enlightenment intellectuals, state administrators, and post-Napoleonic notables.

The view of civil society adopted here is one that looks beneath the surface of institutions—newspapers, commodity markets, local governments, civic associations, business establishments (publishers, commission bureaus)—to access the repertoire of cultural assumptions and social action sustaining them. That this repertoire still embraced many of the disciplinary and paternalistic mechanisms inherited from the Enlightenment project of intelligence provision is undeniable. Access to and control over the gazettes' content was not democratic but structured by small-town market and political relationships favoring notable hegemony. Lurking beneath the continued institutional partnership between state and local notables, however, was a seismic shift in the way power and hegemony were practiced. The evolution of Intelligenz indexed the assertiveness of local civic culture from within the state. By bringing the Enlightenment's encyclopedic sensibility to bloom in community settings, the intelligence gazettes helped "free association" to emerge as both cognitive and social practice.[55] The panoply of their objects of knowledge corresponded, in other words, to the variety in social background among their producers/consumers. The resultant forms of social communication reflected and could even reshape the structure of power in the hometown, both locally and vis-à-vis the state. If one is to understand how the seemingly mundane public spheres of everyday life in Germany contributed to a civic—and eventually political—consciousness instead of reflecting passivity and provincialism, one could do worse than to examine the intelligence gazettes as artifacts of an awakening civil society.

Notes

1. This contrasts with a portrait of hometown provincialism, in conflict with cosmopolitan culture and the state, offered in Mack Walker, *German Home Towns: Community, State, and General Estate 1648–1871* (Ithaca, 1971).
2. Jürgen Habermas, *Structural Transformation of the Public Sphere: An Inquiry into a Category of Bourgeois Society* [1962], trans. Thomas Burger (Cambridge, MA, 1989); Craig Calhoun, ed., *Habermas and the Public Sphere* (Cambridge, MA, 1992).
3. The existing historiography on German civil society remains confined to an elite stratum of policy makers, intellectuals, and cosmopolitan Bürger instead of focusing more deeply on their encounters with local society; epitomized by Reinhart Koselleck, *Preußen zwischen Reform und Revolution: Allgemeines Landrecht, Verwaltung und soziale Bewegung von 1791 bis 1848*, 2nd ed. (Stuttgart,

1989), this tradition continues in the more recent work of Isabel Hull, *Sexuality, State, and Civil Society in Germany, 1700–1815* (Ithaca, 1996). By contrast, Walker, *Home Towns*, foregrounds state-society and cosmopolitan-provincial interactions more successfully.

4. Friedrich Huneke, *Die "Lippischen Intelligenzblätter" (Lemgo, 1767–1799): Lektüre und gesellschaftliche Erfahrung* (Bielefeld, 1989), 49, 196.

5. See Jürgen Voss, "Der Gemeine Mann und die Volksaufklärung im späten 18. Jahrhundert," in *Vom Elend der Handarbeit: Probleme historischer Unterschichtenforschung*, ed. Hans Mommsen and Winfried Schulze (Stuttgart, 1981), 208–33; Jonathan Knudsen, "On Enlightenment for the Common Man," in *What Is Enlightenment? Eighteenth-Century Answers and Twentieth Century Questions*, ed. James Schmidt (Berkeley, 1996), 270–90.

6. That the word "Intelligenz" also referred in this period to the intelligentsia is an infelicitous coincidence, since intelligence gazettes targeted a much broader, humbler audience.

7. Hubert Max, "Intelligenzblatt—Intelligenzwesen," in *Handbuch der Zeitungswissenschaft*, ed. Walther Heide (Leipzig, 1940), 1806–45, here 1806–11; W. Schöne, *Zeitungswesen und Statistik: Eine Untersuchung über den Einfluss der periodischen Presse auf die Entstehung und Entwicklung der staatswissenschaftlichen Literatur, speziell der Statistik* (Jena, 1924), 75–80.

8. Gerhardt Petrat, "Das Intelligenzblatt—eine Forschungslücke," in *Presse und Geschichte II: Neue Beiträge zur historischen Kommunikationsforschung*, ed. E. Blühm and H. Gebhardt (Munich, 1987), 207–31, here 210–2.

9. Justus Möser, "Etwas zur Verbesserung der Intelligenzblätter" [1775], in *Sämtliche Werke* (Oldenburg, 1943), 4:153–155; idem, "Anmerkung wegen dieser Intelligenz-Blätter" [1767], in *Sämtliche Werke* (Oldenbourg, 1955–6), 8:109–10.

10. Roger Chartier, *The Cultural Origins of the French Revolution*, trans. Lydia Cochrane (Durham, NC, 1991), 90; Rolf Engelsing, "Die Perioden der Lesergeschichte in der Neuzeit: Das statistische Ausmaß und die soziokulturelle Bedeutung der Lektüre," *Archiv für Geschichte des Buchwesens* 10 (1970): 788ff.

11. Huneke, *Lippischen Intelligenzblätter*, 86–88, 192, table 1.

12. Thomas Kempf, *Aufklärung als Disziplinierung: Studien zum Diskurs des Wissens in Intelligenzblättern und gelehrten Beilagen der zweiten Hälfte des 18. Jahrhunderts* (Munich, 1991), 106–9.

13. Schöne, *Zeitungswesen und Statistik*, 70–75, 78f., 85f., 90–97.

14. Petrat, "Intelligenzblatt," passim.

15. Anon., *Die Intelligenzblätterkunde für den nicht unterrichteten Privatmann* (Weimar and Berlin, 1802), 21f., cited in Petrat, "Intelligenzblatt," 218 (emphasis in original).

16. See Huneke, *Lippischen Intelligenzblätter*; Kempf, *Aufklärung als Disziplinierung*; Petrat, "Intelligenzblatt"; Winfried Schulze, "Gerhard Oestreichs Begriff der 'Sozialdisciplinierung,'" *Zeitschrift für historische Forschung* 14 (1987): 265–302; Martin Dinges, "The Reception of M. Foucault's Ideas on Social Discipline in German Historiography," in *Reassessing Foucault*, ed. C. Jones and R. Porter (London, 1993), 181–211.

17. Huneke, *Lippischen Intelligenzblätter*, 88ff., has a good analysis of these so-called *gelehrte Sachen*.

18. See note 5, above.

19. Huneke, *Lippischen Intelligenzblätter*, 96, 107ff. for this anecdote.

20. Andreas Gestrich, *Absolutismus und Öffentlichkeit: politische Kommunikation in Deutschland zu Beginn des 18. Jahrhunderts* (Göttingen, 1994), has emphasized negotiation and legitimation—and their limits—as key aspects of publicity and information policy under the absolutist state.

21. *Königlich-Württembergisches Staats- und Regierungsblatt*, no. 25 (1808), 273–76 (§9 of Censur-Ordnung); Staatsarchiv Ludwigsburg (hereafter: StAL) D 5 I Bü 106, Landvogtei Ellwangen to sämtliche Ober- und Stabs-Ämter, 14 December 1803 (on standardization); Hermann Remppis, "Die württembergischen Intelligenzblätter von 1736–1849" (Ph.D. diss., Stuttgart, 1922), 61–65.

22. Hauptstaatsarchiv Stuttgart (hereafter: HStAS) E 146 Bü 2163, Subfasz. "Ein Intelligenzblatt, welches die oberamtl. Ausschreiben in den geeigneten Fällen ersetzen soll," expert opinion of 25 September 1817; StAL D 52 Bü 462, Ober-Censur-Collegium, 24 July 1811; also 2 November 1810; Bü 468 report of 19 September 1812.

23. *Hauskalender* were calendars for peasants, containing harvest dates and religious holidays, astronomical information and statistics on the seasons, and illustrations and miscellaneous practical advice. For Württemberg, see StAL D 5 I Bü 105, "Herausgabe von Hauskalendern für Neuwürttemberg," July 1803–January 1806; in general, Petrat, *Einem besseren Dasein zu Diensten: Die Spur der Aufklärung im Medium Kalender zwischen 1700 und 1919* (Munich, 1991).

24. StAL D 5 I Bü 106, Landvogtei Ellwangen to sämtliche Ober- und Stabsämter, 14 Dec 1803 and 13 March 1804.

25. *Allgemeines Intelligenzblatt für Neuwürttemberg* (1804): 77, 148, 188, 343; (1806): 59, 106.

26. StAL D 7 I Teil II Bü 76, Ritter cover letter of 29 December 1803; ibid., "Ankündigung" of the intelligence gazette, Ellwangen, 23 December 1803; also see Remppis, "Die württembergischen Intelligenzblätter," 59f.

27. HStAS E 146/1 Bü 4718, "Verzeichnisse sämtlicher in Württemberg erscheinender Zeitblätter" for 1826–38 and 1838–48; Remppis, "Die württembergischen Intelligenzblätter," 44–60, 98–108. The counties of Aalen, Brackenheim, Neckarsulm, Neresheim, Tettnang, Weinsberg, and Wiblingen lacked intelligence gazettes. With the exceptions of Aalen and Weinsberg, all were located on Württemberg's borders and were relatively scattered.

28. A proposal to revive the notion of a statewide gazette, combining official announcements and circulars with political and literary articles, never got off the ground. See n. 22 and HStAS E 31 Bü 281, Hauptbericht der Kommission zum Schreibereiwesen, §8, 13–17.

29. Circulars concerned subjects like auctions, bankruptcies, and government-mandated sales. For more on the Schreiber and the analysis in this section, see Ian F. McNeely, "Writing, Citizenship, and the Making of Civil Society in Germany, 1770–1840" (Ph.D. Diss., University of Michigan, 1998).

30. Walter Grube, "Dorfgemeinde und Amtsversammlung in Altwürttemberg," *Zeitschrift für württembergische Landesgeschichte* 13 (1954): 194–219.

31. Remppis, "Die württembergischen Intelligenzblätter," 13, 31, 34; *Wöchentliche Anzeigen* (Stuttgart), No. 1, 17 December 1736.

32. McNeely, "Writing, Citizenship, and the Making of Civil Society," ch. 4; Barbara Vopelius-Holtzendorff, "Das Nagolder Cahier und seine Zeit: Beschwerdeschrift mit Instruktionen für den Abgeordneten zum württembergischen Landtag von 1797," *Zeitschrift für württembergische Landesgeschichte* 37 (1978): 122–78.

33. On administrative culture and official writing, see McNeely, "Writing, Citizenship, and the Making of Civil Society."

34. McNeely, "Writing, Citizenship, and the Making of Civil Society," chs. 6–7; Manfred Hettling, *Reform ohne Revolution: Bürgertum, Bürokratie und kommunale Selbstverwaltung in Württemberg von 1800 bis 1850* (Göttingen, 1990), 31–51, 80ff.

35. HStAS E 31 Bü 281, Hauptbericht; HStAS E 146 Bü 2163, "Intelligenzblatt" proposal.

36. For the case of a Schreiber balking about loss of business, see StAL E 175 I Bü 6243, Oberamt Gerabronn to Jaxtkreisregierung, 12 December 1825.

37. See, for example, StAL D 52 Bü 468, Ober-Censur-Collegium report, 19 September 1812; D 7 I Teil II Bü 76, "Ankündigung" for Landvogtei Rottweil, 23 December 1803; HStAS E 146/1 Bü 4881, announcement for *Süddeutsche Courier* of 29 December 1819.

38. StAL E 175 I Bü 6243, Oberamt Öhringen report, 10 December 1821, and Amtsversammlungs-Protocoll-Auszug, 15 September 1821, §4.

39. Sabine Kienitz, *Sexualität, Macht und Moral: Prostitution und Geschlechterbeziehungen Anfang des 19. Jahrhunderts in Württemberg* (Berlin, 1995), 132–96, treats these rumor networks extensively.

40. HStAS E 31 Bü 281, Hauptbericht (emphasis added).

41. HStAS E 146/1 Bü 4905, printer Bühler appeal to interior ministry, 5 April 1830; Bü 4718, Oberamtmann Reutlingen to same, 27 December 1823.

42. StAL D 52 Bü 462; E 175 I Bü 6243, Ritter proposal of 5 November 1818 and passim.

43. On Haspel, StAL E 175 I Bü 1424, proposal and report dated 3–4 November 1828 for Oberamt Hall, 5 November 1829 for Oberamt Gaildorf; on Commissions-Bureaux, see McNeely, "Writing, Citizenship, and the Making of Civil Society," ch. 7.

44. StAL E 175 I Bü 1425, Stahl prospectus of 5 April 1824.

45. StAL D 1 Bü 975, prospectus for the *Eßlinger Anzeigen für den Bürger und Landmann*, July 1803; D 7 I Teil II Bü 76, Ankündigung for Rottweil, 23 December 1803.

46. StAL E 175 I Bü 1424, Oberamtsverweser Häberle and publisher Kistler at Künzelsau, exchanges of January–February 1837.

47. HStAS E 146/1 Bü 4895, Schnitzer proposal for Wangen, 10 July 1825; StAL E 175 I Bü 1425, Stahl request to Oberamt Gmünd, 24 March 1831; StAL E 177 I Bü 2908, Oberamt Sulz report, 7 November 1849.

48. These and other items from this paragraph are drawn from a sample of the *Öhringer Intelligenzblatt* in 1806–12, 1823–24, and 1835.

49. StAL E 175 I Bü 1425, documents on Raach, Keller, and Dillenius at Gmünd, 1833–44.

50. This terminology and argument are inspired by Benedict Anderson, *Imagined Communities: Reflections on the Origin and Spread of Nationalism* (London, 1991), 9–36, transposing his findings from nationalism to civil society.

51. *Öhringer Intelligenzblatt*, 28 July 1835, 358f.

52. Habermas, *Structural Transformation*; Koselleck, *Kritik und Krise: eine Studie zur Pathogenese der bürgerlichen Welt*, 7th ed. (Frankfurt, 1992); for an excellent critical comparison of these works, Anthony J. La Vopa, "Conceiving a Public: Ideas and Society in Eighteenth-Century Europe," *Journal of Modern History* 64 (March 1992): 79–116.

53. Koselleck, *Preußen*.

54. See, e.g., Walker, *German Home Towns*; Hull, *Sexuality, State, and Civil Society*; and Alf Lüdtke, *"Gemeinwohl," Polizei, und "Festungspraxis": Staatliche Gewaltsamkeit und innere Verwaltung in Preußen, 1815–1850* (Göttingen, 1982).
55. The inextricable linkage of cognition and social action, promoting "invention within limits" (here, the limits of German hometown notable culture) is emphasized by Pierre Bourdieu, *Outline of a Theory of Practice*, trans. Richard Nice (Cambridge, 1977).

6

CLUB CULTURE AND SOCIAL AUTHORITY

Freemasonry in Leipzig, 1741–1830

Robert Beachy

Introduction

WHEN THE YOUNG PHYSICIAN CARL HAUBOLD applied for admission to the Masonic lodge Minerva in 1819, he acknowledged his mentors, including four Leipzig professors and lodge members.[1]

> With hard work and enthusiasm I have pursued the science of medicine, encouraged by the examples of Platner, Rosenmueller, Kühn, and Eschenbach.... After passing my practical exam in 1817, Prof. Dr. Haase, whom I thank as a fatherly friend and mentor, transferred his practice to me. For over a year I have fulfilled my long-desired wish of working in this profession, which stands under the wise leadership of the worthiest doctors of our city. I will never forget the celebrated names of Clarus, Wendler, and Kühn.[2]

Despite his failure to express any interest in Masonic ideology, Haubold's credentials and contacts secured his admission. He underwent initiation rites, swore the secrecy oath, and entered the lodge as an "apprentice" that same year.[3] Haubold's motivations for joining the lodge are striking and reveal a fascinating aspect of

Masonic sociability. Not lofty Enlightenment ideals but the practical and professional advantages of lodge participation inspired the young doctor. Lodge membership complemented the commencement of a medical practice and was the next step in a successful career trajectory. In short, Haubold viewed the lodge as a venue where he might strengthen informal ties with Leipzig's leading physicians, who could promote the young doctor in his private practice or at the university.

Haubold's letter and dozens like it from the internal archives of the Leipzig lodges document a pragmatic element of Masonic sociability that has received little attention. Since the eighteenth century, Freemasonry has evoked images of utopian idealism and arcane ritual or suspicions of political conspiracy.[4] Reflecting these stereotypes, most scholarship on German Freemasonry has focused on the activities of the radical Rhenish lodges and the conspiratorial "Order of the Illuminaten."[5] Historians of the French Revolution, similarly, have identified the lodges with a form of political sociability that undermined traditional authority. Reinhart Koselleck has depicted Freemasonry as a threat to state absolutism—intentional or unwitting—for the simple fact of its secrecy.[6] In the absence of an analysis of the practical aspects of Masonic sociability, François Furet has drawn on the anti-Masonic writings of Augustin Cochin and has gone so far as to cast the French Masonic lodges and other philosophical societies as the "laboratories" of a new democratic sociability. The lodges, according to Furet, were an important source of the totalitarian democracy that produced the Terror.[7]

Against these charges of conspiracy and totalitarian democracy, Margaret Jacob has described the eighteenth century lodges as "schools for constitutional government."[8] Tracing Masonic ideology to its Anglo-Scottish roots, Jacob argues that the lodges "established a constitutional form of self-government, complete with constitutions and laws, elections and representatives."[9] Based on this fund of common values, the continental lodges assimilated diverse groups and forged a social pluralism that undermined traditional prerogatives of birth and estate. But the Masons also confronted the tensions between Enlightenment egalitarianism and the social divisions of the Old Regime, Jacob argues.[10] To mediate members' diverse social and cultural values, the lodges introduced and observed principles of merit. "The lodges mirrored the old order," according to Jacob, "just as they were creating a form of civil society that would ultimately replace it."[11] The defining characteristic of Masonic sociability, in Jacob's analysis, was neither leveling democracy nor conspiracy but "an affirmation of market principles."[12]

Jacob's revision of older scholarship and important analysis of the political significance of Masonic sociability prompt many questions. If the Masons promoted "market principles," as Jacob suggests, how did they exercise this influence? As this essay will argue, understanding the role of Masonic constitutionalism in the inauguration of a new form of civil society requires an analysis of the practices of lodge sociability. Balloting and elections allowed lodge members to choose members and lodge officials, but this Masonic constitutionalism did more than rehearse self-government. As the example of Dr. Haubold demonstrates, the lodges increasingly attracted ambitious members of the mercantile and liberal professions, who joined less for ideological reasons than for the practical advantages of lodge affiliation. Because membership granted access to business and professional networks, the lodges could exert a powerful social control over their own members. Through disciplinary mechanisms undergirded by Masonic secrecy, lodge seniors constituted a social authority that enforced the "market principles" governing an emerging civil society.

An important resource for considering the practical aspects of Masonic sociability lies in the method of traditional German sociology, which long has emphasized the disciplinary mechanisms of modern voluntary associations. Perhaps the first systematic account of Enlightenment sociability came from nineteenth-century legal historian Otto von Gierke, who drew a theoretical distinction between the "corporation"—a group united by craft and estate and sanctioned by absolutist privilege—and a voluntary "association." While the craft guilds conformed to rigid estate barriers, according to Gierke, voluntary associations undermined the corporate and confessional barriers of the eighteenth century and established a system of social and cultural values based on university training, commercial activity, and property ownership.[13] Masonic secrecy received special attention from Georg Simmel, who analyzed its function for lodge cohesion and social control. By threatening exclusion for the betrayal of Masonic arcana, Simmel argued, the Masons enhanced group loyalty and institutional autonomy.[14] Both Max Weber and Ernst Manheim noted the role of Masonic affiliation as a mark of integrity for merchants seeking the confidence of other businessmen.[15] The network of German lodges in the late eighteenth and early nineteenth centuries, Manheim argued, provided merchants with an institution similar to the medieval Hanseatic League.[16] Jürgen Habermas, whose work is rooted in this sociological tradition, has provided the most important account of the emergence of a public sphere and suggests that the Masonic lodges functioned, in part, to regulate the business and professional relations of civic life.[17] By focusing on the dynamics of club sociability, German sociology has underlined how mechanisms of social control including the specific function of secrecy made Masonic affiliation attractive to the mercantile and liberal professions.

Based on sources that have only become accessible since German unification, this essay develops a microhistorical analysis of Masonic practices and discipline.[18] The first Leipzig lodge of 1741 established a novel form of sociability by welcoming burgher elites, confessional minorities, and aristocrats—thereby breaching Old Regime distinctions of confession and estate. This social pluralism was widely mimicked by a range of new cultural clubs and voluntary societies, which by the early nineteenth century had fostered networks of mercantile and academic groups. As this essay contends, it was not Enlightenment ideology but the practical advantages of club membership that attracted new applicants to the Leipzig lodges. Together with diverse Leipzig clubs and societies, the three Masonic lodges came to form the warp and woof of civic life, presiding over a web of cultural, business, and academic affiliations that reflected the city's diverse institutions and actors. This associational culture played a crucial role in enforcing the business and protoprofessional norms of its participants. Not only were Masonic applicants subjected to a thorough vetting process, but successful candidates were monitored for behavior and public comportment following admission. Through the application of explicit and implicit club rules, the Leipzig lodges and associations helped instantiate the social and cultural values of an incipient civil society.

Club Sociability in Leipzig

With its international trade fairs and one of the oldest German universities, Leipzig offers an ideal case study for considering the role of Masonic culture in the civic life of late Enlightenment and early nineteenth-century Europe.[19] Though Leipzig's academic and merchant communities had formed separate clubs since the seventeenth century, the first Masonic lodge introduced a new form of sociability reflecting the example of British Masonic culture.[20] The Grand Lodge of London, founded in 1717—the institutional pinnacle of the Masonic order—sponsored the first German grand lodge in Hamburg in 1737, and Hamburg merchants traveling to the trade fairs likely organized the first Masonic meetings in Leipzig as early as 1737.[21] By 1750, lodges appeared in many larger German court, university, and trade cities, including Berlin, Hanover, Göttingen, Halle, Frankfurt am Main, and Strasbourg.[22] Graf Rutowski, a son of the Saxon Elector-King August the Strong, formed the Saxon Grand Lodge in Dresden in 1738 with a constitutional patent from London, and the Leipzig lodge received its first official charter from Dresden in 1741.[23]

Minerva's published and manuscript membership lists from the mid-eighteenth century reveal the participation of diverse social and confessional groups.[24] Like other German lodges, Minerva attracted both aristocrats and commoners. Until 1770, Saxon and Thuringian nobility accounted for approximately half of Minerva's membership.[25] One explanation for the fraternization of aristocrats with affluent Leipzig bankers and jurists was the mobility of estate properties in Electoral Saxony. The ability of wealthy commoners to purchase the estates of penurious nobles undermined rigid social barriers. Minerva's aristocratic Masons certainly relied on the services of lodge bankers, merchants, and jurists with the resources and legal sanction to purchase their property.[26]

Perhaps the most remarkable characteristic of the first Leipzig lodge was the admission of Calvinist merchants. After members of this religious minority fled France in the late seventeenth century, the Leipzig Consistory and Theology Faculty—bastions of Lutheran orthodoxy—thwarted their attempts to settle in Leipzig. Only with the patronage of the Saxon elector-king could the French traders and their families gain Leipzig residency rights in 1700.[27] Leipzig wholesale merchants were no more hospitable and complained in 1728 that "the foreigners who live here, especially the French merchants, have taken over much of the commerce with Italy, France, Holland, and other provinces."[28] Despite religious intolerance and fears of competition, the Leipzig Masons welcomed these confessional minorities. Long before receiving citizenship rights in 1811, the Calvinists had gained admission to Leipzig's elite circles through clubs and associations. As early as 1741, Masonic sociability provided the first step on this path to acceptance and integration.

As a model for other voluntary associations, the example of the Leipzig lodge was catalytic, and Leipzig Masons founded many new organizations. The Grosses Concert from 1743 represented one of the first subscription concert series in Germany and formed the institutional core of the Gewandhaus Orchestra, whose original directorate in 1781 included five Masons.[29] A faction of Minerva members formed the second abiding lodge, Balduin, in 1776, and disgruntled members from this group founded the third Leipzig lodge, Apollo, in 1801.[30] In 1776, twenty-two Masons helped organize Harmonie, an elite society that restricted membership to equal numbers of merchants and academics.[31] The reading society Gesellschaft Journalisticum began meeting in 1768 and established a detailed set of rules for the purchase and circulation of books.[32] As an extension of the Gewandhaus Directorate, the first Leipzig ball society was formed in 1787. The ball society limited membership to fifty civic notables and their families and specifically excluded aristocrats and army officers.[33]

Although the oldest Leipzig societies catered to urban elites, middling groups increasingly organized their own associations. A second, less exclusive ball society, Concordia, was formed in 1800.[34] Merchants' apprentices and junior partners of major wholesale firms organized "Société" in 1780. Non-elite merchant and academic groups continued to found new clubs into the nineteenth century.[35] A partial list of these groups includes Ressource (1790), Montagsgesellschaft (1790), Donnerstagsgesellschaft (ca. 1800), Amicitia (ca. 1801), Wintergartengesellschaft (ca. 1802), Schachgesellschaft (1806), Zwiebel (1806), Eunomia (1808), Gesellschaft Erholung (1819), Verein Erholung (1820), and Domino-Gesellschaft (ca. 1824).[36] After 1800, the first secular choruses and men's choirs were founded.[37] Leipzig's academic and scientific societies represented another associational genre; two dozen had formed by 1830.[38]

Despite various membership profiles, these associations shared important characteristics with the lodges. As self-governing clubs, the Leipzig associations adopted written charters and rules, admitted applicants through a secret ballot, and elected officials. If established for specific objectives, most groups were emphatically convivial. Many societies stocked libraries and reading rooms and sometimes published books of verse or song for use at club activities. One local satirist, writing in 1799, claimed that "from eight in the morning until ten at night, the celebration never stops.... The Leipziger is never more in his true element than when drinking or attending banquets."[39] In developing the leisure interests of the mercantile and liberal professions, the Masonic lodges and other societies functioned as a seamless and practical extension of work.

Business and Academic Networks

By the early nineteenth century, Leipzig's associations attracted a range of merchants and academics representing the university, law courts, secondary schools, hospitals, churches, and private medical practices. Because club membership vouched for personal integrity and promoted business confidence, merchants were among the most active participants. But the associations also facilitated the professional and scientific contacts of jurists and medical doctors. While academic societies promoted new disciplines or specializations, many groups devoted their efforts to novel cultural pursuits. In documenting the attraction of Leipzig's voluntary associations, the archives of the Leipzig lodges offer a unique source base. Since the Masons permitted their members a single lodge affiliation, moreover, the Leipzig Masons represented the largest discrete bloc of city club participants.

Minerva belonged to a group of the oldest German lodges and was the largest and most elite Leipzig lodge.[40] Among its 247 members in 1816, Minerva still counted thirty-seven landed nobles and six Leipzig city councilors. In its ranks of 144, the second lodge, Balduin, listed a single city councilor and just four nobles.[41] With 107 members, the youngest lodge, Apollo, had neither Leipzig Councilors nor aristocrats among its members (see Figure 1).

Despite differences in size or status, the constituencies of most Leipzig associations were shaped by city commerce. Merchants formed a plurality in all three lodges. With eighty-nine traders in 1816, Minerva had the largest mercantile group, though Apollo's thirty-nine merchants constituted an equivalent percentage. Balduin's sixty-five merchants in 1816 formed nearly half the lodge, giving it the most pronounced mercantile profile.

The constituencies of the Leipzig lodges were nonregional, reflecting influences of both international commerce and the university. Two-hundred thirty-eight, or nearly half of the members of the lodges, lived outside of Leipzig: 152 of Minerva's associates, thirty-nine Balduin affiliates, and forty-seven Apollo members resided in cities other than Leipzig.[42] These Masons hailed from both regional towns and more distant trade and university cities, including Nuremberg, Berlin, Lübeck, Frankfurt/Oder, Königsburg, Riga, Copenhagen, Zurich, Frankfurt/Main, Bremen, Vienna, Hamburg, Rostock, Berlin, Breslau, and St. Petersburg. The lodges maintained an extensive correspondence, providing outside lodges with reports on lodge "business" and with membership fliers.[43] One printed Minerva circular offered guidelines to visiting Masons for gaining

FIGURE 1   Lodges: 1816 Membership Profiles

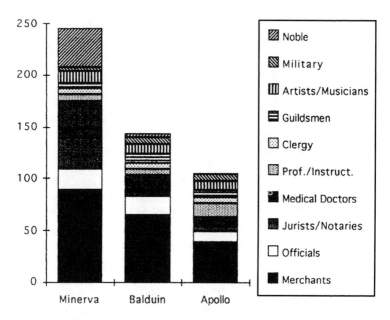

Source: Compiled from the 1816 fliers in GStA Pk: 5.2.L 17 (Apollo), no. 49; 5.2.L 24 (Minerva), no. 116; and the published membership lists, Wilhelm Kunze, *Mitglieder der St. Johannis-Loge Minerva* (Leipzig, 1860); Otto Ehrenberg, *Matrikel der Loge Balduin* (Leipzig, 1926); and *Matrikel der gerechten und vollkommenen St. Johannis Loge Apollo* (Leipzig, 1930).

admission to its own gatherings: "after presenting an identifying certificate, honorable visiting brothers can obtain entrance to the lodge."[44] As members of an international organization, traveling Masons found lodge support in most locales and could switch affiliations when moving to new firms. In anticipation of his own move from Halle to Leipzig, merchant Johann Peter—a member of a lodge in Halle, Zu den 3 Degen—applied to transfer his membership to Apollo.[45]

The connections established through business dealings frequently paved the way for lodge membership: applicants listed employers, partners, or customers for required references. For Gottfried Benedikt Fritsche, the son of a Dessau publisher who worked in the Leipzig publishing firm of Karl Tauchnitz, joining Minerva was an obvious step. Fritsche's employer, Tauchnitz, was already a lodge member and provided the required character reference.[46] Lodge membership likewise offered the advantage of regular contact with civic notables, including prominent merchants. After describing his apprenticeship with firms in Brunswick and Altona, merchant August Wetzel clearly expressed the benefits of membership: "experience has taught me that the worthiest and most prominent men of a city are Masons ... entering a close relationship with these notables, as lodge affiliation requires ... inspires my wish to become a member."[47]

A related attraction of the lodges was their strict enforcement of commercial mores. In an age of few reliable banks, lodge affiliation offered an imprimatur of integrity. One application form for Balduin candidates warned, "we make careful inquiries about you, and after that we vote. If you receive one negative vote with justification, or more than one without, your application is rejected."[48] Apollo was equally forthright in a questionnaire for aspirants, asking, "are you prepared to be expelled, without protest, if just once you prove yourself unworthy of membership?"[49] In a disciplinary action, Minerva lodge officials accused Carl Christian Kob of deceit and admonished: "he should take even greater precautions as a broker, since the other lodges, even more than ours, consist of merchants with whom he has business contacts."[50] After expulsion for bankruptcy from Minerva in 1793, Leipzig merchant Johann Georg Leutsch applied to Apollo in 1802: "I have nearly satisfied my creditors and wish to continue my activity as a Mason in an honorable lodge."[51] But settling debts did not atone for one-time insolvency. Leutsch's appeal was rejected.

Masonic sociability also helped structure academic networks. University-trained professionals formed the second membership bloc in the Leipzig lodges. Minerva's ninety-eight officials, lawyers, medical doctors, professors, and clergy represented the largest proportion of university-trained members among all three groups. Balduin had fifty and Apollo forty-three academics, giving the smaller lodge a larger percentage. In letters of application, recent university graduates thanked teachers and mentors, who were likewise Masons, for their instruction and guidance.[52] For many academics, lodge membership complemented participation in the scientific and academic societies. One recently graduated theologian, August Julius Hermann Vogel, explained that "because no science including theology which has religion as its object, is a closed subject, but rather always seeks new nourishment, I have participated in homiletic, historical, and theological societies, which have pursued their goals under the direction of very worthy teachers."[53] Equally active was young medical doctor and dentist Carl Eduard Hering, who sought lodge membership to complement his participation in Naturforschende Gesellschaft, Kunst- und Gewerbe-Verein, and "other Leipzig societies."[54]

One striking pattern among academic groups was the large number of physicians, surgeons, and dentists active in the lodges. Harmonie had only five medical doctors in 1816; except for the specialized scientific societies, even fewer medical doctors belonged to the other Leipzig associations. In contrast, Apollo had nine medical professionals, Balduin fourteen, and Minerva thirty-six. Like doctor Carl Haubold, whose application is quoted in the introduction, medical student Wilhelm Carl Mann thanked the cadre of Minerva physicians—Clarus, Wendler, and Kühn—for their instruction and guidance in his application letter of 1818.[55] After finishing his practical exams and a three-year training practicum, young physician Karl Hottenroth thanked his mentor, the local medical doctor and a Minerva member, Wilhelm Gottlob Friedrich.[56] Barring the narrow scientific societies, medical practitioners never formed exclusive social clubs like Leipzig's jurists or wholesale merchants. In the absence of specialized associations, the lodges offered medical doctors a combined professional and social venue.

While lodge participation fostered the collegiality of incipient professional groups, for merchants, Masonic affiliation offered access to both local and international business networks. Though the first lodge catered to urban and landed elites, it ignored distinctions of confession and estate. Through the elections and balloting that constituted the practices of Masonic constitutionalism, the values of urban academic and merchant groups gradually displaced traditional markers of the Old Regime. By the early nineteenth century, dozens of new Leipzig associations imitated Masonic governance, creating an associational framework for the integration of middling groups of merchants, publishers, medical doctors, and academics.

Masonic Discipline and Social Control

The ability to punish and exclude members represented the coercive force of club sociability, particularly of its arbiters, the lodge seniors. While the rank and file determined the admission of new applicants, lodge seniors presided over disciplinary proceedings. Through mechanisms of punishment and exclusion, officials enforced the norms of "respectability," an unwritten codex governing market relations, professional conduct, and bourgeois comportment. Though varied by function and structure, voluntary associations played a critical role in the rise of middle-class norms of respectability in nineteenth-century Europe.[57] Leipzig's Masonic lodges expressed these values through a set of institutional practices, which were shared by most voluntary associations. Even the Leipzig Singakademie, or city chorus, required—in addition to a "clear, flexible, and trained voice"—an irreproachable reputation and "moral respectability."[58]

Although other Leipzig societies elected officials, structures of promotion and leadership were most elaborate within the lodges. First-degree Masons, or "apprentices," met monthly for instructional sessions; fewer meetings were required of second-degree members or "journeymen." Only third-degree Masons, or "masters," participated in all lodge activities, including the election of officials and the monitoring of lodge finances.[59] Despite this hierarchy, most novices gained full qualification in three to five years and the right to stand for election to the offices of first and vice-chairmen, secretary, archivist, treasurer, music director, and orator.[60] Through promotion up the Masonic ranks and election by peers, lodge chairmen and officers of these groups gained the recognition of business partners and colleagues.

The breadth of this lodge organization enhanced Masonic authority. By the early nineteenth century, the three Leipzig lodges developed a coordinated system for vetting candidates and monitoring members' activities. Speeches delivered at special events and instructional meetings invoked metaphors of the "brotherly chain," the "family," or the "invisible Church" of Masons, suggesting the extent of local and international communications.[61] Though each lodge maintained a separate house, the groups shared information about internal lodge activities, celebrated holidays together, and exchanged social visits. Programs were organized to avoid scheduling conflicts, and the lodges sponsored regular coffee hours open to all local Masons and their wives.[62] Except for such social events, however, women were excluded from Masonic business and most lodge activities. Within Europe, only the French lodges of adoption welcomed the formal membership and participation of women.[63]

The unwitting effect of inter-lodge cooperation was to facilitate both surveillance and control. When Leipzig jurist Johann Balthasar Küstner applied to Balduin, the lodge seniors worried about his reputation, since they knew he had "expressed interest" in Minerva years before but not gained admission. In a letter to Minerva, the seniors of Balduin requested information on Küstner's application process.[64] Minerva officials responded that "the ballot was not favorable," but added, "for his sake, we note that most voters regretted Küstner's rejection.... Probably had he tried again with our lodge, his attempt would have been successful." With this reassuring word from Minerva, the Balduin Masons voted to admit Küstner.[65]

If members broke lodge rules or committed other offenses, the seniors' objective was rehabilitation. When called to account for rumors of his gambling habit in 1800, jewelry merchant Johann Jacob Stein from Frankfurt am Main confessed his shortcoming, but claimed "masonry has taught me a great deal, and upright Masons will prevent my making the mistake again." Convinced by this response, Balduin officials determined to suspend their investigations, unless rumors should require otherwise: "Since Freemasonry intends to form good men, it is our business to make misled brothers moral again."[66] But on occasions when reprimands did not achieve the desired reform, lodge seniors turned to exclusion. After a three-month suspension for inappropriate behavior, both in and outside of the lodge, Minerva officials barred private instructor Johann Christian Sommer: "Certainly we hoped that this brother would have allowed our lenient punishment to lead to his improvement; our hopes have not been fulfilled; instead he has made himself unworthy of any further consideration by disregarding our rules, telling crude lies, and even making stupid threats."[67] Though his original offense remains unclear, Sommer's inability to satisfy his lodge superiors led inevitably to his expulsion.

Among the most commonly cited offenses were charges of public quarrels or brawling. The seniors of Balduin excluded merchants Caspar Philipp Du Menil, Johann Bodo Meyer, and Christlieb Möbius in 1806, after Du Menil and Meyer assaulted their former business partner Möbius. In a circular announcing their action to other lodges, Balduin officials conceded, "you are probably not unaware of the unpleasant sensation which this has aroused in public.... Expulsion was our only recourse."[68] When medical doctor Ernst Friedrich Baumann attended a public ball on the evening of 13 February 1820 in a popular coffee house, he found himself in a circle of acquaintances including his lodge brothers Dr. Jacob Heinrich Robbi and Johann Vitus Kistner. Robbi provoked his colleague Baumann with insults. When the two agreed to settle their affair outdoors, Kistner and two others intervened and prevented the fight.[69] After deliberating on a written account of the affair, Minerva officials suspended Baumann for two months and Robbi for six. The officials' protocol noted that Robbi's "reputation is not good" and he recently "lost his position as a doctor in the poor house ... the honor of the lodge demands a harsh punishment."[70]

Moral conduct was no less a concern for the lodge seniors. After waiting for a response to his application, Carl Friedrich Kuhn wrote a second letter to denounce the rumors preventing his acceptance. Kuhn admitted to sharing an address with a married woman, but he claimed she had left her philandering husband—a former friend of his—and needed a place to stay. Her character was intact, as was his, Kuhn protested. "By God! I have had no immoral relations with her."[71] Whether true or not, Kuhn's rumored liaison ruined his chances of becoming a Mason. Christian Seidenschnur was punished for both lewdness and public brawling. After fighting with an innkeeper who accused Seidenschnur of flirting with his wife, the Minerva Mason was suspended from lodge activities for a period of twelve months.[72]

The infractions that met most consistently with expulsion, however, were bankruptcy and business failure. Since early nineteenth-century commerce rested on a complex network of trust relations, failure to meet a financial commitment could easily compromise other business associates. Mercantile credit was synonymous with the personal honor requisite for club membership. In one rule-making exception, Balduin officer and merchant Johann Wappler pleaded for associates who were recently expelled for bankruptcy. "These brothers' failure," he argued, "was through no fault of their own but the result of circumstances." Wappler convinced the lodge officers, and his friends were reinstated. Ironically, Wappler himself was excluded for bankruptcy just one year later.[73] In the wake of a European financial crisis in 1826, several Leipzig banking houses closed, and the local clubs lost many members. One prominent wool merchant, Heinrich Wilhelm Campe, entered bankruptcy proceedings, and—without prompting—submitted his letter of resignation to Balduin's seniors: "unfortunate circumstances, which burden me inexpressibly and of which you are aware, move me to perform the sad duty of leaving your brotherly midst.[74] Campe's membership in Harmonie was terminated at the same time.[75] Although business failure was often circumstantial, this offered no excuse. To the end of creating and maintaining a climate of trust and business confidence, bankruptcy represented an absolute evil, and those tainted by it were forced from the fellowship.

But what ultimately distinguished the lodges from other associations was the oath of secrecy sworn by every new Mason. The case of Friedrich Wilhelm Lindner illustrates both the banality of

Masonic secrecy and the fashion in which it enhanced the authority of lodge officials. As a professor of philosophy at the University of Leipzig, Lindner published an innocuous monograph in 1818 purporting to reveal the secrets of the order. Lindner's revelations were unremarkable; the Masonic aura he described as "arising from their secretive-doings with nothing [*Heimlichthun*]."[76] But the reactions to his publication and his own assessment of the lodge officials reveal a great deal. With the book's initial publication, Apollo promptly expelled Lindner. In a response published in the volume's second and third editions, Lindner repeated the familiar claim that Freemasonry was "a state within the state," but his explanation was of greater interest. The Masons, he claimed, practiced a "lodge despotism [*Logendespotie*]." When a member "decries the arbitrariness of the seniors … he is thrown out—the exclusion is reported to all the lodges, and even an upright man and honest burgher is thus branded. First the public asks, what horrible crime did this man commit to be excluded? Secondly, the lodge members are very hierarchical, and they intentionally make his life difficult."[77] No doubt, Lindner described his own treatment here and the lodges' influence on public opinion. By flouting the secrecy oath, he incurred the full wrath of the local lodges. His lucid analysis underlined the role of secrecy in enhancing Masonic discipline and the social authority of the lodge seniors.

Yet Lindner trivialized Masonic secrecy and belittled lodge activities. More worrisome than the loss of lodge membership was the potential damage to credit and career. Since the lodges counted a cross-section of the mercantile and liberal professions among their members, exclusion threatened to undermine reputation and public standing. In sum, the ritual vow of secrecy created a powerful mechanism for enhancing the influence of lodge officials, who constituted a social authority that was recognized and affirmed by a broad stratum of Leipzig's academic and merchant groups.

Conclusion

The stories of Dr. Haubold and Professor Lindner that frame this essay demonstrate the attraction of Masonic membership and the perils of alienating the lodges and their broad constituencies. The larger significance of Masonic sociability was not its potential for conspiracy. Rather, the Masons introduced a novel associational culture that undermined Old Regime distinctions and created a new sociability, which was widely copied by other societies. By the early nineteenth century, Leipzig's many clubs had developed a social profile characterized by the membership of merchants and protoprofessionals, who relied on their lodge and club affiliations for access to informal networks of similarly situated peers. These men viewed club membership as an extension of business and vocation. The pragmatic advantages of club sociability, as early German social theorists have suggested, were secured through mechanisms of discipline, to which every applicant willingly submitted. Club rules did not merely reflect, but actively articulated and enforced, the norms of an emerging civil society. With their members' eager participation, the lodges and other societies inhibited gambling, intemperance, and uncivil public behavior, while promoting social trust and business confidence. These convivial yet practical networks adumbrated the nineteenth-century society and culture of the European middle classes. Indeed, the participants in Leipzig's club culture were prototypes of the "Contemporary man," who, Max Weber claimed, "is without doubt, besides many other things, an associational man [*Vereinsmensch*]."[78]

Notes

This essay is based on research in the internal archives of the Leipzig lodges Minerva, Balduin, and Apollo, which are housed in the Geheimes Staatsarchiv Preussischer Kulturbesitz in Berlin. I extend my thanks to the grand lodges Grossloge A. F. u. A. M. von Deutschland and Grosse Landesloge der Freimaurer von Deutschland for permission to use this material.

1. Clarus, Kühn, Rosenmueller, and Wendler joined Minerva in 1801, 1803, 1808, and 1810, respectively. All four doctors finished their medical training in Leipzig before assuming positions at the University of Leipzig. See *Leipziger Adreßkalender* (Leipzig, 1815), 28, 32, 45, and *Die Institute der medizinischen Fakultät und der Universität Leipzig* (Leipzig, 1909), 19–20. On lodge membership, see Wilhelm Kunze, *Die Mitglieder der St. Johannis-Loge Minerva zu den Drei Palmen* (Leipzig, 1860).
2. Geheimes Staatsarchiv Preussischer Kulturbesitz (hereafter: GStA Pk), 5.2.L 24 (Minerva), no. 161, fols. 14r-v (my translation)
3. Haubold's membership number was 786; Wilhelm Kunze, *Mitglieder der St. Johannis-Loge Minerva*, 24.
4. Johannes Rogalla von Bieberstein, *Die These von der Verschwörung 1776–1945: Philosophen, Freimaurer, Juden, Liberale und Sozialisten als Verschwörer gegen die Sozialordnung* (Frankfurt am Main, 1976).
5. Consider Richard van Dülmen, *Der Geheimbund der Illuminaten* (Stuttgart, 1975); Winfried Dotzauer, *Freimaurergesellschaften am Rhein* (Wiesbaden, 1977);

Helmut Reinalter, *Der Jakobinismus in Mitteleuropa* (Stuttgart, 1981); and the collections edited by Reinalter, *Freimaurer und Geheimbünde* (Frankfurt am Main, 1983) and *Aufklärung und Geheimgesellschaften* (Munich, 1989). One of the best introductions to German Freemasonry is still Norbert Schindler, "Freimaurerkultur im 18. Jahrhundert: Zur sozialen Funktion des Geheimnisses in der entstehenden bürgerlichen Gesellschaft," in *Klassen und Kultur*, ed. Robert Berdahl (Frankfurt am Main, 1982), 205–62.

6. Reinhart Koselleck, *Kritik und Krise: Ein Beitrag zur Pathogenese der bürgerlichen Welt* (Freiburg, 1959); in English, *Critique and Crisis: The Pathogenesis of the Modern World*, trans. Keith Tribe (Cambridge, MA, 1988), 70–73, 91.

7. François Furet, *Interpreting the French Revolution*, trans. Elborg Forster (Cambridge, MA, 1981), esp. 179–80.

8. For Margaret Jacob's critique of Furet, see *Living the Enlightenment: Freemasonry and Politics in Eighteenth-Century Europe* (Oxford, 1991), 12–19.

9. Ibid., 20. On the British roots of Freemasonry, see esp. chs. 2–3, pp. 23–72.

10. Margaret Jacob analyzes the social divisions between the Strasbourg lodges in ibid., ch. 8, pp. 179–202.

11. Ibid., 8.

12. Margaret Jacob, "Money, Equality, Fraternity: Freemasonry and the Social Order in Eighteenth-Century Europe," in *The Culture of the Market*, ed. Thomas Haskell and Richard Teichgraeber (Cambridge, 1993), 102–35, quoted 135.

13. Otto von Gierke, *Das deutsche Genossenschaftsrecht*, 4 vols. (Leipzig, 1868–1913); in English *Community in Historical Perspective*, ed. Antony Black, trans. Mary Fischer (Cambridge, 1990), 11–12, 105–123.

14. Georg Simmel, *Soziologie: Untersuchungen über die Formen der Vergesellschaftung* (Berlin, 1908), 282f.

15. See Max Weber's remarks at the first professional meeting of German sociologists in *Schriften der Deutschen Gesellschaft für Soziologie*, ser. 1, *Verhandlungen der Deutschen Soziologentage*, vol. 1 (Tübingen, 1911), 39–62.

16. Ernst Manheim, *Die Träger der öffentlichen Meinung: Studien zur Soziologie der Öffentlichkeit* (Leipzig, 1933), 105.

17. Jürgen Habermas, *Strukturwandel der Öffentlichkeit* (Darmstadt, 1962); in English, *The Structural Transformation of the Public Sphere*, trans. Thomas Burger (Cambridge, MA, 1989), 35, 50–52. Thomas Nipperdey's essay "Verein als soziale Struktur in Deutschland im späten 18. und frühen 19. Jahrhundert," develops the problematic set forth by Max Weber and others; see *Gesellschaft, Kultur, Theorie: Gesammelte Aufsätze zur neueren Geschichte* (Munich, 1976), 174–205.

18. For a comprehensive guide to the German Masonic materials now housed in the Geheimes Staatsarchiv Preussischer Kulturbesitz in Berlin, see *Die Freimaurerbestände im Geheimen Staatsarchiv Preussischer Kulturbesitz*, ed. Renate Endler, 2 vols. (Frankfurt am Main, 1994–96).

19. The University of Leipzig received its charter in 1409 and the trade fairs their Imperial privileges in 1497. With 32,000 inhabitants in 1800 and just more than 40,000 in 1830, Leipzig trailed Dresden, Berlin, Vienna, Frankfurt am Main, Hamburg, Munich, and Cologne in population.

20. Fraternität, a club of Leipzig jurists, was organized in 1624, and elite wholesale merchants formed the Vertrauten social club in 1680. See Robert Naumann, *Die Fraternität der Notarien und Litteraten in Leipzig* (Leipzig, 1874); and Georg Wustmann, *Die Vertraute Gesellschaft in Leipzig* (Leipzig, 1880).

21. One of the first German Masonic publications, *Der Freymaurer im Jahre 1738* (Leipzig, 1738), confirmed this connection. The Saxon historian C. C. C. Gretschel, who belonged to the Leipzig lodge Balduin from 1830 until his death in 1848, claimed that travelling merchants organized the first Leipzig meetings in 1737. See *Geschichte des Sächsischen Volkes und Staates*, 3 vols. (Leipzig, 1843), 3: 169.

22. See Winfried Dotzauer, "Zur Sozialstruktur der Freimaurerei in Deutschland," in *Aufklärung und Geheimgesellschaften*, ed. Helmut Reinalter, 109–49.

23. See the commemorative history Alwin Bergmann, *Die Grosse Landes-Loge von Sachsen und ihre Bundeslogen* (Dresden, 1911), 7–9.

24. For the membership list from 1741–46 and 1766–1841, see Wilhelm Kunze, *Mitglieder der St. Johannis-Loge Minerva*. Membership lists for the intervening years 1746–66 are in GStA, 5.2 L 24 (Minerva): no. 111 "Matrikel Band I"; no. 360, fols. 10–15. In the first decades, merchant and jurist Masons represented many Leipzig councilors' families including Steger, Hansen, Bose, Faber, Bastineller, Frege, Stieglitz, Bertram, Schmidt, Küstner, Trier, Marche, and Winckler. Aristocratic Masons included members of the families von Bonnigk, von Woelckern, von Kiesewetter, von Miltitz, von Schweinitz, von Ruenau, von Einsiedel, von Vieth, and von Rochow.

25. Like the Hanoverians and Windsors in England, German princes including Frederick the Great and most of the Hohenzollerns were Masons. See Manfred Steffens, *Freimaurer in Deutschland* (Flensburg, 1964), 43–44.

26. One measure of the commercialization of estate properties was declining attendance at the Saxon Diet. Since commoner estate owners were denied Diet representation, the number of nobles represented in the lower house fell rapidly. In 1728, 234 noble estate holders attended the Saxon Diet. But, only 81 nobles were summoned in 1787. See Francis Carsten, *Princes and Parliaments in Germany* (Oxford, 1959), 256; and Rudolf Kötzschke and Hellmut Kretzschmar, *Sächsische Geschichte* (Dresden, 1935), 117–19, 386–91.

27. Among the founding members in 1741 were representatives of the firms of Dufour, Feronce, Conturier, Gontard, and Pallard. Although denied formal citizenship until 1811, the Calvinists were represented in most voluntary societies after 1763. See Paul Weinmeister, *Beiträge zur Geschichte der evangelisch-reformierten Gemeinde zu Leipzig 1700–1900* (Leipzig, 1900), 4–12.

28. Stadtarchiv Leipzig, Ha, VI 1a, "Protocollen der Handelsdeputierten," vol. 7: 1723–28, fol. 506v; and consider the similar complaints of the Leipzig Retailers' Guild in Karl Biedermann, *Geschichte der Leipziger Kramer-Innung* (Leipzig, 1881), 85.

29. The Mason Johann Friedrich Gleditzsch served as the first director of the "Grosses Concert" in 1743. The 1781 Gewandhaus Directorate included three bankers and two Calvinist wholesale merchants who belonged to Minerva. Cf. *Die Gewandhauskonzerte zu Leipzig* (Leipzig, 1981), 20–34; and Alfred Dörffel, *Geschichte der Gewandhausconcerte zu Leipzig* (Leipzig, 1884), 4–6, 230–32; with Wilhelm Kunze, *Mitglieder der St. Johannis-Loge Minerva*.

30. See GStA Pk, 5.2.L 18 (Balduin), no. 1 "Konferenzbeschlüße und Local Statuten, 1776–1801" and 5.2.L 17 (Apollo), no. 17 (Apollo), no. 301 "Protokollbuch 1801–1806."

31. Compare Ernst Kroker, *Gesellschaft Harmonie* (Leipzig, 1926), 18–19, 78; with *Mitglieder der St. Johannis-Loge Minerva*.

32. For the formal rules, see StadtA Leipzig, Vereinigte Journalisten-Gesellschaft, no. 1, fol. 1. A membership list was published in *Gesetzliche Vorschriften ... Gesellschaft Journalisticum* (Leipzig, 1817).

33. StadtA Leipzig, Tanzgesellschaft im Gewandaus, no. 1, fols. 1r-v.

34. See *Zur fünfzigjährigen Jubelfeier der Gesellschaft Concordia* (Leipzig, 1850).

35. *Vorschriften ... der im Jahre 1780 errichteten Gesellschaft Societé* (Leipzig, 1809).

36. See Friedrich Gottlob Leonhardi, *Geschichte und Beschreibung der Kreis- und Handelsstadt Leipzig* (Leipzig, 1799), 665–66; *Leipziger Adreßkalender* (Leipzig, 1815), 234–35.

37. See Friedrich Schmidt, "Das Musikleben der bürgerlichen Gesellschaft Leipzigs im Vormärz (1815–1848)," (Ph.D. diss., Leipzig, 1912), 133–51.

38. Cf. Johannes Müller, *Die Wissenschaftlichen Vereine und Gesellschaften Deutschlands im neunzehnten Jahrhundert*, 3 vols. (Berlin, 1883–1908), 2:326–62; and *Leipziger Adreßkalender* (Leipzig, 1830), 54–75.

39. Gustav Maurer, *Leipzig im Taumel* (1799; reprint, Leipzig, 1989), 117 (my translation).

40. Manfred Steffens, *Freimaurer in Deutschland*, 147–83.

41. Members of Minerva in 1816 included two jurist councilors, Dr. Friedrich Huldreich Siegmann and Dr. Gustav Koch, and four merchant councilors, Christian Heinrich Loth, Johann Conrad Sickel, Carl August Brehm, and Georg Christian Vollsack. The single merchant Councilor in Balduin was Jacob Bernhard Limburger. Compare *Leipziger Adreßkalender* (Leipzig, 1817), 65–66, with Wilhelm Kunze, *Mitglieder der St. Johannis-Loge Minerva* and *Matrikel der Loge Balduin* (Leipzig, 1926).

42. Cf. the 1816 membership lists in GStA Pk: 5.2.L 24 (Minerva), no. 116; 5.2.L 17 (Apollo), no. 49, with Otto Ehrenberg, *Matrikel der Loge Balduin*

43. Apollo sent its printed "Circulair Schreiben" to 115 lodges in 1809. See GStA Pk, 5.2.L 17 (Apollo), no. 21, "Protocoll 3. 1807," fols. 40v–42.

44. GStA Pk, 5.2.L 24 (Minerva), no. 116, noted at the back of the printed membership list from 1816.

45. GStA Pk, 5.2.L 17 (Apollo), No. 70, "Ansuchungs- und Vorschlags-Schreiben" (unfoliated).

46. GStA Pk, 5.2.L 24 (Minerva), no. 165, "Aufnahme Gesuche und Lebensläufe, D/G" (unfoliated).

47. GStA Pk, 5.2.L 24 (Minerva), no. 162, fol. 7 (my translation).

48. GStA Pk, 5.2.L 18 (Balduin), "Personalakten," no. 106, "C" (my translation).

49. GStA Pk, 5.2.L 17 (Apollo), no. 146.

50. GStA Pk, 5.2.L 24 (Minerva), no. 160, "Auschluss des Logenmitglieds Kob, 1809" (unfoliated; my translation).

51. GStA Pk, 5.2.L 17 (Apollo), no. 70 (my translation).

52. One of many examples was the doctoral candidate Franz Wilhelm Meinert, who listed prominent jurists and Minerva members under whom he had studied, GStA Pk, 5.2.L 24 (Minerva), no. 167, fols. 18r-v, 36–37.

53. GStA Pk, 5.2.L 24 (Minerva), no. 168, "Aufnahme Gesuche und Lebensläufe" (unfoliated; my translation).

54. GStA Pk, 5.2.L 24 (Minerva), no. 161, fols. 25–26r.

55. GStA Pk, 5.2.L 24 (Minerva), no. 167, "Aufnahme Gesuche und Lebensläufe, M-R," fols. 5r-v.

56. GStA Pk, 5.2.L 24 (Minerva), no. 164 (unfoliated).

57. Consider Thomas Nipperdey, "Verein als soziale Struktur in Deutschland;" for Britain, F.M.L. Thompson, *The Rise of Respectable Society* (Cambridge, MA,

1988); and for France, Maurice Agulhon, *Le Cercle dans la France bourgeoise 1810–1848* (Paris, 1977).

58. Quoted from "Statuten der Singakademie" in StadtA Leipzig, Singakademie zu Leipzig, no. 1, fol. 3v.
59. Both Minerva and Balduin kept separate protocols of meetings of the three membership groups, GStA Pk: 5.2.L 24 (Minerva), nos. 238–58; 5.2.L 18 (Balduin), nos. 360–84. A calendar for the fiscal year 1807–08 listed forty-three scheduled meetings in the Lodge Apollo, GStA Pk, 17 (Apollo), no. 21, "Protocoll," vol. 3, 1807, fol. 14.
60. See the membership pamphlets published for interlodge distribution, e.g., GStA Pk, 5.2.L 24 (Minerva), no. 116.
61. See the manuscripts of short essays and addresses, GStA Pk: 5.2.L 17 (Apollo), nos. 432, 434; 5.2.L 24 (Minerva), no. 452.
62. Commemorative lodge histories provide much detail on the groups' social activities. See Christian Ludwig Stieglitz, *Geschichte der Loge Minerva* (Leipzig, 1841); Gottlob Schauerhammer, *Freimaurerloge Balduin* (Leipzig, 1926); Edmund Meissner, *Geschichte der g.u.v. St. Johannis-Loge Apollo* (Leipzig, 1905).
63. See Janet Burke and Margaret Jacob, "French Freemasonry, Women, and Feminist Scholarship," in *Journal of Modern History* 68 (September 1996): 513–49.
64. GStA Pk, 5.2.L 18 (Balduin), no. 570, "Allgemeine Mittheilungen," letter from Balduin to Minerva, fols. 20r-21v.
65. Ibid., letter from Minerva to Balduin, fols. 23r-v (my translation).
66. GStA Pk, 5.2.L 18 (Balduin), no. 570, "Allgemeine Mittheilungen," fols. 38r-v (my translation).
67. GStA Pk, 5.2.L 24 (Balduin), no. 207/2, "Ehrengerichtssache ... gegen die Mitglieder Wilgenrothe, Laurentius, und Sommer wegen Disziplinverstössen, 1802–1806," fols. 17r-18r (my translation).
68. See the letter from Balduin to Apollo in GStA Pk, 5.2.L 17 (Apollo), no. 7, "Vermischte Logen Correspondenz für das Archiv," fol. 20r.
69. GStA Pk, 5.2.L 24 (Minerva), no. 207/4, "Auseinandersetzung zwischen den Mitgliedern der Loge, Robbi und Baumann, 1820," fols. 1–4 (my translation).
70. Ibid., fol. 9v (my translation).
71. GStA Pk, 5.2.L 17 (Apollo), no. 70, Kuhn letters dated 26 June 1805 and 10 October 1805 (my translation).
72. GStA Pk, 5.2.L 24 (Minerva), no. 207/5, "Ehrengerichtsverfahren gegen das Mitglied Christian Seidenschnur ..."
73. GStA Pk, 5.2.L 18 (Balduin), no. 235, vol. XVII: "Protocolle: 16.5.1809–1810," fols. 23–24, 77–78 (my translation).
74. GStA Pk, 5.2.L 18 (Balduin), no. 106, "C," Campe letter dated 14 October 1826 (my translation).
75. See Ernst Kroker, *Gesellschaft Harmonie.*
76. I consulted the 3rd ed. of Friedrich Wilhelm Lindner, *Mac-Benac, Er lebet im Sohne, oder: das positive der Freimaurerei* (Leipzig, 1819), quoted from 183 (my translation).
77. Ibid., 185 (my translation).
78. Max Weber, *Verhandlungen der Deutschen Soziologentage* (Tübingen, 1911), 1:53 (my translation).

7

ENERGY, WILLPOWER, AND HARMONY

On the Problematic Relationship between State
and Civil Society in Nineteenth-Century Germany

Daniel A. McMillan

THE POPULAR MOVEMENT FOR GERMAN UNIFICATION reached its zenith in Leipzig on 5 August 1863. Some 23,000 gymnasts from every corner of a politically fragmented Germany had gathered to affirm their faith in national unity, in three and a half days of festivity. Heinrich von Treitschke, later to become a renowned historian, strode to the podium and delivered a stirring address, long remembered as a classic of German political speech. Treitschke celebrated the victory over Napoleon won at Leipzig 50 years earlier. He asked how his compatriots had changed during the intervening years. Without using the term itself, Treitschke described how *civil society* had blossomed: economic stagnation had given way to flourishing commerce and industry; a proud and independent peasantry had replaced the "intimidated" and "abused" serfs of 1813; education had become the property of all the people, rather than the privilege of the few. The citizenry had changed its own attitude and its relationship to the state: "where the state used to be the leader and teacher, now it stands only as a modest helper next to the autonomous energy [*selbstthätige Bürgerkraft*] of the citizens."[1]

Two things had not changed since 1813, Treitschke sadly noted: there was still no German national state. And within the many existing states, royal power frequently violated constitutional principles. Yet Treitschke declared his optimism: "[i]t cannot be that a great, rich, clear-sighted people will forever give up the direction of its government. That mighty energy of the people, which pulses and swells [*wogt*] in all veins of our social life, it will also one day gain control of the German state." The expansion of parliamentary power, he implied, was merely a question of will, of the "people's energy" (*Volkskraft, volksthümliche Kraft*) reaching a sort of critical mass.[2]

Recalling the heroes of 1813, Treitschke claimed that they had defeated Napoleon—a seemingly impossible task—by virtue of their will. "So true it is," he declared, "that a people unerringly reaches that which it seriously and enthusiastically wants." Where their ancestors failed was in resting on their laurels, failing to create a German national state: "this the heroes desired only with pious wishes, with unclear longing, rather than wanting it with that strong passion, that clear perception, which ensure victory." If instead "we are only suffused, man for man, with the passionate conviction that this soil must be inviolate from the hand of the foreigner, if we have truly become the nation of brothers, of which the songs of our choral societies speak ...," then the "cathedral of German unity will stand with its walls firmly anchored."[3]

Treitschke's emphasis on will, energy, and emotion—widespread as these themes were in the language of German politics—reflected salient characteristics of civil society and its relationship to the state in nineteenth-century Germany. The boundary between state and civil society was blurred. Even the most determined liberals abhorred conflict between state and civil society, and sought not so much the autonomy of civil society from the state, but rather harmonious collaboration between the two. Liberals and democrats also expected harmony within civil society. They believed that most or all citizens eventually would unite to embrace a single and transcendent "common good."

This chapter explores the relationship between state and civil society, and the assumption that partisan conflict could be banished, by examining the gymnastics movement. Founded in 1811 to promote national renewal and rebellion against French occupation, the gymnastics clubs were the first political mass organization in modern German history. Most German states banned gymnastics as a revolutionary threat in 1820, and repression decimated the movement after the democratic insurrections of 1849. Nevertheless, gymnastics clubs revived again and again, each time in greater numbers: 150 local groups and about 12,000 members in 1818;

roughly 300 clubs in 1847, growing to perhaps 500 in the revolutionary years 1848–49; more than 1,900 clubs and about 168,000 members in 1864.[4]

From the 1810s through the 1830s, the gymnasts belonged to what contemporaries called the "party of progress" or "party of movement" (as opposed to stasis or reaction).[5] This "party" advocated representative government and national unity. They also supported a host of reforms designed to improve individuals, enhance their dignity, and free them from the putative shackles of tradition and ignorance. Such reforms included expanded public education, municipal self-government, separation of church and state (to limit clerical influence), and the jury trial. The party of progress was not an organized party in the modern sense. Instead, it was a loosely defined community of sentiment, rooted in the urban middle classes, bound together by the press and by voluntary associations such as the gymnastics clubs. In the 1840s this progressive movement, increasingly known as "liberalism," began to split into moderate and radical wings. This division hardened during the 1848–49 period of revolutionary government, producing two mutually antagonistic parties: liberals and democrats. Democrats differed from liberals by insisting on universal (male) suffrage and by favoring an elected executive over a hereditary monarch. The two parties agreed on most other issues, including the central importance of national unity. They also shared basic assumptions about the role of education and character development in political progress.

More consistently than any other kind of voluntary association, gymnastics clubs symbolized the underlying unity of the progressive movement and of the parties that grew out of it. While educated notables articulated policies in state parliaments and the press, gymnastics clubs rallied the urban middle classes behind broadly framed affirmations of nationalist and progressive belief. More than any other kind of voluntary association in the Germanys, gymnastics clubs explicitly strove to augment what Treitschke called the "people's energy," to strengthen the individual and collective will, and to make all Germans love each other "as 'brothers.'"

On the Importance of Being Festive

Gymnasts believed that exercise strengthened and focused the will. They made similar claims for group song and organized festivity, which they helped introduce to German political practice, and which played a large role in political agitation throughout the nineteenth century and into the twentieth.[6] Exercise, song, and festivity produced periods of exaltation or euphoria, comparable to intoxication and in practice (at festivals) often enhanced by drinking alcohol. German liberals and democrats saw a vital role for such altered states in their quest for converts to their political faiths. One of the first to explain the political uses of euphoria was Friedrich Ludwig Jahn, who founded the gymnastics movement. In his *Deutsches Volksthum* (1810)—the first blueprint for a German nation-state—Jahn devoted the bulk of one chapter to explaining how festivals could promote "national sentiment."

"The human being," wrote Jahn, "must arrive at a point where he feels, and becomes aware of, what he is capable of; where he comes alive, catches fire and glows—more surely for what is true, more capably for what is right."[7] It was especially at festivals that people could reach this exalted state, Jahn argued. Karl Theodor Welcker made the same point in the canonical anthology of early German liberal thought that he edited with Karl von Rotteck. Through festivals, he argued, "more can be done practically for religion and Fatherland, for the fulfillment of religious and political duties, than through other means." "The stimulating and inspiring courageous energy, the inner brotherhood, the sanctifying consecration" needed to fulfill civic duties, could not be created through "dead words and rules," through official coercion. "They are generated only through joy and love and in the high points [*Hochzeiten*] of life, and are only strengthened and kept alive through the satisfaction or appropriate reward of noble impulses [*Triebe*] and exertions."[8]

Such "high points of life," Jahn and Welcker suggested, gave people an immediate experience of their best impulses, and also a foretaste of the better world they might create through sustained struggle toward progressive goals. Addressing a festive banquet in early 1849, the Mainz democrat (and future liberal leader) Ludwig Bamberger acknowledged the revolution's prospects for the near future were dim. Nonetheless, he declared, "this gay and joyful gathering ... is the reflection [*Abglanz*] of an age to come, when the sun of truth shall illuminate a world, in which for all children of humanity there is a place at the banquet of life."[9]

The "Beneficial Influence" of Song

The gymnasts' festivals, and other political festivals in nineteenth-century Germany, usually featured some group song; like festivity, song was thought to evoke powerful emotions among the singers, harnessing their euphoria for progressive and nationalist ends. Soon after the movement's founding, gymnasts began to sing every time they met at the place of exercise. They created a distinct genre among the political lyric of the nineteenth century: the *Turnlied*, or gymnastic song. In the 1820s, while gymnastics was banned in most German states as a revolutionary threat, a movement of men's singing clubs took hold in the German states; the singing clubs, of which an estimated 1,100 existed by 1847, were the only widespread type of local association other than gymnastics clubs that were openly identified with the cause of German unity.[10]

Writing in 1861, Frankfurt gymnast Hermann Becker explained that song helped create the desire to work for patriotic ends. Whereas gymnastics produced the will and strength to carry out good deeds, song appealed to "the heart," from whence came the "intention" that then had to be translated into action. Otto Elben, a liberal politician and prominent leader of the singers' movement, made the point more effusively:

> Music exerts upon the human being in all directions of emotional life the most beneficial influence. What wealth of inspiring sentiments are opened to the broad range of [things] which are destined to penetrate to the heart of the singers through song, from the sounds of nature and their glorification, through the realm of art, to the highest goals of humanity!...
>
> The good content of the songs which are offered to the people inspires and educates; playfully, the best and most essential of what is sung implants itself in the heart of the singer; borne by the tones, the content of the text also finds its abode.

As with festivity, the joy of the experience was thought to shape behavior at a level deeper than what Welcker had called "dead words."[11]

Unity through Joy

Exercise was intended to create the sense of joy that was essential to the gymnastics movement's declared purpose in educating citizens. One of the most important lessons to be underscored by this joy was that all members of the club, irrespective of social background, belonged together as brothers, just as all Germans should love each other. Jahn started exercise in 1811 as wild outdoor play among some of his Berlin school pupils. His early collaborator, Eduard Dürre, later reminisced on Jahn's intent: "For Jahn the chief purpose at that time was to see that youth got into the open air, and got used to joyous, youthful companionship. He wanted to unite those who were divided, prevent conflict, and awaken public spirit [*Gemeinsinn*] in the boys of a people that had to shake off its heavy chains."

More than sixty years after Jahn began, Heinrich von Treitschke exhorted his audience in Leipzig to tell their friends back home "how you, in the lively exchange of ideas and feelings, in the exercise of the shared German art of gymnastics and in your heart of hearts, have experienced [*erlebt*] that we belong to each other, that we are *one* flesh and *one* blood."[12] Implicit in Dürre's and Treitschke's remarks was that the sense of community or belonging, once awakened in a small group, could then be transferred to the more abstract level of the nation. Operating on this assumption, both gymnastics and singing clubs strove to submerge differences of social background in a sense of belonging to the group. Like the joy of exercise, song promoted "a sense of belonging" (*gemeinsamen Gefuehls*) among men, in the words of one gymnast. Or as a leading singer named Karl Pfaff declared at a singer's festival in 1827: "[t]he silly boundaries of Estate fall before the power of song; one family, united in harmony, joy and enthusiasm forms the choir."[13]

Gymnasts and singers said that exercise or song erased social differences because both activities required physical capabilities irrelevant to formal education or wealth. As Otto Elben phrased it, "[a]rt knows no difference or privilege of Estate, of lineage, or of wealth, least of all *that* art form which finds its fulfillment in the participation of as many [people] as possible: choral singing, the people's song." If anything, gymnastics actively subverted existing social hierarchies, creating a ladder of achievement within each club that bore little relationship to members' social background. Moreover, as gymnasts liked to point out, all people had more or less the same body, were equal on the physical level and potentially also on the moral level. In 1843 Heinrich Karl Hofmann called for compulsory school instruction in gymnastics, saying it would ensure "for all children of the Fatherland an equal and complete development of their physical and emotional faculties [*Gemüthsanlagen*]." This form of equality would, in turn, "give everyone in the nation, without consideration of Estate or wealth, the opportunity to feel equal to those beside him ... and precisely for this reason to love them more sincerely...."[14]

Willpower and Citizenship

The gymnasts' faith in the power of emotion extended to a curious notion of collective will that mysteriously flowed directly from the sum of individual wills. Leipzig gymnastics teacher Alwin Martens, for example, argued that exercise gave Germans the means to "strengthen the individual will, whose result, an energetic collective character and collective will [*Gesammtcharakter, Gesammtwille*], alone makes a people into a nation." Treitschke declared at the Leipzig festival that a nation "unerringly achieves that which it seriously and enthusiastically wants." The gymnasts likewise asserted that a sufficient degree of will, a proper state of mind, would realize their main political goals. Addressing the first nationwide gymnastics festival at Coburg in 1860, the leading gymnast Theodor Georgii called on all Germans to become gymnasts, to experience "the full feeling of one's strength." If all would come to have this awareness, then anything still oppressing the German people would simply disappear. "Imagine that the whole nation crouches, and thousands of heavy weights lie upon it, and one commands: German people, rise up! and the burdens fall away like chaff."[15]

Strengthening the individual and collective will was not only an end in itself but also part of what the gymnasts saw as their main role in the political process: preparing young men for citizenship. The club in Plauen, which inspired most other gymnastics clubs in Saxony, described itself in 1846 as "a school of the people" that turned male youths into "active citizens of a constitutional polity." By promoting "physical and mental fitness, lawful order, freedom and morality," the clubs took over the state's job of education when most boys left school at the age of fourteen. Later they gave back to the state "men, who, being developed in all ways, are prepared to fulfill the duties—and defend the rights—of citizens."[16] Gymnastics clubs proudly claimed that they gave members practice in the political process: officers were elected annually by all adult members, various misdeeds were judged by internal jury trials, and weekly or monthly meetings were said to teach the rules and skills of parliamentary debate. By uniting members of diverse social background on a basis of formal equality—and by binding them emotionally to each other—gymnastics clubs created a microcosm of the citizenry.[17] Liberal theorists saw such exercises in self-government as a principal function of voluntary associations and as one of the chief means to anchor constitutional government in German society.

A more subtle or indirect component of this education—but one no less important—was molding character. A healthy body meant a healthy mind, as every educated German had learned from cherished Greek classics. Exercise also conferred specific benefits for character development. Self-denial learned on hiking trips with meager rations and Spartan accommodations was one basis for the essential capacity to sacrifice personal interest for the good of the community; similar arguments led liberal theorists to condemn excessive luxury as corrupting the good political order. Exercise developed a surplus of energy, helping the individual rise above his narrow duties to himself and family to work for the good of the community. Intimidating exercises on the high bar or climbing ropes strengthened willpower and courage, the better to assert one's independence against seduction by demagogues or intimidation by tyrants.[18]

Progressives thought that the varied character traits of the ideal citizen were essentially manly, hence gymnastics clubs described their task interchangeably as making citizens or making men. As Moritz Kloss declared in his popular 1846 instruction manual: "[f]rom the regular exercise of the willpower in energetic deeds, and from the awareness of a certain physical strength that develops at the same time, there follows with psychological necessity that moral courage [which is] the noble basis of manliness ..." Kloss went on to explain that "manly character" and "moral courage" were essential for citizenship and concluded that gymnastics led a young man "to that level of moral development ... where he, free of egotistical striving, is always ready and eager to promote the happiness, the honor, the freedom of his people and country, and, if it must be, to make every sacrifice."[19]

Like masculinity itself, this conception of character as the basis of citizenship was politically multivalent and was embraced by state officials and the liberal and democratic opposition alike. The task, as gymnasts and other liberals and democrats often said, was to direct the citizen to a middle way between "servility" and "rebelliousness," between the subject's passivity under despotism and the excesses of revolutionary chaos. Exactly where that golden mean might lie was impossible to specify precisely, but people of opposing political views could still agree that exercise, by shaping character, would make that golden mean easier to find. Calling gymnastics the "lever of freedom," one liberal activist explained in 1847, on the eve of the revolutions, that it "forbids the misuse of strength through the art of learning how to use it." Ernst Steglich, the editor of the movement's journal, explained in 1846 that the goal of all gymnastics was *"the freedom of the gymnast."* By "freedom" he understood the fullest possible use of one's physical and mental powers, and freedom from selfish and ignoble impulses. If anything, Steglich strove to dampen the political militancy of other gymnasts, arguing that gymnastics made its greatest contribution to freedom by strengthening the will; "will" meant, above all, self-control, and self-control was the essence of freedom. If more gymnastics teachers understood this, he continued, then people would gain their *moral* freedom and would stop "lecturing others about [political] freedom." Only when "moral freedom" (*sittliche Freiheit*) became universal could political freedom be established, for "only prejudice and passion are obstacles on the path to freedom."[20]

If Steglich defined "will" as self-control (or even self-effacement), other gymnasts presented it as the underpinning of self-assertion. They envisioned political consequences that moderate liberals like Steglich abhorred. In 1849 a militantly democratic gymnastics club explained its actions in this way:

> We recognize … that the gymnast must protect himself against physical and mental atrophy, that he should strive not only to become stronger in body, but also freer in his opinions, against the ossification of obsolete systems of government. We recognize that the mind which feels the strengthening and energizing of its body begins to look more freely and boldly about itself, and that the man must not be the spineless tool of unscrupulous rulers.[21]

Training young men for citizenship by molding their character thus expressed many variations on the relationship of civil society to the state. These variations fell on a spectrum between obedience and insurrection, in which for most participants harmonious collaboration was the ideal. Altogether the gymnasts straddled the boundary between state and civil society by assuming a task—civic education—that could easily have been reserved to the state.

Shifting the Boundary between State and Civil Society

In Germany before the 1848 revolutions, many kinds of voluntary associations took on similar quasi-governmental tasks. For example, agricultural societies worked with state officials to propagate better farming methods. Others provided modest poor relief and sought to educate the lower classes in habits of thrift and good hygiene, hoping to alleviate the economic misery of the mid-1840s. Associations are therefore said to have gradually shifted the boundary between state and civil society in the German states, undermining monarchical government without directly challenging its legitimacy.[22] The gymnasts took this tendency to its furthest limit, not only in education but in the most sensitive area of policy: military service.

Friedrich Ludwig Jahn had founded the movement to help drive out Napoleon, who had conquered Prussia in 1806, amputated much of its territory, and subjected it to crushing fiscal burdens. Like the reform bureaucrats who reorganized Prussian state and society during these years of crisis, Jahn believed that education, military service, and constitutional government would recast the relationship between state and society: passive subjects would become active citizens, eager to fight in a people's army to save a government in which their elected representatives had a say. Where the Prussian reformers built schools and expanded conscription, Jahn and his followers provided character building and physical fitness supposedly needed for military service. The Berlin gymnasts hurried to volunteer when Prussia rose against Napoleon in 1813, and victory created the enduring myth of a people's war that had both saved and founded the German nation.

From 1813 until the founding of the empire, military service retained powerful emancipatory connotations in German politics. Liberals and democrats of course condemned the standing armies of Prussia and other states: they were needlessly expensive; they could readily be used to repress domestic dissent; the aristocratic officer caste humiliated recruits and promoted habits of subservience. A militia with elected officers, on the other hand, would not only banish ills of the existing system but indeed could do more than any other institution to create active citizens. In 1848 Saxon democrat August Röckel declared that universal military service would "morally uplift and ennoble the entire nation." Responsibility for the common defense would show a citizen that he had "an even *higher* task" than just supporting himself and his family; "it continuously reminds him of his duties and his rights toward the state" and "enhances his awareness of his own worth, ennobles his participation, his interest in the state, and makes him only then a *true citizen of the state*." Gymnastics flourished in the gap between existing armies and the dreams of reformers: governments hoped that exercise would make for healthier conscripts into the standing army, while rejecting the link between service and citizenship rights. Some gymnasts, in contrast, hoped to pave the way for a future militia.[23]

Gymnastics clubs thus trod the line between collaboration and conflict with the state. This helps explain the movement's checkered fortunes. Jahn's following had blossomed to some 150 local groups and 12,000 members by 1818, aided by signs of approval from Berlin and frequent support from state officials at the local level. Jahn was awarded a state pension, two honorary doctorates, and the Iron Cross—and then in 1819 was arrested in the middle of the night and imprisoned for six years. In 1820 almost all German states banned gymnastics entirely, fearing it was a seedbed of insurrection. Official repression ebbed only gradually, and only in a few states, during the 1820s and 1830s. The governments in Bavaria and Saxony began to promote gymnastics in very modest terms. A watershed was reached in 1842 when Prussia lifted the ban and began planning a program of gymnastics in the schools. Only a few clubs were founded in the 1830s, increasing to several dozen in the early 1840s, then mushrooming after 1844 to roughly 300 clubs scattered through most German states by the eve of the 1848 revolution. As the movement blossomed in the 1840s, and as the political and social crisis deepened after 1845, the clubs struck an increasingly militant note, speaking more often about educating citizens than merely improving public health. During the revolutionary years 1848–49, as many as 200 new clubs were founded. Gymnastics clubs became hotbeds of political discussion, and at least one hundred declared support for a democratic republic. An even larger number formed "gymnasts' militias" (*Turnerwehren, Turnercompagnien*), practicing drill and often purchasing firearms. Again, such efforts had widely divergent political implications: some militias were used to suppress rioting mobs; others were conceived as the components of a future militia army. Gymnasts' militias also fought against regular troops in the democratic insurrections of May-June 1849, in Saxony, Baden and the Pfalz.

After the uprisings had been crushed, the German states expanded their efforts to promote exercise in schools, even as they moved to suppress political activity by gymnastics clubs. Gymnastics clubs were banned outright in Frankfurt and in two of the Hessian states. Other governments imposed draconian limits on the clubs' activities and closed those that had compromised themselves politically during the revolution. By 1852 the movement had been reduced to about one hundred clubs, a number that fell further until 1855 or 1856. During the repressive 1850s, the surviving clubs banned political discussion (sometimes called "mental gymnastics") from their meetings, stopped talking about educating citizens, and gave up military drill. Instead they took on a less provocative, quasi-governmental task: protecting the public from fire and flood. Gymnasts had begun forming volunteer fire departments just before 1848. In the 1850s these fire companies became a powerful symbol of the movement's transformation. Gymnastics clubs would no longer engage in "politics"—meaning conflict between parties—but rather would serve the "common good" (*Gemeinwohl*), using their "will-power and physical strength" to rescue fellow citizens in danger. By 1869, one gymnastics club in two supported its own fire brigade or rescue company.[24]

As official repression receded toward the end of the 1850s, and international diplomacy produced new threats and new opportunities, German liberal and democratic nationalism reached a new level of mass participation. Paralleled by growing networks of singing clubs and sharpshooters' associations, the gymnastics movement revived explosively, growing to 1,284 clubs and about 135,000 adult members in 1862, and 1,908 clubs and about 168,000 members in 1864. Chastened by the failed revolution a decade earlier, most gymnastics clubs avoided partisan politics in the 1860s. They concentrated instead on promoting national senti- ment through festivity, song, and exercise; many revived military drill as part of the exercise, hoping that German governments might form volunteer companies in some future "people's war." The war of 1864 between the German Confederation and Den- mark seemed the answer to their prayers; their hopes were dashed when regular armies settled the issue without seeking volunteers, and the popular nationalist movement went into decline. By 1869, the number of clubs had fallen to 1,546 and membership had been reduced by almost one-fourth.[25]

Harmony, Schism, and the Problems of German Democracy

To sum up the discussion thus far, gymnastics clubs mobilized much of the popular support for the progressive movement of the 1810s to 1840s, and for the liberal and democratic parties that grew out of this movement. Together with the singing clubs, they used festivals and song to inspire and unify the citizenry. Gym- nasts used exercise, sociability, and self-government within their clubs to prepare themselves for political participation. Gymnas- tics clubs—like many other associations, but more aggressively than most—assumed governmental functions in the spheres of education and military service. This gradual encroachment on the state's prerogatives shifted the boundary between state and civil society, as Treitschke had noted in his speech of 1863.[26] This chapter argues that the gymnasts' approach to political agitation reflected two basic assumptions about the political process. These assumptions originated among the progressives and their liberal and democratic successors and became pervasive in the parties that developed after them.

The first assumption was that state and civil society would naturally coexist in harmony, working together in a project of general progress. As John Keane has shown, the conceptual distinction between state and civil society came later to German political theory than to its French and Anglo-American counterparts. German theorists were also much less willing to countenance an open antagonism between state and civil society and rarely sought the liberation of civil society from the state's influence. Keane attributed this national difference to (among several factors) "the fragility of a political culture of citizenship—expressed in the idea (which contrasts sharply with the British *citizen* and the French *citoyen*) of the *Staatsbürger*, the passive subject whose egoism is restrained and whose liberty, prosperity and spiritual identity are guaranteed and defined from above through the state and its laws."[27]

As the gymnasts repeatedly demonstrated, citizens of the German states were hardly as passive before 1848 as some historians assume. Moreover, gymnastics was only the most flamboyant among countless forms of civic activism. Keane and other scholars underestimate the importance of such activism, because they assume that a sharp and mechanical separation of state and civil society is the norm. Thus they see only passivity in the German aversion to conflict between state and society. Yet in Germany the relationship between state and civil society was understood in organicist terms, and harmony was widely assumed to be the norm. Germans did not lack an idea of active citizenship; what they lacked, instead, to a great degree, was the French and Anglo-American glorification of the individual's autonomy and freedom from state interference. This national difference can be seen in the comparatively weak German tradition of abstractly formulated individual rights, as compared to France or the United States, where catalogues of rights have been constitutive of the political tradition.[28]

The German deficit of rights did not mean citizens lacked the desire to participate, to determine their own political fate. It merely reflected their trust in the state and their hope for active collaboration in a common movement toward social and cultural progress. The state was not readily seen as the first enemy of freedom, because "freedom" meant actively contributing to the common good; to serve in a democratically organized militia could be the consummate expression of "freedom" for a liberal or democrat. The expectation of harmony created unacknowledged obstacles on the road to representative government; in particular, a clear transfer of power from monarchies to the people's representatives was seldom recognized as a goal. Liberal constitutional thought posited a "dualism" between the hereditary monarch and the elected parliament, assuming that the two institutions would determine policy together. Liberals never explained who would have the decisive say if crown and parliament could not agree on some important issue.[29]

The liberals' road map for German political development lacked an important milestone of progress: parliamentary control over the executive. Liberals (and many democrats) therefore found it useful to talk endlessly of "willpower" and "the people's energy," to imagine progress as a gradual improvement of civil society by imperceptible degrees. Eventually citizens would have enough say in government that Germany would be a "free" polity, without citizens having to struggle against the state for control of the levers of power. Treitschke declared in 1863 that "the future of Europe belongs" to "true democracy." He meant by this the manifold forms of civic activism and collective self-improvement that had taken hold in Germany since Napoleon's defeat, and in particular the way associations had gradually supplanted the state in some areas of public policy. Upon assessing this progress, Treitschke proclaimed, any reasonable observer "will feel his heart swell with joy, like the youth who, in a moment of quiet reflection, profoundly moved, avows to himself: I have become a man."[30] Political nationhood was thus like manhood—such gendered metaphors were ubiquitous in German political discourse—and indeed a manhood miraculously achieved without rebelling against the paternal state.

The foregoing argument requires one qualification: militant democrats did give up their expectation of harmony between state and civil society. Thousands joined the insurrections of May and June 1849. Democratic clubs became the most numerous of political associations during Germany's revolutionary years, numbering an estimated 950 clubs and a half-million members.[31] However, the democratic movement declined sharply after the revolution ended. For the next fifty years, democratic parties enjoyed only minimal support in the German electorate. This weakness may demonstrate how widespread the expectation of harmony between state and society had become.

The second widespread assumption about politics—shared by liberals, democrats, and their progressive forebears—was that civil society could be harmoniously unified behind a single party. The early progressives had recognized only one legitimate party, namely the "party of progress." This party allegedly represented an idealized general interest of the whole community. It would valiantly battle all other parties, which supposedly represented only selfish interests or the forces of obscurantism. Karl von Rotteck, for example, divided opponents of the "party of progress" into six categories: those who did not see that natural law must dictate positive law; men gripped by an irrational fear of revolution; aristocrats and others who clung to their traditional privileges; people "whose God is merely the most immediate material interest"; "deplorable weathervanes" who changed their opinions from day to day, influenced or intimidated by others; and men who supported progress but were overly timid.[32] Believing that all human beings were fundamentally good—and therefore would join the progressive camp sooner or later—progressives did not consider themselves intolerant. Their liberal and democratic successors espoused a similar faith in their respective parties, denying the legitimacy of their opponents.[33]

The very existence of the gymnastics movement reflected this importance of harmony (or even unanimity) in German political culture. As Treitschke did in his 1863 speech, they spoke of a unified national will, to be created through exercise, festivity, and song. As the fourth of his "gymnastic laws," Friedrich Ludwig Jahn had prohibited his followers from "thinking of hatred or rancor" toward each other when exercising or when travelling to and from the place of exercise.[34] Succeeding generations of gymnasts strove mightily to impose harmony within their ranks. Gymnasts classified outsiders as "friends/enemies of gymnastics" (*Turnfreunde, Turnfeinde*): they welcomed every German who would join them or at least praise them, but they ridiculed any who rejected gymnastics, accusing them of being ignorant, cowardly, weak, effeminate, slavish toward authority, or opposed to "progress."[35] In this sense the gymnasts' vision of civil society—like that of other liberals and democrats—was not particularly *civil*.

Civility in politics means tolerance, the willingness to accept disagreement and regulate conflict. This is something very different from a unified "collective will." Civility implies interaction on the plane of calculation and interest, not on the emotional level of Treitschke's "nation of brothers."

A lack of civility caused few problems so long as censorship and other restraints on political life muted the expression of diverging views. After the March revolutions of 1848, however, a wide spectrum of competing parties emerged. Even as the gymnastics movement flourished in this climate, growing from 300 clubs to perhaps 500, antagonism between liberals and democrats broke it apart. Delegates to a July 1848 conference in Hanau tried to establish a national umbrella organization of gymnastics clubs. The democratic clubs insisted that any such organization proclaim that a democratic republic was the proper form of government for a united Germany. Losing a vote on this issue, 91 to 81, the democratic clubs walked out and formed a rival umbrella group.

The democratic gymnasts had not given up the basic expectation of harmony; instead, they had insisted on it too strongly, seceding so as to at least have consensus within their own ranks. In dozens of towns across the Germanys, the local gymnastics club would split into two or three clubs: one explicitly democratic, the others liberal or politically agnostic. This schism was mirrored by the bitter antagonism between democratic and liberal parties during the revolutionary years. In the 1860s, most gymnasts escaped this conflict by suppressing discussion of divisive issues within their clubs. Gymnastics remained a political movement, in that clubs ritually affirmed their "progressive" sentiment and demand for national unity. Otherwise they left "politics" (defined as partisanship) to clubs affiliated with political parties. While self-censorship banished discord among the gymnasts, the problems of German party politics were just beginning.

By 1849, Germany's distinctive five-party system had already taken shape: conservatives, Catholics, liberals, democrats, and socialists. Although each party grouping varied over time in strength, together the parties defined the political spectrum until Hitler seized power in 1933. The stability of the German party system reflected its rigidity: each party presented itself as the sole bearer of the nation's transcendent general interest and rejected the other parties as illegitimate. Perhaps because the early progressive movement had originated the concept of party in Germany, all parties took on the progressives' expectation of harmony and intolerance of dissent. Each party sought to develop a harmonious community of supporters; the German parties became anchored in "social-moral milieus,"[36] each party having its characteristic social base, network of associations, and worldview. To choose a party was not merely to embrace a set of policies; it was to define one's self as a particular kind of person.

During the years of the German Empire (1871–1918), antagonism between parties took precedence over the question of parliament's power vis-à-vis the imperial crown. Liberals joined Bismarck in trying to crush political Catholicism in the 1870s. This campaign (the notorious *Kulturkampf*) only rallied Catholic voters to the embattled Center Party, creating an enduring Liberal-Catholic antagonism. The liberal right wing then supported repressive legislation against the socialists. After this law was allowed to lapse in 1890, the Social Democrats grew to become Germany's largest party, taking one-third of the votes in the last national election before World War I. The socialists became almost a separate civil society, with a hermetically sealed network of unions, pubs, and voluntary associations.[37] Rejecting imperial politics and society, longing for a revolutionary utopia, the Social Democrats were, in turn, ostracized from the already fragmented national political community.

Divided against itself by antagonisms between the parties, the German parliament was in no position to wrest power from the imperial crown. The parties' internecine conflict reinforced their inherited reluctance to challenge the state and subordinate it to the will of civil society. For these and other reasons, Germany alone among central and western European states did not make the transition to parliamentary government until war and revolution destroyed the old order in 1918. The gymnasts can hardly be blamed for this national misfortune. However, they reflected and reinforced important assumptions about civil society, state, and politics. These assumptions became pervasive in German politics and did much to delay the advent of a German democracy.

Notes

1. Heinrich von Treitschke, "Zur Erinnerung an die Leipziger Völkerschlacht," in *Deutsche Reden*, 2 vols., ed. Theodor Flathe (Leipzig, 1893), 1: 561–62.
2. Ibid., 564–65.
3. Ibid., 567, 567, 566.
4. The following discussion of the gymnastics movement is based on my doctoral dissertation: "Germany Incarnate: Politics, Gender, and Sociability in the Gymnastics Movement, 1811–1871" (Columbia University, 1997).
5. Karl von Rotteck, "Bewegungs-Partei und Stillstands-Partei," in *Staats-Lexikon oder Encyklopädie der Staatswissenschaften* 15 vols., ed. Karl von Rotteck and Karl Theodor Welcker (Altona, 1834–1843), 2:558–65.
6. A wide range of political festivals is surveyed in Dieter Düding, Peter Friedemann, and Paul Münch, eds., *Öffentliche Festkultur: Politische Feste in Deutschland*

von der Aufklärung bis zum Ersten Weltkrieg (Hamburg, 1988); also Manfred Hettling and Paul Nolte, eds., *Bürgerliche Feste: Symbolische Formen politischen Handelns im 19. Jahrhundert* (Göttingen, 1993).

7. Friedrich Ludwig Jahn, *Deutsches Volksthum* (Lübeck, 1810), 341–42.

8. Karl Theodor Welcker, "Feste, Festspiele, Volksfeste, griechische, deutsche, englische," in *Staats-Lexikon*, vol. 5, 490–491. German democrats held similar views, as seen, for example, in the articles on "Bürgersinn, Bürgertugend" and "Deutsche Volksfeste" in Robert Blum, et. al., eds., *Volksthümliches Handbuch der Staatswissenschaften und Politik: Ein Staatslexicon für das Volk*, 2 vols. (Leipzig, 1848–51), 1: 174, 269–70.

9. Ludwig Bamberger, *Erinnerungen* (Berlin, 1899), 159.

10. On the singers' movement, and its similarities to the gymnastics movement, see Dieter Düding, *Organisierter gesellschaftlicher Nationalismus in Deutschland (1808–1847): Bedeutung und Funktion der Turner- und Sängervereine für die deutsche Nationalbewegung* (Munich, 1984), esp. 94–107.

11. Hermann Becker, "Gesang in Turn-Vereinen," *Deutsche Turn-Zeitung: Blätter für die Interessen des gesammten Turnwesens* (Leipzig, 1856–1939), 1861: 271–74; Otto Elben, *Der Volksthümliche deutsche Männergesang* (reprint of 1887 edition, Wolfenbüttel, 1991), 150.

12. Dürre quoted in Carl Euler, *Friedrich Ludwig Jahn: Sein Leben und Wirken* (Stuttgart, 1881), 186; Treitschke, "Zur Erinnerung," 565, original emphasis.

13. Becker, "Gesang in Turn-Vereinen," 271–74; Pfaff quoted in Elben, *Männergesang*, 152.

14. Elben, *Männergesang*, 152; Ernst Steglich, "Was ist das Ziel der Turnerei?" in *Der Turner: Zeitschrift gegen geistige und leibliche Verkrüppelung* (Dresden, 1846–52), 1846: 65; Heinrich Hoffman, "Turnen, Turnerei, Turnkunst," in *Staats-Lexikon* (Altona, 1843), 15: 477–78.

15. Martens quoted in O. H. Jaeger, "Ein Turnervermächtnis," *Deutsche Turn-Zeitung* (1863), 332–34; Theodor Georgii, *Das erste deutsche Turn- und Jugendfest zu Coburg den 16.-19. Juni 1860: Ein Erinnerungsblatt für Deutschlands Turner* (Leipzig, 1860), 38.

16. Plauen report in *Der Turner* (1846), 74.

17. On practice in parliamentary debate, A. Schürmann's history of the influential Leipzig club, in *Deutsche Turn-Zeitung* (1871), supplement to no. 47, esp. p. 20; on several aspects, Bormann, "Die Entwickelung des Turnwesens in Sachsen," *Deutsche Turn-Zeitung* (1888), 89–92, 103–6; an example of elaborate club rules, including procedure in internal jury trials, is in the Plauen club's model for other clubs, *Voigtländisches Turnbüchlein* (Plauen, 1844); on learning citizenship by having all members obey a common law, Steglich, "Ziel der Turnerei," 67.

18. On liberal theorists such as Karl Welcker and Robert von Mohl, see Wolfgang Hardtwig, "Strukturmerkmale und Entwicklungstendenzen des Vereinswesens in Deutschland 1789–1848," in *Vereinswesen und bürgerliche Gesellschaft in Deutschland*, ed. Otto Dann (Munich, 1984), 35–37; Karl von Rotteck, "Luxus," in *Staats-Lexikon*, 10: 293–311, especially 303–4; on rising above selfish desires to work for the common good, K. Badewitz, "Ueber den Nutzen der Leibesübungen für Handwerker," *Der Turner* (1849), 162–63.

19. Kloss, *Pädagogische Turnlehre oder Anweisung, den Turnunterricht als einen wesentlichen Theil des allgemeinen Erziehungs- und Unterrichtswesens zu behandeln* (Zeitz, 1846), 19–21.

20. Richard Glaß, "Die körperliche Erziehung ist der Hebel der Freiheit! Turnrede an das deutsche Volk," in *Vorwärts! Volks-Taschenbuch für das Jahr 1847. Unter Mitwirkung mehrerer freisinnigen Schriftsteller Deutschlands*, ed. Robert Blum (Leipzig, 1847), 171; [reprinted as vol. 5 of Sander L. Gilman, ed., *Robert Blum: Politische Schriften* (Nendeln, Liechtenstein: KTO, 1979)]; see also Steglich, "Ziel der Turnerei."

21. Report from Hainichen, *Der Turner* (1849), 54.

22. Hardtwig, "Strukturmerkmale und Entwicklungstendenzen," 37; Thomas Nipperdey, "Verein als sozialer Struktur," in *Geschichtswissenschaft und Vereinswesen*, ed. H. Boockmann, et al. (Göttingen, 1972), 29–42, esp. 40–42.

23. August Röckel, *Die Organisation der Volksbewaffnung in Deutschland* (Dresden, 1848), 5, original emphasis. When Johannes Schulze of the Prussian education ministry began the initiative that led to the state's decision to promote gymnastics, he originally cited military preparedness and general patriotism as benefits, commenting approvingly on the gymnasts' festivals; although the War Ministry approved Schulze's plan, Interior Minister von Rochow objected to linking gymnastics with military service and patriotism, and these themes were removed from the plan that the king ultimately approved: Edmund Neuendorff, *Geschichte der neueren deutschen Leibesübung*, 4 vols. (Dresden, 1932–36), 3: 307–18.

24. Report of the club in Markranstädt, *Deutsche Turn-Zeitung* (1858), 54–55; D. G. M. Schreber, "Die Turnanstalt als Schule der Männlichkeit," *Neue Jahrbücher der Turnkunst* (1858), 169–70; 49 percent of gymnastics clubs had either a fire brigade or rescue company in 1869, according to the movement's third statistical yearbook, as analyzed by Michael Krüger, *Körperkultur und Nationsbildung: Die Geschichte des Turnens in der Reichsgründungsära—eine Detailstudie über die Deutschen* (Schorndorf, 1996), 69.

25. Georg Hirth, ed. *Statistisches Jahrbuch der Turnvereine Deutschlands* (Leipzig, 1863), xxxv–xxxvii; Hirth, ed., *Zweites statistisches Jahrbuch der Turnvereine Deutschlands* (Leipzig, 1865), xli; Ferdinand Goetz, ed. *Drittes statistisches Jahrbuch der Turnvereine Deutschlands* (Leipzig, 1871), xxxviii.

26. "[W]here the state used to be the leader and teacher, now it stands only as a modest helper next to the autonomous energy [*selbstthätige Bürgerkraft*] of the citizens." In Flathe, *Deutsche Reden*, 562.

27. John Keane, "Despotism and Democracy: The Origins and Development of the Distinction between Civil Society and the State," in *Civil Society and the State: New European Perspectives*, ed. John Keane (New York, 1988), 63.

28. Rainer Wahl, "Rechtliche Wirkungen und Funktionen der Grundrechte im deutschen Konstitutionalismus des 19. Jahrhunderts," in *Moderne deutsche Verfassungsgeschichte (1815–1914)*, 2nd ed., ed. Ernst-Wolfgang Böckenförde (Königstein i.T., 1981), 345–71.

29. On this conception of freedom through and in the state (rather than from it), Paul Nolte, "Bürgerideal, Gemeinde und Republik. 'Klassischer Republikanismus' im frühen deutschen Liberalismus," *Historische Zeitschrift* 254, no. 3 (1992), 625–26; on liberals' continuing ambivalence about parliamentary power, James J. Sheehan, *German Liberalism in the Nineteenth Century* (Chicago, 1978), esp. 44–48, 115–16, 131–33, 212–13.

30. Treitschke, "Zur Erinnerung," in Flathe, *Deutsche Reden*, 563.

31. And these figures include only those clubs that joined an umbrella organization, the "Central March Association." Jonathan Sperber, *Rhineland Radicals: The Democratic Movement and the Revolution of 1848–49* (Princeton, 1991), 192.

32. Rotteck, "Bewegungs-Partei und Stillstands-Partei," 562–63.

33. On the liberal concept of "party," see Nolte, "Bürgerideal, Gemeinde und Republik," 635–36, 644–45; an example of liberal intolerance is found in Paul Pfizer, "Liberal, Liberalismus" in *Staats-Lexikon* (1840), 9: 713–30, esp. 729–30; a democratic example is the article "Partei," in Blum, et al., eds. *Volkstümliches Handbuch* 2: 138–39.

34. Jahn published his "gymnastic laws" (*Turngesetze*) in 1816; they were to regulate the conduct of all gymnasts, so as to make them models for others: Jahn and Ernst Eiselen, *Die deutsche Turnkunst* (1816; reprint East Berlin, 1960), 181.

35. See, in particular, ch. 4 of my dissertation, "Germany Incarnate."

36. A term coined by M. Rainer Lepsius, in his path-breaking essay "Parteisystem und Sozialstruktur: zum Problem der Demokratisierung der deutschen Gesellschaft," in *Deutsche Parteien vor 1918*, ed. Gerhard A. Ritter (Cologne, 1973), 56–80; also: Thomas Nipperdey, "Grundprobleme der deutschen Parteiengeschichte im 19. Jahrhundert," in Nipperdey, *Gesellschaft, Kultur, Theorie* (Göttingen, 1976), 89–112.

37. See esp. Vernon L. Lidtke, *The Alternative Culture: Socialist Labour in Imperial Germany* (New York, 1985).

PART IV

THE LIMITS OF INCLUSION

The Basis of Society

8

CIVIC CULTURE, WOMEN'S FOREIGN MISSIONS, AND THE BRITISH IMPERIAL IMAGINATION, 1860–1914

Steven S. Maughan

I N LATE VICTORIAN BRITAIN, women significantly advanced their influence in the foreign missionary movement. Not only did the numbers of overseas female missionaries increase substantially, but both in Britain and in the field advocates for women's missions also effectively promoted a strategy for the cultural transformation of indigenous societies that stressed the importance of female agency. This strategy drew on British assumptions about feminine influence in the family and legitimized the activity of British women in foreign service. It also enabled female missionary advocates to expand their roles as experts on social and imperial policy and theorize an extended set of public roles for all women that drew on the lessons provided both by religious and imperial experience. By the opening decade of the twentieth century, all of the major denominational missionary societies had established popular and successful women's branches. Explaining how women's missions rose to prominence after 1860 is important to understanding the foreign missions that Victorian Britain produced and the impact that missionary activity had on the civic life and imperial imagination of the late nineteenth century. For in the creation of women's missions lay relative independence and access to public culture that allowed female missionaries and their supporters to assume roles as legitimate participants in both religious and civil society. In these roles they set many of the terms of debate regarding the nature of indigenous societies and the "civilizing" processes operating through the family that were taken up by feminists, colonial reformers, and indigenous nationalists in the decades that followed.

Because of the centrality of churches as social institutions, religious assumptions and discourse were of considerable importance to public culture and politics in nineteenth-century Britain.[1] Religious activity supported an expanding civil society in Britain owing to legacies of the late seventeenth century: religious toleration and general social consensus about the desirability of free associational life.[2] British civil society legitimized the formation of voluntary associations, the most widespread and influential being associated with churches and religious groups. While the religious discourse of the era was vigorously contested between a national church—which retained considerable power and influence in public institutions, but not a monopolistic relationship to the state—and several groups of Nonconformists, these conflicts only amplified the relevance of religious institutions. Perhaps the most important organizations through which the adherents of sectarian British religion advanced their public rivalries were the freely supported voluntary societies. And the foreign missionary society was arguably the most successful class of voluntary society in manipulating and extending the religious associational network upon which so much of Victorian public life depended.[3]

By the Victorian era, solidification of the middle-class codes of respectability that evangelical religion endorsed increasingly shut women out of public political life. At the same time, ideas about the "nature and mission" of women encouraged them to extend the "domestic" sphere beyond the home. Because of this cultural formation, women became engaged with social problems through charitable voluntary action, exploiting an inconsistency in Victorian domestic ideology by embracing the set of opportunities that could be defined as "domestic" both in Britain and in the Empire.[4] Voluntary religious and philanthropic associations provided the primary opportunity for women, particularly the growing numbers of middle-class women, to play increasing roles in public life and engage questions of imperial expansion and domination.[5] Women's voluntarism engaged issues of social concern both at home and overseas. Therefore it is not surprising that it was through imperial reform movements—antislavery, missionary settlements, colonial social and legal reform—that many women first entered into debates surrounding public policy.[6] Advocacy for foreign missions, and more specifically for indigenous female education, had an important role to play in extending women's domestic duty beyond the purely private sphere of the home.[7] Foreign missions evoked both religious and imperial enthusiasms. When combined with social opportunity, the missionary cause allowed women to develop the ideologies and experience that gave them legitimacy to pronounce publicly upon the overseas activities of the British.

The development of women's public voice on missionary subjects was, however, a slow and uneven process. Institutionally, women's support for missions was associated with the several foreign missionary societies of sectarian British Protestantism, established in the era of the French Revolution and Napoleonic wars. The chief societies were founded at roughly the same time: the Baptist Missionary Society (BMS) in 1792, the London Missionary Society (LMS) in 1795, the Church Missionary Society (CMS) in 1799, and the Wesleyan Methodist Missionary Society (WMMS) in 1816.[8] Their provenance in an age of apocalyptic vision and global conflict ensured that two forces would bulk large in their contribution to the construction of Victorian civic culture: "enthusiastic" Christianity and empire.

By the 1840s the missionary movement had come to enjoy a centrality in the religious consciousness of the growing commercial and industrial middle classes.[9] Missionary societies were part of a fundamentally competitive denominational system and paralleled other interdenominational rivalries over education, methods of social reform, and state support of Anglicanism.[10] As one of the most popular classes of Victorian charity, missionary societies had a powerful impact on domestic culture through their well-publicized formulations for evangelizing and "civilizing" the peoples that came under British influence in the nineteenth century. By the turn of the century British missionary societies had a combined income of approximately £2 million annually and directed more than 9,000 missionaries abroad. Additionally, missionary societies had mass-circulation periodicals, the largest society, the CMS, alone distributing 2.5 million magazines and 5 million papers and tracts in 1899.[11]

Women came to have a crucial role in defining and prosecuting foreign missions both as active agents in the field and as subjects of theorizing about families and social change. Missionary societies, which were at the center of religious associational life, were quite naturally deeply concerned about imperial matters. As many recent

studies have emphasized, imperial matters had a profound, continuous, and lasting effect on British domestic culture at large.[12] Missionary activity provided an important rationale for women's
interest in British overseas activity. The doctrine of evangelical
Protestantism emphasized the freedom that Christianity gave Western women to improve manners, morals, and civilization. When
linked to foreign work, evangelical belief had a strong resonance
with the socially conservative British women who dominated the
religious associational networks of the major denominations. As
advocates for the destruction of "native" barbarism in favor of
feminine philanthropic voluntarism, religious women increasingly entered public debates with a prescription for extending
civil society to the empire. Thus, in addition to spreading religious
belief and dogma, nineteenth-century British missionaries were
also concerned to replicate British assumptions about liberal, progressive "civilization" abroad.[13]

It is important to note that this prescription, while cast nominally in the terminology of classical liberalism, came to be increasingly influenced by missionary theories of conversion, spiritual
advance, church order, and the social change presumed necessary
to support Christian communities. These theories came to have a
profound impact on British self-identity. Missionaries defined
their own culture against the evocative examples of foreign cultures and found in the comparative condition of British women
the proof of the superiority of Christian liberalism.[14]

Yet missionary ideology was not simply a product of British religious doctrine and cultural beliefs. Over the course of the nineteenth century, British Protestants responded to the deeply foreign
conditions and cultures that missions brought to their attention
and the imperial means used to establish British hegemony overseas. Thus missionary ideology was generated out of a complex
interaction of influences—domestic religious culture, shifting gender relations, imperial anxieties, exposure to foreign cultures—
that intertwined reflexively in a feedback relationship of domestic
and imperial factors and imperatives.

In the first half of the century, missions to the poor and indigent
in Britain itself were of paramount importance to the Christian
public. In the second half of the century, interest and support for
foreign missions grew to challenge the earlier preeminence of domestic concerns.[15] A crucial aspect of this process was the growing
visibility of women and women's missions within the movement
as missionaries refined gender-based strategies for cultural transformation in colonized societies. From about 1860, women's mis-

sions entered a period of expansion that increased rapidly until the turn of the century. The rapid extension of women's missions in the ensuing decades was partially a response to the Indian rebellion of 1857.[16] But it also drew heavily on the enthusiasm generated by a new wave of revivalism prominent in the British Isles after 1859.

By the 1880s, missions to women by women were accepted widely by the boards of missionary societies because they offered a "maternalist" strategy for "civilizing" that did not fundamentally challenge the female subordination held dear by traditionalist clerics. From fewer than a hundred unmarried female agents in 1870, their number expanded to 1,627 in 1899, making single females the most rapidly expanding sector of missionary recruitment late in the century. Simultaneously, the clerics who dominated the missionary societies began for the first time to publicly acknowledge the importance of the wives of male missionaries to the effort overseas. Tabulations that for the first time include missionary wives indicate that on the eve of the new century women made up at least 56 percent of missionaries fielded by the five major denominational societies.[17]

After 1880, as women's missions entered their decades of most vigorous growth, their very success began to generate competition and criticism. From outside the movement, feminists, secular social reformers, and indigenous nationalists challenged missionaries for the role of legitimate defenders of "native" women. Within the movement, traditionalist evangelicals began to attack the public roles of female missionaries by defining women's leadership in civil and religious society as a dangerous symptom of "modernist" infidelity to scripture. By the turn of the century, female missions began to evoke a multipronged reaction. While early female missionary work had been an exotic and comparatively independent sphere of work for women, the advancing wave of women's professionalism in both Britain and the empire began to rapidly extend women's opportunities in secular realms.[18] These changing circumstances meant that by the end of the Edwardian era, enthusiasm and recruitment for women's missions had peaked. Evangelical theology and culture, which initially had provided a crucial rationale for women's entrance into civic culture in the Victorian era, had come by the early twentieth century to erect barriers to women's leadership and authority in public life.

* * * *

In THE FIRST HALF OF THE NINETEENTH CENTURY, women's roles in foreign mission stations were limited largely to the activities carried out by missionary wives, daughters, sisters, and aunts.[19] While women in Britain provided the backbone of organization and finance that supported the societies, these services went largely unacknowledged in the clerically dominated culture of denominational Christianity.[20] Yet women, especially the wives of missionaries and clerics, were crucial to sustaining the overseas operations of a burgeoning missionary movement. Drawing on enthusiasm generated by the antislavery movement, the major missionary societies saw a sharp upturn of both income and recruits; the CMS alone sent out more than 100 missionaries between 1830 and 1839.[21] And because the missionary movement matured at the same time and in the same places as early Victorian family-based capitalism, the same male-dominated civic elites who defined urban public life also controlled the missionary movement, relegating women to roles of unobtrusive hard work with little public presence.[22]

Nevertheless, women and families were of considerable importance to the way social transformation in indigenous communities was theorized. Baptist missionaries in Jamaica, for example, argued that missionary wives, through their education of "heathen" women and their positive domestic example, would encourage the morality, free association, and free labor that slavery had destroyed. Families were imagined as the fundamental units of society and social change as well as the crucial agency of spiritual and cultural change.[23] The major denominations all used similar arguments to construct a special, although dependent, sphere for women in the mission field, especially married women.[24]

Evangelical culture could be rigid and puritanical. But it also held within it styles of charisma that under the right conditions allowed the construction of innovative female roles in both religious and secular society.[25] In particular, it assumed that women were suitable for ministering to women, children, and especially girls. This assumption provided an argument for female work outside of the home. But there remained a tension between the evangelical insistence on the spiritual equality of the converted and the demand that believers exhibit fidelity to established social hierarchy and the clear gender roles presumed to be demonstrated by scripture. While spiritual equality did not necessarily imply social equality, the ambiguity of what it authorized allowed women to contest more restrictive definitions of the feminine sphere to encourage useful, serious, spiritual work for women outside of the home.[26]

Drawing on imperatives to evangelize, missionary wives launched new efforts to reach Indian women in the 1820s. These concentrated almost exclusively on the instruction of "native" girls and sometimes were carried out even by unmarried women.[27] By the 1840s missionaries had developed a coherent strategy for female education that encouraged British women to extend their domestic talents outside the home.[28] Women's missionary societies initially were founded with the limited goal of supporting female mission teachers for girls' schools. The earliest were the Society for Promoting Female Education in the East, in 1834, followed by the Indian Female Normal School and Instruction Society (IFNS) in 1852.[29] Both operated primarily as auxiliaries to the denominational societies, supplying teachers and submitting to clerical oversight in the field. In effect, the early Victorian missionary imagination defined civilization, and women's roles within its civic life, in the classical liberal terms of the eighteenth century: women were denied equal status in civil society, although assigned theoretically crucial supporting roles in maintaining the families upon which the fortunes of free, rational, independent, middle-class men were presumed to depend.

In the second half of the nineteenth century, however, women transformed their place in the missionary movement. At least three factors enabled women to construct roles as both relatively independent single missionaries in the field and definers of the culture of imperialism at home: growing demographic pressure applied by increasing numbers of women in British society; the rise of revivalist theologies used by women to expand their activity in the name of religion; and growing imperial opportunity.[30] Thus, by 1888 a female delegate at the London Missionary Conference could comment approvingly on the "need of women, and especially of unmarried women, in the foreign field itself."[31]

By the 1880s women's missions were routinely considered as a crucial component of missionary work. Vigorous public advocacy for exclusively female missions using unmarried women dates from the mid-Victorian period with the foundation of women's branches at the major denominational societies.[32] Missionary societies supported the creation of women's branches by drawing on arguments about the supposed deleterious effect that indigenous women had on their own families. Removing the "corrupt" ideas held by "heathen mothers" and thus regenerating "native" families rapidly became a central concern and resulted in new strategies to change religious and moral instruction within the indigenous family.[33] In the process of defining this new "mission," the public roles and freedoms of English women were explicitly defined in opposition to what Western commentators argued were the debilitating conditions suffered by the non-Western wife and mother. Mary Weitbrecht, CMS missionary wife and prolific writer on missions and India, insisted on "the greater liberty" of Western women compared to those of "the East," a liberty that was dependent upon Christian influence.[34]

Three interlocking developments in the 1860s led to these rapid and radical changes in the position and expectations of women's missionary activity. First, the rise of a new spiritual radicalism, drawing heavily on American revivalism, provided a stronger religious rationale for insisting on the spiritual equality of women and helped undermine older and stricter evangelical definitions of the "female" sphere. Second, a new focus on reforming the Indian home combined with the growth of imperial anxiety following the 1857 rebellion to provide both a unique realm for women's activity and a reinforced desire within the evangelical community to rebuild Indian society from the family upwards. Third, a rapid transformation in accepted public roles for women in England itself, especially in the realms of charity and social reform, provided a rationale for the semiprofessionalized expansion of the work of "independent" women overseas.[35] The combination of these three forces allowed missionaries to develop women's work beyond the relatively restricted levels of the early Victorian period.

The first of these determinants, the new wave of revivalism in North America, jumped the Atlantic in 1859 and 1860 to produce revivals in the British Isles. The message of American revivalists like Charles Finney, James Caughey, and Phoebe Palmer was that an earnest presentation of Christian truth would miraculously infuse recipients with the power of the Holy Spirit without regard to gender. While largely dismissed by mainline clergy, especially Anglicans, this message found a warm reception in "holiness" conferences, beginning with the annual evangelical gatherings at Barnet.[36] By the 1870s this new style of evangelicalism had spread in Anglican circles. From 1875 annual Keswick holiness conventions attracted upwards of 2,000 largely middle-class Anglican evangelicals who increasingly saw foreign missionary work as the obvious project in a new "pentecostal season." Revivalistic influences spread in Nonconformist and especially Methodist circles through the work of revivalist and rescue associations like the Salvation Army, founded by William and Catharine Booth in 1865 with an emphasis on spiritual charisma and female evangelism.[37] One of the most significant elements of this new spirituality was the important role it gave to the laity and, as members of the laity, to women. The more prescriptive cultural norms of the "Age of Atonement" (Hilton) began to crumble as socially inclusive and active ideals of revivalism contributed to a new evangelical Age of Incarnation.[38] With this "incarnationalist" doctrine came special emphasis on callings for men and women fired by the Holy Spirit: lay preaching, platform speaking, visible and often autonomous public charity work.

The second determinant, the changing attitudes toward India and the Indian family, came from the evangelical assessment of both the causes of the Indian rebellion in 1857 and the nature of the Indian home. For British religious commentators, Indian home life was determined by the conditions of the *zenana*, the exclusively female apartments of many high-caste Hindu and Islamic households. Inaccessible to male missionaries, enterprising missionary wives began visiting zenanas in the 1830s, gaining entry by offering to teach the occupants needlework skills.[39] This was work, it was emphasized, that could only be done by women—a sphere God had opened specially and exclusively for their talents.[40] The argument in favor of zenana work was reinforced after 1857 because it meshed closely with evangelical assessments of the rebellion. While most civilian officials in India, like the official classes in England, interpreted the Indian Mutiny as a reaction against rapid Western cultural reform, the evangelical community preached that shirking of religious duty in India had led to chastisement by God.[41] In the absence of any immediate hope for cooperation from the Colonial government to Christianize through education or preaching, the alluring idea of pacifying and elevating a rebellious population through a reformation of family life went hand in hand with the notion of converting the next generation of men through the agency of their mothers. Evangelicals always emphasized that social change would come by focusing on individuals and their moral development, conversion by conversion. In India the lesson of experience seemed to be, in the words of Maria Charlesworth, that "until we raise the women of India, but little can be done in morally elevating the men."[42] Commentators like Charlesworth assumed that the women of the zenana, parallel to the Christian middle-class women of Britain, exemplified the condition and potential of the women and the families of the entire society.

Support for developing an exclusive female sphere of missionary activity was reinforced by the third determinant: the growing role of independent women in domestic charity in Britain. While manuals for spinsters and other "surplus women" in the period advocated "religion and restraint," female foreign missions assumed public roles for women just as active as those of the growing vocation of nursing advocated by the "war hero" Florence Nightingale or the slum visitations of Ellen Ranyard's Bible Women. Martha Vicinus has identified these developments as the transformation of the virginal, self-sacrificing, but passive woman into the woman of active spirituality and passionate social service exemplified by the unmarried female nurse and charity worker.[43] Thus when evangelical theology, imperial opportunity, and the incipient drive toward active and professional identities for women in England combined in the 1860s, women's missions became an avenue for religiously conservative women to legitimately claim a civic role in the name of empire.

* * * *

AS ATTITUDES TOWARD WOMEN'S PUBLIC WORK changed rapidly in Britain itself, the attraction of zenana visitation and female home visitation in the slums of British cities reinforced each other. In India, as a veteran missionary wife recalled, the most rewarding aspects of female missionary work arose out of "house-to-house visitation among ... [Indian] women. Their horizon is bounded by the four walls of the Zenana, and dreary, monotonous and dull are all their lives."[44] The description of the zenana woman presented a vision antipodean to what committed, charitable, activist Christian women in Britain asserted their role should be. Rather than being frivolous, superstitious, and useless—the example ostensibly presented by the zenana—women should be serious, Christian, and useful—the example presented by the zenana missionary and the English parish visitor. The prerogatives of charity mandated an extension of these special qualities of women to the public realm.

By the 1870s supporters of women's missions consistently deployed images of the zenana to develop a coherent ideology based on the English middle-class domestic ideal.[45] Examples of Indian domestic arrangements graphically demonstrated the superiority of the Western, and particularly the British, domestic model. Supporters of missions to females often took the Indian zenana as an example of the results of a separate-spheres ideology put into practice, but without an emphasis on the natural moral influence that women should exert through the domestic sphere. Thus upper-class Indian women lay in dissipated isolation, unable to influence husbands and brothers, unable to affect public morality through charitable action.

"Class" was critical to the levels of empathy that zenana images generated. Upper-class Indian women were the subject of attention. Early supporters of zenana work emphasized the oppressiveness of zenana existence through comparisons to the physical comforts of British ladies.[46] Perhaps worst of all, Indian women were entirely bound by the capricious whims of a single man rather than by the generalized norms of civilized behavior that, missionaries argued, had issued from the historic Christian appreciation of the strengths and limitations of women themselves. It was this appreciation, supporters of women's missions maintained, that had liberated Western women within the domestic sphere and allowed their influence to extend beyond it where public needs corresponded with private vocations.[47] Seen in this way, the zenana represented more than just a primitive holdover from the past. It also served as a cautionary example. In the zenana, English middle-class men and women could imagine the results of a rigid ideology that rigorously limited women to a physical private space rather than allowing domestic economy and philosophy to flow into the public realm.[48]

By the 1880s women's work in foreign missions had expanded significantly in Africa and China and with it the types of examples mission propagandists could use to advance domestic support. The zenana, and the "imprisoning" of all non-Western women that it implied, became the standard core of missionary constructions of "oriental" women in the second half of the nineteenth century.[49] The 1890s were the heyday of women's missions, and the rhetoric of the movement was refined as examples of African and Chinese domestic life became readily available for comparison to the British home. African homes purportedly demonstrated what happened when women were thrown into public life as laborers and drudges shamefully exploited by indolent males. As Dr. G. R. M. Wright, CMS missionary to Uganda, emphasized in his fund raising speeches in Britain, the contrast between African and British women defined the need for action: "No one even thinks of giving ladies the first place there. They live in superstitious terror, they ... have no position at all."[50] Moreover, the plight of Chinese women suggested the problems arising when women were treated as mere commodities, "piece[s] of goods bought and sold" as chattels.[51]

Through these examples, missionaries and their supporters imagined the extremes bracketing the British domestic norm. On one side were the excesses of the private, which led to seclusion and an extinguishing of women's domestic genius, as in Indian zenanas. On the other were the excesses of the public, which led to exploitation of women as unprotected labor and chattels in the harsh African and Chinese societies. Either extreme was believed to produce excesses highly detrimental to women. These arguments paralleled those of British feminists, who championed an evolutionary change in civil society away from primitive male force and toward morality as a basis for order.[52] Yet arguably the message spread through religious channels reached far more women and was more subtly persuasive than that voiced by feminists. In virtually all the rhetoric of the times, the role of the Western woman was to improve "heathen" women as part of a developmental schema whereby historical forces begun in the West would sweep the world: "Woman has always been the slave and drudge of man," Mrs. Thompson explained at the London 1888 Centenary Conference, "but now through the influence of the Gospel she is raised to be man's helper and equal."[53] In the missionary vision, however, the implied contradiction between being both an "equal" and a "helper" was not explored. For missionary observers, the presumed dangers that the "weaker sex" faced in the brutal world of market forces suggested the wisdom of thankfully accepting the unequal and "nonpolitical" roles that gave Western women comparative advantages in the public realm.[54]

By the late-Victorian era, evangelical theology, imperial concerns, and changing social conditions had combined to increase the role of women in both the home support and the overseas operations of foreign missions to a level of overwhelming importance. Advocates of expanding women's responsibility in mission administration indicated that in most English parishes women did most of the work and nearly all the door-to-door collecting.[55] The CMS Gleaners' Union, whose 70,000 members had spearheaded the much vaunted late-Victorian expansion of the society, was almost entirely the preserve of women. By 1910, 970 of its 1,128 secretaries (86 percent) were women.[56]

Women were equally crucial abroad. The "new era" in late-Victorian missionary recruitment rested heavily on the successful enlistment of single female missionaries. Between 1880 and 1900, the total number of CMS missionaries in the field increased from 252 to 889; of the 637 new missionaries, 331 (or 52 percent of the increase) were single women.[57] When both single women and missionary wives are considered, the numbers are striking: in the BMS women made up 56 percent of missionaries in the field, in the CMS and the LMS 55 percent, and in the WMMS 45 percent. When the numbers of agents employed by the Church of England Zenana Missionary Society and the Zenana Bible and Medical Mission, independent societies closely associated with the CMS, are added to the figures for the CMS, single women accounted for 41 percent of all missionaries employed by the society.[58]

While women's missionary work in the 1880s and 1890s was an important component of the general success of British missionary activity, it also was a source of rising tension within the missionary societies and the evangelical subculture. As the number of female missionaries increased, the clerical secretaries of missionary societies became interested in the questions of authority and church government that women's activities raised. A series of contests between female missionaries and clerical missionary bureaucrats occurred in the 1880s and 1890s that, on the whole, resulted in the subordination of women's missions to male clerical authority.[59] However, the resulting more complete incorporation of women's missions into the bureaucratic structure of the mainline societies only partially solved the problem of maintaining enthusiasm for female missions while providing a place for women within traditional church hierarchy. And by the turn of the century, female missions faced three new challenges to their continued success. Theology, imperial opportunity, and domestic conditions—which had favored the growth of women's missions after 1860—now began to erode the earlier successes of women within the missionary movement.

First, from around the turn of the century, "modernist" challenges to orthodox Christianity—which disputed the authority of scripture and the divinity of Christ—split the ranks of evangelicals into fiercely warring parties.[60] The authority of women became a hotly contested point in this doctrinal conflict. With the slow waning of interest in "zenana evangelization," evangelical conservatives questioned the appropriateness of social service in the mission field that women had engaged in as educators, doctors, and nurses. In this context the power given to women through radical evangelical practice rapidly ebbed as evangelical conservatives fought what they saw as the larger battle of scriptural infallibility. One of the most telling examples of this development occurred in the CMS, where women's attempts to advance their organizational authority were thwarted first by bureaucratic indifference and later by vigorous conservative evangelical opposition to allowing women into "positions of governance." The result was that women remained barred from the CMS General Committee until 1917.[61]

Second, the social authority with which evangelical women spoke about Indian and other indigenous women was eroded as other groups asserted their own claims to represent the women of the empire, often tapping into the ideological complex originally constructed by missionaries. As early as the 1860s some committed Christian women interested in Indian social reform, such as the influential Mary Carpenter, had sought to advance Indian women's education as an issue separate from Christian proselytizing. By the

1890s, Margaret Noble, Margaret Gillespie Cousins, and others were embracing Hinduism and Indian culture as they advanced agendas for Indian social reform.[62] British feminists also increasingly adopted Indian women as a "special imperial burden." Feminists, like missionaries, drew on an ideology that emphasized comparison between Western and Eastern women to provide indications of Western women's position and progress.[63] And women with professional ambitions increasingly challenged missionaries as educators and service providers, a contest exemplified in the 1870s and 1880s when professional women seeking a secular rationale for the freedom to practice medicine by female doctors protested the monopoly held by missionary societies over women's medical work in India. Such confrontations allowed women outside missionary circles to define themselves as part of the male professionalized rational world, rather than the female religious emotional one, and undermined earlier rationales for women's public activity upon which the missionary societies had relied.[64]

Such professionalizing of the realms of social service had a broad effect as missionary arguments about the transformative value of women's familial influence began to lose force in the light of newer arguments for imperial and national efficiency that emerged in the wake of the Boer War.[65] Even within missionary circles, progressives associated with the growing Student Volunteer Missionary Union increasingly argued for institutional and public educational strategies rather than for the earlier domestic strategies that had been dependent upon access to upper-class Indian houses, which, after all, had produced few converts.[66] Slowly, the claim to a uniquely domestic mission in India lost force as other missionary fields were opened and as women became more enmeshed in professionalized mission strategies that emerged in the institutional environment of hospitals and schools.[67] Perhaps most important in the mission field, nationalists claimed indigenous women as their special responsibility. In India they attempted to remove women from Western contact and the authority of the colonial regime, thus insulating Indian culture and buttressing their own political and social authority.[68]

Third, the growing range of occupations open to women in Britain by the Edwardian era meant increased competition for missionary recruiting. The claims of groups outside of the missionary subculture to represent indigenous women had changed the imperial opportunities open to missionaries, yet such claims were part of a broader set of professionalizing forces that provided greater opportunities to women. This changing environment made it more difficult for missionary advocates to claim the interest and commitment of women. By the Edwardian era, the movement that at one point had promised women adventure, uniqueness, and considerable freedom overseas began to pale in comparison to other openings for women in the professions and in the work force. Evidence from the CMS shows that after 1900 the society had increasing difficulty recruiting the University women it most coveted because of a prevalent idea that the CMS was "very old-fashioned and narrow in its views."[69] Even in its training homes for women of "deficient background," the CMS found itself faced with demands for more sophisticated academic treatment in subjects such as Christian apologetics, eschatology, and comparative religious study, all of which were poorly served by the evangelical emphasis on emotional rather than intellectual spirituality.[70] While many women found roles as professional administrators in the mission field, the emotionally sustaining evangelical theology that earlier had directed women from conservative religious homes into the mission field was increasingly contested in a society more open to gender mobility.

After the turn of the century, conservative evangelicalism ceased to be effective as a mobilizing ideology for women's independent public work. This shift was partly a result of the internal erosion of the ideal of a unique women's mission—conducted by women for women—which was replaced by programs emphasizing professional administrative efficiency. These programs fed on the systematized study of missionary methods, in vogue in the universities, that reinforced trends in the mission field. Institutionally based strategies were favored in settled mission stations and offered new opportunities to women. However, these new roles increasingly were contested by conservative evangelicals and ecclesiastical authorities. Women gained practical experience and administrative authority abroad, but they found resistance to a parallel extension of these powers in England from the conservative evangelical clergy who controlled both the societies and the most important supporting congregations. Male secretaries at the CMS argued that the experiment of women's committees begun in the 1890s had failed; but as female administrators noted, this was because, "through lack of means by which to gain information, [women's committees have] not had a fair chance at gaining the knowledge necessary for their work."[71] Continued male professional prejudice was buttressed by growing numbers of protofundamentalist clergy for whom women's advancement signaled the victory of "modernist" heresies. Thus women's horizons became restricted within the missionary movement in comparison to the burgeoning opportunities in society at large.

* * * *

WOMEN'S WORK IN THE MISSIONARY MOVEMENT, like most women's work within the churches, formed a middle ground between a more radical feminism and traditional definitions of domesticity and propriety. In the case of foreign missions, ideals for women's involvement in public life were expanded at mid-century by making clear linkages to women's "knowledge" about foreign cultures and endorsing the passionate activism characteristic of charismatic evangelicalism. The middle ground established between radical feminism and restrictive domestic patriarchy was ideologically located through the lessons provided by the Indian zenana and African and Chinese families. While women's missions drew heavily on ideas of a divinely ordained domestic hierarchy, they were also open to those increasingly professionalized pursuits outside the home that could be defined as appropriate for women. For the women of the mid-Victorian evangelical subculture, the license provided by holiness theology was a crucial opening to public space. In turn, this opening reinforced the sense of imperial need and the broader growth of women's social roles in secular realms. By the 1890s missionary strategies focusing on women had widespread currency in Britain. Their popularity opened crucial areas of public debate regarding imperial and domestic matters to women of the most religiously conservative subcultures. Missionary activity directly affected far more women than many other imperial issues, and it brought women to a position of indispensability in the massive Victorian missionary endeavor itself.

This change in the position occupied by women in foreign missions gave all women a place and a voice in the ongoing religious competition that made up such a significant part of nineteenth-century British civil debate. Within the movement, women's independent roles were persistently advocated, and slowly advanced, and although this advocacy fell far short of more progressive forms of feminism that demanded equality, missionary ideas about families had a direct impact on women in conventional middle- and even working-class homes.[72] For women to carve out a secure position within the movement, they first had to define as women's work those tasks that they could perform better than men and that were open to them through an ideology which divided the world into separate spheres. In an ironic twist of the operation of Victorian gender norms, women expanded their public roles by defining themselves as specialists in the more circumscribed realm of the domestic. When this paradigm was extended overseas—earliest and most extensively in missionary activity—religious women found a channel for public activity justified within the restrictive standards of their religious subcultures.

As women's association with the missionary movement grew, their appropriate public roles became an important issue in the shifting debates over how to define both the convert societies that missionaries attempted to construct and the British civil society that was presumed to be their model. While religion legitimized women's role in the missionary movement, the actual work performed by women and their expanding public roles eventually came to challenge the moral and social boundaries that religious doctrine and institutions sought to uphold. Over time, the emancipatory potential embodied in religious society was overcome by traditional forces emphasizing hierarchy and order so that religious ideology ceased to operate as an effective vehicle for the expansion of women's activities in the broader society.

Thus, evangelical religion had an ambiguous function in the history of civil society. Initially, when operating in an atmosphere of largely uncontested imperial opportunity and restricted opportunities for women outside of charitable voluntarism, Protestantism played a crucial role in the expansion of civil society through force of zeal. Despite its patriarchal and dogmatic elements, a crucial feature of missionary enthusiasm was its mobilization of interest in empire as a justification for feminine activism. As other forces came to challenge the social authority of revealed religion—professionalism, feminism, indigenous nationalism, liberal Christianity—the earlier revivalist evangelical consensus shattered, producing conservative protofundametalist variants that resisted further expansion of public authority for women.

Yet the ongoing process of defining the roles of empire, mission, and women continued, leaving behind what was perhaps the greatest contribution of the foreign Protestant missionary movement in the second half of the nineteenth century: the transfer of a substantial portion of British women's pre-existing interest in community, child care, and women's welfare to foreign mission work. In the process, women of conservative evangelical backgrounds claimed a place in public debates about British society and empire and forged ideologies that idealized maternal contributions to civil society. In this way the charitable concerns of women formed the nucleus of the "civilizing" discourse about "progress" that the British world vision encompassed in the high imperial age. Foreign missions served to funnel these concerns into the empire and the "regions beyond." While the several Victorian religious denominations did not, in stated theory, endorse extending the public roles of women, competition between them, operating within the context of evolving Victorian Protestant theology, shifting social attitudes to female public activity, and the anxieties produced by imperial challenges, provided at a crucial time a field of opportunity for the extension of women's roles in religion, in the professions, and in civil society at large.

Notes

I would like to thank participants at the North American Conference on British Studies, Vancouver, 1994, for their comments on an earlier version of this piece. Research on this subject was made possible by grants from the Center for European History at Harvard University, the Krupp Foundation, and the Fulbright Fellowship Program.

1. See John Wolffe, *God and Greater Britain: Religion and National Life in Britain and Ireland, 1843/1945* (London, 1994); Boyd Hilton, *The Age of Atonement: The Influence of Evangelicalism on Social and Economic Thought, 1795/1865* (Oxford, 1988); G. I. T. Machin, *Politics and the Churches of Great Britain, 1869–1921* (Oxford, 1987); Leonore Davidoff and Catherine Hall, *Family Fortunes: Men and Women of the English Middle Class, 1780/1850* (London, 1987); J.P. Parry, *Democracy and Religion: Gladstone and the Liberal Party, 1867/1875* (Cambridge, 1986).
2. John A. Hall, "In Search of Civil Society," in *Civil Society: Theory, History, Comparison*, ed. John A. Hall (Cambridge, 1995), 14–15, 21–22.
3. Jeffrey Cox comments on the changing relationship between "modern" Western religion, state power, foreign missions, and the voluntary society in "The Missionary Movement," in *Nineteenth-Century English Religious Traditions*, ed. D. G. Paz (Westport, CT, 1995), 200–204.
4. The literature on separate spheres is voluminous. For a pioneering synthesis, see Davidoff and Hall, *Family Fortunes.*
5. See F. K. Prochaska, *Women and Philanthropy in Nineteenth-Century England* (Oxford, 1980), 8–17 and *passim*; Margaret Strobel, *European Women and the Second British Empire* (Bloomington, 1991); Nupur Chaudhuri and Margaret Strobel, eds., *Western Women and Imperialism: Complicity and Resistance* (Bloomington, 1992). Scholarly attention to British female missionaries is inadequate and does not match attention given to their American counterparts. However, see Fiona Bowie, Deborah Kirkwood, and Shirley Ardener, eds., *Women and Missions: Past and Present: Anthropological and Historical Perceptions* (Providence, 1993).
6. See Clare Midgley, *Women Against Slavery: The British Campaigns, 1780/1870* (London, 1992); for later in the century, when attention shifted to women in India, see Antoinette Burton, *Burdens of History: British Feminists, Indian Women, and Imperial Culture, 1865/1915* (Chapel Hill, 1994).
7. David Savage, "Missionaries and the Development of a Colonial Ideology of Female Education in India" *Gender and History* 9, no. 2 (1997): 208–11.

8. The LMS was largely supported by Congregationalists; the CMS, by evangelical Anglicans. Wesleyan Methodists had been active for two decades prior to centralization under the WMMS. The fifth major society, the Society for the Propagation of the Gospel (SPG), was a High Church organization that had been in operation since 1701, although until the 1830s almost exclusively among English colonists. Although more than fifty missionary societies existed in Britain and Ireland in 1900, representing many denominations and independent missionary associations, the five major denominational societies controlled 72 percent of domestic giving to missions and 59 percent of the missionary force (94 percent if the Salvation Army, with its large number of lay missionaries, is excluded). James S. Dennis, *Centennial Survey of Foreign Missions* (Edinburgh, 1902), 22–25. For the origins and operation of these missions, see Steven S. Maughan, "'Mighty England Do Good': The Major English Denominations and Organisation for the Support of Foreign Missions in the Nineteenth Century," in *Missionary Encounters: Sources and Issues*, ed. Roberts Bickers and Rosemary Seton (London, 1996).

9. Brian Stanley, *The Bible and the Flag: Protestant Missions and British Imperialism in the Nineteenth and Twentieth Centuries* (Leicester, 1990), 78–80.

10. Stuart Piggin has noted that support for missions among evangelicals tended to encourage ecumenical cooperation. However, between the denominations, the sectarian reality was dominant, especially at the local level when competitive attitudes toward Anglicanism are considered. "Sectarianism vs. Ecumenism: The Impact on British Churches of the Missionary movement to India, c. 1800/1860," *Journal of Ecclesiastical History* 27 (October 1976): 387–402. Cf. David Savage, "Evangelical Educational Policy in Britain and India, 1857/60" *Journal of Imperial and Commonwealth History* 22, no. 3 (1994): 432–61 and Wolffe, *God and Greater Britain*, 40–42.

11. Dennis, *Centennial Survey*, 257–60; "Report of the Centenary Review Committee: Section XI," in *Centenary Review Reports* (private printing, 1899), 78, CMS Archives, G/CC b 15, University of Birmingham, Birmingham, England. Anglican figures suggest that this amount represents about 12.5 percent of total church contributions. From 1860 to 1884, Anglican giving to foreign missions of £10,100,000 made them the third largest Anglican charity, behind £35,175,000 for church building (43.1 percent) and £21,362,041 (26.2 percent) for elementary education. *Official Yearbook of the Church of England, 1888* (London, 1889), xv. Proportions were similar within the Congregational churches. Hugh McLeod, *Religion and Society in England, 1850/1914* (New York, 1996), 147.

12. Most notably, see John MacKenzie, *Propaganda and Empire: The Manipulation of British Public Opinion 1880/1960* (Manchester, 1984); MacKenzie, ed., *Imperialism and Popular Culture* (Manchester, 1986); and successive volumes in the Manchester Studies in Imperialism and Popular Culture series.

13. For an instructive exploration of one "Westernization" theme in missionary thinking, see Brian Stanley, "'Commerce and Christianity': Providence Theory, the Missionary Movement, and the Imperialism of Free Trade, 1842/1860," *Historical Journal* 26, no. 1 (1983): 86–89; and Andrew Porter, "'Commerce and Christianity': The Rise and Fall of a Nineteenth-Century Missionary Slogan," *Historical Journal* 28, no. 3 (1985): 597–621.

14. On parallel strategies among Victorian feminists, see Burton, *Burdens of History*, 6–8.

15. McLeod, *Religion and Society*, 145–9. See also Wolffe, *God and Greater Britain*, 215–18.

16. Emancipation in the United States and the backlash following the 1865 Morant Bay revolt in Jamaica helped shift attention away from the Americas. Clare Midgley, "Ethnicity, 'Race' and Empire," in *Women's History: Britain, 1850/ 1945* ed. June Purvis (London, 1995), 259, 263.

17. This percentage includes female missionaries sent out by the independent Church of England Zenana Missionary Society and the Zenana Bible and Medical Mission, who were under the direction of the CMS in the field. Unmarried women made up 23 percent of the missionaries of the five societies. Figures for the entire British missionary force are somewhat lower (women 39 percent; unmarried women 18.5 percent), chiefly because of the large number of short-term "unprofessional" male lay missionaries sent out by the Salvation Army. Dennis, *Centennial Survey*, 22–24, 257.

18. See Martha Vicinus, *Independent Women: Work and Community for Single Women, 1850/1920* (Chicago, 1985).

19. Their contributions are largely ignored in missionary publications and records. Rosemary Fitzgerald, "A 'Peculiar and Exceptional Measure': The Call for Women Medical Missionaries for India in the Later Nineteenth Century," in *Missionary Encounters: Sources and Issues*, ed. Robert A. Bickers and Rosemary Seton (Richmond Surrey, 1996), 176–78; and Deborah Kirkwood, "Protestant Missionary Women: Wives and Spinsters," in *Women and Missions: Past and Present: Anthropological and Historical Perceptions*, ed. Fiona Bowie, Deborah Kirkwood, and Shirley Ardener (Providence, 1993), 23–42.

20. Eugene Stock, *The History of the Church Missionary Society: Its Environment, Its Men and Its Work*, 4 vols. (London, 1899, 1916), 4:517 and *passim*. Frank Prochaska, "Little Vessels: Children in the Nineteenth-Century English Missionary Movement," *The Journal of Imperial and Commonwealth History* 6, no. 2 (1978): 103–18.

21. Stanley, *Bible and Flag*, 78–80.

22. Miss Rainey, Free Church of Scotland, quoted in James Johnson, ed., *Report of the Centenary Conference on the Protestant Missions of the World*, 2 vols. (London, 1888), 2:143. On the middle classes, capitalism, and gender relations, see Davidoff and Hall, *Family Fortunes*, 107–92, 429–36.

23. On the establishment of free convert villages in Jamaica constructed according to racial, class, and gender hierarchies, see "Missionary Stories: gender and ethnicity in England in the 1830s and 1840s" in Catherine Hall, *White, Male and Middle Class: Explorations in Feminism and History* (New York, 1992), 241–45.

24. On the LMS, e.g., see Rosemary Seton, "'Open Doors for Female Labourers'": Women Candidates of the London Missionary Society, 1875/1914," in *Missionary Encounters: Sources and Issues*, ed. Robert A. Bickers and Rosemary Seton (Richmond Surrey, 1996), 51. See also Midgley, *Women against Slavery*, ch. 5.

25. An earlier example of this can be found in the realm of primitive popular religion, in which women had a long tradition of prophesy and preaching. As Deborah Valenze has shown, by the 1850s this role was rapidly waning in the context of changing social and class structures. Valenze, *Prophetic Sons and Daughters: Female Preaching and Popular Religion in Industrial England* (Princeton, 1985), 274–81.

26. Middle-class ideology in Victorian Britain was always being negotiated, as Mary Poovey has demonstrated in her analysis of how inconsistencies in Victorian gender ideology provided opportunities for women to construct new social opportunities. Poovey, *Uneven Developments: The Ideological Work of Gender in Mid-Victorian Britain* (Chicago, 1988).

27. From very early in their history, the denominational missionary societies sent some unmarried female missionaries into the field to fill specific educational posts. Prior to 1887 the CMS sent out 103 single women, roughly 40 percent of whom were widows or daughters of missionaries; the other 60 percent were women sent to run girls' schools in well supervised mission stations. Early female missionaries often quickly married in the field. Eugene Stock, *An Historical Survey of Women's Work in C.M.S. at Home and Abroad* (London, 1907), 12.

28. Savage, "Female Education in India," 208–9.

29. The Calcutta Female Normal School took the IFNS name when it reorganized to tap domestic British support in 1861. Minutes, 15 July 1861, Calcutta Female Normal School, London Committee Minutes, 1859/65, Interserve Archives, CM 1, London. It changed its name again to the Zenana Bible and Medical Mission shortly after 1880. On the female education society, see Margaret Donaldson, "'The Cultivation of the Heart and the Molding of the Will ...': The Missionary Contribution of the Society for Promoting Female Education in China, India, and the East," in *Women in the Church*, ed. W. J. Sheils and Diana Wood, vol. 27 of *Studies in Church History* (Oxford, 1990), 429–42.

30. See Vicinus, *Independent Women*, 3–5, 294.

31. Johnson, *Centenary Conference*, 2:143.

32. The WMMS was the first to form a Ladies Committee, in 1858, followed by the High Church Anglican Society for the Propagation of the Gospel, in 1866, the BMS, in 1867, and the LMS, in 1875. While the most influential evangelical society, the CMS, did not form its own independent Women's Committee until 1895, it was deeply involved in the work of the IFNS from the time it reorganized as a London-based society in 1861. It was also the patron society of the Church of England Zenana Missionary Society when it split from the IFNS in 1880 to form a distinctively evangelical Anglican women's organization. For more detail on this process and differences of denominational style within it, see Steven S. Maughan, "'Regions Beyond' and the National Church: Domestic Support for the Foreign Missions of the Church of England in the High Imperial Age, 1870/1914" (Ph.D. diss., Harvard University, 1995), ch. 3.

33. Maria Louisa Charlesworth, *India and the East; or, a Voice from the Zenana* (London, 1860), 4–5; see also [Mary] Weitbrecht, *The Women of India and Christian Work in the Zenana* (London, 1875), 47–48, on the necessity of transforming Indian society through women and their families.

34. *The Women of India*, 1. Anna Davin has commented on the shifting focus in the nineteenth century from women as wives to women as mothers, but primarily in analysis of the later development of explicitly imperial concerns about declining population and eugenics. Davin, "Imperialism and Motherhood," *History Workshop Journal* 5 (Spring 1978): 12–14.

35. On independent women in religion, see Vicinus, *Independent Women*, ch. 2.

36. The Barnet Conference was organized by Anglican Vicar William Pennefather, who was also involved in the early organization of the IFNS and later the Mildmay Deaconess Institution. Stock, *The History*, 2:31–33; on Pennefather's early association with the IFNS, see Meeting, 7 May 1862, Calcutta Female Normal School, London Committee Minutes, 1859–1865, Interserve Archives, CM 1; on the early Barnet Conferences, see Robert Braithwaite, *The Life and Letters of Rev. William Pennefather* (London, [1878]), 305–20.

37. See D. W. Bebbington, *Evangelicalism in Modern Britain: A History from the 1730s to the 1980s* (London, 1989), 151–52, 159–65; on the importance of Keswick and

late-Victorian missions, see Andrew Porter, "Cambridge, Keswick and Late Nineteenth Century Attitudes to Africa," *The Journal of Imperial and Commonwealth History* 5 (1976): 5–34.

38. Hilton, *Age of Atonement*, 5–6, 361–72.

39. Anon., *How the Zenana Missions Began* (c.1890), 4–5, Baptist Missionary Society Archives, zenana pamphlets box, Regents Park College, Oxford.

40. C. B. Lewis, *A Plea for Zenanas* (c.1866), 6–7, BMS Archives, "B.Z.M. Papers" volume.

41. *The Indian Crisis: A Special Meeting of the Church Missionary Society at Exeter Hall* (1858), 18–20, 31. For domestic Christian reactions to the Indian Mutiny and their contrast to "official" views, see Stanley, "'Commerce and Christianity,'" 86–89.

42. Charlesworth, *India and the East*, 4. The idea that the mothers and women of India were the key to the conversion of India continued to have considerable force. See, e.g., the reference to influential linguist Sir Monier Williams's assertion that Christianity would make little progress in India until female missionaries had free access to the women of India. E. R. Pitman, *Lady Missionaries in Foreign Lands* (London, c.1889), vii.

43. Vicinus, *Independent Women*, 3, 5, 13.

44. Mrs. Ferguson, address to a public meeting, 25 October 1878, in *Proceedings of the General Conference on Foreign Missions held at the Conference Hall, in Mildmay Park, London, in October, 1878*, ed. by the Secretaries to the Conference (London, 1879), 309. For parallel portrayals of Indian women in feminist periodicals, see Burton, *Burdens of History*, 66–67.

45. As Janaki Nair has shown, the image of the zenana had considerable capacity to carry a variety of ideological messages at different times for different audiences. Janaki Nair, "Uncovering the Zenana: Visions of Indian Womanhood in Englishwomen's Writings, 1813/1940," *Journal of Women's History* 2, no. 1 (Spring 1990), 8–34.

46. Zenana existence generally was portrayed as: devoid of pleasures and benefits that Western arts, commodities, and true religion brought to the English household; experience akin to "the home-bred canary … never [knowing] how to stretch their wings into open air"; and one that destroyed the natural kinship that women should feel because of the unnatural jealousies that polygamy bred. Lewis, *A Plea for Zenanas*, 1–3.

47. J.C. Parry, *What is a Zenana? A Paper Read at the Zenana Breakfast held at the Baptist Mission House in London, 24th April, 1872* (London, 1872), 5–6.

48. Cf. Nair, "Uncovering the Zenana," 16–18. The theme of women as "prisoners innocent" yet "still the commander of Indian life" suggests both that women need to be drawn into the public realm so that their "superstition" can be assailed and that they may then provide the key to constructing a moralized Christian public realm that will convert and "civilize." George Ensor, *"Help These Women": A Plea for the Work of the Church of England Zenana Missionary Society* (London, 1894), 4–7.

49. "'Daybreak Workers' Union leaflet," CEZ Girls leaflets, ca. 1900, Church of England Zenana Missionary Society Archives, CEZ G/EC1/5C, University of Birmingham, Birmingham, England. The pioneering work on Western constructions of the "orient" is Edward Said's influential *Orientalism* (New York, 1978). While Said alludes to the influence of missionaries, he largely ignores them, suggesting they are simple functionaries of British imperial institutions.

50. 1893 "Uganda" speeches notebook, pp. 50–52, Dr. Gaskoin Richard Morden Wright Papers, CMS Archives, Acc 134 F/2. Wright also emphasized that women often were beaten to death in Uganda for trivial offenses against men (p. 33). The imagery of women in Africa was strongly influenced by its connection to earlier antislavery efforts and the attention drawn by David Livingstone to the continuation of slavery in East Africa under the direction of "Mohammendans." For emphasis on the buying and selling of family members in Africa, see Emma Raymond Pitman, *Central Africa, Japan and Fiji: A Story of Missionary Enterprise, Trials, and Triumphs* (London, 1882), 16. For further imagery of women as the "chattels of men," see Minna C. and G. A. Gollock, *Half Done: Some Thoughts for Women* (London, 1916), 49.

51. Rev. W. S. Swanson, English Presbyterian Mission, Amoy, quoted in Johnson, *Centenary Conference*, 1:400. For an earlier emphasis on female infanticide and superstition, see Harriet Warner Ellis, *Our Eastern Sisters and Their Missionary Helpers* (London, c.1883), 120.

52. Burton, *Burdens of History*, 79–80.

53. Mrs. Thompson, LMS Matabeleland Mission, quoted in Johnson, *Centenary Conference*, 1:446.

54. Just as there were shadings of radicalism in feminist circles, so there also was no clear separation between evangelicals and feminists, as the career of Josephine Butler, especially in the campaign to repeal the Indian Contagious Diseases Acts, reveals. Burton, *Burdens of History*, 127–69.

55. Georgina A. Gollock, *The Contribution of Women to Home Work of the C.M.S.* (London, c.1912), 5.

56. Similar percentages held in its Young People's Union, its Medical Mission Auxiliary, and so on throughout the local organization of the society. And Gollock also implies percentages of female members and contributors were probably even higher. Gollock, *Contribution of Women*, 5–8.

57. *Proceedings of the Church Missionary Society ... 1879/80* (London, 1880), xii–xiii; Eugene Stock, *History of the CMS*, 4:465. These figures do not include missionary wives, since their numbers were not tabulated in 1880. In 1900 the total CMS missionary force, including wives, was 1,238.

58. Figures calculated from Dennis, *Centennial Survey*, 22. Also see note 17.

59. The women's branches of the WMMS and the BMS were dominated by the wives and daughters of society secretaries. In 1890 women achieved thirty three seats on the LMS governing board of 295 members, but at the expense of losing control over women's work to male-dominated subcommittees. Among Anglican women, who accounted for roughly 70 percent of the female missionary force in 1900, however, there were vigorous clashes over Anglican clerical authority and female missions. By 1895 Anglicans had four uneasily coexisting agencies for women's missionary work: the IFNS (ZBMM), CEZMS, CMS, and SPG. Maughan, "Regions Beyond," ch. 3.

60. Bebbington, *Evangelicalism*, 181–228.

61. M. C. Gollock, "Memo. on the C.M.S. Women's Department," 1914, CMS Archives, G/C 26 A; Reports I and II, "Representation of Women on Committees," February 1914, CMS Archives, G/AP 2; Joan Bayldon, *Cyril Bardsley, Evangelist* (London, 1942), 34–35. These conflicts were part of a greater set of divisions between liberal and conservative evangelicals after 1900 that eventually led to a schism in the CMS, with the formation of the fundamentalist Bible Churchman's Missionary Society in 1922. Kenneth Hylson-Smith, *Evangelicals in the Church of England, 1734/1984* (Edinburgh, 1988), 252–55.

62. Barbara Ramusack, "Cultural Missionaries, Maternal Imperialists, Feminist Allies: British Women Activists in India 1865/1945," in Nupur Chaudhuri and Margaret Strobel eds., *Western Women and Imperialism: Complicity and Resistance* (Bloomington, 1992), 120–6.

63. Antoinette Burton, "The White Woman's Burden: British Feminists and 'The Indian Woman,' 1865/1915," in Nupur Chaudhuri and Margaret Strobel eds., *Western Women and Imperialism: Complicity and Resistance* (Bloomington, 1992), 137–39.

64. Antoinette Burton, "Contesting the Zenana: The Mission to Make 'Lady Doctors for India,' 1874/1885," *Journal of British Studies* 35, no. 3 (1996): 368–97.

65. See G. R. Searle, *The Quest for National Efficiency: A Study in British Politics and Political Thought, 1899/1914* (Berkeley, 1971), chs. 2 and 3.

66. *World Missionary Conference, 1910: Report of Commission III: Education in Relation to the Christianization of National Life* (Edinburgh, n.d.), 6–7, 368–70.

67. Jeffrey Cox has identified this trend in the women's work of the Cambridge Mission to Delhi as part of a broader set of developments in Anglicanism. "Independent English Women in Delhi and Lahore, 1860/1947," in *Religion and Irreligion in Victorian Society: Essays in Honor of R.K. Webb*, ed., R. W. Davis and R. J. Helmstadter (London, 1992), 172–73.

68. Partha Chatterjee, "Colonialism, Nationalism and the Colonized Woman: The Contest in India," *American Ethnologist* 16, no. 4 (November 1989), 622–33.

69. Interview with Agnes de Sèlincourt, "Special Committee to Consider the Ladies' Training Homes' Curriculum, &c.," 12 November 1906, Sub-Committee Minutes, 1904/23, p. 85, CMS Archives, G/CS 4.

70. Interview with Miss Outram, "Special Committee to Consider the Ladies' Training Homes' Curriculum, &c.," 5 November 1906, Sub-Committee Minutes, 1904/23, pp. 79–80, CMS Archives, G/CS 4.

71. "Memo. by Miss Baring-Gould," 1914, pp. 1, 3–4, CMS Archives, G/C 26 A.

72. Evidence from oral history suggests that in the late-Victorian and Edwardian eras as much as 35 percent of urban working-class women attended church frequently. Middle-class attendance would run considerably higher. McLeod, *Religion and Society*, 69.

9

THE VILLAGE GOES PUBLIC

Peasants and Press in Nineteenth-Century Altbayern

John Abbott

Here and there was found a respected man in the village, who received a newspaper at his house through the mail. This was known to everyone in the area, and seen as something excep-tional. But now many attend to the happenings in the world, and whoever can't afford his own newspaper goes to the tavern, sits himself near the light and reads three times a week.

— Ludwig Thoma, *Andreas Vöst* (1905)

BÜRGERLICHE *GESELLSCHAFT* AND THE BAUERN, civil society and the peasantry: these categories struck many German observers of the latter nineteenth century as dissonant and incompatible. Civil society, however defined, suggested social mobility, individual freedom, and at least moderate economic liberalization.[1] Against these tenets, the peasantry often appeared as civil society's anti-thesis, the immovable object to its irresistible force. The very word *Bauer* connoted a way of life fixed by heredity, bound by tradition, and inescapably narrow in the compass of its economic calcula-tion. Indeed, some dictionaries depicted Bauer and *Bürger* as anto-nyms, an opposition that, while grounded in old town-country distinctions, conveyed a wider complex of meanings: boorish, ignorant, clownishly rustic, the Bauer provided the stereotypical counterpoint to *bürgerlich* civility and cultivation.[2] Alongside the nobility, the peasantry represented the obdurate survival of an older social order, one rooted in estate instead of class. As such the German peasant symbolized a mode of existence that in its very nature seemed inimical to the dynamics of social mobility, self-improvement, and civility.

These oppositions were not unique to the nineteenth century. Across Europe, town and country had long viewed one another across ramparts constructed of mutual distrust and incomprehension. But it was precisely this wary coexistence that nineteenth-century social and political development had increasingly begun to dislodge. The force of urban growth and industrial development provided continual stimulus in renegotiating town-country relations, even as state-building, the emergence of political parties, and the consolidation of the political nation worked to uproot and overwhelm older governing structures rooted in territorial autonomy and social compartmentalization. In this way, the sprawling horizontal clutter of the ancien régime—its political landscape segmented and subdivided by dynasty and estate, town charter and communal membership, seigneurial jurisdiction and ecclesiastical domain—was increasingly reconfigured into the more integrated, consolidated structures of the modern state. In the course of this epochal shift, the opposition of town and country resurfaced within the emerging spaces of national politics, no longer chiefly the stuff of parochial dispute, but as a touchstone of national interest and political definition.[3]

What was distinctive in the German case was the fragmentary, staggered development of this national political space and the ways in which this process interacted with the historical self-understanding and social vision of Germany's aspiring political classes. The outcomes of the 1848 revolutions represent a significant clarifying point. In the ferment of *Vormärz* political thought, the German peasantry had been accorded a respectable role: the antique village of Germania was an essential ingredient in the stewing of nationalist mythologies, even as growing anti-aristocratic sentiment prodded intellectuals to go out and "discover" those social strata hitherto rendered invisible by aristocratic privilege and prestige.[4] Liberal notions of the *Volk* were usually sufficiently expansive to include the Bauern; for the radical wing of the German democratic movement, the peasantry was considered vital to the popular energies to be unleashed by the "social question."[5]

Such hopes seemed partly realized when, in early 1848, peasant uprisings in several German lands helped precipitate the revolutionary crises to follow. Yet these rebellions, evanescent and local in their concerns, remained largely unconnected to more sustained political activity that, whether revolutionary or reformist, was centered primarily in urban areas.[6] At the Frankfurt National Assembly there reportedly was only a single person, among the eight hundred delegates present, designated as a "Bauer" (although in reality he was more likely a steward from Austria); he is not known to have spoken out in its proceedings.[7]

The course of the revolution, and the demoralizations of its defeats, prompted searching political reassessment among contemporaries, including those middle-class intellectuals emerging from the wreckage of their aspirations.[8] The events of 1848–49 had forced upon them the recognition, not only of their own isolation, but of the formidable chasms still separating the nascent political nation from its fragmented social constituencies. This instance of recognition crystallized in a transfigured discussion over the cognate problematic of civil society and state.[9] It occurred within an intellectual ambience hardened by the encounters of 1848, one soured upon romantic notions of the Volk and "universal brotherhood swindles" and primed for the unsentimental claims of scientific social theory. The two most cogent doctrines emerging from this period, Marxian socialism and the social-political conservatism associated with Wilhelm Heinrich Riehl, owed much of their influence to the manner in which they captured the pessimism of the moment and thus the attentions of political aspirants who, in retreating from a dispiriting present, sought renewal and solace in the images of, respectively, a utopian future and an idealized past.

For all their fundamental differences, Marx and Riehl shared an underlying theoretical aim: to dispel the "illusion of politics" by elevating society to analytical primacy, and to establish a social-scientific foundation for subsequent political activity.[10] Both men's thought illustrated as well the broader post-1848 inclination to view civil society in more class-specific terms than before: as "bourgeois society," increasingly shaped by the interests and outlook of an ascendant *Bürgertum*. Marx and Riehl viewed this ascent with profound ambivalence; each sought a resolution of this ambivalence via theoretical solutions grounded in appeals to history. And each came, by very different routes, to a strikingly similar assessment of the small-holding peasantry.

Marx's pronouncements, made in his critique of the French counterrevolution, suggested that peasant smallholders lacked the economic interdependence required to constitute a civil society. As a "simple addition of homologous magnitudes," they lacked the social articulation required for meaningful political self-representation, so that "their representative must at the same time appear as their master, as an authority over them." Thus they provided the authoritarian state its continued social foundation and legitimacy.[11] Riehl's account of the peasantry, far more cultural in its observations and arguments, drew much the same conclusion. Riehl viewed rural life as the natural confluence of landscape, folk custom, and communal norms; these imbued the peasantry with a native wisdom impervious to the conceit of reform. With conspicuous relish, he noted the failure of those German radicals who in 1848 had attempted to democratize local government in the countryside. They had not realized that the rural community "was not merely political, but also a social corporation," whose members invariably would choose, under even the freest circumstances, to remain "aristocratic, socially exclusive, not democratic."[12] In his 1851 *Die bürgerliche Gesellschaft*, Riehl championed the peasantry as the chief social bulwark against the upstart dynamism of the "Fourth Estate" haunting Europe; it was precisely the peasants' naive adherence to custom and belief, their indifference to appeals to reason and freedom, that recommended them to this role.[13]

The views of Riehl and Marx were symptomatic of a larger shift in Germany's post-1848 political landscape, by which the left arrived at a more exclusive, sectarian approach to the "social question" even as the outlines of a very different social politics— broader, incipiently *völkisch* in its dimensions—were taking shape on the conservative right.[14] The peasantry figured centrally on both ends of this exchange, as a benchmark issue of grand strategy and ideological definition. To the already considerable chasms separating town and country—cultural and linguistic as well as economic—German political culture now added its own symbolic baggage, as partisans of the right and left alike acquired a proprietary interest in perceiving the Bauern in essentialist terms, as the more or less natural residue of a premodern order, existing alongside but always somehow apart from civil society.

Even today, historical scholarship remains powerfully beholden to these assumptions; this is especially so in respect to post-1848 historiography, in which old notions of "rural idiocy" die hard.[15] Thus, for example, Riehl's affectionate depiction of the peasant mentality as "naive instinct and tradition"[16] finds latter-day expression in the assertion, by a leading historian of Weimar agrarian politics, that the "individual countrydweller" of the 1920s "remained culturally illiterate" and, politically, unreflexively servile.[17] Even avowedly revisionist approaches of recent years, devoted to reestablishing the Bauern as independent historical agents, have staked their arguments almost exclusively to economic categories and developments, highlighting the strides towards modernity suggested by peasant economic adaptation while in effect conceding the realm of rural culture to a half-baked folkloric exoticism.[18] In this view, occupational associations, particularly those of the peasant cooperative movement, signal the forward advance of the Bauern, while "the village"—spatially isolated, culturally undernourished and lacking in civic differentiation—remains a traditionalist backwater noteworthy mainly for its indifference to any recognizable historical process, save perhaps that of secular decline.[19]

Yet the story of "the village" over the latter nineteenth and early twentieth century is less one of decline than of transition and redefinition. If the rate of transformation—whether in respect to economic performance, popular literacy, associational life, or political participation—lagged behind that of urban areas, what unsettled and invigorated rural populations was the perception of unprecedented change. And their response to these challenges, to the relentless *Verbürgerlichung* of rural relations, is best seen when viewed in connection with the expanding writ of civil society and through the lens of its analytic categories. Among these categories is the public sphere, which, as formulated by Jürgen Habermas, offers a valuable conceptual window onto the political dynamics associated with civil society. Habermas's account of this "bourgeois public sphere" is centered in an emerging realm of discussion and debate, unfettered by state regulation, involving private persons who, through their own volition, "come together as a public"; the product of their exchanges is an acknowledged "public opinion" that increasingly impinges upon government affairs and upon the legitimacy of the state itself. In this manner, the self-assertion of private persons—to break free of tutelage and "make public use of their own reason"—is joined through the medium of public debate into a powerful institutional, and moral, argument for political freedom, by which civil society might best determine and represent "its" better interests.[20]

To be sure, this Habermasian model has yet to find much application in rural social history. Indeed, the concept of a rural public— viewed as a realm of freedom, and not merely as the absence of privacy—remains essentially unexamined. One of the few to have addressed this issue was none other than Riehl, who in the 1850s entertained the possibility of a rural public, if only to reject it. Riehl's argument rested on two main points: the austere intimacy of the village community, with its dense intertwining of (hierarchical) private status and (ritualized) public behavior, allowed for no significant separation between social and political life.[21] Under such circumstances, politics was not the function of an autonomous realm of free discussion but the expression of an organic communal agreement. "Where a townsman would speak of a consensus decision as a product of 'public opinion,'" Riehl explained, "the Bauer would say, 'the whole community says so.'"[22]

Riehl's second point concerned the ways in which this "whole community" expressed itself: here he emphasized the low educational levels in rural areas and the related issue of clerical leadership and authority. In this, Riehl drew upon his familiarity with the rural regions of Altbayern: Upper Bavaria, Lower Bavaria, and the Upper Palatinate. These were areas marked by the preponderance of small and medium-size peasant proprietors in agriculture and by the authority of the Catholic church in public matters. In the lower clergy of these regions, most of them "peasants with some religious training," Riehl perceived "a really curious phenomenon": "It was these singular people who mainly saw to it that the Bavarian people went from the seventeenth century directly to the nineteenth, without having noticed anything from the eighteenth."[23] This was no mere rearguard maneuver against the Enlightenment; it marked the emergence of a clerical stratum that, with its demotic style and rough-hewn pragmatism, would figure centrally in the development of rural public life over the nineteenth century.

For all Riehl's polemicist vinegar and hyperbole, these observations largely hold true for the time in which they were written.[24] Indeed, the rural regions of mid-century Altbayern amply support the proposition that a weak state and a weak civil society often went hand in hand. Here a narrowly based ministerial bureaucracy maintained a tenuous, often strained connection to local communities. Communal governments, for their part, existed largely to defend local interests from the world outside—not least the incursions and exactions of the state. Functioning principally as executive bodies, policing the village in accordance with customary law and paternalist notions of the common good, these local councils—their membership as a rule restricted to the rural patriciate—afforded little space for civic participation or input from the broader community.[25]

This picture contrasts sharply with the lively civic culture in Württemberg over much the same period, as reflected in the emergence of the *Intelligenzblätter* described in Ian McNeeley's contribution to this volume. By way of comparison, there were, as of 1848, only thirteen such Intelligenzblätter for all of Bavaria, most of them appearing in Swabia and the Franconian provinces. Upper Bavaria, the Upper Palatinate, and Lower Bavaria boasted only one such paper each, with a postal circulation of sixty-six, forty-six, and "unknown," respectively.[26] Such figures graphically illustrate the narrow social bases of the state bureaucracy in the provinces and its lack of organic contact and public dynamism.

The complement to distant bureaucracy and weak local government was a generous space of protopolitical interaction presided over by the Catholic church, its offices, and parish organization. The meager civic infrastructure characteristic of rural areas assured the priest a wide-ranging local preeminence. The lowly status of rural schoolteachers, for example, kept them largely in the priest's shadow, and indeed in his employ, supplementing their miserable salaries largely by performing menial church tasks; only in the last decades of the nineteenth century would rural schoolteachers emerge, in the teeth of opposition and controversy, as significant public personalities in their own right.[27] Moreover, a desultory educational system meant continuing low levels of popular literacy.[28] This, in turn, ensured clerics—often the most literate members of the community—a vital role as intermediaries in local affairs and, increasingly, with the outside world.

Over the nineteenth century, as economic development, state regulation, and increasing political participation introduced new complexities and challenges to local communities, it was the clergy that most readily stepped into the breach, assuming an imposing multiplicity of roles and competencies. Whether explaining election law to parishioners,[29] mediating between rural doctors and communal poor-relief agencies,[30] supervising local school curriculum and teacher performance, launching credit cooperatives, or otherwise promoting agricultural improvements,[31] clerics made themselves indispensable to post-1848 rural adaptation and change—even as most continued to denounce, from their pulpits, the myriad evils of the modern world. This clerical role in turn augmented, and was reinforced by, the ceremonial importance of the clergy in village social life, whether in respect to holidays (at least nominally dependent upon religious observance) or to occasions—baptisms, weddings, funerals—defined by church ritual.[32] Even tavern life was heavily dependent upon these occasions, as signified by the usual adjacency of the tavern to the parish church in rural areas.[33] And while the tavern represented one potential arena for sociability free of clerical interference, its internal protocols—by which economic distinctions determined one's table companions, and separated one *Stammtisch* from the other—placed serious restrictions upon even this public venue: the invisible walls separating the village from the outside world were often coextensive with the walls segregating its inner spaces.[34]

To stress the centrality of the church to village life is not to deny the more or less autonomous traditions and value systems sustained by rural folk.[35] The point is that this autonomous culture had little acknowledged *public* legitimacy; it instead remained beholden to a semiprivate sphere of custom and social negotiation. One of the more storied peasant traditions, the autumn charivari known as *Haberfeldtreiben*, helps illustrate the point. These consisted of boisterous gatherings outside of selected homes in the dead of night, often threatening "rough justice" upon those seen as having transgressed community norms. Occasionally these crowds lashed out at social superiors, including clerics and, in exceptional cases, the nobility. Yet even the most radical such episodes remained essentially subterranean affairs; public recognition came only in those cases in which, after the fact, the state prosecuted participants for especially serious transgressions. The most celebrated such instance came in 1893, in the aftermath of the "Miesbacher Haberfeldtreiben," in which hundreds were arrested and sentenced to lengthy prison terms for their attacks upon a noble estate.[36]

Even as this episode marked the tradition's climax, it also signaled its terminus. For the final spasm of Haberfeldtreiben mobilization coincided with the emergence in 1893 of a new kind of peasant politics and activism across Bavaria, a *Bauernbewegung* (peasant movement) sustained by raucous public assemblies, vehement oratory, newspaper vendettas, and open confrontations with local authority. The conventions that had defined the Haberfeldtreiben—conspiracy, elaborate rituals, and nocturnal stealth— no longer connected to any vital social function. In their place had arisen a critical mass of public activity, by which a growing number of Bauern announced their intention to represent themselves in all political matters. This upsurge led to the creation of an aggressively populist party, the Bavarian *Bauernbund* (Peasants League), and a badly shaken Catholic political establishment. While vociferous in its advocacy of agrarian economic interests, this eruption of peasant protest was no less an angry rejection of both clerical *Vormundschaft* (tutelage) and, as many Bauernbündler saw it, the widespread presumption of peasant passivity and *"Dummheit."* With its penchant for frequent public assemblies, impassioned political debate, and fiercely partisan journalism, the Bauernbewegung of the 1890s introduced many thousands of peasants to the novelties of public life. In its wake, Bavaria's rural regions would never be the same.[37]

The sudden appearance of this movement, in regions heretofore considered strongholds of clerical influence, caught contemporaries off guard; ever since, explanations for its radical departures have mainly pointed to economic factors, in particular the drastic decline in grain prices during 1892–94. Certainly perceptions of economic decline helped fuel the Bauernbund movement. Yet the economistic explanation remains unsatisfactory on several counts,[38] not least because it posits a peasantry simply *forced* into political life. The optic of the public sphere, on the other hand, helps explain why peasants were suddenly *able* to undertake such action, and, indeed, why they might have wanted to.

At first glance, the antecedents for this rural public sphere are not obvious. Measured by associational activity, rural Altbayern was exceptionally backwards before 1893. There was relatively little economic organization to speak of: the first Raiffeisen credit cooperatives were established in Lower Bavaria only during 1892.[39] Public organization, such as it was, typically consisted of local fire brigades, established in most rural areas only during the 1870s.[40] With their formal membership and uniforms, the fire brigades greatly expanded the ranks of rural civic participation; the staging of fire drills, often drawing upon the combined forces of many villages and hamlets, became the occasion for great parades, followed by open gatherings, speechifying, and the raffling off of farm animals or other prizes.[41] For all the retrospective familiarity of such scenes, to participants at the time they represented a novel departure. Though the fire brigades often were justified by invoking the Christian principle "love thy neighbor as thyself,"[42] they nonetheless represented a highly visible, participatory local function independent of church authority, a venue by which villagers could rehearse and celebrate an essentially civic identity.

But this incipient civic realm as yet generated little overt politicization. Over the 1870s and 1880s, it coexisted with, but did not seriously challenge, the commanding public role and presence of the church, its parish organization and offices. Political associations were few and far between: in Lower Bavaria, the predominantly rural province that was the epicenter of the Bauernbund movement, there were only eleven such associations in 1892, most of them clerically dominated, spread across a handful of provincial towns.[43] Electoral participation was similarly stagnant: in the Reichstag elections of 1881, 1887, and 1890, Lower Bavaria mustered the lowest voter turnout rates of any province in the German Reich.[44]

The dynamic exception to these dismal indices is found in provincial newspaper publishing. Between 1874 and 1884, the circulation of newspapers published in Upper Bavaria (excluding Munich), Lower Bavaria, and the Upper Palatinate more than doubled, from 54,397 copies to 113,169. By 1898, these totals had nearly doubled again, amounting to 201,300 copies.[45] The causes of this provincial expansion were not wholly internal to the provinces themselves. They entailed a complex, protracted interaction between city, town, and country, of which three broad phases can be discerned.[46] The initial phase was dominated by the larger cities—Munich and Augsburg—whose major newspapers provided the sinew for a widely dispersed, if thinly based, reading public broadly associated with liberal political interests. The second phase, beginning during the 1860s, witnessed a growing number of newspaper ventures launched in the larger provincial towns; these aimed for a more local readership of townsmen and the patriciate of the surrounding countryside. The final phase saw the emergence of a decidedly more rural press, based in small towns and heavily pitched to the populations of surrounding villages. This small-town/rural press took root over the 1870s and 1880s; its growth was predicated on an expanding rural commerce that, in the form of advertising revenue, could help underwrite smaller-scale newspaper enterprise.[47] This final, expressly rural phase is illustrated by the table below, which charts newspaper publishing trends within the province of Lower Bavaria.

Table 1 Circulation of Newspapers Published in Lower Bavaria, 1876–1898 (number of newspaper titles given in parentheses)

	Total		Towns		Rural Districts	
1876	(18)	26,930	(7)	22,900	(11)	4,030
1884	(22)	37,340	(9)	29,420	(13)	7,920
1887	(33)	40,205	(9)	28,550	(24)	11,655
1890	(35)	46,620	(10)	30,400	(25)	16,220
1893	(36)	51,046	(10)	31,650	(26)	19,396
1896	(38)	54,580	(10)	28,976	(28)	25,604
1898	(35)	57,600	(8)	28,539	(27)	29,061

Source: Bayerisches Hauptstaatsarchiv, Ministerium des Innern, 46671, 46673, 46674, 46675, 46676.
Note: "towns" category includes all newspapers published in Landshut, Passau, Straubing, and Deggendorf.

There is of course no automatic correlation between where a newspaper is published and who is reading it. The Lower Bavarian towns of Landshut, Passau, Straubing, and Deggendorf were small by most standards; each was surrounded by considerable rural hinterland, and their newspapers certainly catered to this audience.[48] But while such town-based newspapers often enjoyed broad dispersion in rural areas, this was very much a one-way street. Rural newspapers, with their rustic accents and largely parochial concerns, only rarely transcended their intended local audiences. One can assume, then, that the surge in rural publishing demonstrated by the figures in the table represents a corresponding leap in rural readership.

The local dimensions of this growth are illustrated by developments in the Lower Bavarian district of Eggenfelden.[49] As late as 1886, there had existed only one newspaper in the area, the vaguely liberal *Eggenfeldener Wochenblatt*, which, consisting mainly of reprints from big-city papers, had for several years maintained a fairly constant circulation of around 700 copies.[50] In 1887 two new papers appeared, and area readership jumped sharply. In 1888, *Wochenblatt* circulation had risen to 1,030 copies, while those of its competitors combined for 790. In 1889, the total circulation of all three papers had climbed to 2,292; in 1892, to 3,330. Of the new papers, the clerical *Rotthaler Anzeiger* proved the fiercest challenger; by 1894, its circulation outstripped that of the *Wochenblatt*, and its publisher had launched another venture, the *Niederbayerischer Bauer*, a weekly that soon boasted a circulation of 5,200 copies.

The chief catalyst in creating a rural newspaper readership in Bavaria was the Catholic press. Popular journalism had not come readily to the Catholic establishment; indeed, Church leaders for long looked upon the press as a liberal infestation: intrinsically vulgar, suspiciously modern and, in its very topicality, unavoidably profane.[51] Yet by the mid-1860s—after nearly a decade of liberal political advance, coupled with the ominous shifts in power between Prussia and Austria—the consensus within Catholic circles began to shift, and the press came to be seen as a "necessary evil," even as a "great power" (*Großmacht*), that had to be mastered.[52] Within a very few years—in a development closely linked to the emergence of the Catholic Center Party—an expanding cadre of Catholic newspapermen had launched a vibrant, extensive press network. In Bavaria in 1871, there were a total of 37 Catholic papers, with a circulation of 80,000; by 1881, the corresponding figures were 63 and 150,000; by 1903, 100 and 283,000.[53] By the end of the century, as a Social Democratic commentary noted, the Catholic press had become the dominant force through-out Bavaria's provinces, so that its "readership suffers from a surplus of Catholic press production" and from an acute competition for readers among its ever-proliferating titles.[54]

If the creation of this press represents a remarkable achievement, the achievement was matched by an equally remarkable presumption: that the church could somehow manage to steer, contain, and control the dynamics unleashed by this burgeoning Catholic publicity. Though parish priests generally welcomed the emergence of local newspapers, seeing them as a useful extension of their own powers, it was precisely at the parish level that the press's cumulative effects would be most destabilizing. This problem was alluded to in a leading Catholic daily, the *Augsburger Postzeitung*, in a series of 1883 articles addressing the new challenges presented by "this reading-mad era." In order to keep one step ahead of their flocks, whose interests were presumably being met by the "local and provincial press," clerics were strongly advised to subscribe to a more sophisticated paper—"one that views the times from on high"—presumably such as the *Postzeitung* itself. This approach suggested that, by preserving an intellectual edge over lay audiences, the clergy might hope to maintain control over what already was becoming an unmanageable diversity of opinion.[55]

But ultimately the problem would elude the grasp of even the most adroit, well-read parish priests. It was in its essence insoluble: in having legitimated the Catholic press among its constituency, the church in effect had legitimated the reading of newspapers in general. Drawing distinctions over what constituted permissible opinion would henceforth grow immeasurably more difficult.[56] In great measure this was due to schisms and disputes emerging from within the Catholic press itself; here the social heterogeneity of the church's constituency as well as fissures between lower and upper clergy, and between the Center Party's publicists and its parliamentary deputies, all found extravagant journalistic expression. Especially nettlesome were those populist figures—agrarian, conservative, democratic—associated with the ultramontane movement, who after 1871 found themselves in repeated conflict with an increasingly conciliatory Catholic political establishment. Among these was Johann Baptist Sigl, whose *Bayerisches Vaterland* from 1869 onwards doggedly scourged the Bavarian authorities, state and church alike. Another was Julius Marchner, whose *Neue freie Volks-Zeitung* combined splashy graphics and scandal mongering with crusading journalism. Sigl's and Marchner's Munich-based papers, often courting the fringes of legality, were products of calculated outrageousness, brazenly flaunting their disdain of Prussian interests, of militarism, of parliamentary chicanery and business-as-usual.[57] These kinds of messages, joined with a vigorous advocacy of agrarian interests, played well in the provinces: Sigl's paper, especially, enjoyed active support from the rural clergy, who provided the backbone to his paper's system of provincial reports. These small-town or rural dispatches, in their immediacy and frequent scurrility, stretched the local limits of permissible opinion to the breaking point; thus did papers like the *Vaterland* and *Volks-Zeitung* work to expand the range of possibilities for rural newspapermen seeking to make their own controversialist mark.

From such motley quarters, rural audiences gained a growing familiarity with political debate during the 1880s and 1890s. The medium of reading, and the querulous "community of print" it conjured, opened the interior spaces of the village—at least those involving male heads of households—to new, broader denominators of discussion and opinion.[58] What was distinctive about Lower Bavaria was that this politicization of village sociability occurred within an otherwise stagnant field of associational and political party life. As the pace of discussion quickened—at markets, taverns, and other social venues—it found no meaningful outlet or constructive expression in existing political structures. This was a circumstance that, coupled with the mounting economic distress of the early 1890s, invested peasant discontents with an exceptional fury. A Lower Bavarian observer noted in the *Neue freie Volks-Zeitung* in January of 1893 how:

> During the previous Landtag session, it quite frequently happened that when several men gathered together, men who subscribed to a newspaper, one would say to the other, "So how's it going?" I can no longer read the reports from the Landtag, there's nothing to them but pay hikes [for the deputies], always pay hikes, where has it gotten to with these people, whatever happens I'd just as soon burn the newspaper from sheer rage![59]

A few months later, men such as these would be caught up in the nascent Bauernbund insurgency. It was in Lower Bavaria that the movement would enjoy its greatest popular support, as measured in electoral strength and grassroots activity. It was also here that the movement assumed its most radical form, as shown by the violence of its rhetoric, the volatility of its public assemblies, and the scathing anticlericalism of its spokesmen.[60]

Newspaper culture left its mark on early Bauernbund leaders. A visit to Franz Wieland's farmhouse in 1894 revealed "a table piled high with newspapers."[61] Police reports noted that Georg Eisenberger "reads an exceptional amount. He is supposed to keep up with no less than sixteen newspapers, reading them deep into the night, as well as during work."[62] Movement agitators invariably impressed upon audiences the importance of the press, and Bauernbund journalism—especially the derisive, provocative sort practiced by Albert Gäch—was crucial in feeding the habits of controversy and indignation that helped sustain the movement. Contemporary observers often remarked upon this centrality of the press: for example, the protagonist of the 1898 novella *Centrum oder Bauernbund?* becomes a Bündler (and an all-around lout) after reading disreputable papers in the local tavern.[63]

Though the Bauernbund insurgency subsided by the end of the decade, men such as Wieland, Gäch, and Eisenberger would serve as model and inspiration for subsequent generations of rural Bavarians, as "intellectually self-made men" (*geistige Selfmademen*) of humble origins who had dared to rouse the popular will against economic and political injustice.[64] Indeed, the Bauernbund would prove a remarkably durable vehicle for continuing peasant protest, launching a new round of insurgency in the years prior to the First World War, playing an important role in Bavaria's revolutionary upheavals of 1918–19, and reemerging as a potent force during the Weimar Republic.[65]

The clashes of the 1890s were not simply the result of populist pressures "from below"; they grew out of the conflicted development of the nineteenth-century rural public. As late as the early 1890s, this public was still largely the domain of rural clerics, who had taken on a daunting array of competencies and functions. Yet the foundations of their dominance were being undermined by other public practices in the countryside. The spread of a contentious newspaper culture, in particular, acted as a leavening in rural affairs: newspapers splintered lay community opinion, subverted paternalist notions of the common good, and popularized in their stead the particularity of interest. By such means, Bavaria's provincial press gradually spurred the reconstitution of rural public opinion upon new, more rationalistic foundations. This transformation ultimately reacted back upon the position of the rural clergy itself, bringing it by the early 1890s to a decisive juncture. Whereas over much of the nineteenth century the priesthood had successfully adapted to modernity through an incremental agglomeration of political roles and civic functions, henceforth it could maintain its pastoral authority only through their gradual divestment. This dilemma inspired sharply divergent responses among clerics and rural folk alike. In many cases, new spaces were opened for local political expression and activity, while in others a protracted clerical reaction took hold. In the clash of these outcomes is seen much of the white heat and volatility of the populist awakenings in rural Bavaria over the 1890s, and the enduring bitterness that followed in their wake. Clerical censorship and censoriousness, the threatened withholding of sacraments to Bauernbund activists and their families, the frequent pulpit appeals for female parishioners to bring their husbands back to the Center and the church—acts such as these fostered a latent distrust of the Center Party and clerical establishment in many rural households and communities, for decades to come. These resentments provided subsequent Bauernbund political departures with enduring reservoirs of sympathy and support.

The Bauernbund nonetheless remained a minority party, especially outside its Lower Bavarian strongholds. Other rural regions in Bavaria coalesced instead around a reconstructed Center Party organization; the instrument of this rapprochement was the *Christlicher Bauernverein* (Christian Peasants Association), a loyalist countermovement. Initially a defensive reaction to the Bauernbund insurgency,[66] the Bauernverein eventually grew into a powerhouse ensemble of peasant cooperatives, schools, self-help services, and political association. For all its dynamism, it was from the beginning strongly hierarchical, with well-established lines of authority and little of the egalitarian, participatory character that so marked the Bauernbund. Yet its own impact upon rural life was hardly less momentous. Far from being a one-dimensional instrument of co-optation, the Bauernverein became an important vessel for social renegotiation and cultural adaptation. While enjoying the support of the clerical establishment, it presented breakthrough opportunities to a new Catholic lay leadership, a dynamic cohort defined more by university than by seminary education.[67] This new leadership—personified by men such as "Peasant Doctor" Georg Heim—stressed a technocratic complex of virtues: efficient organization, modern accounting methods, peasant literacy, and (within limits) worldly knowledge. Theirs was a paternalism based more upon self-improvement than piety; as key representatives of a rising meritocracy grounded in Catholic lay institutions, they began to displace the worldly authority of the clergy in rural areas.[68] Casting themselves in the garb of tradition, they represented the triumph of essentially bürgerlich values and relations in the countryside; indeed, the Catholic associational infrastructure introduced after 1893 would became the principal agent of rural Bavaria's gradual modernization.

* * * *

THE ABOVE ARGUMENTS have stressed both the importance of a rural public sphere in the making of civil society and the crucial role newspapers played within that process. These points have been made by reference to the experience of Altbayern and especially Lower Bavaria: regions that well before Wilhelm Heinrich Riehl had been regarded as exceptionally laggard in their conditions and culture. Yet even here the forces of print culture and newspaper publishing—stereotypically regarded as urban activities par excellence—came to intervene in decisive ways. What of other German regions? Clearly the question of the rural press goes well beyond Bavaria's borders. During the decades on either side of 1900, there occurred throughout Germany a great flourishing of provincial, small-town newspaper publishing; over this time, these papers, with circulations running from several hundred to three thousand copies, captured a share of German newspaper publishing not seen before or since.[69] This is a story largely yet to be told; its retrieval would go far in illuminating the dimensions and dynamics of the rural public and of its stormy relationship to Germany's fateful trek toward civil society.

Notes

1. See John Keane, "Despotism and Democracy," in *Civil Society and the State*, ed. Keane (London, 1988); Manfred Riedel, "Bürger, Staatsbürger, Bürgertum," in *Geschichtliche Grundbegriffe: Historisches Lexikon zur politisch-sozialen Sprache in Deutschland*, ed. Otto Brunner et al. (Stuttgart, 1972), 1:672–725. My own concerns lie more in the untidy intersections between German civil society discourse, the political problematic of *Volk* and *Staat*, and the debate over *ständisch* versus liberal principles of social organization.
2. See Johann Andreas Schmeller, *Bayerisches Wörterbuch*, 2nd ed., 3 vols. (1872–1877; reprint, Munich, 1985), 1:187. Nineteenth-century reformers generally preferred the term *Landwirt* to describe agriculturalists of a newer sort: the Landwirt was rational, improving, and connected to the land via occupational choice, not hereditary circumstance. See also H. Muth, "'Bauer' und

'Bauernstand' im Lexicon des 19. und 29. Jahrhunderts," *Zeitschrift für Agrargeschichte und Agrarsoziologie* 16 (1968): 72–96.

3. See, e.g., Kenneth Barkin, *The Controversy over German Industrialization, 1890–1902* (Chicago, 1970) and Klaus Bergmann, *Agrarromantik und Großstadtfeindschaft* (Meisenheim am Glan, 1970). Dan White, *The Splintered Party: National Liberalism in Hessen and the Reich, 1867–1918* (Cambridge, MA, 1976); David Hendon, *The Center Party and the Agrarian Interest in Germany, 1890–1914* (Ph.D. diss., Emory University, 1976).

4. John Gagliardo, *Pariah to Patriot: The Changing Image of the German Peasant 1770–1840* (Lexington, KY, 1969), 263–83; Werner Conze, "Bauer, Bauernstand, Bauerntum," in Brunner et al., *Geschichtliche Grundbegriffe*, 1:407–39.

5. Franz Mehring, *Geschichte der deutschen Sozialdemokratie* (Stuttgart, 1897), 1:36–39.

6. Jonathan Sperber, *Rhineland Radicals: The Democratic Movement and the Revolution of 1848–1849* (Princeton, 1991), argues that, in the Rhineland at least, certain rural regions provided the democratic movement its most consistent support. In most regions, however, the enduring impact of the revolution was to deepen, and politicize, urban-rural divisions.

7. Günther Franz, *Geschichte des deutschen Bauernstandes* (Stuttgart, 1970), 265.

8. To emphasize the perception of defeat is not to declare the revolution a wholesale failure. See the judicious assessment by Hans-Ulrich Wehler, *Deutsche Gesellschaftsgeschichte, 1815–1845/49* (Munich, 1987), 759–79.

9. Florian Simhart, *Bürgerliche Gesellschaft und Revolution: Eine ideologiekritische Untersuchung des politischen und sozialen Bewußtseins in der Mitte des 19.Jahrhunderts: Dargestellt am Beispiel einer Gruppe des Münchner Bildungsbürgertums* (Munich, 1978); Mack Walker, *German Home Towns* (Ithaca, 1971), 417–25.

10. Regarding Marx, see especially Francois Furet, *Marx and the French Revolution* (Chicago, 1988), 3–96. Riehl's views regarding the separation of "bürgerliche Gesellschaft" from "politische Gesellschaft" are forcefully put in Wilhelm Heinrich Riehl, *Die Naturgeschichte des Volkes als Grundlage einer deutschen Social-Politik*, Volume 2, *Die bürgerliche Gesellschaft* (Stuttgart, 1858), 4.

11. I am taking a minor liberty here: Marx's famous disparagement, from *The Eighteenth Brumaire of Louis Bonaparte*, posits a peasantry incapable of fully constituting itself as a *class*. Yet the political conclusion Marx draws in this passage—that the political aberration of Napoleon III could be explained only by reference to freakish social anachronism, embodied in the small-holding peasantry—reveals the continued impress of the civil society-state dialectic inherited from Hegel, a dialectic that remained central, albeit via a transformed vocabulary, to Marx's thought. See Schlomo Avineri, *The Social and Political Thought of Karl Marx* (Cambridge,1968), 13–25, 168–70; and George Lichtheim, *Marxism: An Historical and Critical Study* (New York, 1982), 41–50.

12. Wilhelm Heinrich Riehl, *Die Naturgeschichte des Volkes*, vol. 1, *Land und Leute* (Stuttgart, 1858), 103f.

13. First published in 1851, *Die bürgerliche Gesellschaft* was subsequently reprinted as vol. 2 of Riehl's *Die Naturgeschichte des Volkes* (Stuttgart, 1858), the edition consulted here. See also Conze, "Bauer," 431–35; and the percipient summary of Riehl's thought and career by David Diephouse, in the introduction to his abridged translation, *The Natural History of the German People* (Lewiston, ME, 1990).

14. Regarding German Social Democracy's "dead end" vis-à-vis the peasantry, see Hans Georg Lehmann, *Die Agrarfrage in der Theorie und Praxis der deutschen*

und internationalen Sozialdemokratie (Tübingen, 1970), 64–236. For conservative responses to the social question, see Elmar Roeder, *Der konservative Journalist Ernst Zander und die politischen Kämpfe seines "Volksboten"* (Munich, 1972); Simhart, *Bürgerliche Gesellschaft und Revolution*, 148–90; and Hermann Beck, "Conservatives and the Social Question in Nineteenth-Century Prussia," in *Between Reform, Reaction and Resistance: Studies in the History of German Conservatism from 1789 to 1945*, ed. Larry Eugene Jones and James Retallack (Providence, RI, 1993), 61–94.

15. Ian Kershaw, *Popular Opinion and Political Dissent in the Third Reich: Bavaria 1933–1945* (Oxford, 1983), 62, recounts the "shocking" results of an Upper Bavarian survey of newspaper readership: in the rural portions of Rosenheim district, "45 percent of families in late 1939 were still not taking a newspaper" (in contrast to the town of Rosenheim, where "every family" reportedly did so). These figures are presented as "evidence of the customary peasant aloofness from politics." At what point, however, do the 55 percent in rural areas who *did* receive a paper become historically relevant?

16. Riehl, *Die Naturgeschichte*, 2:61.

17. Dieter Gessner, "The Dilemma of German Agriculture during the Weimar Republic," in *Social Change and Political Development in Weimar Germany*, ed. Richard Bessel and Edgar Feuchtwanger (London, 1981), 140.

18. Ian Farr, "Tradition and the Peasantry," in *The German Peasantry: Conflict and Community in Rural Society from the Eighteenth to the Twentieth Centuries*, ed. Richard J. Evans and W. R. Lee (New York, 1986), for its repeated conflations between "tradition" and peasant culture (and admonition against "culturalist" approaches). Robert Moeller's *German Politics and Agrarian Politics 1914– 1924* (Chapel Hill, 1986) strains to depict the peasant as rustic *homo oeconomicus*; his argument implies an all-too-clean separation between "economic" categories and those cultural processes associated with household and social reproduction.

19. Important exceptions are works that examine the intersections between popular religion and nineteenth-century politics. See David Blackbourn, *Marpingen: Apparitions of the Virgin Mary in Nineteenth-Century Germany* (New York, 1994); Werner Blessing, *Staat und Kirche in der Gesellschaft* (Göttingen, 1982); and Jonathan Sperber, *Popular Catholicism in Nineteenth-Century Germany* (Princeton, 1984).

20. Jürgen Habermas, *The Structural Transformation of the Public Sphere: An Inquiry into a Category of Bourgeois Society* [1962], trans. Thomas Berger (Cambridge, MA, 1991).

21. Riehl, *Die Naturgeschichte*, 1:102f.

22. Ibid., 101.

23. Ibid., 204.

24. Blessing, *Staat und Kirche*, esp. 82–98.

25. W. R. Lee, *Population Growth, Economic Development and Social Change in Bavaria* (New York, 1977), 265–71.

26. Johann Brunner, "Die bayerische Postzeitungsliste von 1848," in *Zeitschrift für bayerische Landesgeschichte* (1930), 481–85.

27. Christian Weinlein, *Der Bayerische Volksschullehrer-Verein: Die Geschichte seiner ersten 50 Jahre, 1861–1911* (Nuremberg, 1911), 380–383; Blessing, *Staat und Kirche*, 71, 122ff., 171–74, 221f.

28. As late as the 1840s, an estimated 40 to 50 percent of all adults in some Upper Bavarian districts could not sign their names. Lee, *Population Growth*, 344–47.

29. See, e.g., Friedrich Hartmannsgruber, *Die Bayerische Patriotenpartei, 1868–1887* (Munich, 1986), 44ff.

30. Staatsarchiv Landshut (hereafter: StAL), 164/1 4794, Beschwerde des Arztes Dr. von Kammerloher gegen den Arzt Dr. Gäch in Schwarzach, 1879.

31. Alois Hundhammer, *Die landwirtschaftliche Berufsvertretung in Bayern* (Munich, 1926); Dr. Ernst Hohenegg, *Die Landesorganisation des landwirtschaftlichen Genossenschaftswesens in Bayern* (Munich, 1927).

32. This dependence is found, for example, in the annual *Kirchweih* (church consecration) celebration observed in many parts of Lower Bavaria. A three-day occasion for revelry, dance, and drink, long divorced from any actual religious function, this most profane of social events nonetheless remained linked, if only nominally, to religious observation. See Felix Dahn, "Volkssitte," in *Bavaria: Landes- und Volkskunde des Königreichs Bayern*, vol.1, *Ober- und Niederbayern* (Munich: 1860), 990–1006, here 995ff.

33. Enterprising tavern owners could stage dances, but these evenings of *Tanzmusik* were as a rule sharply condemned by the clergy as an assault upon the morality of youth. See the treatment in the pro-clerical novella by J. Werax, *Centrum oder Bauernbund? Zeitgemäße Erzählung* (Kempten, 1898), 12.

34. Joseph Schlicht, *Bayerisch Land und Bayerisch Volk* (Straubing, 1875), 100ff., describes the internal segregation typical of the *Wirtshaus*, by which the size of one's properties determined one's social companions. Larger-scale Bauern enjoyed a table of their own, followed by, in descending order of status, tables for medium-holders, smallholders, dwarf-holders, and day laborers.

35. Hermann Hörger, *Kirche, Dorfreligion und bäuerliche Gesellschaft* (Munich, 1978), 323f., 340–348.

36. Helga Ettenhuber, "Charivari in Bayern: Das Miesbacher Haberfeldtreiben von 1893," in *Kultur der einfachen Leute*, ed. Richard van Dülmen (Munich, 1983), 280–308.

37. See Ian Farr, "Peasant Protest in the Empire: the Bavarian Example," in *Peasants and Lords in Modern Germany*, ed. Robert Moeller (London, 1986), 110–39; Anton Hochberger, *Der Bayerische Bauernbund 1893–1914.*(Munich, 1991).

38. George Vascik, "Crisis or Transformation? Confronting the Myth of Agricultural Depression in Wilhelmine Germany," *Essays in Economic and Business History*, 14 (1996): 91–103.

39. The credit cooperative movement was at the time far more advanced in Franconia and Bavarian Swabia. Marion Hruschka, *Die Entwicklung des Geld- und Kreditwesens, unter besonderer Berücksichtigung der Sparkasse im Raum Straubing-Bogen 1803–1972* (Straubing, 1990), 241ff.

40. Strictly speaking, the fire brigades were not voluntary associations at all but the product of state intervention from the early 1870s. Once the brigade movement took hold, however, it aroused passionate support from even remote rural areas. See StAL, 164/12 4021, which charts the brigades' rapid growth in Mallersdorf district, where by 1879 the prefect could boast, "there are now, thank God, forty fire brigades, 1,629 men strong."

41. See reports in the *Kurier für Niederbayern*, 22 September 1876, and the *Landshuter Zeitung*, 13 June 1876.

42. *Straubinger Zeitung*, 4 April 1874.

43. Bayerisches Hauptstaatsarchiv, Ministerium des Innern (hereafter: BHStA M Inn), 38989, 66308.

44. For electoral participation rates, see *Statistisches Jahrbuch für das Königreich Bayern* (Munich, 1894). Reich-wide comparisons from Gerhard A. Ritter and Merith Niehuss, *Wahlgeschichtliches Arbeitsbuch* (Munich, 1980).

45. Figures compiled from the data in BHStA M Inn, 46671, 46673, 46674, 46675, 46676 (Pressestatistik).

46. Additional discussion in my dissertation, "Peasants in the Rural Public: The Bavarian Bauernbund 1893–1933" (University of Illinois, Chicago, 1999).

47. Technical innovations in press machinery and paper manufacture also played a role in lowering production costs. Advertising support for local papers was not entirely of local provenance. After 1871, an advertising supplement—the "Allgemeine Anzeiger für das Königreich Bayern"—became available for insertion in local papers; its press run was around 110,000 copies, for inclusion in more than 90 provincial papers. Heinz Starkulla, *50 Jahre Verband Bayerischer Zeitungsverleger 1913–1963* (Munich, 1963).

48. In 1864, e.g., of the 2,550 circulation for the *Kurier für Niederbayern* (Landshut), 850 copies were distributed within Landshut itself, 1,700 sent through the mail to outlying areas. BHStA M Inn, 46670.

49. The population of Eggenfelden district, composed of 759 settlements, numbered 20,214; all newspapers were published in the town of Eggenfelden, population 2,237 (1880 census figures).

50. The *Eggenfelder Wochenblatt* carried little local news, mostly reprinting "so-called political roundups and dispatches from other political newspapers." BHStA M Inn, 46671, 46673, 46674.

51. Michael Schmolke, *Die schlechte Presse: Katholiken und Publizistik zwischen "Katholik" und "Publik," 1821–1968* (Münster, 1971), esp. 60, 306.

52. Hartmannsgruber, *Patriotenpartei*, 265–68.

53. Karl Bachem, *Vorgeschichte, Geschichte und Politik der Deutschen Zentrumspartei* (1929; reprint, Darmstadt, 1967), 4:155.

54. *Münchner Post*, 24 July 1901.

55. *Augsburger Postzeitung*, 6 and 8 October 1883.

56. See again the *Augsburger Postzeitung* series, 6 and 8 October 1883, for its suggestions as to how to temper and contain the increasingly rancorous exchange of opinion in the Catholic press: *In dubiis libertas* called for more open-mindedness over those "questions, especially from social and political fields, over which the church has not spoken out, and therefore in which, up to a certain point, opinion is open." This was followed by *In omnibus charitas*, which called for introducing a little "Christian love" into the often brutal "methods of struggle" employed by Catholic against Catholic.

57. Sigl and Marchner, while standing on the radical edges of the Catholic press, were at the same time leading practitioners of *Revolverjournalismus*, an admixture of sensationalism, sentiment, scurrility and populism. Another leading *Revolverjournalist* was Anton Memminger. Sigl would later play an early (if erratic) leading role in the Bauernbund movement, as would Memminger and his Würzburg-based *Neue Bayerische Landeszeitung*; the *Neue freie Volks-Zeitung* would become its leading newspaper. In 1881, these three newspapermen alone were charged in nearly one-half (44 of 89) of all government cases against the press. BHStA M Inn, 46672.

58. In rural Bavaria, the usual restrictions against female participation in public life were invested with particular force. This owed largely to the continued importance of household labor to most peasant enterprises; indeed, in the decades before the First World War, family labor grew increasingly central to farming operations. See *Die Landwirtschaft in Bayern* (Munich, 1910), 80–83.

59. *Neue freie Volks-Zeitung*, no. 13, January 1893.

60. See the stenographic records of the speeches of Bauernbund leaders Franz Wieland and Albert Gäch in StAL, 164/9 2339; also StAL, 164/1 5849, 5378; StAL, 164/5 1071, 1073.

61. "Die Bauernführer Wieland und Dr. Gäch," *Neue freie Volks-Zeitung*, 16–17 August 1894.

62. BHStA M Inn, 73455.

63. Werax, *Centrum oder Bauernbund?*, 6ff. Cf. the discussions of popular literacy and politics in Ludwig Thoma, *Andreas Vöst* (1905; reprint, Munich, 1961), 110–18.

64. Franz Wieland was especially venerated by later Bauernbund activists; after his death in 1901 he became the object of a posthumous personality cult. See the report from the village of Safferstetten, *Niederbayerischer Anzeiger*, 12 April 1904, of a successful "Wieland Celebration" held—much against the wishes of area clergy—in the local tavern. The evening was capped by the hanging of Wielands's portrait on the tavern's wall. The phrase "geistige Selfmademen" appeared in a Peasants Council memorandum of 3 December 1918, cited by Karl Ludwig Ay, *Die Enstehung einer Revolution* (Berlin, 1968), 208.

65. See Hannsjörg Bergmann, *Der Bayerische Bauernbund und der Bayerische Christliche Bauernverein, 1919–1928* (Munich, 1986).

66. On the early phases of the CBV, see StAL, 164/1 5850; on the clergy's initial reactions to the Bauernbund insurgency, see *Deggendorfer Donaubote*, 5 April, 1893, found in StAL, 168/5 1071.

67. Dr. Georg Heim set the leading example; he was followed by, among others, Drs. Sebastian Schlittenbauer, Alois Hundhammer, Michael Melchner, Josef Baumgartner, and Alois Schlögl.

68. See Abbott, "Peasants in the Rural Public."

69. Otto Groth, *Die Zeitung*, vol. 1, *Allgemeine Zeitungskunde* (Mannheim, 1928), 207f., 253f.

10

RELIGION AND CIVIL SOCIETY

Catholics, Jesuits, and Protestants
in Imperial Germany

Róisín Healy

I N JANUARY 1914 the Shopkeepers' Association of Osnabrück, in
Lower Saxony, was looking forward to a lecture entitled "Modern Trends in Christianity," to be held on 3 February in the town
hall. The proposed lecture was never given, however, because the
director of the municipal police banned it just more than a week
in advance.[1] The speaker, Otto Cohausz, was a Jesuit priest, and,
according to a law of 4 July 1872, Jesuits were not allowed to give
lectures that touched upon the subject of religion. The police ban
provoked an angry response from Catholics, who disagreed with
the so-called Jesuit Law.[2] A compromise solution was reached in
time for Cohausz to honor his commitment to the Shopkeepers'
Association. He was allowed to deliver a lecture on a nonreligious theme.[3]

Such incidents occurred all over Germany from 1872 until 1917,
when the Jesuit Law was repealed. In fact, the proscription of religious lectures was the least of the restrictions imposed on Jesuits.
The law forbade Jesuits from establishing order houses, defined as
a community of more than two Jesuits living in the same house,
and dissolved existing houses. The law further provided for residency restrictions on individual Jesuits, restrictions that were not

contingent on any violation: provincial police forces were authorized to compel Jesuits of German citizenship to leave a particular administrative area and to expel Jesuits of foreign citizenship from the empire. The Federal Council (Bundesrat) specified that Jesuits were prohibited from all activities in churches and schools and from giving missions.

The Jesuit Law represented more than restriction of the religious activities of Jesuits, however. It provided a moment in the articulation of particular understandings of civil society, especially the relationship between tolerance and freedom. Although the term "civil society" had lapsed by the late nineteenth century, issues central to it remained important in public discussion.[4] In addition to a vibrant associational life, John Hall has identified tolerance or "living with difference" as a constitutive element of civil society.[5] The ban on Jesuit religious activities would seem to run counter to this spirit of tolerance. While legal restrictions on religion were nothing new, the Jesuit Law of 1872 contrasted with growing liberalization of the public sphere at this time. It marked a hiatus in the gradual extension of civic freedoms by German states in the nineteenth century. With one stroke, the Jesuits were divested of the civic freedoms enjoyed by most male citizens in the newly unified empire—freedom of assembly, freedom of movement, and freedom of speech. As a result of the law, Jesuits were confined to the private sphere. They were entitled to venture out only to give lectures on nonreligious academic topics and in choosing a residence were dependent on the sympathy of provincial officials.[6] As a result of the ban, 737 Jesuits went into exile.[7]

Yet while the state was acting contrary to civil society's spirit of tolerance in approving the Jesuit Law, at the same time it was meeting demands from major groups within civil society. The initiative for the law came not from the government but from religious and political associations. Their call for restrictions did not necessarily violate civil society. Unqualified tolerance is not a requirement of civil society. Concern for the protection of innocents, for instance, leads to limits on tolerance; hence the proscription of child pornography. Civil society can be conceived as the space in which an appropriate balance between such concerns and demands for freedom is worked out, or, as Adam Seligman puts it: "the proper conceptualization of the social good and its relation to individual rights, responsibilities, and freedoms."[8]

This chapter focuses on the debate about the Jesuit Law to investigate what it was about the character of civil society in Imperial Germany that militated against toleration of the Jesuit order. It explores why the Jesuit order was seen to threaten civil society and why a legal ban on its activities was considered necessary. More broadly, it analyzes the role of religion and confessional rivalry in shaping the balance between individual rights and tolerance. I will argue that, in the case of the Jesuit debate, religious convictions and confessional prejudices encouraged a balance that reduced individual rights in favor of the social good. Because this social good was defined in confessional and exclusionary terms, civil society became a space where religious tolerance was undermined.

Motives for Exclusion: The Anti-Jesuit Case

Anti-Jesuits justified religious intolerance in the name of civil society. Far from viewing the Jesuit Law as an affront to civil society, the majority of anti-Jesuits understood the law as a bastion of civil society. They accepted the principle that rights must be measured against the social good. Theologian and prominent anti-Jesuit Willibald Beyschlag wrote:

> In today's constitutional state nobody has absolute freedom of self-development, rather the freedom of every individual and corporation, whether it is called "Roman church" or otherwise, is limited by the rights of others and the needs of the whole for its existence. And this whole, the state, decides the limits of self-development for everything that enjoys its authority and protection.[9]

To understand why such severe limits were placed on the self-development of Jesuits, it is necessary to consider the relationship between civil society and exclusionary practices, the influence of the German liberal Protestant tradition on the anti-Jesuit movement, and the reputation of the Jesuits.

The exclusionary impulse of the law did not represent a new departure in the history of civil society. The voluntary associations that formed the "social institutions" of civil society used the space offered by civil society to decide a balance between individual rights and the social good that favored their particular prejudices and interests. Indeed, the emergence of civil society often went hand in hand with a narrowing of public roles for women, Jews, and the lower classes.[10] Even where such groups were offered more freedoms, inclusion was not based on the principle of equal rights but was contingent on good behavior. In the same way that the burghers of the German home towns—small towns that enjoyed a high degree of self-government within the Holy Roman

Empire—denied undesirables the rights of citizenship, members of civil society had limited the spread of their privileges.[11]

It is significant but not surprising, therefore, that the impetus for the Jesuit Law came from a series of voluntary associations. The Old Catholic Congress, which had broken with the Roman church in 1870 over papal infallibility, Protestant and liberal associations, and Freemasons demanded restrictions on the activities of Jesuits.[12] Politicians then endorsed the impetus created by these extraparliamentary associations. A bill introduced into the Reichstag by the right-wing liberals, the National Liberal Party, proposed a permanent ban on the Jesuits and was approved by a large majority, including left-wing liberals and conservatives.[13] Socialists allied with the Catholic Center Party in opposing the bill.

While the Jesuit Law attracted broad support, the particular prejudices and interests that animated the anti-Jesuit movement were rooted in the liberal Protestant tradition. The experience of German liberal Protestants in the mid-nineteenth century reinforced concern that the social good, which they saw through the lens of their own interests, might suffer from an indiscriminate concession of individual rights. Hence they became increasingly prepared to support state repression. Their ideology developed from a tradition of hostility to authoritarianism within the Lutheran Church. Liberal Protestants were dissatisfied with both the constitutional relationship between the church and state and the conservative outlook of most Protestant church governments in midcentury. Their reform program included the transfer of authority from provincial consistories to local congregations, a greater voice for the laity, freedom for theological research, and tolerance for a broad spectrum of doctrinal beliefs. Beginning in the 1860s, church leaders made some concessions, with the partial devolution of authority from provincial church organs or consistories, whose members were often government-appointed, to smaller local organs known as synods, where the laity had a greater voice.[14] But when reforms turned out to favor conservatives, the majority of liberals came to see the state as a bulwark against reactionary church governments.

Liberal Protestants also saw the state as an ally against their other enemy—Catholicism. While their immediate target was the orthodox Protestant establishment, the logic of their critique made the Catholic Church an obvious enemy. Liberal Protestants believed that priests controlled the minds and actions of parishioners and that ultramontanism threatened the autonomy of the modern state. Liberals interpreted the Syllabus of Errors of 1864 as a direct attack on liberalism and modernity and the Declaration of Papal Infallibility as an instruction to Catholics to disregard their secular leaders. Suspicions of disloyalty intensified after 1871 because Catholics had favored a *kleindeutsch*, or Austrian-led, approach to German unification.

The Protestant Association, an elite organization founded in 1863 and active in the anti-Jesuit movement, was typical of liberal Protestantism. The association was committed to a liberal mode of thought, characterized by "an affinity to the new, orientation toward the future, belief in progress to more freedom, justice, and reason."[15] This commitment to liberalism was evident in the association's defense of a host of civic rights, such as freedom of belief and conscience, and in its campaign against authoritarianism in the churches. As an international movement, political Catholicism appeared incompatible with a national state.[16]

Liberal Protestants' enthusiasm for the anticlerical and anti-Catholic legislation of the *Kulturkampf* of the 1870s illustrates the extent to which they were prepared to renounce toleration for the sake of the protection of their interests and the promotion of their prejudices. The *Kulturkampf* ran counter to civil society, as Hall understands it. Liberals endorsed the shift of functions from the churches, which were part of civil society, to the state and the inscription of their anti-Catholic prejudices in law. The *Kulturkampf* proceeded along two fronts. It consisted of a transfer of functions such as marriage and school inspection from civil society to the state and, at the same time, an attempt by the state to shield itself from challenges from the realm of civil society, especially from Catholics. The Jesuit Law was one of several laws that frustrated the Catholic Church in expressing its opinion publicly and encouraged it to adopt a nationalist ethos; others included a ban on the discussion of political issues from the pulpit and a requirement that German priests pass examinations in German culture.

Although Bismarck abandoned the *Kulturkampf*, repealing and modifying much of its legislation after 1878 in response to Catholic opposition, liberal Protestants continued to defend it. The Protestant League was founded in 1886 in an attempt to preserve its spirit and the remaining legislation. The league was the most active anti-Jesuit organization throughout the period and quickly developed into a mass organization.[17] It was sympathetic to the liberal wing of the Lutheran Church and had close relations with the National Liberal Party.

Liberal Protestants regarded anti-Jesuitism as a natural extension of their commitment to liberalism and Protestantism. The reputation of the Jesuits as ruthless agents of clericalism and ultramontanism encouraged liberal Protestants to see them as their archenemy. But the liberal Protestants of nineteenth-century Germany were by no means the first to vent against the order. At one time or another, the Jesuits had been expelled from nearly every state in Europe; the pope had felt obliged to dissolve the order in 1773 because it was so unpopular. Liberal Protestants and reform-minded Catholics alike associated the Jesuits with everything that the Enlightenment rejected—tradition, conservatism, backwardness, superstition, ultramontanism, scholasticism, curialism, and despotism. The unwillingness of the Jesuits to reform their theology and their continued monopoly on education at second and third levels in many Catholic areas angered both those who wished to promote secularization and devout Catholics who were encouraging the church to adapt to the changing needs of society.[18]

Opposition also was rooted in popular myths about the Jesuits. The Jesuit, along with the Jew and the gypsy, had been a favorite figure in the litany of popular enemies since the foundation of the order in 1540. According to myth, the driving force behind the Jesuits was power, whether for themselves or the papacy. Greed and lust were natural sidelines. The religious life provided merely the best opportunity for the host of illicit and immoral activities attributed to them, such as depriving widows of fortunes, hearing intimate details of married life in confession, and assassinating kings. The cartoon story, *Pater Filizius*, composed by satirist Wilhelm Busch in 1872, described how the eponymous Jesuit tried to wheedle an inheritance from an elderly woman by means of poison and attempted murder.[19] In justification of his portrait of Jesuits, the author explained to his publisher that the cartoon "simply expressed the most current desires of the state."[20]

Anti-Jesuit language drew on ideas of civil society as well as on popular myth. It depicted civil society as a triumph over Jesuitism. Anti-Jesuits condemned the Jesuits for failing to respect values associated with civil society—tolerance and personal autonomy. In addition to tolerance, Hall and Seligman view personal autonomy as a constitutive element of civil society. Hall argues that civil society must allow individuals the freedom to make mistakes.[21] Seligman describes civil society as: "that arena where—in Hegelian terms—free, self-determining individuality sets forth its claims for satisfaction of its wants and personal autonomy."[22] Anti-Jesuits further argued that Jesuits constituted a threat because they rejected the existing relationship between public and private that was the precondition for civil society. Anti-Jesuits insisted that the temporal authority of the state was supreme, that the husband had total command in the home, and that voluntary associations had to respect the authority of both.

Yet anti-Jesuits also defined the social good in confessional terms. They identified tolerance, personal autonomy, and a particular ordering of public and private as Protestant. They insisted that religious toleration was a product of the Christian pluralism inaugurated by the Reformation. They lauded Luther as the advocate of personal autonomy. Protestant clerics further respected the authority of fathers and husbands within the home. Finally, Protestantism was a natural ally of the nation-state.[23]

Anti-Jesuits elevated their confessional vision of the social good to a universal one, maintaining that it coincided with the German national tradition: the Protestant social good was also the German social good. A history professor at Karlsruhe, Arthur Böhtlingk, wrote in 1903 that Luther "is not just our religious, but our intellectual, in short, our national reformer. Both our poets and thinkers, our classics and our heroes all are rooted in him. Who disparages him, wants to hide his work, can only do this by cutting our whole intellectual culture and our national state at the roots."[24]

This association of civil society with Protestantism was inherently exclusionary. It had serious implications for Catholics generally, and Jesuits in particular. Only by abandoning their religious traditions could Catholics aspire to civil society. And until they accepted civil society, they did not deserve the benefits of civil society—protection by the state. As leaders of the Catholic assault against tolerance, personal autonomy, and the existing public/private divide, Jesuits were highly dangerous. Tolerance of a group that attacked civil society could only weaken civil society. Beyschlag explained the logic: "Tolerance is patience with regard to the weak and the errant, it is to restrain oneself from influencing them by means other than truth and love; but to allow the enemy of my fatherland to enter is not tolerance but treachery."[25]

A few examples of the charges made by anti-Jesuits will illustrate how values associated with civil society were used to justify religious intolerance. Anti-Jesuits claimed that Jesuits were intolerant of those who disagreed with their religious views, especially Protestants. The latter, by contrast, were far more tolerant. A physician, Georg Lomer, wrote on the eve of the First World War: "Whoever is familiar with Protestantism knows also that it treats its opponent with comparatively far greater tolerance and objectivity than the opponent treats it."[26] This charge of intolerance was particularly serious because anti-Jesuits blamed confessional heterogeneity for the delay in achieving the unification of German states. The dominant Borussian school of history, practiced by Johann Gustav Droysen, Hermann Baumgarten, and Hermann von Treitschke, described unification as the triumph of Protestantism over Catholicism.[27] Anti-Jesuits highlighted the role of the Jesuits in frustrating unification. A leading Protestant theologian in Heidelberg, Adolf Hausrath, celebrated Germany's victory over France in 1871 as "a victory of German Enlightenment over ultramontane spiritual enslavement ... of the Protestant over the Jesuitical spirit."[28]

Anti-Jesuits maintained that the order was founded for the express purpose of destroying Protestantism, that it committed atrocities against Protestants, and that it continued to foment religious conflict. A schoolteacher, Lieberknecht, claimed that Loyola hated heretics and had turned the Jesuits into a *"Kampforden,"* or fighting order, against Protestants.[29] Anti-Jesuits pointed to links between Jesuits and anti-Protestant atrocities, such as the St. Bartholomew's Day Massacre of 1572, which marked the start of a six-week campaign of slaughter by Catholics of perhaps as many as 12,000 Huguenots throughout France. One author claimed that while the Jesuits were not directly responsible for the massacre, their way of thinking contributed to it.[30] Jesuits continued to "disturb the confessional peace" in the nineteenth century. A Protestant League pamphlet suggested a Catholic priest, Stöck, had rebaptized a Protestant child, implying he believed that the Protestant baptism had been invalid. The priest had received his training in Jesuit colleges in Austria, in Feldkirch and Innsbruck.[31]

Another typical charge was that Jesuits rejected the principle of personal autonomy. Not only did Jesuits persecute Protestants for professing a different set of religious beliefs, they also suppressed all independent thought on the part of Catholics. Protestantism, on the other hand, fostered personal autonomy. Historian Karl Lamprecht was typical of his colleagues in depicting the Reformation as a crucial moment in the historical development toward personal emancipation. Lamprecht made the idea of subjectivity characteristic of a historical period of "Individualism": "It was Luther, who cleared the way for Individualism in the most profound regions of spiritual life, in the religious and philosophical, in that he placed the individual person before the divine principle directly, without the intrusion of any sacral institution."[32] Jesuits had a very different agenda. Members of an anti-Jesuit committee from Saxony declared in a protest resolution in 1892 that they wanted to live with Catholics as one people but felt that Jesuits endangered "civil freedom, as well as freedom of belief and conscience ... and our whole German culture, which has grown from the ground of the Reformation."[33]

A favorite related charge was that Jesuits themselves had no personal freedom because they owed "cadaver-like" obedience to their superiors. Beyond making Jesuits into highly effective cogs in a malicious machine, this charge created a counterimage to Luther's drive for personal autonomy. Jesuits epitomized the damage wrought by restrictions on self-development and disqualified themselves from civil society: if Jesuits were not independent individuals, but more like children bound to obey their parents, then they could add little to public discussion. Böhtlingk condemned the level of obedience demanded with all the indignation of a rational, free-thinking individual. He explained what "cadaver-like" obedience meant:

> The obedience demanded of a Jesuit, unlike a servant or even an ordinary soldier, consists not simply of carrying out tasks or commands of his superior; the level of obedience that leaves room for one's own thoughts is not sufficient; the Jesuit has not fully complied with the order's demands, until he has surrendered his own free will so completely to that of his superior that he feels and thinks as his master and knows no wishes of his own.[34]

Another aspect of personal autonomy that Jesuits rejected was objective scholarship. Because they adhered to a set of dogmas, Jesuits could not pursue the truth. Protestants, by contrast, had a natural inclination toward free scholarship. As Lomer put it: "Not for nothing has Protestantism become the intellectual mother of modern scholarship, which draws its strength primarily from its freedom from prejudice."[35] The same author insisted that Jesuits do not love truth but the "truth of the order."[36] In a speech to the Protestant League, church superintendent Christian Friedrich Meyer argued that the German Volk stood for scholarship, whereas Jesuit scholarship was not free but prescribed by the pope.[37]

According to anti-Jesuits, Jesuits rejected personal autonomy in areas where it was essential—in associational life, moral decisions, and scholarship. They also failed to respect necessary limits on their interference in other areas, particularly in the state and the family. Anti-Jesuits claimed that by rejecting the authority of the state and the integrity of the family, Jesuits challenged the particular ordering of public and private necessary for civil society. By exerting excessive influence on wives and servants, Jesuits undermined the master's control of his household. By rejecting clericalism, Protestantism had protected the private realm.

The confessional symbolized the transgression of public/private boundaries so disliked by anti-Jesuits. It represented a liminal space between the state and the household, but it operated according to rules very different from those of civil society. For liberal Protestants, it represented a unique opportunity for Jesuit mischief. The author of a Protestant League pamphlet, Carl Fey, argued that Jesuits said in confession what they could not say in public without fear of repression. Moreover, he alleged that Jesuits used the confessional to incite Catholic servants against Protestant masters and Catholic landlords against Protestant tenants.[38] Another anti-Jesuit accused Lehmkuhl, a Jesuit theologian, of encouraging priests to prey on the weaknesses of women in the confessional with a view to seducing them. The same author claimed that priests caused strife in families by urging women, whom they considered generally more pious than men, to impose their beliefs on their husbands, even if the latter were nonpracticing Catholics or Protestants.[39]

In addition, anti-Jesuits charged that Jesuits failed to accept the authority of the state and rejected the subordination of voluntary associations, which included the churches and religious orders, to the state. Instead they pledged obedience to the head of the order known as the general and the pope, who in turn tried to assert their authority over the state. On the other hand, Protestantism, organized on a national or subnational basis, constituted a natural ally of the modern state. Indeed Protestantism had fostered the national consciousness that inspired political unification. The accusations made by a liberal pastor in Stuttgart, Traub, are typical. He argued that the Jesuits had only one goal—absolute domination of the world. Traub quoted a Jesuit writer's assertion that the pope was the highest earthly authority. Jesuits were dangerous to the state, he continued, because of their special allegiance to a foreign power, the pope. Traub then quoted Treitschke, who declared: "The Jesuit order is incompatible with the existence of the modern state.... [B]lind obedience, sworn to a foreign leader, is intellectual serfdom and, indeed, leads to the constant interference of secret foreign powers in the life of the state."[40]

Challenges to Exclusion: The Pro-Jesuit Case

While the anti-Jesuit case resonated with all Protestants, many conservative Protestants felt that their church suffered as a result of the Jesuit Law and were sympathetic toward repeal. The rejection of the

Jesuit Law was part of a broader shift in favor of religious pluralism. Orthodox Protestants moved from support for the state's role
in the church in midcentury to a desire for independence of the
church from the state by the end of the century. This shift was the
product less of ideological conviction than necessity, however. They
felt that the state had turned against them. The *Kulturkampf* eroded
some of the churches' powers in accordance with the liberal agenda.

Some orthodox Protestants saw the Jesuit Law as evidence of
the institutionalization of the liberal church agenda, which they
felt damaged Protestantism and Christianity generally. One conservative pastor complained in 1894 that the law was like a certificate of poverty: its existence implied that the Protestant church
was unable to fight its own battles, to beat Catholicism by rational
argument.[41] A conservative paper in Baden condemned the law,
arguing that police measures were not appropriate to deal with
religious matters.[42] Friedrich von Bodelschwingh, a prominent
conservative pastor, echoed this sentiment: "I think it is very damaging for the Christian church, when it calls on the state to protect
and help it in spiritual matters."[43] Some orthodox Protestants even
believed that Catholics might be allies in the struggle against athe-
istic ideas inside and outside the church. The president of the
Higher Consistory of the Lutheran Church of Bavaria pointed out
that the empire had room for all kinds of marginal views, including anarchism and monism, and thus should value men who call
themselves after Jesus.[44]

While such Protestants were sympathetic to Jesuit suffering, the
majority of the order's supporters were drawn from the Catholic
community. Unified by the experience of persecution in the *Kulturkampf* and relieved of anti-ultramontanes by the secession of the
Old Catholics, the Catholic community provided greater support
than ever for the Jesuits in the late nineteenth century. The abandonment of the Anti-Socialist Law, an exceptional law directed
against socialist activity, strengthened Catholics in their demands
for repeal of the Jesuit Law after 1890. Jesuits played an important
role within the Catholic community in nineteenth-century Germany, even during the operation of the ban. Their schools, located
just outside the German borders, attracted the sons of the Catholic
elite. Thousands of Catholics attended their missions.[45] Jesuits
engaged many of the important political and social questions of
the day in their journal, *Stimmen der Zeit*, and in public lectures. The
program of a Symposium on Social and Political Questions held at
Mönchen-Gladbach in 1892 included several lectures by Jesuits on
the following topics: "The Responsibility of the State with Special

Focus on Macro-economic Policy"; "Socialism"; "The History of the Socialist Movement in Germany"; and "The Social Question in Literature and Art."[46]

The Catholic Center Party, the People's Association for Catholic Germany—a mass organization founded in 1890—and a small number of Jesuit scholars led the campaign to have the order readmitted to Germany. Jesuit Bernhard Duhr was the most prolific defender of the order. He wrote numerous works that deflated claims of Jesuit wrongdoing. The most famous was his *Jesuitenfabeln*, of which four editions were published, before it was abridged and reprinted. It consisted of a list of myths or fables about the Jesuits, followed by rebuttals.[47] Otto Cohausz also gave lectures all over Germany in which he criticized the Jesuit Law.[48] Jesuits showed their disdain for the law by repeated violations. Hundreds of missions were held in Germany despite the ban.[49]

In their campaign against the law, Jesuits and their supporters defined the social good in confessional terms, too. They posited a commitment to Christianity, especially Catholicism, as a prerequisite for toleration. Like anti-Jesuits, Catholics had their own hierarchy of undesirables. Socialists came highest on the list, followed by Jews and by liberal Protestants. Orthodox Protestants were the most acceptable of all non-Catholics, because they supported dogmatism and authoritarianism. Yet Catholics, like anti-Jesuits, drew on the language of civil society when possible.

The Catholic defenders of the Jesuits denied that Jesuits were intolerant of Protestantism and maintained, rather, that they were the victims of intolerance. In an attempt to shame Protestants into repealing the law, Cohausz ended his pamphlet on the Jesuit question with Christ's injunction from the crucifix: "father, forgive them, for they know not what they do."[50] A Catholic politician, Martin Fassbender, challenged the use of historical examples to show Jesuits rejected religious tolerance. Tolerance was a recent concept and should not be applied to the past. Like many other pro-Jesuits, Fassbender also refuted specific historical charges of intolerance. He rejected the claim that the order was founded to root out Protestantism.[51] Duhr refuted the charge that Jesuits were engaged in witch trials or sought to convert Protestant princes by illicit means. He also provided evidence that the popular missions held in the two decades before the Jesuit Law did not disturb the peace. In fact, he maintained, they contributed to the suppression of the revolutionary spirit of 1848.[52]

But supporters of the Jesuits were not committed to extending tolerance unconditionally. They depicted the repeal of the Jesuit

Law as a question of parity rather than pluralism. Numerous resolutions and pamphlets argued that the Jesuit Law was unfair because other groups they believed dangerous were allowed to operate without legal restrictions. The Catholic daily *Germania* complained that the Jesuit Law was an insult to Catholics, in that it placed Jesuits in a position inferior to prostitutes and pimps; there was no suggestion of concessions to prostitutes.[53] A Catholic regional paper conceded that the Jesuits were more anti-Protestant than most orders but denied that this attribute justified an exceptional law against them. Socialists were also anti-Protestant but were free since the Anti-Socialist Law was removed. The Protestant League was anti-Catholic, but this fact hardly justified the expulsion of all its members.[54]

Groups who rejected Christianity were especially begrudged. In this sense, anti-Jesuit claims of religious intolerance on the part of Jesuits were true. A Catholic author, Heiner, contrasted the treatment of Jesuits and atheists. He criticized the lack of public indignation over restrictions on Jesuits: "If one were making such an argument against Jews, Freemasons, Social Democrats or even anarchists, the whole world would be shocked and aghast, from the most balanced professor to the simplest man, about such a stark, incredible injustice and enslavement of a free person and citizen."[55] A committee of the Constance Club, a Catholic organization in Dortmund, ended an appeal to the Prussian cultural minister—against a ban on lectures by a Jesuit, Granderath—by emphasizing:

> the drastic fact, that here in Dortmund, as everywhere, the fundament of throne and altar is undermined every week in numerous meetings, that a Dr. Rüdt and similar persons have been able to spread the principles of atheism openly and unpunished, but that—provided the police ban remains in force!—the educated Catholic bourgeoisie which is committed to the constitution and monarchy, is deprived of the opportunity to have people of *its* choice explain the basis of their worldview, on which our present political and social order ultimately rests.[56]

Jesuits implicated Protestantism in the rise of socialism. One popular Jesuit lecturer, Pesch, declared to the Catholic People's Association that, while atheism was characteristic of socialism, it originated in scholarly circles. Pesch implied that liberal Protestants were responsible for the decline of religion. In a reference to the biblical scholarship of David Friedrich Strauß and his successors, Pesch complained that, once Christ was robbed of his divinity, it was no wonder that people began to lose faith in God entirely.[57]

Anti-Semitic attitudes, too, were common among Catholics. In 1862 Bishop Ketteler, the principal advocate of social Catholicism, had decried the corrupting influence of Jews as well as capitalism and industrialism on the economy, family, and public morality. Catholics believed that Jews threatened "discipline, modesty, family integrity, and ecclesiastical authority."[58] The *Kulturkampf* did not result in any lasting sympathy for the historical sufferings of Jews. In trying to prove their Germanness after 1878, Catholics emphasized their anti-Semitism.[59]

Supporters of the Jesuits also refuted the charge that the order rejected personal autonomy. They focused less on the obedience of members than on their moral theology. Defenders of the order were especially careful to rebut the claim that Jesuits believed that the ends justified the means. A Center Party deputy, Dasbach, offered a reward for anyone who could find such a statement among Jesuit writings. Paul Graf von Hoensbroech, an ex-Jesuit who had converted to Protestantism, claimed the reward, but his claim was rejected by a German court.[60] Duhr devoted much of his *Jesuitenfabeln* to disproving charges that Jesuits condoned lying, equivocation, and perjury.[61]

Duhr was one of many writers who challenged charges of Jesuit disloyalty to the state and disrespect for national German culture. But he insisted on a Christian frame of reference. He insisted that the Jesuits had promoted culture, as he understood it: "Culture we understand as the entire development of human capabilities in material and intellectual affairs in the direction desired by God."[62] Duhr argued that in their intellectual activities Jesuits promoted both God and nation. He argued that "the struggle for Germanness against cosmopolitanism stands out as a major theme in the poetic literature of German Jesuits."[63] Another Jesuit, Huonder, writing under a pseudonym, pointed to contributions by Jesuits to German culture in Africa and Asia: Jesuits working there remained *kerndeutsch*, or German to the core.[64]

Conclusion

The charges made by anti-Jesuits were not entirely without foundation. The Jesuits were no paragons of religious tolerance. They believed in limits on personal autonomy, insisting on the importance of clerical guidance for the laity, especially through missions. Neither did the Jesuits embrace nationalism. The order endorsed ultramontanism in the nineteenth century and energetically promoted

Catholic piety. On the other hand, the claims of anti-Jesuits were exaggerated. A government observer at the Mönchen-Gladbach symposium found the claims of anti-Jesuits hollow: "While the lectures and discussions were firmly rooted in Catholicism and one cannot agree with all the statements made by the speakers, at the same time nothing was said that might undermine the confessional peace and state institutions."[65] Jesuits and their supporters emphasized their enthusiasm for the newly unified polity. They saw no contradiction between loyalty to the papacy and to the state. The Jesuit Pesch praised both the emperor and the pope as champions in the fight against social democracy.[66] A meeting of Catholics in Erfurt against the Jesuit Law concluded with toasts to the emperor and pope.[67] Such endorsements were intended to rebut the charge of disloyalty to the state, but they also reflected a traditional Catholic recognition of the layered nature of personal identity, the compatibility of subnational, national, and international allegiances. The Catholic Center Party was a firm advocate of particularism as well as a defender of international Catholicism.

Germany was not alone at this time in placing restrictions on Jesuits. Geoffrey Cubitt has documented the series of anti-Jesuit measures taken in nineteenth-century France. French anti-Jesuits echoed their German counterparts in many of the charges against the Jesuits. They maintained that the Jesuits were a secret society, incompatible with modern state and society. And they, too, looked to the state to institutionalize anti-Jesuitism. French anti-Jesuits had a very positive view of the state, seeing it as "the active embodiment, the political protector, and the moral guardian of society."[68] Anti-Jesuits in France had greater reason to suspect Catholics of disloyalty to the state. Catholics traditionally had been hostile to the French republic and were reluctant to endorse it even after the first *Ralliement* of the 1890s. Whereas German anti-Jesuits sought to counter Jesuit influence in the church as a whole, they focused their attack on the Jesuits' role in education. Republicans believed Jesuits sought to undermine the republic and replace it with an ancien régime-style monarchy. The Jesuits were an unauthorized order in France, and there were repeated efforts to expel them from schools. A measure in 1880 intensified restrictions on Jesuits: they were banned from cohabiting and teaching.[69]

The *Kulturkampf* was a particular instance of a general conflict over the relationship between church and state throughout Europe. But the German case was particularly acrimonious. Signs of secularization were obvious, but the laic culture of France had not yet arrived in Germany.[70] Most importantly, Catholic-Protestant tensions ran high. German liberals and anti-clericals were not usually secular, like most of their French counterparts, but in many cases motivated by religious concerns. By contrast, confessional conflict declined in Britain, although many of its subjects, as in Germany, associated Protestantism with their national identity. By the mid-nineteenth century, the British government had abandoned most of its anti-Catholic legislation. Concentrated in evangelical movements, anti-Catholicism became increasingly marginalized, except in Ulster.[71] But there the stakes were higher. For Ulster Protestants, home rule for Ireland meant "Rome rule," government by a Catholic majority, a fate never implied in the admission of Jesuits into Germany.

Although a majority of Reichstag members voted in favor of repealing the Jesuit Law five times between 1893 and 1913, the Prussian-dominated Federal Council refused to repeal the law until 1917. Only the prospect of defeat in war persuaded the Prussian government to yield to the demands for repeal. The proclamation of "civil peace" by Emperor William II at the start of the war had emphasized the need for equality and national unity. The immediate impetus to repeal was the need to grant a concession to the Center Party in order to counter a lapse of morale among Catholic workers in 1917.

The debate about the Jesuit Law in Imperial Germany highlights the fragility of tolerance in a confessionally divided society. While civil society provided the space for a lively debate about the balance between individual rights and the social good, in this case the space was filled by religious prejudice. The Jesuit debate also illustrated the problematic consequences of institutional links between state and civil society. It is not surprising that, as a partner of the Protestant Church in the "throne and altar" alliance, the Prussian state endorsed the inscription of Protestant prejudice into law. However, the anti-Jesuits' emphasis on the rights of the state to defend itself against subversion also strengthened the state's position vis-à-vis civil society. When the government decided to repeal the law, anti-Jesuits found themselves ill-prepared to contest Jesuits according to the methods of civil society. Their reliance on state coercion had sharpened their power to mobilize like-minded Protestants but had dulled their capacity to convert Catholics to their ideology. By contrast, the experience of state coercion had honed the political skills of Jesuits, leaving them better equipped than ever to defend their cause in civil society after 1917.

Notes

1. Geheimes Staatsarchiv Preußischer Kulturbesitz (hereafter GSPK), RG 77/ 413/14/13, Trott zu Solz (Prussian Cultural Minister) to Bethmann-Hollweg (Reich Chancellor), 29 January 1914. The police ban was issued on 23 January 1914.
2. Bundesarchiv Potsdam (hereafter BAP), R43/900, Gröber (Catholic Center Party deputy) to Bethmann-Hollweg (Reich Chancellor), 26 January 1914.
3. GSPK, RG 77/413/14/13, Trott zu Solz to Bethmann-Hollweg, 29 January 1914.
4. John Keane, *Civil Society and the State: New European Perspectives* (London, 1988), 1.
5. John A. Hall, ed., *Civil Society: Theory, History, Comparison* (Cambridge, 1995), 15.
6. The repeal of paragraph two of the law in 1904 ended residency restrictions.
7. Bartholomew Murphy, *Der Wiederaufbau der Gesellschaft Jesu in Deutschland im neunzehnten Jahrhundert* (Frankfurt am Main, 1985), 362.
8. Adam B. Seligman, *The Idea of Civil Society* (Princeton, 1992), 9.
9. Willibald Beyschlag, *Gehören die Jesuiten ins deutsche Reich? Ein Beitrag zur Tagesfrage*, 4th ed. (Berlin, 1903), 54.
10. For a discussion of the limits of civil society see Belinda Davis, "Reconsidering Habermas, Gender, and the Public Sphere: The Case of Wilhelmine Germany," in *Society, Culture and the State in Germany, 1870–1930*, ed. Geoff Eley (Ann Arbor, 1996). Dagmar Herzog has also explored the contrast between liberal appeals for freedom for men and the defense of the continued repression of Jews and women in *Intimacy and Exclusion: Religious Politics in Pre-Revolutionary Baden* (Princeton, 1996).
11. Mack Walker, *German Home Towns: Community, State, and General Estate, 1648–1871* (Ithaca, 1971).
12. Ernst Rudolf Huber, *Deutsche Verfassungsgeschichte seit 1789*, 4 vols. (Stuttgart, 1969), vol. 4: 704.
13. E. R. Huber and Wolfgang Huber, *Staat und Kirche im 19. und 20. Jahrhundert* (Berlin, 1976), 546.
14. Armin Müller-Dreier, "*Konfessionelle 'Selbstbehauptung' und 'nationale' Politik: Der Evangelische Bund zur Wahrung der deutsch-protestantischen Interessen im Kaiserreich (1886–1914)*" (Ph.D. diss., University of Hamburg, 1995), 24.
15. Gangolf Hübinger, *Kulturprotestantismus und Politik: Zum Verhältnis von Liberalismus und Protestantismus im wilhelminischen Deutschland* (Tübingen, 1994), 7.
16. Dieter Langewiesche, *Liberalismus in Deutschland*, cited in Hübinger, *Kulturprotestantismus*, 38f.
17. Müller-Dreier calculates membership grew from 80,000 in 1891 to 468,435 in 1911. See *Evangelischer Bund*, 85f.
18. Richard van Dülmen, "Antijesuitismus und katholische Aufklärung in Deutschland," *Historisches Jahrbuch* 89 (1969): 52–80.
19. Wilhelm Busch, "Pater Filuzius: Eine allegorische Geschichte," *Sämtliche Werke*, ed. Rolf Hochhut (Gütersloh, 1956).
20. Harold Just, "Wilhelm Busch und die Katholiken: Kulturkampfstimmung im Bismarck-Reich," *Geschichte in Wissenschaft und Unterricht* 2, no. 74 (1974): 72.
21. Hall, *Civil Society*, 27.
22. Seligman, *Idea of Civil Society*, 5.
23. The link that anti-Jesuits assumed between civil society and Protestantism may owe something to the way in which Scottish Enlightenment discourse was translated into German. Fania Oz-Salzberger shows that the translator of

Adam Ferguson's *Essay on the History of Civil Society* into German drew on terminology from Pietism, mainstream Protestantism, and sentimentalism; see *Translating the Enlightenment: Scottish Civic Discourse in Eighteenth-Century Germany* (Oxford, 1995), 157–64.

24. Arthur Böhtlingk, *Die Jesuiten und das deutsche Reich: Zeitgemässes* (Frankfurt am Main, 1903), 16.

25. Beyschlag, *Gehören die Jesuiten*, 50.

26. Georg Lomer, *Ignatius von Loyola, vom Erotiker zum Heiligen: Eine pathographische Geschichtsstudie* (Leipzig, 1913), 7.

27. Wolfgang Hardtwig, "Von Preussens Aufgabe in Deutschland zu Deutschlands Aufgabe in der Welt: Liberalismus und borussianisches Geschichtsbild zwischen Revolution und Imperialismus," *Historische Zeitschrift* 231 (1980): 265–324.

28. Uriel Tal, *Christians and Jews in Germany: Religion, Politics, and Ideology in the Second Reich, 1870–1914* (Ithaca, 1975), 45.

29. Lieberknecht, *Wider die Jesuiten*. Wartburgheft 66 (Berlin, 1912), 7f.

30. Anon., *Die Wahrheit über die Jesuiten* (Berlin, 1900), 35f.

31. Anon., *Wider den Priester Stöck und die Jesuiten: Gedanken über die gerichtliche Verhandlung vor der Strafkammer in Trier gegen den katholischen Priester Stöck wegen Entführung eines evangelischen Kindes* (Leipzig, 1893), 5f.

32. Karl Lamprecht, *Deutsche Geschichte*, cited in Roger Chickering, *Karl Lamprecht: A German Academic Life (1856–1915)* (New Jersey, 1993), 128.

33. Politisches Archiv des Auswärtigen Amtes, R9316, 1: cited in Dönhoff (Prussian ambassador to Saxony) to Caprivi (Prussian Foreign Minister), 29 December 1892.

34. Böhtlingk, *Die Jesuiten*, 8.

35. Lomer, *Ignatius von Loyola*, 7.

36. Ibid., 1.

37. Christian Friedrich Meyer, *Der Jesuitenorden und die deutsche Volksseele*. Wartburgheft no. 66 (Berlin, 1913), 15.

38. Carl Fey, *Unsere Lage und unsere Aufgaben nach dem Fall des §2 des Jesuitengesetzes*. Flugschrift des Evangelischen Bundes no. 223 (Leipzig, 1904), 11.

39. Karl Souverain, *Der Jesuit im Beichtstuhle: Dreimaldrei Briefe an einem katholischen Prälaten* (Bamberg, 1913), 14, 44–50.

40. Hermann von Treitschke, *Politik*, cited in Th. Traub, *Die Jesuiten: Material zur Jesuitenfrage* (Berlin, 1912), 28.

41. *Protestantische Stimmen über das Jesuitengesetz* (Berlin, 1894), 49, 72.

42. Heinrich Krueckemeyer, *Der Jesuiten-Lob(!) aus Gegners Mund: Eine Zusammenstellung von Aussprüchen hervorragender Protestanten und Gegner der katholischen Kirche über den Jesuitenorden* (Danzig, 1902), 42.

43. Friedrich von Bodelschwingh, *Wie kämpfen wir siegreich gegen die Jesuitengefahr?* (Bethel bei Bielefeld, 1904), 3.

44. Speech in Leipzig, 30 May 1912, described in *Positive Union*, 9 November 1912.

45. Murphy, *Wiederaufbau der Gesellschaft Jesu*. Archiv der norddeutschen Provinz der Gesellschaft Jesu, O/VI/97 Volksmissionen und Volksexerzitien.

46. GSPK, RG 77/413/14/11.

47. Bernhard Duhr, *Jesuitenfabeln: Ein Beitrag zur Culturgeschichte* (Freiburg, 1891), abridged as *Hundert Jesuitenfabeln: Volksausgabe der Jesuitenfabeln* (Freiburg, 1913).

48. These lectures attracted much official attention, because the authorities had to decide if they were illegal. See BAP, R43/899.

49. Archiv der Norddeutschen Provinz der Gesellschaft Jesu, Section O/VI/97.

50. Otto Cohausz, *Das Glaubensbekenntnis der Jesuiten: Appell an alle rechtlich denkenden Deutschen, besonders an allen Protestanten* (Dortmund, 1912), 30.
51. Martin Fassbender, "Der Kern der Jesuitenfrage," *Die Zukunft* 22, no. 16 (1913): 308–10.
52. Bernhard Duhr, *Die Stellung der Jesuiten in den deutschen Hexenprozessen.* Görres Gesellschaft zur Pflege der Wissenschaft in katholischem Deutschland, Vereinsschrift für 1900 (Cologne, 1900); *Die Jesuiten an den deutschen Fürstenhöfen des 16. Jahrhunderts* (Freiburg, 1901); *Aktenstücke zur Geschichte der Jesuiten-Missionen in Deutschland, 1848–1872* (Freiburg, 1903).
53. *Germania*, 21 May 1912.
54. *Märkische Volkszeitung*, 8 October 1890.
55. Franz Xaver Heiner, *Der Jesuitismus in seinem Wesen, seiner Gefährlichkeit und Bekämpfung, mit besonderer Rücksicht auf Deutschland* (Paderborn, 1902), 133.
56. GSPK, RG 76/IV/1/17/A/II. Letter, Dortmund, 5 April 1892, emphasis in original.
57. *Bergisch-Märkische Zeitung: Organ der Centrumspartei*, 10 February 1892.
58. Tal, *Christians and Jews*, 93.
59. Ibid., 95.
60. For an account of this trial see: from Hoensbroech's perspective, *Der Zweck heiligt die Mittel als jesuitischer Grundsatz erwiesen von Hoensbroech* (Berlin, 1903); from Dasbach's perspective, Georg Frider, ed., *Dasbach gegen Hoensbroech: Widerlegung d. Beweismaterials d. Grafen Paul v. Hoensbroech in d. Streitfrage, ob die Jesuitenlehren: Der Zweck heiligt d. Mittel. 2. Antwort auf d. 3. Aufl. D. Schrift d. Grafen Paul v. Hoensbroech*, 2nd ed. (Trier, 1904).
61. Duhr, *Hundert Jesuitenfabeln*, 28f.
62. Ibid., 23.
63. Ibid., 35.
64. A. Camerlander, *Sind die Jesuiten deutschfeindlich? Ein Beitrag zur Geschichte des Deutschtums im Ausland* (Freiburg, 1913), preface.
65. GSPK, RG 77/413/14/11.
66. GSPK, RG 76/IV/1/13/17/A/II, report by Abraman, 10 January 1892.
67. *Germania*,18 December 1890.
68. Geoffrey Cubitt, *The Jesuit Myth: Conspiracy Theory and Politics in Nineteenth-Century France* (Oxford, 1993), 168.
69. Ibid., 166.
70. Gangolf Hübinger, "Confessionalism," in *Imperial Germany: A Historiographical Companion*, ed. Roger Chickering (Westport, CT, 1996), 259.
71. D. G. Paz, *Popular Anti-Catholicism in Mid-Victorian England* (Stanford, 1992), 301.

11

PROSTITUTES, CIVIL SOCIETY, AND THE STATE IN WEIMAR GERMANY

Julia Roos

A MAJOR ISSUE IN THE CURRENT DEBATE about civil society concerns the role of voluntary associations and other forms of political self-organization in the rise of a democratic public sphere.[1] While initial studies largely focused on the growth of a public sphere among privileged, propertied men, more recent scholarship has drawn attention to the political activities of groups like the women's and ecological movements.[2] However, there is still a tendency in this literature to downplay the pivotal role within civil society of those whom dominant moral standards classify as outcasts. The history of prostitutes' political organization in Weimar Germany aims to overcome this blind spot. This essay intends to show that a form of civil society emerged among prostitutes in the late 1920s. Implicitly posing a radical challenge to traditional gender roles and ideologies, this "outcast civil society" is crucial for understanding the fate of Weimar social policy.

Recent studies of Weimar welfare policies have stressed the continuity of authoritarian state interventionism from Imperial Germany to National Socialism.[3] The expansion of the Weimar welfare state into the areas of health, sexuality, and reproduction, it has been argued, continued antiliberal traditions in German politics because it subordinated individual rights to the interests of the abstract collectivity of the *Volk*. While it is important to point to the negative impact of social hygiene and eugenics on social legislation during the 1920s, it nevertheless is problematic to focus exclusively on antidemocratic tendencies in Weimar social policy. This study of the reform of prostitution policy in Bremen during the Weimar Republic suggests that the extension of welfare policies into the areas of health and sexuality had important *positive* implications for individual rights as well. Weimar's 1927 legislation against the spread of sexually transmitted diseases, while containing problematic disciplinary provisions, nonetheless granted prostitutes crucial civil rights previously denied them. The law generated a new form of civil society among women traditionally ostracized by important segments of the population. Significant opposition to this aspect of the anti-venereal disease (anti-VD) law on the part of the police and conservatives points to the problems faced by innovative social policies challenging traditional views of sexuality and gender. In my view, this opposition constitutes an important facet of the resurgence of right-wing authoritarianism in Weimar's final years.

From Police Regulation to Hygienic Control

During the Weimar Republic, socio-hygienic concerns about the negative impact of sexually transmitted diseases (STDs) on public health and the birthrate increasingly influenced the debate about prostitution. Anxieties over the dangers of STDs temporarily united Social Democrats, feminists, and some conservatives in the effort to replace the system of state-regulated prostitution with comprehensive measures against the spread of sexually transmitted diseases.[4] This politically diverse alliance often proved precarious; the Left's demand for a more liberal approach to prostitution was strongly opposed by the "moral Right." However, a broad consensus picturing STDs as a threat to population growth ultimately paved the way for crucial reforms of prostitution policy in the Weimar period.

In 1927, a new law for combating venereal diseases, the *Reichsgesetz zur Bekämpfung der Geschlechtskrankheiten* (RGBG) abolished the nineteenth-century system of police control known as "regulationism."[5] Under the old system, the "morals police" (*Sittenpolizei*) supervised prostitution on the basis of police regulations which ranged from the registration of prostitutes to the de facto licensing of brothels.[6] This system subjected registered prostitutes to numerous infringements on their personal liberties. For example, health checks for STDs were required. Both registered and "clandestine" prostitutes found to be infected had to undergo compulsory medical treatment. While the women were subjected to rigid and humiliating controls, their customers evaded screening for venereal infection.

In contrast to the old system, the new anti-VD law extended the scope of hygienic supervision beyond the small group of prostitutes. Like the Norwegian and Danish anti-VD laws on which it was modeled, the RGBG aimed to control the spread of sexually transmitted diseases throughout the population.[7] It not only ensured free medical treatment for persons without means but also made possible the compulsory hospitalization of "negligent" patients unwilling to continue their treatment. A person who knowingly infected others with STDs could be punished with up to three years in prison. The same applied to someone who, prior to marriage, had not informed the prospective spouse of his or her venereal infection.[8] Although prostitution ceased to constitute a crime, the law simultaneously declared brothels illegal. It also banned prostitution from towns of less than 15,000 inhabitants and from zones immediately contiguous to schools and churches.[9] The practice of concentrating prostitutes in special streets or blocks also was forbidden. Persons suspected of spreading sexually transmitted diseases had to present certificates to the local health office proving that they had undergone regular checkups, a provision that affected primarily prostitutes.

The RGBG shifted authority from the police to public health officials and physicians. Medical experts and health officials now were in charge of the supervision of persons infected with STDs and of "risk groups" like prostitutes. Orders to arrest so-called "negligent" patients and prostitutes trying to evade medical examination had to be issued by the health office. Thus, in the area of the *hygienic* control of prostitution, the police were demoted and largely ceased to function as an independent force. For prostitutes, the new law resulted in a certain liberalization: they now had the right to choose private physicians and were better protected legally against arbitrary arrests.

The passage of the anti-VD law constituted a victory for the "abolitionist" opponents of state regulated prostitution. After many setbacks, the German abolitionist movement finally achieved its dual aim of establishing equal standards of sexual morality for both sexes and of liberating prostitutes from the arbitrary power of the morals police.[10] But abolitionism itself had been transformed since its inception around the turn of the century. Feminist abolitionists of the 1920s were more concerned with social hygiene (for example, the negative effects of sexually transmitted diseases on the birthrate) and the control of sexual behavior than their predecessors before the war. In the interwar period, Germany witnessed the triumph of what Alain Corbin calls "neo abolitionism, which combined abolitionist theory with the supposed need for health supervision."[11] Weimar feminists continued to criticize the sexual double standard inherent in the system of state-regulated prostitution. Yet they increasingly tried to discredit the institution by linking it to fears about the "nation's pollution" through the spread of STDs. By potentially stigmatizing diseased people, this strategy indeed represented a "bewildering ... combination of emancipatory and repressive ideas."[12] Because they tended to be preoccupied with socio-hygienic goals, German abolitionists supported the 1927 anti-VD law despite its repressive features.

Clearly, the RGBG was an ambiguous victory, as ambiguous as the politics of abolitionism had been from the outset—continually oscillating between liberal individualism, feminism, social reform, and conservative social purity concerns.[13] Stressing the negative aspects of the law, Gisela Bock has argued that it paved the way for economic exploitation and brutal persecution of prostitutes under National Socialism.[14] Yet this view ignores important improvements in prostitutes' overall situation after the passage of the anti-VD law. The following discussion of the effects of the 1927 prostitution reform in Bremen—with references to similar developments in Frankfurt and Leipzig—demonstrates that, despite its problems, the RGBG supported prostitutes' emancipation in significant ways. Most important, the new law helped generate novel forms of political self-organization among Weimar prostitutes.

Prostitutes, Civil Society, and the State in Bremen

The northern German city-state of Bremen offers an excellent case study for the history of Weimar prostitution policy. The Bremen arrangements served as a model for state-regulated prostitution elsewhere in the country. In the 1910s and 1920s, defenders of state regulation praised the hygienic provisions of the Bremen system and advocated their implementation at the national level. Similarly, critics often paid special attention to the shortcomings of police-controlled prostitution in the city in order to highlight the bankruptcy of regulationism. Because the Bremen model played such a prominent role in German controversies about the reform of prostitution policy, the history of prostitution there reflects issues and trends central to the national debate.

After 1878, the Bremen police confined prostitution to a single street in the city providing room for up to seventy-five prostitutes.[15] What became known nationally as the "Bremen System" of *Kasernierung*—the geographical isolation of prostitutes under close medical supervision—was distinguished from similar institutions elsewhere by its hygienic efficiency and by the absence of a brothel economy in the regulated area. Nevertheless, like state-regulated prostitution in other German cities, it subjected registered prostitutes to a catalogue of repressive rules regulating every detail of their daily lives.[16] The women had to obtain permission from the police if they wanted to leave the city or visit a museum, the theater, or the hospital. Strict prescriptions defined the kind of clothing they had to wear when outside the Helene Street area. Prostitutes were banned from certain public places and from using public transportation. Within the Helene Street complex, the women were not allowed to engage in social activities such as sharing common meals. The price the women in the Helene Street paid for a modicum of economic independence was the status of pariah.

From the perspective of the defenders of the system of police regulation, the Bremen model was especially attractive because of its thorough sanitary provisions. A police physician examined all registered prostitutes twice a week.[17] After 1905, the prostitutes had to supply their customers with prophylactics that they purchased from the city at wholesale prices—an unusual measure at a time when contraceptives were still banned in public under the penal code's obscenity clause.[18] Kasernierung as practiced in Bremen seemed to prove the socio-hygienic case for state regulation. In 1911, the city presented the "Bremen System" at the International Hygiene Exhibition in Dresden, stressing its sanitary efficiency.[19] Against the backdrop of the debate about an anti-VD law during the First World War, the influential German Society for the Suppression of Venereal Diseases (DGBG) formally endorsed the Bremen model and, in a petition to the *Reichstag*, recommended its adoption on a national scale.[20] Bremen's success in advertising its model of Kasernierung is also revealed by the fact that the brothels established by the German military command during the First World War (the so-called *Etappenbordelle*) were operated according to the "Bremen System."[21]

In the Weimar period, however, supporters of regulationism in Bremen and elsewhere increasingly came under public pressure to defend their views. In some states, abolitionism triumphed before the national anti-VD law became effective—for instance, Hamburg abolished police-controlled prostitution as early as 1921.[22] In Bremen, regulation endured until it became illegal in 1927, which was largely a result of the Social Democrats' absence from the state government between 1920 and 1928.[23] Due to the Bremen political elite's strong support of state regulated prostitution, abolitionism gained momentum only relatively late.[24] But by the mid-1920s, the Bremen model of regulation suffered from a serious loss of credibility and popular support. In June 1924, seventeen-year-old Elisabeth Kolomak, who had been arrested for solicitation and forced to undergo compulsory medical treatment, died in the municipal hospital as a result of diagnostic errors.[25] For more than three months during which her physical state continuously deteriorated, Kolomak was treated for syphilis with the chemotherapeutic Salvarsan, a medication whose negative side effects were still largely unexplored.[26] At the national as well as the local level, her death became a powerful symbol for the brutal nature of police-controlled prostitution. Nationwide attention to the case was heightened by publication, in the winter of 1926, of a diary based on Kolomak's experience. The author, who turned out to be the girl's mother, sharply criticized the Bremen morals police and blamed them for Elisabeth's death. Publication of the fictitious diary strengthened the position of abolitionists in the Reichstag, where the final draft of anti-VD legislation was being debated.[27]

In her analysis of Bremen feminists' reactions to the Kolomak incident, Elisabeth Meyer Renschhausen has stressed their feelings of solidarity with the lower-class woman, whom they saw as a symbol of the victimization of the whole female sex in a misogynist society. Meyer Renschhausen suggests that moral issues connected to prostitution gave rise to a "united front of women" transcending class and party differences.[28] This interpretation neglects the prejudices expressed by many middle-class female reformers in their statements about prostitutes. Closer examination of the Bremen parliamentary debates about the abolition of *Kasernierung* shows that leading women abolitionists ultimately aimed at eradicating the "social scourge" of prostitution in general, not just the system of state regulation. This goal implied that prostitutes had to be reintegrated into society by means of persuasion or, if necessary, by force. Thus, for instance, when in April 1926 the abolitionist and delegate of the German Democratic Party, Minna Bahnson, motioned to close down the Helene Street operation, she also demanded that "totally obstinate, depraved, and work-shy girls" be punished with prolonged prison sentences and confined to special workhouses.[29]

Bremen feminists reacted with hostility to prostitutes' first efforts at political self-organization. In the spring of 1926, more than fifty prostitutes petitioned the Bremen senate in defense of certain material protections included in the Helene Street system.[30] In their response to the petition, female abolitionists argued that those women unwilling to return to a respectable life should no longer enjoy the "loving protection of the state," which had misled them to think of their occupation as a proper middle-class (*gut buergerliche*) profession.[31] These remarks reveal the intolerant and paternalist attitude with which many abolitionists confronted prostitutes resisting schemes for social and moral reform. The Bremen parliamentary debate illustrates that prostitutes' interests were in many ways opposed to those of middle-class women. The abolitionists' class prejudices imposed strict limitations on the sense of a "bond of sisterhood" between the two groups. This conflict between feminists and prostitutes points to a division within Weimar civil society separating its "respectable" members from representatives of what may be called an "outcast civil society" radically challenging predominant notions of sexual morality and propriety. While Weimar feminists attacked the sexual double standard inherent in state-regulated prostitution, their attitude toward prostitutes remained highly ambivalent. To a certain extent, abolitionists could identify with prostitutes as *passive victims* of male oppression.[32] Ultimately, however, they were unable to accept prostitutes as *independent*, self-confident political *actors*. Feminists shared many of middle-class men's prejudices about the alleged lack of sexual morality in the lower classes.[33] But they had other motives, as well. As women, Weimar feminists had only recently gained equal political rights and broader access to the public sphere. This might have been one reason why they were especially concerned about distinguishing themselves from prostitutes—those other "public women" closely associated with misogynist images of female vice and corruption. Because the prostitute, as the "quintessential female figure of the urban scene" (Judith Walkowitz), could serve antifeminists as a prime example of the "polluting" impact of women on politics, middle-class feminists may have felt a special need to establish their moral superiority over prostitutes.[34] Seen from this perspective, feminists' support of prostitutes' exclusion from "respectable civil society" not only expressed certain class prejudices but can also be interpreted as part of their striving to legitimate themselves in a public sphere still dominated by men.[35]

Conflicts about the status of prostitutes became even more evident after the anti-VD law became effective in October 1927. In defending the reform, political organization among prostitutes soon took on a new intensity. In the context of heightened anxieties about social stability and public mores, negative attitudes surfaced in popular and official responses to the liberalization of prostitution policy introduced by the new law. On 4 November 1927, the "Bremen System" of state-regulated prostitution was abolished, and Helene Street was turned into a regular residential area.[36] Complaints about prostitutes' continuing presence in the street soon reached the authorities. Members of the Social Welfare Bureau (*Pflegeamt*) were largely unsuccessful in convincing the former inhabitants to assume a "respectable" lifestyle. About half of the registered prostitutes remained in their apartments and pursued their old profession, and two of them even acquired real estate on the street.[37] Efforts aiming at the social reintegration of the prostitutes failed miserably.[38] The RGBG, rather than providing a solution to the problem of prostitution, seemed to many to exacerbate it. Prostitution, formerly tolerated only within a single, closed-off street, now became a more conspicuous part of public life visible to everybody.

Strong opposition to the new legislation came from the police. Police officials emphasized that the RGBG "tied their hands" in the effort to suppress prostitution. The anti-VD law indeed imposed important restrictions on the police's ability to arrest women for street soliciting. A general clause stated that only those forms of solicitation violating "public mores and feelings of decency" constituted a criminal offense. Such a formulation was clearly open to interpretation, and the majority of Bremen court decisions rejected arrests made on these legal grounds.[39] The judges' liberal attitude, Bremen police officials complained, undermined the effective public control of prostitution.

Disagreements between the police and the courts about the new legal situation concerning prostitution were typical of other German states as well.[40] Thus in 1928 the state supreme court (Oberlandesgericht) of Saxony annulled numerous convictions of Leipzig prostitutes for street soliciting. The judges argued that a prostitute's solicitation of men in public—even if pursued in a conspicuous, sexually explicit manner (*"nach Dirnenart"*)—did not constitute a sufficient basis for an arrest because prostitution was now legal. Further proof (such as a bystander's complaint to the police) was needed to show that someone had actually been seriously offended by the woman's behavior. However, such complaints were notoriously rare; between 1927 and 1931, the Leipzig police received fewer than ten legal complaints from citizens about having been harassed by a streetwalker.[41] Like their Bremen colleagues, police officials in Leipzig sharply criticized the state supreme court's "lax" interpretation of the new law and proposed to ban "unruly" prostitutes from the city. Not everywhere in Germany did judges subscribe to the Saxon court's liberal position toward prostitution.[42] Nevertheless, the examples of Bremen and Leipzig show that after 1927 the law provided an important new means for prostitutes to defend themselves against the police.

These cases also shed light on certain conflicts between liberal-minded courts and the police over the issue of the state's role in the public sphere. By emphasizing that individual citizens rather than policemen should decide whether a prostitute's behavior offended public morals, the Saxon supreme court implicitly supported a liberal concept of the public sphere substantially restricting the state's authority to intervene in this matter. This interpretation contrasted sharply with the police's extensive and often arbitrary powers under regulationism. The introduction of new controls on police constituted a legal gain not only for prostitutes but for Weimar civil society in general. Among representatives of the police, concern about their loss of authority led to a strong reaction against the 1927 reform of prostitution policy.

Crucial to the conservative backlash against the reform was the growth of a radical *outcast civil society* among prostitutes after 1927. In Bremen, former registered prostitutes displayed a novel self-confidence vis-à-vis the state reflected in the women's decision to hire a lawyer for the protection of their newly won rights against police transgressions. A report of the health bureau written in January 1932 disapprovingly mentioned that women suspected of prostitution now had their own "legal defense association."[43] Prostitutes' effort to protect their rights collectively by sharing a legal counsel was a new form of political organization causing considerable unease and insecurity among Bremen bureaucrats. In 1931 the police faced several lawsuits for illegal arrests brought against them by the women's lawyer, and police officials expressed great concern that the court might decide in the prostitutes' favor.[44] The growing political awareness among prostitutes was not a development unique to Bremen. In March 1931, the Saxon Ministry of Labor and Welfare (*Sächsisches Arbeits- und Wohlfahrtsministerium*) also reported efforts among prostitutes to form associations in defense of their rights.[45] In September 1927, Frankfurt prostitutes organized picket lines and protested the health office's order that they resume their regular health checks at the municipal hospital.[46] After consultations with their lawyer, the women declared that they were determined to oppose the measure, which in their eyes constituted an "illegal continuation of police control." They believed that "the new law with its provisions for compulsory medical treatment is only applicable to diseased prostitutes refusing to consult a physician" and emphasized their right to a doctor of their own choice.[47] The prostitutes' collective protest forced the health office to issue a statement defending its policy and led to a public debate about the issue. Even if ultimately most of the women accepted the health checks' legality, their organization had put considerable pressure on Frankfurt officials.

It is difficult to reconstruct prostitutes' own views of the anti-VD law's impact on their lives. A collection of thirty-five interviews with former brothel inmates conducted in 1928 offers certain limited glimpses at their attitudes.[48] Among the ten women expressing opinions about the new system, three rejected it mainly, because they feared abolition would lead to increased competition with nonprofessionals. Seven, however, considered the law an important improvement of their situation. Thus, Ella Ziegler from Karlsruhe declared that she was "happy about the new law" because it opened up the possibility of returning to a normal life.[49] Ziegler stressed that she wished to "live again like a human being, not an animal."[50] Frieda Maurer, too, supported the reform because it would end the social isolation of prostitutes, who now "counted again as human beings instead of being locked away."[51] Most of the women welcomed the new law because it ended their dependency on the brothel. Not all of them took a remorseful position towards their profession. For instance, thirty-four-year-old Ida Schuesser told the interviewer that she was in favor of the law because "afterwards, one did not need to become the embodiment of virtue and still could lead a more humane and sophisticated life."[52] These examples show that at least a certain group of prostitutes supported the RGBG because it offered them new rights and freed them from the inhumane elements of regulationism.

This aspect of the new law deserves special attention. While it is true that the anti-VD law included highly problematic provisions infringing on the personal freedom of people infected with sexually transmitted diseases, it also had important liberalizing implications for prostitution policy. For the first time, prostitutes enjoyed a range of civil liberties enabling them to challenge the power of the police over their lives. Though still subjected to certain restrictions, such as the required regular health checks, they no longer were fair game for the vice squad. Interpretations of the RGBG stressing its repressive character often fail to adequately acknowledge the crucial improvements in prostitutes' civil status after 1927.[53] The anti-VD law broke with the traditional practice of branding prostitutes as social outcasts living in an essentially extra-legal sphere. This was a vital precondition for the growth of a civil society among prostitutes during the final years of the Weimar Republic. However, the radicalism of this *outcast* civil society not only challenged police authority but also threatened middle-class notions of sexual morality often shared by members of *respectable* civil society. Prostitutes thus remained relatively isolated politically and encountered widespread hostility in their efforts at self-organization. Ultimately, prostitutes' increasing politicization was one of the main factors prompting demands for a reversal of the 1927 prostitution reform.

"A Symbol of Crisis"

Against the backdrop of the world economic crisis, prostitution became an even more visible, pressing problem in Bremen. By 1933, about 27 percent of the work force was unemployed.[54] In the early 1930s, the public debate about prostitution assumed increasingly shrill overtones. Conservatives now saw an opportunity to attack the liberalization of prostitution policy and called for a strengthening of police powers in order to "clean up the streets." During the Bremen parliamentary elections of November 1930, the fight against prostitution became a crucial issue. Conservative politicians such as the female delegate of the German People's Party, Dr. Luerssen, demanded harsh repression of street soliciting "in the interest of the youth."[55] While Social Democratic and liberal women reformers defended the RGBG against conservative critiques, they accused the police of failing to consistently enforce its provisions in order to heighten public anxieties.[56] Whether this accusation was justified, the police clearly were involved in lobbying for new legislation to counteract the more liberal course of prostitution policy since 1927. In response to increasing public demands for harsher measures against street soliciting, the Bremen parliament in 1931 approved a repressive new custody law. Undermining the RGBG, the law allowed the police to detain prostitutes for up to twenty-four hours and subject them to medical exams at the health bureau.[57] During the first six months after the enactment of the new law alone, 186 women arrested for street soliciting had to undergo compulsory health checks.[58] Prostitutes did not accept this return to regulationist practices without protest. Not only did they physically resist the police, but they continued to defend their legal rights with the help of a lawyer.[59]

In the early 1930s, attacks on the 1927 law increased substantially. Thus, in June 1932 the National Women's Advisory Council (Reichsfrauenbeirat) of the Catholic Center Party petitioned the Minister of the Interior (*Reichsinnenminister*) to reintroduce the criminal persecution of *any* kind of street soliciting, a demand subsequently supported by the Department of Youth of the Rhine Province and by the Prussian State Council.[60] In their petition, the Catholic women's leadership claimed that prostitution had increased dramatically not only because of the impoverishment of large parts of the population but also due to the courts' "fatefully lenient" interpretation of paragraph 16 RGBG which had made police intervention against prostitutes' "impertinent demeanor" effectively impossible. Under the pressures of the economic crisis and the social disruptions it created, tolerance for prostitutes and other stigmatized groups rapidly eroded. National Socialists appealed to widespread fears of Weimar's alleged "moral decline" when they demanded a radical "national renewal" hostile to the democratic values and institutions of the Weimar Republic.[61] In Bremen, prostitution played an important role in Nazi propaganda as a symbol of the existing political system's weakness and corruption. During September 1931, the *Bremer Nationalsozialistische Zeitung* dedicated a series of articles to the "vice problem" and its allegedly devastating effect on the younger generation's sense of morality.[62] In its campaign for a drastic "cleansing" of prostitutes from the city, the paper claimed support from officials and citizens' associations. Liberal prostitution policies ultimately provided a powerful polemical instrument to those promoting the resurgence of a strong authoritarian state—like that established by the Nazis in 1933.

Conclusion

The growth of an outcast civil society among Weimar prostitutes throws new light on the nature of Weimar social policy. Studies stressing exclusively continuities from the welfare policies of the 1920s to Nazi racism tend to ignore the anti-VD law's crucial role in mobilizing prostitutes. Similarly, an analysis inspired by Michel Foucault's critique of the modern welfare state as simply a locus for the deployment of repressive forms of "bio-power" risks missing the improvements in prostitutes' civil status through Weimar social reforms. Prostitutes' efforts at political self organization cannot be adequately captured within Foucault's negative conception of the institutions of civil society, which he unambiguously interprets as integral components of the power mechanisms of normalization.[63]

While prostitutes gained important new liberties during the 1920s, the broad reaction against their movement also illuminates certain weaknesses of Weimar democracy. It points especially to the problematic exclusion of outcast groups from respectable civil society and to the restrictive effects this exclusion had on the development of a democratic public sphere in the Weimar period. The abolition of state regulation of prostitution had not only emancipated prostitutes from arbitrary police powers but at the same time had limited police authority in the public sphere in a way generally conducive to the stability of a democratic political life. Conservative calls for the strict suppression of street soliciting, gaining momentum in the early 1930s, thus constituted more than an attack on prostitutes' rights: arguably, they also helped pave the way for the return of the state's role as a repressive regulator of public life after 1933. After the Nazi takeover, the liberalization of prostitution policy was fundamentally reversed.[64]

The study of Weimar attitudes toward prostitution illuminates certain comparative issues in the history of modern feminism. Using abolitionism as a case in point, Richard Evans has claimed that the German women's movement lacked the liberal-individualist orientation characteristic of its British counterpart.[65] Early twentieth-century German abolitionists were exceptional in their acceptance of illiberal political ideas such as eugenics and in their support for state interventionism: "Concern for the dignity of the individual woman had been replaced by concern for the future of the race. Suspicion of the state had yielded to a readiness to see in it the highest expression of the unity of the people."[66] Such a dichotomous contrast between German feminists' outlook and the liberal-individualist goals of feminist movements elsewhere is problematic. As recent scholarship on the relationship between women's movements and welfare-state formation in the early twentieth century shows, feminists in all major western countries increasingly used the state to further their political goals.[67] Similarly, the shift toward social hygiene in debates about prostitution and the growing obsession with sexually transmitted diseases as "racial poisons" constituted international trends rather than an exclusively German development.[68] Evans's characterization of abolitionism outside Germany as based on liberal-individualist principles also fails to capture the movement's ambivalent impact on the lives of prostitutes. In countries like England and the United States, where abolitionists were most successful in fighting state-controlled prostitution, prostitutes often faced increased pressures after the abolitionist victory had been won. As Judith Walkowitz has pointed out, British abolitionism ultimately gave way to a repressive campaign for social purity integrating many former abolitionists. Prostitutes' lives became more marginalized and precarious.[69] Seen from this comparative perspective, German abolitionists' turn towards socio-hygienic aims remains worrisome but hardly exceptional.

Notes

For their helpful comments on various versions of this essay, I would like to thank Geoff Eley, Donna Harsch, Mary Lindemann, Fritz Ringer, Frank Trentmann, and especially Bill Scheuerman.

1. In this essay, "civil society" refers to a sphere of autonomous political activity that may be—and often is—directed at the state but remains based on forms of political association and self-organization outside the state apparatus. See Jean L. Cohen and Andrew Areto, *Civil Society and Political Theory* (Cambridge, MA, 1992).

2. Paradigmatic for subsequent scholarship was Jürgen Habermas, *The Structural Transformation of the Public Sphere: An Inquiry into a Category of Bourgeois Society* (Cambridge, MA, 1991), which chronicles the rise of a (male) "bourgeois public sphere." For a richer picture and analysis of civil society, see Cohen and Arato, *Civil Society and Political Theory*.

3. See, e.g., Paul Weindling, *Health, Race and German Politics between National Unification and Nazism, 1870–1945* (Cambridge, 1993). For a critique of an exclusive focus on continuities, see Atina Grossmann, *Reforming Sex: The German Movement for Birth Control and Abortion Reform, 1920–1950* (Oxford, 1995), esp. vi–viii.

4. See Weindling, *Health, Race and German Politics*, 357–59; and Cornelie Usborne, *The Politics of the Body in Weimar Germany: Women's Reproductive Rights and Duties* (Ann Arbor, 1992), 109–12.

5. The RGBG took effect on 1 October 1927. See *Reichsgesetzblatt*, part I (Berlin, 1927): 61–63.

6. The regulations varied greatly from one German city to another. For the impact of regulationism on prostitutes' lives, see Lynn Abrams, "Prostitutes in Imperial Germany, 1870–1918: Working Girls or Social Outcasts?," in *The German Underworld: Deviants and Outcasts in German History*, ed. Richard J. Evans (London, 1988), 189–209; see also Richard Evans, "Prostitution, State and Society in Imperial Germany," *Past & Present*, no. 70 (1976): 106–29.

7. For a discussion of the Scandinavian laws, see Alfred Blaschko, "Prostitution," in *Handwörterbuch der Staatswissenschaften*, vol. 6 (Jena, 1910): 1245–46; the Danish anti-VD law is reprinted in Abraham Flexner, *Prostitution in Europe* (New York, 1914), 445–52; for similar but more limited legislative developments in the U.S., see Allan M. Brandt, *No Magic Bullet: A Social History of Venereal Disease in the United States since 1880* (New York, 1987), esp. 143–44.

8. According to paragraph 5 of the RGBG, the criminal persecution of persons who had infected others with STDs was possible only if the damaged party filed a claim.

9. This so-called *Kirchturmparagraph* ("church-tower paragraph"; paragraph 16.4 of the RGBG) constituted a concession to the conservative parties and was highly controversial among liberals and Social Democrats. See, for instance, Marie Elisabeth Lüders, "Befreiung von Krankheit und Lüge," in *Die Frau* 34 (1927), 304.

10. For a contemporary account, see Anna Pappritz, "Die abolitionistische Föderation," in *Einführung in das Studium der Prostitutionsfrage*, ed. Anna Pappritz (Leipzig, 1919), 220–60; see also Evans, "Prostitution, State and Society"; and idem, *The Feminist Movement in Germany, 1894–1933* (London, 1976); see also the local study of the Hanover abolitionist movement by Nancy R. Reagin, *A German Women's Movement: Class and Gender in Hanover, 1880–1933* (Chapel Hill, 1995), 147–72; and idem, "'A True Woman Can Take Care of Herself': The Debate over Prostitution in Hanover, 1906," *Central European History* 24, no. 4 (1991): 347–80.

11. Similar trends existed in France during this period. Unlike their German counterparts, French neo-abolitionists were unsuccessful in substituting hygienic control for regulationism. See Alain Corbin, *Women for Hire: Prostitution and Sexuality in France after 1850* (Cambridge, MA, 1990), 342.

12. Ann Taylor Allen, "Feminism, Venereal Disease, and the State in Germany, 1890–1918," *Journal for the History of Sexuality* 4, no. 1 (1993): 29. See also Evans, *Feminist Movement*, 162–66.

13. See Corbin, *Women for Hire*, 216–20. Compare also Judith R. Walkowitz, *Prostitution and Victorian Society: Women, Class, and the State* (Cambridge, 1991), 246–52; and idem, "Male Vice and Female Virtue: Feminism and the Politics of Prostitution in Nineteenth-Century Britain," in *Powers of Desire: The Politics of Sexuality*, ed. Ann Snitow, Christine Stansell, and Sharon Thompson (New York, 1983), 419–38.

14. See Bock, "'Keine Arbeitskräfte in diesem Sinne': Prostituierte im Nazi-Staat," in *"Wir sind Frauen wie andere auch!" Prostituierte und ihre Kämpfe*, ed. Pieke Biermann (Reinbek, 1980), 70–106. I refer here to Bock's interpretation that "[o]n the basis of the 1927 law, the state under National Socialism openly and systematically constituted itself as a pimp: profiteer of women's labor and collector of their wages" (p. 86, my translation).

15. See Dr. Stachow, "Die Kontrollstrasse in Bremen," *Zeitschrift für Bekämpfung der Geschlechtskrankheiten*, special ed. (Leipzig, 1905): 77–87; and Hermann Tjaden, *Geschlechtskrankheiten und Prostitution in Bremen und ihre Bekämpfung* (Bremen, 1922). See also Monika Mohrmann, "Staatlich reglementierte Prostitution," in *Bremer Frauen in der Weimarer Republik, 1919–1933*, ed. Staatsarchiv Bremen (Bremen 1991), 129–53.

16. For copies of the registration form and the police regulations, see Staatsarchiv Bremen (StAB) 4,21-414.

17. See Stachow, "Die Kontrollstrasse," 80–81.

18. Section 3 of paragraph 184 banned the advertisement and display of contraceptives. See Usborne, *Politics of the Body*, 11. The legalization of advertising for contraceptives came only with the 1927 anti-VD law.

19. For official arguments in favor of the Bremen system, cf. the various remarks by Hermann Tjaden in *Verhandlungen der Sachverständigenkommission der Deutschen Gesellschaft zur Bekämpfung der Geschlechtskrankheiten*, ed. by Deutsche Gesellschaft zur Bekämpfung der Geschlechtskrankheiten (Leipzig, 1916), 11–72. See also Tjaden, *Geschlechtskrankheiten und Prostitution*.

20. See Tjaden, *Geschlechtskrankheiten und Prostitution*, 17.

21. For a criticism of this practice, see Stalmann, "Das Bremer System," *Mitteilungen des Schleswig-Holsteinischen Provinzialvereins zur Hebung der öffentlichen Sittlichkeit* 3, no. 3 (1916).

22. See Gaby Zürn, "'A. ist Prostituiertentyp:' Zur Ausgrenzung und Vernichtung von moralisch nicht-angepassten Frauen," in *Verachtet—Verfolgt—Vernichtet: Zu den vergessenen Opfern des NS-Regimes*, ed. Projektgruppe für die vergessenen Opfer des NS-Regimes (Hamburg, 1988), 130–132.

23. For a discussion of Bremen party politics during the Weimar Republic, see Inge Marssolek and Rene Ott, *Bremen im Dritten Reich: Anpassung, Widerstand, Verfolgung* (Bremen, 1986), 41–57.

24. For the history of Bremen abolitionism, see Elisabeth Meyer-Renschhausen, "The Bremen Morality Scandal," in *When Biology Became Destiny: Women in Weimar and Nazi Germany*, ed. Renate Bridenthal, Atina Grossmann, and Marion Kaplan (New York, 1984), 87–108; and Meyer-Renschhausen, *Weibliche Kultur und soziale Arbeit: Eine Geschichte der Frauenbewegung am Beispiel Bremens, 1810–1927* (Cologne, 1989), 271–372.

25. Official reactions to the public controversy about this case are documented in StAB 4,21-422. For the repercussions of the Kolomak case, see Meyer-Renschhausen, "The Bremen Morality Scandal."

26. Salvarsan was invented in 1909; it replaced older treatments of syphilis with mercury and hot vapor baths. See Brandt, *No Magic Bullet*, 40.

27. For the effect of the book on debates in the Reichstag, see *Verhandlungen des Deutschen Reichstags*, vol. 391 (Berlin 1927), 8683.

28. Meyer-Renschhausen, "The Bremen Morality Scandal," 105.

29. *Verhandlungen der bremischen Bürgerschaft* (Bremen, 1926), 154; 215 (my translation). Bahnson's proposal was representative of the views of leading Weimar feminists who campaigned for a national custody law (*Bewahrungsgesetz*) aiming at the control of prostitutes and other people allegedly unable "to lead an ordered and responsible life." See, e.g., Anna Pappritz, "Das Bewahrungsgesetz," in *Die Frau* 32 (1925): 270–272.

30. The wording of the prostitutes' parliamentary motion seems to have been lost. The original motion is contained in neither the protocols of the Bremen parliament nor in the related archival files I examined. The prostitutes' specific claims can be reconstructed indirectly from the speeches of several parliamentarians. See also Meyer-Renschhausen, "The Bremen Morality Scandal," 108, n. 54.

31. *Verhandlungen der bremischen Bürgerschaft* (Bremen, 1926), 219.

32. For a discussion of the political limitations of this approach, see Judith Walkowitz, "Male Vice and Female Virtue."

33. See, e.g., Klara Thorbecke, "Über den Sittlichkeitsbegriff in der sozialen Unterschicht," in *Die Frau* 31 (1924): 137–43.

34. See Walkowitz, *City of Dreadful Delight: Narratives of Sexual Danger in Late-Victorian London* (Chicago, 1992), esp. 21–24.

35. On the limitations of women's emancipation in the Weimar period, see Renate Bridenthal and Claudia Koonz, "Beyond *Kinder, Küche, Kirche*: Weimar Women in Politics and Work," in Bridenthal et al., *When Biology Became Destiny*, 33–65.
36. See the street file StAB 3-S.8b-Helenenstrasse. See also the administrative account of the implementation of the RGBG in Bremen (c. 1930) in: StAB 4,130/1-R.I.1.-17.
37. See the report of the State of Bremen Health Bureau to the senate of January 1932, in: StAB 4,130/1-R.I.1.-17.
38. See the 30 January 1929 report of the Social Welfare Department for the years 1927 and 1928 in: StAB 4,130/1-R.I.3.-5.
39. See the report of the Bremen head of police of 2 November 1928 in: StAB 4,130/1-R.I.1.-17.
40. See Leopold Schäfer, "Prostitution und Rechtsprechung," in *Mitteilungen der Deutschen Gesellschaft zur Bekämpfung der Geschlechtskrankheiten* (hereafter: *Mitteilungen DGBG*) 27 (1929): 412–31.
41. See the report of the Leipzig police official G. Heiland at a 1931 conference about the effects of the anti-VD law on prostitution: "Sachverständigenkonferenz am Mittwoch, den 15. April 1931 in Berlin: Das Straßenbild nach Inkrafttreten des RGBG," in *Mitteilungen DGBG* 24 (1931), esp. 80–81.
42. For instance, the conservative interpretation of paragraph 16 of RGBG through the Bavarian supreme court sharply contrasted with the Saxon ruling. See Schäfer, "Prostitution und Rechtsprechung," esp. 414–15.
43. The correspondence between the police and the prostitutes' lawyer is documented in StAB 4,130/1-R.I.1.-24. See also the report of the health bureau to the senate in January 1932 mentioning the "legal defense association," in: StAB 4,130/1-R.I.1.-17.
44. See the report of police official Bollmann at a meeting at the Bremen health bureau on 28 August 1931, in: StAB 4,130/1-R.I.1.-24.
45. The Saxon report is mentioned in a letter of the Bremen health bureau to the senate of January 1932, in: StAB 4,130/1-R.I.1.-17. For the widespread reaction among the German public against prostitutes' increased self-assurance after 1927, see Bock, "'Keine Arbeitskräfte in diesem Sinne,'" 76–77.
46. For a discussion of the prostitutes' protests, see "Gesundheitskontrolle der Prostitution," *Volksstimme: Organ der Sozialdemokratie für Südwestdeutschland* 38, no. 230 (1 October 1927); "Die Untersuchung der Prostituierten," *Volksstimme* 38, no. 233 (5 October 1927); "Die von der Straße leben," *Volksstimme* 39, no. 28 (2 February 1928); "Polizei und Prostituierte," *Arbeiterzeitung* 4, no. 229 (30 September 1927); and "Polizei und Prostituierte," *Arbeiterzeitung* 4, no. 231 (3 October 1927).
47. Cited in "Gesundheitskontrolle der Prostituierten," *Volksstimme* 38, no. 230 (1 October 1927), my translation.
48. See Elga Kern, *Wie sie dazu kamen: 35 Lebensfragmente bordellierter Mädchen nach Untersuchungen in badischen Bordellen* (Munich, 1928). The women came from different German cities and regions.
49. I am using Kern's *changed* names of the women interviewed; all translations in this paragraph are my own.
50. Ibid., 95.
51. Ibid., 100.
52. Ibid., 109.
53. An example of an exclusively negative evaluation of the new law is Bock, "'Keine Arbeitskräfte in diesem Sinne.'"

54. Marssolek and Ott, *Bremen im Dritten Reich*, 30–31.

55. *Bremer Nachrichten*, 14 November 1930, my translation. The debate is also documented in: StAB 4.130/1-R.I.1.-24.

56. See the account of a discussion about the RGBG at a meeting of the Bremen branch of the League for the Protection of Motherhood and Sex Reform (*Bund für Mutterschutz und Sexualreform*) in *Bremer Volkszeitung*, 15 December 1930.

57. See *Gesetzblatt der Freien Hansestadt Bremen* 36 (1931): 189. The police administration had worked on blueprints of this law since 1930. See StAB 4,130/1-R.I.1.-24.

58. See the report of the health bureau to the Bremen senate, January 1932, in: StAB 4,130/1-R.I.1.-17.

59. For correspondence between the lawyer representing a group of prostitutes and the police, see StAB 4,130/1-R.I.1.-24.

60. See "Der Widerstand gegen das Gesetz zur Bekämpfung der Geschlechtskrankheiten," *Der Abolitionist: Organ des Bundes für Frauen- und Jugendschutz (Deutscher Zweig der Internationalen Abolitionistischen Föderation)* 31, no. 5 (1 September 1932): 67–69; see also Dorothea Karsten, "Prostitution und Straßenbild: Neue Gesetzliche Bestimmungen," *Freie Wohlfahrtspflege* 7 (1932): 310–15.

61. For a discussion of the negative effects of the "moral agenda" on Weimar democracy's stability, see Richard Bessel, *Germany after the First World War* (Oxford, 1993), 220–53.

62. See *Bremer Nationalsozialistische Zeitung*, 10–15 September 1931, in: StAB 4,130/1-R.I.1.-24.

63. See Michel Foucault, *Discipline and Punish: The Birth of the Prison* (New York, 1977), esp. 222–24; and idem, *The History of Sexuality*, vol. 1, *An Introduction* (New York, 1980). For a critique of Foucault's somewhat one-dimensional view of civil society, see Cohen and Arato, *Civil Society and Political Theory*, 255–98.

64. For National Socialist attitudes toward prostitution, see Wolfgang Ayaß, *"Asoziale" im Nationalsozialismus* (Stuttgart, 1995), esp. 184–96.

65. See Evans, *Feminist Movement*, esp. 162–66.

66. Ibid., 163.

67. See Seth Koven and Sonya Michel, "Womanly Duties: Maternalist Politics and the Origins of the Welfare State in France, Germany, Great Britain, and the United States," *American Historical Review* 95 (1990): 1076–108; see also Allen, "Feminism, Venereal Disease, and the State."

68. For France, see Corbin, *Women for Hire*, esp. 262–75; for the United States, see Ruth Rosen, *The Lost Sisterhood: Prostitution in America, 1900–1918* (Baltimore, 1982). For similar developments in Britain, see Frank Mort, *Dangerous Sexualities: Medico-Moral Politics in England since 1830* (London, 1987), esp. 179–83.

69. See Walkowitz, *Prostitution and Victorian Society*. Rosen offers a similar analysis of the American situation in *Lost Sisterhood*.

PART V

POLITICAL CULTURE AND
SOCIAL CITIZENSHIP

12

Oligarchs, Liberals, and *Mittelstand*

Defining Civil Society in Hamburg, 1858–1862

Madeleine Hurd

Only a few years after the unification of Germany, German liberals found themselves embattled, their program for a just society attacked. They had sought to create a citizenry of formally equal males, united in education, culture, and political maturity, well able to debate and direct the actions of a neutral state. This polity, they complained, was being destroyed by corporatist factions working to divide Germany's citizens into state-dependent interest groups. The liberals' enemies were legion. In 1874, a Hamburg editor decried the "ultramontane" who served the "overweening priest class"; the socialists' "Evangelium … grounded specifically on the egoism of the workers"; and the "agrarian politicians," with their one-sided consideration of the farming estate. Finally, and perhaps most worryingly, there were the adherents of "artisanal politics"—the petite bourgeoisie, or *Mittelstand*—who were "caught up in one-sided interests" which were unacceptable at a time when the empire was beset by particularist demands from every side.[1]

The image of a minority of liberals fighting a rising tide of economic and political protectionism, a "flight from freedom" spearheaded by a frightened petite bourgeoisie, has become a standard in Germany history.[2] It presents, perhaps, an oversimplified view of the conflict between liberal and Mittelständlich social groups and worldviews. Their relationship was, I argue, more complex. This can be seen in mid-century Hamburg, where liberals and Mittelstand were both allies and competitors. They collaborated in an attempt to unseat Hamburg's mercantile oligarchy. But they disagreed on means; and herein lay a fundamental political division. The liberals appealed to (what they conceived of as) an individualized electorate; their most trusted weapon was the pressure of reasonable public opinion. The anti-oligarchic Mittelstand relied, instead, on the economic power and group ethos of petite bourgeois estates. The economic clout of Hamburg's mercantile families was, they argued, best countered by the mobilization of popular corporatist groups. Liberals sought to divide economic, state, and political power; representatives of the Mittelstand saw them as inextricably mixed.

These disagreements reflected very different worldviews. Hamburg's liberals—a loosely defined group, united primarily by attitude—sought to establish a political system that, in its reality and norms, resembled what Jürgen Habermas has termed the "bourgeois public sphere." In Hamburg, the public sphere consisted of a male, middle-class associational world, complemented by newspapers, pamphlets, and public speech. Its norms presupposed an ongoing, public discussion between educated males able to evaluate arguments purely on their logical merit. This public sphere, which would mobilize public opinion on behalf of rational consensus, was to replace the oligarchy's privileged, personalized state. The new, liberal government would be accountable, transparent, and neutral.[3]

It would also be libertarian. The state would cease its interference in the economy; and it would withdraw the legal privileges that allowed sub-state corporations to pervert economic and political life. The free market would end the privileges that created local monopolies, guilds, and tariff-protected manufactures. These sub-state corporations robbed men of their personal autonomy, diminished prosperity, and harmed the public. They also impeded political debate. Guild members could bring nothing useful to politics, for they could not divide their economic and political personae. The state's disengagement from civil society would free the latter for the achievement of personal and general prosperity, while delivering political life to the impersonal play of disinterested public debate.[4]

State-financed public education was the one exception to the liberals' libertarian ideal. Rational debate required a general understanding of the "natural laws" of science, economy, and society, while shared knowledge of the nation's high culture would further the abolition of particularist interest. Secular primary schools—and their sisters, the educational voluntary associations—freed men politically. They taught their pupils to penetrate the lies of the tyrant, the obfuscating superstitions of the church, and the simplistic teachings of communism. The individual was freed from state and corporation in his economic life; education gave him mental autonomy.[5]

Not everyone shared these norms. Hamburg's plutocratic elites questioned the division of economic and political identities: those who maintained a city's economy deserved a weightier political voice. Economic and political responsibility, they felt, were linked. Members of the Mittelstand—small producers and skilled workers, current and ex-guild members—were similarly uneasy about the proposed division between economy and politics. They did not reject the idea of the public sphere. Like the liberals, they used newspapers, public speech and assembly to mobilize public opinion; like them, they preferred a transparent and neutral state to political secretiveness, elite privilege, and patronage. They joined the liberals in a concerted attack on the local mercantile elite. But there was one part of the liberal vision with which they could not be reconciled. Many small producers and skilled workers were die-hard opponents of the liberal ideal of an atomized economic order; they held corporatist organizations to be essential to a functioning democracy.

Representatives of Hamburg's Mittelstand rejected the liberals' distinction between the political and the economic citizen. Political and economic power, public sphere and civil society, could not be so easily disengaged. Free trade and the free labor market would, they argued, destroy the independent producers and, hence, individual integrity. How could one reconcile the despairing, impoverished wage slave with the liberals' autonomous political citizen, the rational and independent public debater? Not education, but independent work, was the key to political citizenship. The mature, moral political citizen was created not through educational leisure but through independent, skilled work. A man's pride in his trade, his economic autonomy and "estate honor," were essential sources of public morality. Hence the need for guilds; for guilds alone guaranteed the transition from dependent wage worker to independent producer, allowing the worker become the self-reliant neighbor and family father essential to civil society and state.

Liberals refused to acknowledge these arguments. By the 1870s, indeed, the Hamburg liberals' response was to lump guild-friendly Mittelstand with Lassalleans and pro-tariff agrarians: all, according to liberal rhetoric, merely chased state privileges, in an orgy of self-indulgent egoism. But this moralistic rejection of Mittelstand claims marked the end of a long tradition of liberal-Mittelstand cooperation. During the 1840s and 1850s, liberals had seen the Mittelstand as their natural allies against an arbitrary, oligarchic state. In Hamburg, they had joined the Mittelstand in fighting the local Senators, the self-recruiting representatives of the mercantile patriciate.

Fighting Hamburg's Oligarchic Senate

Hamburg's grand-bourgeois Senators had long dominated city politics. They both initiated and enforced laws; they controlled the budget, the police, the justice system, and Hamburg's chief administrators, the so-called notables. The rest of Hamburg's citizenry was relegated to the assemblies of "Propertied *Bürger*" (*Erbgessessene Bürgerschaft*)—the voice of Hamburg's property-owning small businessmen, skilled workers, petite bourgeoisie and professionals. Bürger assemblies could only approve or dismiss Senatorial initiatives. If they dismissed an initiative, a combined Senate-Bürger commission was assigned the task of deliberating the matter. Such commissions were weighted—as was the entire system—in favor of the Senate. The Bürger could do little more than advise.[6]

The Senators' high social position made them difficult to challenge. According to city bureaucrat Julius Eckardt, members of the mercantile patriciate were linked not only by intermarriage and business ties but by shared loyalties deriving from common educational background, morality, and "special customs and ways." Senators were aware of their privileges within and duties to the Hanseatic city. When it came time to elect representatives to trans-German parliaments (in 1848 and 1867), Hamburg Bürger sent merchants; for it was upon the merchants, conservatives argued, that Hamburg's prosperity and prestige depended. According to Eckardt, their collective consciousness of service to the "father city" gave this group a sense of being "born to rule"; others were second-class "co-citizens." Or, as a satirist in the liberal newspaper *Reform* put it in 1857, "I've often heard merchants praise themselves: we alone are capable of governing, only the merchant understands administration, how to handle money, to pass laws."[7]

This self-importance appeared in the Senate's handling of the democratic constitution submitted by Hamburg's 1849 Constituent Assembly. Senators objected to the constitution because, as they put it, insufficient representation was given those interests upon which the city's well-being depended. Senators argued, accordingly, that the constitution was decisively opposed by an important and influential part of the population. This part might be numerically inferior, but it was "certainly of greater weight." Consideration for the public weal, the writers concluded, was the Senate's primary moral duty; it outweighed the Senate's obligation to honor its promises to Hamburg's Constituent Assembly.[8]

The Senators' patriarchal view was roundly condemned by the Constituent Assembly's liberals. The Senate, they answered, seemed to consider Hamburg citizens "underage children, whose actions had to be controlled according to the good-will of a strict father." They advocated, as an alternative, the independent voter with "an open ear for the well-meaning voice of experience and [who] weighs every careful warning with great care, but who in the end—fully conscious that he himself must answer for the consequences—bases his decision upon the results of his own deliberation."[9]

In 1849, the liberals lost. The Senate insisted on compromises and, finally, called in Prussian reinforcements. In 1858, however, the liberalization of Prussian politics gave Hamburg's Bürger a new chance. In January 1858, the Propertied Bürger met and demanded constitutional reform. The Senate was forced to establish a joint commission to determine the election modus of a new, constituent City Council (*Bürgershaft*). The commission's proposal was formally accepted by assemblies of Hamburg's Propertied Bürger, which thereby formally dissolved themselves. Elections were held; the resultant Constituent City Council had the task of negotiating a new, permanent constitution with the Senate. None of this occurred without strife, much of which focussed on the liberals' visions of a new social and political system. The Senate remained resistant to a widened franchise; while the liberals' attempts to reshuffle and recombine Hamburg citizens created discontent among the liberals' Mittelständlich allies.

The Liberal Vision of Society

The liberals' vision of the proper Hamburg society was evident in the laws they advocated within the Constituent City Council, convened in November 1859. It is worth jumping ahead, briefly, to the laws and issues promoted by the Constituent Council's liberals, for these demonstrate liberal priorities. The new council had a strong liberal minority. It at once set out to promote the liberal vision of a citizenry guided not by a well-meaning patriciate, nor by group allegiance, but by individualized, educated reason. Council liberals sought to mobilize voters for a new, liberal Hamburg. To do this, they exploited Hamburg's evolving public sphere. They could call on organizations such as the Association for the Education of Workers, the Association of Young Teachers, the Citizens' Club, the Society for the Promotion of Freedom of Conscience, and a variety of free-trade organizations. Associational activities were publicized by left-wing newspapers. These faithfully reproduced meeting minutes and speeches, well-spiced by editorials, commentaries, and letters to the editor. The liberals used these resources to promote their ideal of the self-reliant, mature, and autonomous Hamburg citizen. In the process, they fought to separate state, religion, and economy—the public and civil spheres of citizenship.

Religious freedom was a liberal priority. In Hamburg, only Christians enjoyed full civil rights, while Lutherans were often granted additional, informal state favors. Liberals sought to erase this state-sponsored social divide. In early 1859, City Council liberals registered strong opposition to a Senatorial proposal that the city fund renovation of the Lutheran church St. Nicolai. This use of state funds, liberals argued in newspapers, the Citizens' Club, and the City Council, meant state endorsement of a specific religious group. Would the government allocate proportionate monies to Catholic churches and to synagogues? Let the Nicolai be repaired by private subscription.[10]

A renovated Nicolai, answered Senate-friendly council members, would serve Hamburg's public. The state had a duty to combat irreligiousness, the breeding ground of demagoguery. The new church would inspire not only churchgoers but other passersby—including workers, "whom culture can scarcely reach." The work of renovation had already attracted many spectators. Once finished, the church would contribute to Hamburgers' civic pride and public morality.

Liberals agreed that the public could use moral education. But they questioned the means. The Nicolai would not educate the public in anything worthwhile: on the contrary, its Gothic architecture represented the outmoded stance of the "darkest" and "most ignorant" Middle Ages. Further—according to council member G. R. Richter, prominent member of the powerful Educational

Association for Workers—one had to have a correct understanding of public opinion. Large crowds at the recently held Schiller Festival represented true public sentiment; but crowds at public executions, lining the street when the Tsar visited or viewing the work of the Nicolai were mere expressions of curiosity. Hamburg liberals differentiated between informed public attention and vulgar gawking; as they did between proper methods of instructing the public in moral and civic duties and those that belonged to a dark, "Gothic" past.[11]

Not public monuments to Protestant Christianity, but secular education, held the key to civil morality. Universal education would unite Hamburg citizens. It would bind the Bürger together in enlightened reason and associational habit, overcoming both religious and occupational divides. The particular role entrusted to education reinforced liberals' outrage when the city's public teachers' association decided to exclude Jewish teachers. "Such a thing," expostulated council member G. L. Ulex, "in the year 1859!" The teachers' association had argued that if state and public morality were "fundamentally Christian," then public schools were "upheld by the spirit of Christianity": consequently, "honest Israelites" had no place in a public teachers' organization. Council members Ulex (president of the Educational Association for Workers) and teacher Johannes Halben (cofounder of the Society for Freedom of Conscience and prominent in the Educational Association for Workers) used city newspapers to protest against this religious view of civil morality and citizenship. They branded the teachers' decision a dishonor to the father city. In the past, wrote Halben, schools had been expected to create obedient, religious citizens. But surely things were different now. "Oh my contemporaries! What has humanity done to you, that your first and dearest desire is not—to be good human beings?"[12]

School director Dr. Anton Rée, former president of both the Society for Freedom of Conscience and the Association for the Social and Political Interests of the Jews, was in fervent agreement. Religious divisions had no place in the school. Secular primary education, Rée believed, was necessary to a healthy citizenry. He lectured the Society for Freedom of Conscience on the connection between freedom of belief and political freedom. Other teachers agreed. Moral instruction, teacher F. D. Wex reminded the society in 1865, was possible without religion. Not religion, but secular schools, would create a free, public-spirited, united people, able to transform the state into a manifestation of morality.[13] Schooling, Rée told the society's members, ought also to ignore all differences in estate; for, as he lectured the Educational Association for Workers, universal, secular education would give everyone the freedom to lay the foundations for a happy future and thus lessen the division between rich and poor.[14]

Rée dedicated his professional and political life to this ideal. After a long struggle with the Jewish community, on which he depended for funding, his school was opened to both Christians and—with the help of charity organizations and scholarships—working-class boys. Shared schooling, Rée believed, would unite "the entire population" in "a more similar character in language, manners, morals, and worldview."[15] As Rée told the German Reichstag in 1880,

> If … the children of the poor and the children of the rich sit together on the same school-bench … if they learn to know and love each other during their early years … then you would not see the subsequent mutual lack of understanding between the worker and the well-to-do. [Education would] unite the estates with … the bond of similar forms of association and language.[16]

No one could persuade him, Rée told a Hamburg audience, that it was for nothing that rich and poor had shared school-benches in his school. The energy of the poor rubbed off on the rich; the poor child, in turn, gained finer manners. This ideal inspired Rée to employ women teachers. Women's nature, he believed, was closer to the children's, while their very fine manners had a powerful educational effect on the school's "raw elements."[17]

For liberals, the creation of an individualized but mutually sympathetic and enlightened citizenry also derived from correct forms of adult association. Germany's many workers' educational associations were also schools in liberal citizenship. When, in 1848, Berlin's Artisans' Association called for a Workers' Congress, it invited those associations that promoted workers' spiritual and moral citizenship, seeking to "deepen insight, spread morality" and "create brotherliness."[18] Hamburg's Educational Association for Workers fit this model. It provided practical education: in 1860, when Hamburg's shoemaker journeymen presented their guild with their own sickness insurance scheme, a letter to the editor describing the event attributed the journeymen's success to their membership in the association. But the association supplied more than skills. It also taught workers self-respect. As a keynote speaker put it in 1859, the association's soul was anchored in the knowledge that the true worker was one who had learned not to objectify himself as a tool; who, even while laboring, stood above his work. Education, finally, provided political liberation. For, in the opinion of association chairman Franz Appel, speaking in 1852, "an educated people cannot be repressed, it will not tolerate enserfment."[19] Workers gained necessary experience in educated and cultural citizenship through the association's lectures, classes, and festivities. Enlightened leisure promoted both personal liberation and citizenship bonds. "Raw, brutal" festivities were to be replaced by "more noble and honorable types of pleasant pastimes"; for, according to Appel and Ulex, workers' traditional recreation— dancing, frequenting public houses and bars, and playing games of chance—destroyed "every noble impulse." The ties of enlightened citizenship were acquired during off-hours association; this was no time for debauchery.[20]

Attempts to substitute the bonds of secular education and respectable associational culture for group identities derived from family, religion, or occupation took vivid expression in Hamburg's 1859 Schiller Festival. Hamburg liberals exulted in the cultural wave that they hoped would engulf religious, geographical, and estate divides. According to one newspaper poet, devotion to Schiller would raise both those who were in the dust and those who stood "before the golden calf"; all would join in celebrating "ye land of thinkers"—"German land!" For, as a Hamburg editor put it, Schiller stood for "true freedom," undarkened by popishness or despotism. Those who followed him would be "worthy members of a free state," capable of "manly deeds."[21]

Manliness was integral to the liberal public sphere. As S. Israel told members of the anti-Semitic teachers' association: "just come here, you slaves, you supporters of delusion and intolerance, you'll find your man!" When a public meeting reached a conclusion that a Hamburg editor found uncongenial, he accused participants of "lacking in maturity, even manliness." Voters, according to another editorial, demanded "manly determination" in the face of the Senate's attempts to "rob us of our priceless goods."[22]

Women had a special place in this free, manly culture. Civic virtue was propagated at home as well as in public. Women had attended, and had a seat on the board of, the Society for Freedom of Conscience: it was important that women, too, receive secular education. For, as a society lecturer put it, one must consider her high calling: as mediator between hearth and humanity, as educator of boys. "The church and its regiment is incapable of fulfilling the education of women"; women deserved "deep-going, intellectual education," directed not toward expertise, but idealism, patriotism, and faith in humanity.[23]

Schiller enthusiasts also stressed woman's role as educator. According to one journalist, the Schiller Festival had served to unite men, bringing them together in concert halls and meetings. But the private world of home and women had played a role, as well.

> But to you, ye German *women* and *mothers*, remains a further, as yet unfulfilled sphere of action! Take ye the festival, which the nation is celebrating, *into the house! Make it a celebration of the house, of youth, of children!* … I speak to women of all estates…. So! Deck out your workroom in his honor, put his picture, his bust on a festively decorated birthday table…. And now, ye mothers, when you read Schiller to your children, they'll answer that Schiller was a Schwabian poet, a "south German." At this moment, when narrow souls and small hearts want to convince us that the German spirit is not one, but divided, let … women of north and south Germany … firmly join hands, and promise … to educate our sons and daughters as German men, as German women.[24]

This celebration of culture's ability to overcome particularist and estate divides was more than flowery language. Left-wing editors pointed to the artisans' "enormous" participation in Hamburg's Schiller procession. Ulex told members of the Educational Association for Workers that their contribution to the procession had gained the "artisan estate" public acknowledgement for its dedication to "justice and morality" and willingness to "battle for freedom and fatherland."[25] Hamburg's skilled workers expected to be treated as valued participants. A newspaper advertisement addressed to "Friends, Comrades in Artisanship and Celebration!" called the recent "German *Volksfest*" and the massive participation of artisans therein a celebration of work and workers. Those who wished to remember the occasion—as they would, when their wander-years had passed and they sat, as honored masters, in their family circle—could buy an inexpensive book on the subject, of the advertiser's own composition, from the directors or "fathers" of journeymen's common houses. Organized workers also demanded that their contributions be properly acknowledged. A letter in the liberal newspaper *Reform* complained that workers had paid for the flags and emblems borne by the workers' corporations in the Schiller procession. The flags and emblems were now on display, but the evening entry fee was beyond the workers' purse. Workers were good enough when it was a matter of participating in the parade, concluded the writer; but now it seemed that the Festival Committee wanted nothing more to do with them.[26]

Organized workers were, as yet, liberal allies. The secession of Lassalleans from the Educational Association for Workers—

precipitated, in fact, by a dispute over a flag—was delayed until 1864. In the meantime, however, other clouds darkened the skies of Hamburg's cultural harmony. The debate over how to elect the Constituent City Council, and the subsequent election campaigns, had taken place immediately after the Schiller Festival; and, as the elections progressed, it became apparent that not everyone agreed with the liberals' version of the ideal society.

The Radical Mittelstand's View of Society

Liberals sought to create a citizenry of enlightened males who, stripped of their particularist identities, were reunited in shared rational and cultural values. Once this was achieved, Hamburg's government could be run by compromise and negotiation, as enlightened public opinion corrected legislative error. Not all Hamburg citizens were equally convinced of the political capacities of an atomized, enlightened electorate. Many Hamburg Senators held that politics could not be divorced from estate. Different economic occupations produced different types of knowledge; and this influenced people's ability to recognize the public weal. The city's Mittelstand agreed. The electorate could not be so individualized, and so united; for one's occupation influenced one's politics. The Senate, for example, was run by a few powerful families. Their interests were always opposed to those of the bulk of Hamburg's citizens, the small producers, artisans and property owners. Let the Constituent City Council, therefore, consist only of representatives of the Mittelstand; and let these deal with the Senate through confrontation and ultimata rather than through the diffuse pressure of enlightened public opinion.

Self-declared representatives of the Mittelstand distrusted the liberals' tactics. In August 1859, a joint commission of Senators and liberals, established in January to decide how to elect this Constituent City Council, proposed a very Senate-friendly electoral system. All tax-paying Bürger would receive the vote; but roughly one-third of the council would be elected by Hamburg's "notables"—that is, Senate appointees to prominent administrative posts. Notables, the radicals feared, would be pro-Senate and pro-merchant.[27] In Fall 1859, assemblies of Propertied Bürger met to debate the commission's proposal. At the first, stormy meeting, popular radical Dr. Alfons Trittau condemned it as a "parody of a representative system." A small number of highly placed merchants, he complained, was seeking to control the future City

Council. It was necessary to stop one estate from ruling over others. The Bürger, he concluded, had to fight back. The Propertied Bürger could refuse to allot taxes at the end of the year, or simply withhold Senators' wages. One thousand men, demonstrating before the government buildings, would shake the Senate's nerve. He swayed the meeting, which rejected the proposal.[28]

Liberals were dismayed. Dr. Hermann Baumeister urged the Propertied Bürger to moderation. Things were not so bad. A substantial number of City Council notables, he argued, was no great evil: notables would add expertise and thoroughness to City Council discussions. Anyway, the old "medieval" division of Hamburg by estates no longer applied, and so there was no danger that the notables would constitute an overbearing mercantile presence. All were workers now, whether in the office, workshop, or study. Other liberals stressed the corrective power of public opinion. Teacher Dr. Wichard reassured doubters: as long as the City Council's meetings were public, the press and the gallery would guard against the abuse of representative mandates. Trust, urged one editor, in "the tireless, forward-pushing human spirit ... It does not let itself be tied down by written paragraphs."[29]

This did not convince the radicals. They considered the commission's liberal members traitors; and, after the majority of the Propertied Bürger approved the commission's electoral proposal, seceded from the newly created Liberal Voters' Association. This transformed the City Council elections of 1859 into a three-way battle. The Senate, of course, was represented by the conservatives. The more "liberal" reformers were organized in the Liberal Voters' Committee; their primary mouthpiece was the newspaper *Reform*. The more radical, Mittelstand-friendly group was mobilized in the Citizen's Voters' Committee, and enjoyed the support of the left-wing newspaper *Freischütz*.

As City Council elections proceeded, the division became, ever more clearly, a divorce between those who sought to use public persuasion and compromise to usher in a new political order and those who believed that politics were profoundly affected by estate antagonisms. Liberals urged the benefits of negotiation and gradualism: even a conservative City Council constitution would make it possible to enact urgently needed reforms in Hamburg's schools, justice system, economy, and administration. The liberals' reliance on the gradual effects of an increasingly enlightened public opinion worried the radicals. Their spokesmen prioritized the constitution. The Citizens' Committee insisted that all candidates for the Constituent Council demand the immediate implementation of a relatively democratic constitution; this was the only way to combat the Senate's concentrated power. "THEN"—as Trittau urged voters—"you can ask for the rest of it—reforms in justice, administration, tax reduction, Volk education."[30] This meant, moreover, electing men from the right social group. The current struggle, Trittau told voters, pitted the "people's party" against "Stock Exchange men." Only the Mittelstand represented Hamburg's "uncompromising, incorruptible citizenry"; only the Mittelstand truly opposed the estates of merchants and lawyers.[31] As the *Freischütz* put it, "The Liberal Committee is just a Stock-Exchange coterie, that represents the so-called Free-Trade Party and the Mercantile Lawyer-Association.... We want ... independent Bürger, who don't flirt with the Senate, nor are paid with the gold of the Stock Exchange matadors or the North-German Bank."[32] Hamburg's "Mittelstand," the *Freischütz*'s editor repeated, was the true representative of Hamburg; it must not allow itself to be deceived "by the cunning merchants and still more cunning lawyers.... Voters! Hamburg Bürger!" It was time to show that they could defend their rights against "Hamburg's great merchants and *Standesherren* [gentlemen of estate]."[33]

In late fall 1859, the *Freischütz* editors went a step further. They appealed to the successor of the Propertied Bürger, the Property Owners' Association, bidding it join the radicals in nominating only artisans ("No merchants! No lawyers!"). The Property Owners' Association maintained strong relations to Hamburg's guilds. The guildmasters (*Aelterleute*) were publicly worried about the political future. Had not the Mittelstand been better represented by the assemblies of Propertied Bürger, asked the guildmasters' election advertisements. Now Hamburg's representatives were taken mostly from the "Merchants' Estate" and the "Free Trade Party." Don't make the goat gardener, nor the wolf shepherd, warned guildmasters; small businessmen must vote for their fellow Bürger, before it is too late.[34]

The Property Owners' Association had, in fact, asked the guilds to join it in creating a common City Council candidacy list. Both association and guilds were invited to collaborate with the Citizens' Committee. *Reform* editor and free trade activist H. S. Hertz, who witnessed a preliminary meeting between radicals, guildmasters, and property owners, was shocked. He used the occasion to protest, according to *Freischütz*'s report on the meeting, that "he was a free trader and an opponent of all guilds, which only represent outmoded traditions, he wanted a free market and therefore it was inadmissible ... to turn to the guildmasters ... The relation of the Property Owners' Association to the guilds will incite the

Mittelstand against the rich free-traders."[35] Trittau, who was the property owners' legal consultant, responded that "it was natural, that the property owners tried to join with the Mittelstand." The Property Owners' Association had always represented the Mittelstand, he argued; the "high gentlemen of the Stock Exchange" kept their distance. And if the Property Owners' Association wanted to contact the Mittelstand, it "had to turn to the guildmasters; there is no other organ of the Mittelstand. The guilds are the organized representatives of the Mittelstand." It was a matter of protecting the rights of the Mittelstand against the merchant estate, repeated Trittau. Hertz reiterated his regret that Hamburg should be full of such incitement of one estate against another.[36]

There obviously was more at stake, here, than competition between class-conscious radicals, idealistic liberals, and oligarchic Senators. Political divisions overlapped with economic power. Neither Trittau, nor O. J. Nagel, president of the Property Owners' Association, nor Hamburg's guildmasters endorsed the liberal free market. Senators, by contrast, joined liberals in promoting free trade. Liberals believed that free trade and a free market would bring the city greater prosperity and freedom. It also would lessen state intervention in the economy, which would further individualize and liberate the citizenry. Liberal council members' first item of business, once the constitutional battle was resolved, was to work with Senators to abolish Hamburg's guilds. Mittelstand representatives responded with anger, in a hard fight against what they perceived as a self-interested, undemocratic alliance between liberal free-traders and merchants.[37]

Liberal historians often have joined their Marxist counterparts in dismissing the anti-free trade Mittelstand as either self-interested or reactionary. Hamburg's liberals agreed: guilds had no place in a modern parliamentary state. They were involuntary; they were legal entities, based on occupation; they retarded individual development and fulfillment. They also hampered productivity. They could offer neither communal feeling, morality, nor freedom. As City Council member Hermann Baumeister put it, their principle was "*Zwang* [force], their content *Verbot* [to forbid]."[38]

The Case for Guild-Based Political Citizenship

Recent scholars have been less contemptuous of the Mittelstand's defense of economic corporations. Guild members, they emphasize, were often socially progressive. In 1848, the Frankfurt Master

Artisans' Congress demanded progressive income and inheritance taxes, state pensions, and state employment of those in "involuntary poverty"; these planks were formally underwritten by Frankfurt's Journeymen's and Workers' Congresses. Journeymen also joined masters in championing free and equal education—in order, as the masters put it, "that art and science become the people's common possession, rather than a monopoly of wealth"; for "[a]s soon as the future Minister sits at the same school-bench as the artisan, the true people's state is founded."[39]

Masters' political and social radicalism included the defense of a regulated economy. In a basic disagreement with liberals, masters emphasized that citizenship derived from the experience of work. Leisure-time education, although desirable, was no key to civil morality. Guilds, which were built on the experience of shared work, were superior sources of social mores. They protected the worker's right to control the product of his work, to become "his own"—an essential condition for political maturity. The self-ruling master stood in sharp juxtaposition to both the enslaved factory worker and the untrained, mobile capitalist. No matter how educated, how cultured these were, the independent master would always be more important to society.[40]

The Frankfurt Master Artisans' Congress, held in 1848, and the various petitions submitted in 1861 in defense of Hamburg's guilds give a cogent presentation of the guild members' worldview. Liberals held that young men learned to be citizens through school, through the culture taught them by (the liberals hoped, adequately educated) mothers, and through the self-education and political activity of voluntary associations. Masters artisans held quite another view. The ascent into manhood and citizenship was three-tiered: apprentice, journeyman, master. The master, in his role as father and teacher, introduced apprentices to the morality, manliness, and maturity of skilled labor. The apprenticeship years, the masters maintained, were "the most important time for the human": they established character. "Only a hard-working, thrifty, obedient apprentice will make a good husband and father, an able citizen." It was the master's job to train the apprentice, both in skill and manhood. This parenting was, of course, all-male; women, who were unskilled, could not train apprentices.[41]

The habit of work determined a man's character, but, in the end, full citizenship came only with economic independence. The abolition of guilds would destroy men's ability to reach such independence. The capitalists' beloved free market deprived the worker of the chance of independence; it condemned him not only to poverty but to despair. Members of the Masters' Congress regularly coupled the words "slave" and "proletariat"; a journeyman who adopted the name of worker had, they held, renounced his rights. The journeyman had to learn to feel like an independent artisan—not a day worker, a factory worker, the slave of a money-master. For only the man who had found a place in the economy, who was self-supporting, could know "true freedom."[42]

The progression from apprentice to master was—as masters admitted in 1848—not always easy. The main problem, they concluded, was not the guilds, the unfree labor market, or tariffs. In this, the free-traders—and their allies, the "theoreticians," publicists, ideologues, and bureaucrats who often dominated city councils and state parliaments—were mistaken. But the artisan would (as the 1848 congress put it) defy the "falsifying mouth of the poet … the tinted glasses of the learned bureaucrat," for only the artisan could judge from work experience.[43] This experience told them that overproduction, not guilds, was to blame for unemployment and poverty. There were too many apprentices and journeymen, not enough customers to sustain them as masters. The solution, the Masters' Congress concluded, was to curtail production through emigration, provide state employment of the poor (on infrastructure and agricultural projects), and impose restrictions on the right to sell manufactured goods, to employ labor, to set oneself up as a manufacturer, and to marry. Marriage should be allowed only to those able to support a family. The proper protection of guilds, masters hastened to add, would ensure enough general prosperity to put marriage within the reach of all.[44]

There was, however, a second and more dangerous cause of artisanal distress. Capital—and its users, the factory owner and the speculator—were destroying the artisans. In congresses held both in Hamburg and Frankfurt, master artisans condemned capital's ability to reduce artisans to "slaves." Artisans must be freed from the "slave-chains of gold power" imposed by the "money aristocrats, the great Moloch, capital, that bears down heavily on the artisan estate." To enact free trade, to allow capital to rule, would mean that the ownership of money—rather than hard work and skill—would determine a man's success in life. "Only the state can conquer the capitalist, the manufacturer, who makes workers into slaves," and thus give the artisans a chance to achieve freedom, independence and prosperity. Hard work, and the rights of work, had to be legally protected.[45]

Merchants were handled equally harshly. Merchants, argued the Frankfurt Masters' Congress, profited from the sale of the worker's craft, while forcing the artisans into debt; it was necessary to fight the *Herrschaft* (dominance) of money. The artisan produced; the merchant did not. The artisan was impoverished; the merchant drove golden carriages and drank champagne. The merchants, as one master summed it up, were the cancer on the activity of the artisan.[46] In 1861, Dr. Hermann Baumeister assured Hamburg's artisans that the free market would benefit them: with diligence and enterprise they too could become minicapitalists. Masters could not agree. Their rejection of the liberal economic system was anchored in the essential difference between capital and skill. Capital, responded Hamburg masters, was transferable, while skill inhered in the artisan. Capital was mobile; the artisan was tied to his neighborhood. The merchant, speculator, and factory builder were like "migratory birds—today here, tomorrow there," pushed by the powerful "impulse of speculation." The artisan was chained to the soil where he had settled, his skill his only capital, hard work his only motor. The master was the stable element in the state organism. He was worthy of state protection; masters, like guilds, provided a key impulse toward "morality, order, and hard, skilled work."[47]

In 1865, liberals joined with Senators in dissolving Hamburg's guilds. Former guild members now faced an economic order that contradicted the Mittelstand's definition of manliness, citizenship, and moral economy. They also lost political power; council seats were no longer reserved for guildmasters. The imposition of free trade, orchestrated by a combined mercantile-liberal alliance, deepened the Mittelstand's distrust of liberals. Their suspicions were not softened by the fact that the liberals, although triumphant in the City Council elections, remained unable to force the Senate to implement a democratic constitution.

The *Mittelstand* Vanquished

In April 1860, the Senate finally proposed a constitution. Its reactionary clauses caused general outcry. Again, radicals urged confrontation; again, the liberals decided to compromise. Members of the Constituent City Council agreed to participate in yet another joint Senate-council commission. An undemocratic constitution was the generally anticipated result. The council meeting that decided on negotiation was both tempestuous and depressed. Many urged confrontation. Artisan J. F. Martens accused the Senate of holding council members for fools; Senators would never have dared propose such a constitution to the Propertied Bürger. Trittau warned council members of a turning point in the Senators' centuries-long struggle to vanquish the Propertied Bürger. If the City Council compromised now, it would betray the mandate given it by the Propertied Bürger; to make further concessions was simply to debate how best to put slavery into constitutional form. But *Reform*'s repeated calls for the public to express its displeasure in mass citizens' meetings had little effect. Public opinion, as later editors reluctantly concluded, still needed enlightenment. The liberals' political tools had proved impotent.[48]

But what was to take their place? Shortly after the City Council's compromise decision, the Property Owners' Association called a meeting of all interested ex-Propertied Bürger. Trittau told the meeting that it would have been better had sovereignty remained with the old, "medieval" assemblies of Propertied Bürger. A petition was circulated, encouraging property owners—in their character as Propertied Bürger—to deny the legitimacy of the City Council's compromise commission.[49] Predictably, these corporatist measures met with liberal disapproval. Dr. H. May expressed his displeasure in *Reform*. Trittau, he wrote, wanted to revive outmoded forms, ancient ghosts, in his battle against the Senate. But this was not the way to the goal; it would be reached, perhaps more gradually, but all the more securely, through negotiation. For, as even *Freischütz* put it, "backwards is backwards"; and they had no time to go backwards, at the behest either of the Senate or the old Propertied Bürger.[50]

Mittelstand representatives disagreed. The issue was not progress, but justice. As a letter to the editor put it in November 1859, that great giant, the Assembled Propertied Bürger, had died—and those who had insulted him, calling him the brainless, contemptible servant of glovemakers and tailors, had declared themselves his heirs. "At his death-bed, sorrowing, stand his disinherited children—the small producers and businessmen of the Mittelstand." They had been promised adequate representation in the new City Council—"But as the giant lay in agony, after he had been given some doses of opium to lighten his suffering, it was suggested that his successors be almost exclusively merchants and lawyers, and—he said YES, because his tongue was already paralyzed." In vain did the giant's legal heirs seek to undo this injustice, the writer continued. They were accused of inciting unrest, of being bad people. Those who had faithfully stood by the giant were unable to save him from his most bitter enemies.[51] The people, the skilled workers and petite bourgeoisie of

Hamburg, had been disinherited; and the new City Council was unwilling to help.

The Mittelstand's contribution to the democratic struggle, coupled, as it was, to attempts to use guilds to enforce social and political justice, was given short shrift by the liberals. When the corporatist Mittelstand reappeared in the 1860s and 1870s, Hamburg liberals condemned it as villainous: motivated (as liberal commentators put it in 1878) by "crass egoism," nakedly self-seeking, the enemy of freedom, bearing a banner with the motto "Backwards!" Against it stood healthy common sense, humanitarianism, the unprejudiced, intelligent, forward-striving, truly liberal part of society.[52] Many historians, sympathetic to libertarian liberals and their struggles, have agreed. They have lumped the Mittelstand with the *Junker*, Center Party, and pro-tariff groups, which together transformed Germany's public sphere into a degenerate arena of state-dependent interest groups. But, as a study of the years following 1858 indicate, Hamburg liberals, at least, were not altogether candid: they had once benefited from the corporatist power of one of the groups whose enmity they protested. Their deep prejudices against economic corporations could, by this reading, have prevented the creation of an effective pro-democracy front.

In Britain, as Frank Trentmann shows, liberal free trade was less controversial. There was a general consensus: "little men" could only benefit from the repeal of protection and the attendant downfall of tariff-bloated monopolies and plutocratic oligarchies. Free trade, it was held, promoted voluntary associations, the foundation of democracy.[53] Britain's small producers did not consider the country's (long-deceased) guilds a source of civil morality. Association, cooperation, even consumption—all, it was felt, promoted by free trade—would be enough to create an autonomous and harmonious citizen body. Free trade united, rather than divided, Britain's liberal-democratic front.

The German left reached no such consensus on the beneficial effects of free trade. Many saw the free market as the harbinger of political progress, prosperity, and personal autonomy. Many reasoned, like the British, that free trade would explode unjust, state-sponsored monopolies. But others equated free trade and the free market with the final triumph of mercantile and financial oligarchies. The division of state from civil society, guild members claimed, was a capitalist-serving sham. There was similar disagreement on the role of free association. Liberals ranked the experience of association with that of primary education, twin engines of individual autonomy. Members of the Mittelstand were more interested in the autonomy derived from skilled and responsible work; guild members' "estate honor" was more important than voluntary association. This divided liberals and Mittelstand. It also divided liberals from Germany's increasingly well-organized workers. The long-cherished ideal of work-based morality, the nexus of politics and economy, lent ideological impetus to Germany's strong socialist movement.

In 1843, Karl Marx had celebrated the liberation of the "political spirit" from civil society. The overlap between state and civil society, so typical of feudal society, was dissolving. He characterized the evolving public sphere as the domain of the abstract, moral man working for the general concerns of the people. The particularistic, sensual, self-interested man had been relegated to civil society. Civil society was affected by the new divide between political and economic life, however; for "[t]he bonds which had restrained the egoistic spirit of civil society were removed along with the political yoke." And the newly unfettered egoism of civil society influenced the supposedly rarified and abstract world of politics. The modern state's main task was, after all, the enforcement of civil rights—that is, providing the legal (and police-state) infrastructure necessary to maintain the inequalities between, and the exploitation of, the inhabitants of civil society.

> None of the supposed rights of man ... go beyond the egoistic man, man as he is, as a member of civil society; that is, an individual separated from the community, withdrawn into himself, wholly preoccupied with his private interest and acting in accordance with his private caprice.... Species-life itself—society—appears as a system which is external to the individual and as a limitation of his original independence. The only bond between men is natural necessity, need and private interest, the preservation of their property and their egoistic persons.[54]

Marx condemned all efforts to reengage state and civil society: guild members' attempts to retain the old order were doomed. But he shared their repugnance for the liberals' civil society. Education and culture were insufficient to overcome the ill effects of the individual's estrangement from the community. As Germany's social democrats were to demonstrate, liberals rejected or neglected these dissenting worldviews at their peril. They were unable to democratize either Hamburg, or Germany, on their own. They may have done well to pay more heed to the alternative civil and political society proposed by Hamburg's "rightful heirs."

Notes

1. Editorial in *Hamburg Nachrichten*, 3 January 1874.
2. E.g., the classic by James Sheehan, *German Liberalism in the Nineteenth Century* (Chicago, 1978), 175ff.
3. Jürgen Habermas, *The Structural Transformation of the Public Sphere*, trans. Thomas Burger (1962; Cambridge, MA, 1996), 7ff., 42–43, 53–56, 86–87, 137; Craig Calhoun, "Introduction," and Geoff Eley, "Nations, Publics, and Political Cultures: Placing Habermas in the Nineteenth Century," in *Habermas and the Public Sphere*, ed. Craig Calhoun (Cambridge, MA, 1992).
4. Habermas, *Structural Transformation*, 55, 74.
5. Ibid., 137.
6. Herbert Kwiet, "Die Einführung der Gewerbefreiheit in Hamburg 1861 bis 1865" (Ph.D. diss., Hamburg Universität, 1947), 14–27, 44–53; Hans-Wilhelm Eckardt, *Privilegien und Parlament: Die Auseinandersetzungen um das allgemeine und gleiche Wahlrecht* (Hamburg, 1980), 27ff.
7. Julius Eckhardt, *Lebenserinnerungen* (Leipzig, 1910), 2:47–48, 199–201, 208–10; *Reform*, 28 November 1857; Wolfgang Schmidt, "Arbeiter und Bürger in der Revolution von 1848/49 in Hamburg," in *Arbeiter in Hamburg*, ed. Arno Herzig, et al. (Hamburg, 1983); *Reform*, 25 November 1867, 9 August 1867, 30 August 1867; see also Richard J. Evans, *Death in Hamburg: Society and Politics in the Cholera Years, 1830–1910* (Oxford, 1987).
8. Werner von Melle, *Gustav Heinrich Kirchenpauer: Ein Lebens- und Zeitbild* (Hamburg, 1888), 343, 358, quote 365.
9. Hermann Baumeister et al., "Denkschrift über die Verfassung des Freistaates Hamburg vom 11. Juli 1849," quoted in Melle, *Kirchenpauer*, 348–49.
10. City Council debates and speeches, *Reform*, 18 February 1860, 25 February 1860.
11. City Council debates and speeches, *Reform*, 25 February 1860, 29 February 1860.
12. Ulex and Halben in *Reform*, 24 December 1859, 2 November 1859; see also *Reform*, 14 December 1859, 9 January 1860; D. Schlie, *Dr. Anton Rée: Zur Würdigung seiner Bestrebungen und Verdienste* (Hamburg, 1891), 51.
13. Anton Rée, *Wanderungen eines Zeitgenossen auf dem Gebiete der Ethik* (Hamburg, 1857), quoted in Schlie, *Dr. Anton Rée*, 107; also Rée, *Ueber die Pflicht: Einige Definitionen nebst einer Schlußbemerkung für Pädagogen* (Frankfurt, 1875): *Freischütz*, 1 December 1859, 12 January 1860; *Reform*, 11 January 1860, 14 October 1865.
14. *Reform*, 14 October 1865, 30 March 1875.
15. Anton Rée, *Die allgemeine Volkschule, oder Standeschulen?* (Hamburg, 1866), 16.
16. Schlie, *Dr. Anton Rée*, 69–71. See also Manfred Asendorf, "Der Hamburger Pädagoge und Politiker Anton Rée," *Sonderdruck aus Beiheft 6 des Instituts für Deutsche Geschichte*, Universität Tel-Aviv (1984), 11.
17. Anton Rée, "Rede des Herrn Dr. Anton Rée," *Fremdenblatt*, 11 September 1888; Anton Rée, *Stiftungsschule von 1815 zu Hamburg: Schuljahr 1889/90* (Hamburg, 1890), 11.
18. *Neue Rheinischen Zeitung*, 22 June 1848; *Das Volk*, 20 June 1848, reproduced in Deiter Dowe and Toni Offermann, *Deutsche Handwerker- und Arbeiterkongresse, 1848–1852* (Berlin, 1983), 42, 44.
19. *Reform*, 24 March 1860, 31 October 1859; Toni Offermann, "Arbeiter, Bürgertum und Staat in Hamburg 1850–1862," in Herzig et al., eds., *Arbeiter in Hamburg*, 126 (quote).
20. Franz Appel, *Bildungs-Verein für Arbeiter* (Hamburg, 1895), 5, 7, 10–11.

21. *Reform*, 7 November 1859; *Freischütz*, 24 October 1859.
22. S. Israel, *Freischütz*, 7 January 1860; editorials in *Freischütz*, 9 August 1859, and *Reform*, 25 April 1860.
23. *Reform*, 23 January 1860. For women's participation, e.g., *Reform*, 4 February 1860.
24. *Freischütz*, 15 October 1859, emphasis in original.
25. *Reform*, 7 November 1859, 19 November 1859.
26. *Reform*, 21 December 1859, 10 December 1859.
27. Kwiet, "Die Einführung der Gewerbefreiheit," 47.
28. *Freischütz*, 9 August 1859.
29. *Freischütz*, 11 August 1859, 13 August 1859. This is one of the few times that *Freischütz* took the liberal position.
30. *Freischütz*, 8 November 1859, emphasis in original. For the liberals, e.g., *Freischütz*, 18 October 1859, 22 October 1859, 29 October 1859, 5 November 1859.
31. Alfons Trittau, *Freischütz*, 9 August 1859, 11 August 1859, 18 October 1859.
32. *Freischütz*, 27 October 1859.
33. *Freischütz*, 12 November 1859, emphasis in original.
34. *Freischütz*, 22 November 1859, 17 November 1859.
35. *Freischütz*, 3 November 1859.
36. *Reform*, 7 November 1859.
37. Kwiet, "Die Einführung der Gewerbefreiheit," 48, 109.
38. Quote, [Hermann Baumeister], "Bericht des von der Bürgerschaft am 20. März 1851 niedergesetzten Ausschusses zur Prüfung einiger die Gewerbefrage betreffenden Anträge vom 24.12.1861," (Hamburg, 1861), 10; see also Dr. Asher, "Bericht der von … Hamburger Gesellschaft zur Beförderung der Künste und nützlichen Gewerbe ernannten Commission zur Untersuchung der Gewerbe-Verhältnisse in Hamburg," 21 January 1861, 48–49, quoted in Kwiet, "Die Einführung der Gewerbefreiheit," 93, 114–18.
39. *Entwurf einer allgemeinenen Handwerker- und Gewerbe-Ordnung für Deutschland: Verathen und beschlossen von dem deutschen Handwerker- und Gewerbe-Congreß zu Frankfurt am Main in den Monaten Juli und August 1848* (Hamburg, 1848), 31. See also *Denkschrift über den Entwurf einer allgemeinen deutschen Gewerbe-Ordnung des Handwerker- und Gewerbe-Congresses: Verfaßt von dem allgemeinenen deutschen Arbeiter-Congreß zu Frankfurt am Main in den Monaten August und September* (Darmstadt, 1848), 15–16; "Aufförderung … zur Beschickung eines in Berlin vom 20. bis zum 26. August abzuhaltenden Arbeiter-Parlamentes," *Das Volk*, 27 June 1848, 41ff., reproduced in Dowe and Offermann, *Deutschen Handwerker- und Arbeiterkongresse*, 44–45, 192–94, 209. For rehabilitation of the petite bourgeoisie, e.g., Geoffrey Crossick and Heinz-Gerhard Haupt, eds., *Shopkeepers and Master Artisans in Nineteenth-Century Europe* (London, 1984), 52, 72–73; Friedrich Lenger, *Zwischen Kleinbürgertum und Proletariat: Studien zur Sozialgeschichte der Düsseldorfer Handwerker, 1816–1878* (Göttingen, 1986); Dieter Langewiesche, *Liberalismus in Deutschland* (Frankfurt, 1988), 7–38.
40. *Entwurf einer allgemeine Handwerker- und Gewerbe-Ordnung*, 16, in Dowe and Offermann, *Deutsche Handwerker- und Arbeiterkongresse*, 185.
41. "Gutachten der in supplicis unterzeichneten Aelterleute in Betreff des vom Gewerbe-Auschuss der Bürgerschaft abgestattete Berichte" (January 1862), quoted in Kwiet, "Die Einführung der Gewerbefreiheit," 119, 123–24, 199; *Entwurf einer allgemeine Handwerker- und Gewerbe-Ordnung*, 14; G[eorge] Schirges, ed., *Verhandlungen des ersten deutschen Handwerker- und Gewerbe-Congresses gehalten zu Frankfurt a.M. vom 14. Juli bis 18. August 1848* (Darmstadt,

1848), 163, 165; *Verhandlungen der ersten Abgeordneten-Versammlung des nord-deutschen Handwerker- und Gewerbe-Standes zu Hamburg, den. 2.-6 1848* (Hamburg, 1848), in Dowe and Offermann, *Deutsche Handwerker und Arbeiterkongresse,* 59, 131, 184.

42. *Verhandlungen des ersten deutschen Handwerker- und Gewerbe-Congresses,* 39; *Verhandlungen der ersten Abgeordneten-Versammlung ... Hamburg,* 16, 23, in Dowe and Offermann, *Deutsche Handwerker- und Arbeiterkongresse,* 14, 18, 68, 93.

43. *Entwurf einer allgemeinen Handwerker- und Gewerbe-Ordnung,* 10; *Verhandlungen der ersten Abgeordneten-Versammlung ... Hamburg,* 23; *Verhandlungen des ersten deutschen Handwerker- und Gewerbe-Congresses,* V, 7–8, 111, 162, in Dowe and Offermann, *Deutsche Handwerker- und Arbeiterkongresse,* 18, 47–48, 53, 129, 182.

44. *Entwurf einer allgemeinen Handwerker- und Gewerbe-Ordnung,* 18, 32; *Verhandlungen der ersten Abgeordneten-Versammlung ... Hamburg,* 22, 24; *Verhandlungen des ersten deutschen Handwerker- und Gewerbe-Congresses,* 32, 41, 47, 65, 72–78, 82, 98–99, 102–4, 111–12, 152, 156, 187, 201, 210, 249–51, in Dowe and Offermann, *Deutsche Handwerker- und Arbeiterkongresse,* 17, 18, 65, 69, 73, 81, 84–87, 89, 97, 99–100, 104, 124, 126, 149, 153, 173–74, 193–94.

45. *Entwurf einer allgemeinen Handwerker- und Gewerbe-Ordnung,* 13; *Verhandlungen des ersten deutschen Handwerker- und Gewerbe-Congresses,* 51, 77, 85, 256; for journeymen, *Das Volk,* 27 June 1848, 41ff., in Dowe and Offermann, *Deutsche Handwerker- und Arbeiterkongresse,* 44, 74, 87, 97, 176, 208.

46. *Verhandlungen der ersten Abgeordneten-Versammlung ... Hamburg,* 97; *Verhandlungen des ersten deutschen Handwerker- und Gewerbe-Congresses,* 25, 35–36; in Dowe and Offermann, *Deutsche Handwerker- und Arbeiterkongresse,* 62, 65–66, 97.

47. "Offenes Sendschreiben an die Gesellschaft ... zur Abwehr des von Herrn Dr. Asher abgestatteten Commissionsberichten ... von den Aelterleuten der hiesigen Aemter und Brüderschaften" (June 1861), 59–60, and "Gutachten der in supplicis unterzeichneten Aelterleute," 8, quoted in Kwiet, "Die Einführung der Gewerbefreiheit," 11, 99; see also City Council debate covered in *Reform,* 8 February 1862. Antimercantile rhetoric reappeared in 1867, when·the radical Mittelstand (including Trittau) fought a free-trading front of liberals and merchants over national elections and whether Hamburg would join the Customs Union; see, e.g., *Reform,* 6 February 1867, 8 July 1867, 12 July 1867, 5 August 1867.

48. Debate covered in *Reform,* 14 April 1860; see also *Reform,* 16 April 1860, 25 April 1860; on the need to "enlighten" public opinion in the face of another abuse of power by the Senate, *Reform,* 23 August 1865, 6 November 1865, 6 December 1865.

49. *Freischütz,* 21 April 1860; *Reform,* 28 April 1860.

50. *Reform,* 30 April 1860; *Freischütz,* 1 May 1860.

51. *Freischütz,* 26 November 1859, emphasis in original.

52. *Reform,* 3 December 1878, 28 December 1879.

53. Frank Trentmann, "Civil Society, Commerce, and the "Citizen-Consumer": Popular Meanings of Free Trade in Modern Britain," in this volume.

54. Karl Marx, "On the Jewish Question" (1843), in *The Marx-Engels Reader,* ed. Robert Tucker (New York, 1878), 41ff., quotes 45, 43. See also Habermas's illuminating discussion of Marx's views, in *The Transformation,* 122–23.

13

CIVIL SOCIETY, COMMERCE, AND THE "CITIZEN-CONSUMER"

Popular Meanings of Free Trade in Modern Britain

Frank Trentmann

I

"[E]VERY CIVILIZED MAN must regard murder with abhorrence. Not even in the defense of Free Trade would I lift my hand against a political opponent, however richly he might deserve it."[1] Bernard Shaw's caricature of a liberal Englishman contained more than a grain of truth. To Bertrand Russell in 1903, the very "purity and intensity of public spirit" depended on Free Trade; indeed, the liberal activist-philosopher felt "inclined to cut my throat" if the forces of tariff reform were to triumph in the "fiscal controversy."[2] Free Trade was at the very center of British political culture. In contrast to continental societies, Free Trade in Britain dominated as value system and policy. It acted as a *Weltanschauung* and a collective identity to broad social and political groups, ranging from the liberal Free Trade Union and the more exclusive Cobden Club and conservative Free Food League to popular movements such as the two-million-strong cooperative movement and the People's League Against Protection.

Freedom of trade had been linked to civil society in Enlightenment thought, but it was not until the late nineteenth century that it reached an apotheosis as a popular ideology and movement. The "fiscal controversy" that erupted in 1903 opened an important chapter in the popular history of civil society in which older affinities between "civil society" and "commerce" were revived, revised, and, ultimately, lost. This essay is an attempt to listen to the popular voices of Free Trade, and to reclaim the ideas, values, and languages that tied it to civil society. Rather than offering a political or economic narrative, then, it will suggest a re-reading of Free Trade as a public debate about civil society, its history, constitution, and boundary to state and economy. How did contemporaries imagine the relationship between civil society and political economy? What was the place and knowledge of Free Trade in popular views of the development of the social? Finally, how did visions of the social relate to ideals of citizenship?

II

Free Trade, as a social cause and movement, depended on the recycling and construction of ideas, symbols, and narratives that provided an internal culture of shared knowledge and identity.[3] In the collective identity of radical movements, the strengthening of civil society and the coming of Free Trade were closely intertwined. At the outbreak of the battle over protection in 1903, Mrs. Bury, vice-president of the Women's Cooperative Guild, reminded a women's mass meeting that "Cooperation and Free Trade started together, and they had jogged along successfully."[4] This positive association was based on a historical memory of "1846," the repeal of the corn laws. The construction of this memory was a crucial cultural achievement, for it refashioned popular understandings of the history of civil society and political economy, suppressing a more complex past of the earlier tension-filled relationship between Chartism and the Anti-Corn Law League.[5]

The role of a radical narrative emerges vividly from George Holyoake's "The Days of Protection," a piece of historical memory by the old cooperator widely circulated in the Edwardian campaign. When Joseph Chamberlain finally launched the tariff reform crusade, Liberals were quick to turn to Holyoake for an account of "the condition of the workmen in England before Free Trade and the changes you have observed since that time." Rather than simply following the Liberal editor's request to focus on "the increase in … purchasing power,"[6] Holyoake, who remembered the era of "Repeal," offered a set piece of radical collective memory. The longer history of free associations was compressed and directly linked to Repeal. Readers were told of a protectionist past in which society had been colonized by capitalism, leaving no space for societal self-organization or the development of the "self." Workers and the starving poor were not counted as members of society; indeed they had "never learned to think much of [them]selves." Free Trade marked a turning point in the history of civil society and democratization. It led to the recognition of autonomous social groups, and it provided laborers with "a more generally-recognized position in the State," "having rights which should be respected ... [and] having interests which should be consulted."[7]

Political rights, however, remained embedded in an antistatist outlook. Social autonomy and self-limitation went hand in hand in the cooperative approach to laissez-faire. Cooperation, in Holyoake's oft-cited words "took no man's fortune, it sought no plunder,... it gave not trouble to statesmen,... it subverted no order,... it asked no favour.... It meant self-help, self-dependence."[8] This negative view of the state reflected a positive, utopian vision of the cooperatives as a separate, self-regulating social order. Cooperatives would distribute the wealth created by Free Trade and, in turn, strengthen civil society, protecting its groups from state interference and dependence. Indeed, assisted by the Free Trade environment, cooperatives had apparently grown into indispensable nurseries of democracy—in terms of social inclusion as well as political participation. In her attack on tariffs in the popular collection *Labour and Protection* (1903), the cooperator Rosalind Nash concluded that

> Co-operation is in fact democracy in action, and apart from its economic achievements it forms a training-ground in the democratic qualities which the ballot-box demands—disinterestedness, forbearance, confidence, the capacity for responsible action and judgment. Can anything be more valuable to a democratic State than a movement which guarantees to a great mass of the people some share, at any rate, in every economic advance, and which amply repays its successive gains by political and municipal service, and by an extension of its missionary work among the poor, not to speak of the larger and happier range of life, and the gain to character which it brings to the individual?[9]

This voluntarist-democratic project ran through the cooperative educational curriculum, which offered courses in cooperation, citizenship, history, and political economy.[10] The two-million-strong cooperative movement played an indispensable role in assisting the elite, but impoverished, Cobden Club by disseminating popular literature and organizing mass rallies.[11] In the cooperative literature, the repeal of the corn laws was represented as the beginning of "the progress of the people," the landmark of a new social geography, in which cooperatives, friendly societies, and trade unions cultivated social autonomy, trust, and solidarity.[12]

The cooperative narrative of democratization and social autonomy was complemented by the historical memory of the "Hungry Forties" constructed in the Edwardian period. Individual laborers' memories of suffering were fused into a collective experience of a protectionist *Hungry Forties*, the title of a volume initiated by Cobden's daughter, Jane Cobden Unwin, in 1904. A "people's edition" was issued the following year. By 1912 the penny edition had sold 110,000 copies, the bound copy another 100,000. They established the term as a public symbol. The "Hungry Forties" offered a movement story of the heroic achievement of Cobdenites and a frame of interpretation highlighting the civilizing function of Free Trade. Significantly, this narrative borrowed both from liberal middle-class icons and from biblical images so central to the Victorian language of melodrama that had appealed to the powerless. Retrospectively, repeal stood for the final triumph of the virtuous: in the concluding words of Brougham Villiers, it had delivered the nation from "Egyptian bondage."[13]

The insertion of "1846" into a story of Britain's quasi-biblical mission elevated Free Trade from economics to the larger plane of the social. Free Trade was a natural mark of human progress. The recycling of Cobden's "cheap loaf" as an icon of national liberty and progress in public ritual and popular print reminded Edwardians that a civilizing achievement was at stake as much as cheap food. References to the uncivilizing effect of protection in other societies, especially the dark counterimage of reactionary militarism and barbaric consumption of black bread, horseflesh, and dog meat in Imperial Germany, suggested just how fragile this achievement was; it ignored the fact that in Germany tariffs were relatively low and that social inequality had decreased more than in Britain.[14] This ideological view of the other was an integral part of Free Trade. "If this country wanted German tariffs," Lloyd George warned audiences repeatedly "it must have German wages ... German militarism, and German sausages.... They could not have British freedom and British wages along with German Protection."[15]

Free Trade language was not merely a rhetorical exercise: it had important implications for the ideological structure of political debate. Political economy was divided into mutually exclusive terms of national development: societies had a stark choice between unilateral, pure Free Trade linked to a liberal polity or protection coupled with autocracy. The combination of democracy and high tariffs across the channel in the French Third Republic (and across the Atlantic in the American republic) disappeared from the political imagination. The complex history and political economy of tariffs was simplified into a universal, transhistorical truth equating protection, poverty, and social anarchy.[16] Free Trade discourse thus closed the space for alternative ways of imagining political economy and collective identity as well as alternative policies, such as reciprocity or social trade regulation. The Liberal leader Campbell Bannerman used the Cobden centenary in 1904 to preach this binary view of competing societal systems:

> [we] stand to-day at the parting of the ways.... One road ... leads to Protection, to conscription, to the reducing of free institutions to a mere name ... And the other road leads to the consolidation of liberty and the development of equity at home, and to treaties of arbitration and amity ... and the lightening of taxation, which presses upon our trade and grinds the faces of the poor.[17]

This narrative structure, then, made it possible to dissociate Free Trade from free market. It would be too simple to reduce Free Trade to a "technique by which market capitalism was justified to working men," in McKibbin's words.[18] The stories in *Hungry Forties* expressed an alternative popular imagination of political economy. One laborer concluded his critique of protection with a radical critique of middlemen and called for the "Co-operative Commonwealth, to fight for rather than against each other," urging that "land should be the bedrock on which national burdens rest."[19] Significantly, Jane Cobden Unwin turned her energies to supplementing Free Trade with "Free Trade in Land," which she promoted as completing her father's attack on monopoly and social dependence. The popularity of land reform and the inflated expectations of resettling an independent peasantry—all within a pure Free Trade economy—indicate how open (or limited by the standards of liberal economics) the understanding was of capitalist development based on open markets and the international division of labor.[20]

Popular Free Trade, then, was far removed from a stereotypical "Manchester liberalism." For all the praise of Free Trade's contribution to wealth, the relationship between commercial capitalism and civil society remained open to debate. In contrast to the high intellectual separation of economic theory from moral science in the Victorian period, moral and social considerations remained integral to popular political economy. Here the relationship between commerce and civil society remained ambiguous, continuing the eighteenth-century debate between favorable assessments of the "douceur" of commerce (Montesquieu) and warnings of its tendency "to break the bands of society" (Ferguson).[21] A late Victorian cooperator, for instance, simultaneously advocated Free Trade and denounced economic liberalism: "What next shall we say of the evils of competition? What of the immoralities of greed and its gospel, 'Get all you can, buy in the cheapest market and sell in the dearest, no matter at what cost to the comfort of your employes [*sic*], or the health of your customers?"[22] The cooperative answer separated the social qualities of free exchange from the economic qualities of competitive exchange. Free Trade was not merely a defense of Gladstonian finance but an offensive movement for a new social order based on truly "free, clean, and beneficent" trade as the "three laws of a healthy State." It reflected a remarkable trust in the power of social agencies to immunize social relations against the competitive dynamics of a capitalist economy.

The notion that under Free Trade the social could develop apart from the market left its mark on the imagination of political economy, high and low. It renders it problematic to view the survival of Free Trade in terms of "modernizing" ideas. As well for the Liberal government that returned to power on the coattails of the tariff controversy in 1905, the economy, though imperfect, was self-regulating *and* differentiated from society and politics—and as such not accessible to outside knowledge, planning or prognostication by politicians.[23] Tellingly, Lloyd George, when president of the board of trade, compared the economy to the weather, equally "difficult to understand and appreciate. All you know is that it is like the tide."[24] The image of separate systems helps to explain what appears paradoxical from today's perspective. For it made it possible in the public debate to extract a distinct social function of Free Trade, indeed, made it difficult to imagine it as part of a transfer system that might subordinate civil society to the imperatives and culture of the market—in the very period when, thanks partly to Free Trade, capitalism expanded more freely than at any time since.

III

The radical divorce of Free Trade from capitalist principles of free market and possessive individualism left its legacy on new movements and ideologies at the turn of the century. It would be misleading, however, to stop the analysis here and to presume that this influence was static. In contrast to the recent emphasis on radical-liberal continuity,[25] we can see the fiscal debate as a site of contestation where alternative views of political economy were formulated. In popular Free Trade before the First World War some beliefs and values, like internationalism and opposition to militarism and aristocratic privilege, overlapped and assisted collaboration, but there were also fresh currents leading away from inherited traditions. This dynamic tension can be heard in the competing voices in the young Labor Party that, on one hand, tied Free Trade to international peace but, on the other, called for a more "national" political economy and rejected the link between freedom of commerce and civilization for its imperialist erosion of native societies.[26] Equally significant was an imaginative shift within liberalism itself that reexamined the subject of the development of the social in a modern political economy by focusing on the dialogical relationship between consumption and citizenship.

In the "new liberal" writings of J. A. Hobson an economic critique of the market pointed toward a social ideal of the "citizen-consumer." For Hobson, the "unearned surplus" exposed the notion that competition benefited the consuming public as a myth of Manchesterite traders. This critique has attracted attention from historians of economic thought, but equally interesting is the historical sociology of modernity underlying it. For Hobson, the evolution of unreformed capitalism pointed toward the end of liberal civilization. It promoted bureaucratization, commercialization, a growing division of labor, the standardization of human mind and body, and a widening separation of home from work, family from labor, and individual from community: civil society was in danger of being turned into mass society.

By fusing historical economics and Ruskinian romanticism, this new liberal critique of "modernization" transcended an older liberal equation between "civilization" and commerce and restored a more ambivalent understanding shared by eighteenth-century observers like Ferguson.[27] Free Trade was defined as a collective arrangement, part of an "organic" order, fostering a "social will" among individual citizens that would help them replace a culture of selfish individualism with considerations of community, reciprocity, and welfare. Rather than acting as a benign agent of individual interest, trade fostered other-regarding "higher" interests that reconciled societal and individual needs.

Divorced from what Hobson saw as the producer-bias of classical economics, Free Trade plus the redistribution of "unearned income" would allow for the development of qualitative (rather than quantitative) consumption. "Everything in human progress will be found to depend upon a progressive realisation of the nature of good 'consumption.'"[28] Turning the consumer from a passive object into an active citizen—educating a "citizen-consumer" in Hobson's words—would reverse an advancing division of labor and strengthen "organic" human relations over bureaucratic and materialist ones. The arts of consumption and production, leisure and work, would be reunited and the "spirit of machinery" replaced with "individual thought, feeling, [and] effort." The resulting "increased regard for quality of life" would make it possible to "escape the moral maladies arising from competition": the ethics of the market would be transformed into "generous rivalry in cooperation."[29] By raising more community-minded individuals, "higher" consumption functioned as an enlightenment agency weaving together new bands of civic life and activating democratic sensibilities weakened by industrial mass production.

From a comparative perspective, this vision of civic consumption stands in striking contrast to the better-known productivist utopias of labor power abroad. Frederick Taylor and German social liberals, like Friedrich Naumann, were fascinated by corporate industrialism and a modernist vision of stripping labor of its cultural and social dimensions for the sake of a productivist "calculus." Organizing the world of labor required extracting it from the worlds of civil society and politics. "Standing above the titanic struggle of classes," as Rabinbach has argued, this "social vision comprised a concept of work expunged of all political and social experience."[30] Hobson's utopia of social harmony looked instead to an organic reintegration of moral, social, and political elements by reuniting the consumptive and productive sides of human activity. Instead of depending on keeping politics "out," social harmony would be safeguarded by fostering those features and habits of civil society that would replenish the liberal polity with responsible, participatory citizens.

This new liberal vision of a Free Trade society looked toward a network of small workshops and intimate firms drawing on artistic skills and catering to a plurality of tastes—with the exception of a few trades considered suitable for standardized mass production.[31] "Scientific management," or Taylorism, was considered wasteful and alienating. As Hobson elaborated in *Work and Wealth* on the eve of the First World War, any gains from standardized production would be short-lived and outweighed by the loss of "factors of human value," namely, "initiative, interest, variation, experiment, and personal responsibility." The "automatism," "drudgery," and "regimentation" would create a generation of "motor-men." Scientific management threatened to create both standardized producers and standardized consumers. And it was by degrading consumption that it would ultimately erode a liberal society. A modernist nightmare presented itself:

> the "scientific manager" ... with the assistance of the bio-psychologist ... would discover and prescribe the precise combination of foods, the most hygienic clothing and housing, the most appropriate recreations and the "best books" for each class, with a view to the productive efficiency of its members. He would encourage by bonuses eugenic, and discourage by fines dysgenesic marriages among his employees.[32]

To connect this pessimistic assessment of "modernization" to fears of an irreparable separation of the consumptive and productive elements of humanity helps us better understand widespread anxieties about the decline of civilization. Productivist ideals were so threatening precisely because they were identified as part of a broader trend away from individual freedom and social solidarity toward moral degeneration and social collapse. At the very moment mass democracy was advancing, technocratic management might leave individuals numb and vulnerable to the power of the jingoist mass media and "degenerate" commercial leisure.[33] The moral dispositions of educated, liberal, responsible citizens were at risk.

Interestingly, Hobson's advocacy of Free Trade invoked the metaphor of the socially minded consumer rather than the older liberal one of the merchant as an agent of peace.[34] This shift in the social meaning of Free Trade did not prevent "new liberals" from cooperating with traditional Cobdenites or from idolizing Cobden as *"the international man"*; Hobson chose the latter as the subtitle for his 1919 biography, while Hobhouse served as the first secretary of the Free Trade Union in 1903–04. Yet the tendency among historians to see such elements as evidence of continuity within radicalism and Cobdenism[35] has obscured the revisions these ideas underwent. For progressive Edwardians, like Hobson, the positive proclivities of Free Trade rested in generating conscious, other-regarding qualities, rather than in the unintended consequences of self-interested actions reconciled by the invisible hand.

This social vision of trade left its mark on internationalism. Indeed, one reason that this vision could be imagined, I would argue, was that freedom of trade did not appear inherently connected to a global economic system promoting mass production, nor to the growing disharmony between consumption and production following from regional specialization. In contrast to the familiar case for an advancing international division of labor, Free Trade went hand in hand with what Hobson envisaged as "social progress": "There must be a progressive recognition of the true relations, between the products which can be most economically raised upon each portion of the soil, and the wholesome needs of mankind seeking the full harmonious development of their faculties in their given physical environment."[36] Comparative advantage and specialization were qualified by the balanced development of the organic interests of humanity in different societies.

IV

While defended for maximizing wealth, Free Trade represented no surrender to market culture. Instead it appeared as an arrangement that strengthened civil society's resistance to economization. This civil society-oriented conception formed an essential background to Free Trade's appropriation by emancipatory popular politics. We have already noted the popular correlation between Free Trade and a rich associational life and active citizenship. Two related sets of questions can now be opened up for further inquiry. First, what were the moral dispositions associated with Free Trade, and what does this reveal about the imagined nature and future of civil society? Second, what was the relationship between civil society and liberal polity embedded in these assumptions?

Until the First World War, Free Trade was widely believed to protect society from new forms of social oligarchy, plutocratic power, and economic concentration. To both popular liberals and treasury officials, combinations, trusts, and cartels were purely political creatures, unviable in a liberal economy.[37] This was one background to the identification of Free Trade with the cause of "the people" and "toilers." When the *Daily News* advertised the foundation of The People's League Against Protection in December 1903, it typically contrasted the populist nature of Free Trade with the protectionist habitat of "Park-lane millionaires … and the wire-pullers of Trusts" in America.[38]

In fact, Free Trade was believed to check the materialist and individualist traits of capitalist society. To the old liberal industrialist Hugh Bell, the United States typified the social degeneration following naturally from tariffs: "I do not desire to have a crop of millionaires; I do not wish for a population striving for wealth at any cost."[39] Free Trade was associated with an ideal of social harmony based on virtues of moderation and reciprocity, not yet with the profit motive of the corporate firm. Protection, G. K. Chesterton warned, was a "new creed of materialism run mad." A combination of Free Trade and land reform, the *Daily News* told its liberal readers, was the only way to save the nation from "decadence," the social anemia of city life, and "racial decay."[40]

Instead of creating self-interested individuals, Free Trade was imagined to foster social solidarities. By preventing hidden fiscal handouts to "rent-seeking" groups, it guaranteed transparent, "visible" relations both between members of society and between them and the state, especially in the potentially explosive areas of taxation and food distribution. Alluding to memories of speculators and hatred under the corn laws, the editor of *Hungry Forties* warned that protection, by nature, was "a force making for social disintegration."[41] One reason for the unpopularity of Chamberlain's proposal to spend part of the tariff revenue on old-age pensions was that it would have introduced a dangerous invisibility into the relationship between state and society. Redistributing public income was feared to produce an avalanche of selfish demands, a lack of responsibility among its citizens, and a crisis of ungovernability—a diagnosis not so dissimilar from recent critiques of the welfare state.[42]

But Free Trade also was understood as a social agency that directly fostered mutual assistance, reciprocity, and civic-mindedness. One manual worker concluded his memories of the "Hungry Forties" with a denunciation of protection as "an immoral policy because it substitutes 'Do unto others as *they do unto you*,' for the Golden Rule, 'Do unto others *as ye would* they SHOULD do unto you."[43] The collective belief in Free Trade as an indispensable catalyst of right moral dispositions was important, not least because it helped overcome the "free-rider problem" for the Free Trade movement. Bertrand Russell, to take an upper class example, saw the fiscal issue as a "chiefly moral" one and began a long career in political activism in 1903 feeling "that morally England is on trial."[44] Free Trade improved the character of citizens. Transcending qualities of material self-interest, Free Trade in social and international relations was an educational, civilizing force moving the world toward a higher consciousness.[45] The prominent references to a concern for the poor, the cheap loaf, and the Sermon on the Mount reflected this vision of social solidarity. This had less to do with a positive view of the market than with a positive understanding of civil society, in which Free Trade helped to widen and deepen areas of public-spirited citizenship, social service, and social autonomy. Popular political economy, then, can be seen as a complement to aspects in social thought, recently highlighted by Jose Harris, in which social reform functioned as a form of ethical exchange involving personal relationships embedded in secondary associations and voluntarist agencies, promoting not only material welfare but active citizenship.[46]

This had implications for the scope and substance of democratization. There is a symmetry in the vision of civil society's relative autonomy from both the economy and from the political system. To favor Free Trade meant to favor the institutional separation of politics from society: political reform before the First World War focused on territorial representation and universal suffrage, not on functional representation. This reflected, partly, a constitutional fear of special interests. It also mirrored a constructive view of society as a terrain and target of democratization. Free Trade provided a setting for society to reform itself in a way that would strengthen liberal democracy.[47] I have noted earlier the strong belief in a congruence between liberal political economy and associational life. This could be tied to a Tocquevillian notion of civil society as "schools of democracy," leaving a space for associations, such as the cooperative movement, to inculcate their members with the civic habits of cooperation, reciprocity, and responsible action.

As a normative conception of the politics of civil society, Free Trade can be seen to anticipate some features that recently have been highlighted as characteristic of "new social movements." It combined a "politics of identity" and a "politics of influence," as opposed to a strategy of capturing the political or economic system directly by means of interest aggregation.[48] It helped society to act on itself, assisting the formation of new social norms and solidarities, and extending spheres of public discussion and civic involvement. Like the closely related Edwardian peace movement, Free Trade understood itself as enhancing civil society's influence on political life from the outside by mobilizing public opinion and raising the "standard of public life." In this fashion, it could present itself as an extra-institutional forum of political influence for the unrepresented "consumer" interest.

The Free Trade politics of civil society were no unmixed democratic success, however. The "consumer" interest was defined by moral and gendered assumptions that limited Free Trade's emancipatory horizon. On one hand, the fiscal controversy created a forum for political action by disenfranchised women. Both as activists and symbols, women created a link between domestic anxieties about higher prices and fears about "corrupt public life," in the words of the Women's Cooperative Guild.[49] Edwardian posters showing a conservative Chancellor of the Exchequer invading a poor woman's home highlighted the importance of Free Trade to the autonomy of the private sphere from interference by the state.[50] In the early-Victorian movement for the repeal of the corn laws, women already had played a political role as extra-parliamentary representatives of a "virtuous" private sphere.[51] Now in the Edwardian campaign bodies like the Women's Cooperative Guild, with more than 360 branches and 18,000 members, pushed the domestic side of Free Trade into the public sphere, linking it directly to demands for enfranchisement.[52]

On the other hand, women's role in Free Trade remained mainly that of the housewife; even women activists rarely referred to women as workers or individual consumers. Annie Esplin of the Free Trade Union stressed that tariffs in Germany undermined the stability of the family by forcing married women into the workforce, to their own and their children's detriment.[53] The progressive liberal vision also remained strongly gendered. After all, industrial modernity was condemned by Hobson for breaking up the female domain of the household and pulling women into the world of work, thus corrupting "female" skills and senses: "The exigencies of factory life are inconsistent with the position of a good mother, a good wife, or the maker of a home."[54] While the development of "good" consumption aimed to replace the routine of mass production with more creative and fulfilling occupations, like carpentry, the anticipated reintegration of work and leisure was a male preserve. It was predicated on a pronounced gendered division to restore those "female" caring qualities vital for the future of family life and the British race.[55]

Free Traders had little sympathy with the expansion of popular consumer culture—the department store, commercial advertising, sports, and public entertainment—that had gathered pace since the 1870s. Rather than appreciating the opportunities that mass leisure or shopping offered individuals for exploring their selves and creating new group identities,[56] Hobson condemned them as the breeding grounds for a "new bastard culture" driven by selfish materialism and eroding family life, civic associations, and the bonds of moral cohesion between individuals. Free Traders' ideal of intimate civil society was distinctly hostile to new consumerist spaces of the public sphere, which were condemned as the dangerous outgrowth of anonymous mass production, the artificial desires created by advertisement, and a new feudal culture of conspicuous consumption;[57] indeed, leisure was at times charged with sapping popular interest in political economy.[58] The rights of the consumer, therefore, remained narrowly defined in liberal terms of necessities ("the people's food") and creative self-perfection (carpentry, books) rather than extending to individuals' unlimited freedom to explore new desires in an expanding consumer culture.

Moreover, the particular nature of "identity" and "influence" favored by Edwardian radicals and liberals set clear limits to the further democratization of state and economy. The "politics of influence" remained tied to the parliamentary representation of a supposedly organic public interest. As the cooperative vision of civic education illustrates, this was a view of political education that was rooted in civil society. The "democratic state" depended on the social capital raised within associations outside the state. The emancipatory vision of Free Trade targeted civil society itself and reinforced a way of thinking about civil society in terms of institutional distance *from* the state. While Free Traders would split over the question of voluntary and compulsory principles in Edwardian social legislation, there was not yet support for constructing more direct institutional bridges *between* state and civil society, whether by directly assisting social self-organization or by opening up the political system to the needs and interests of particular social groups. Civil society and liberal polity were congruent: under the sheltering umbrella of Free Trade, they flourished naturally, without direct support from or institutional links to the state.

The defense of the economy as an autonomous system put economic policy (and its social consequences) beyond the scope of direct political participation. By equating the public interest with the indivisible consumer, Free Trade cemented a view of other social interests as factional forces from which the political system needed to be insulated. This made the paradigm of "the consumer" especially appealing to sections in the state, symbolized by the treasury doctrine of taxation for revenue only to protect the freedom of all consumers alike. By equating public and consumer interests, Free Trade spoke not only to "toilers" and "mothers" but to entrenched political interests as well, seeking to preserve the autonomy of the political from the claims of social groups. It thus also was able to serve an elite vision of politics that inverted the radical link to participatory democracy. For many conservative Free Traders, the most deplorable aspects of Chamberlain's tariff reform were political, not economic; in fact, some did not rule out revenue tariffs. Tariff reform, Robert Cecil warned, would replace the political world of public-minded representatives and independent men with that of "shibboleths & excommunication," led by an "impulsive and unscrupulous demagogue ... [and] a theory of politics which would soon drive all self-respecting persons to other pursuits. It is American Bossism in its worst form."[59] Free Trade sheltered a parliamentary system based on deliberation and elite representation of an imagined "public" interest from the influence of particular social interests. Thanks to the separation between civil society and political society, Free Trade was able to offer a home for conservative as well as radical democratic ideas.

V

The decade after the First World War saw the dissociation of civil society from Free Trade. This was a complex process rather than a linear one. The defeat of protection in the 1923 election appeared to confirm liberal hopes that Free Trade could be revived as a popular ideology. This proved a short-lived illusion. For while the workings of party politics delayed the introduction of a general tariff until 1931, Free Trade was gradually losing its social and cultural support. Its agitational network never recovered from the war. The Cobden Club suffered a hemorrhage of members.[60] The fate of the Free Trade Union reflected the split in the Liberal Party, as some, like business politician Alfred Mond, began to question the subordination of producer to consumer and support the soft protectionist "safeguarding of key industries." By the time of the world depression, Free Trade was no longer at the core of the collective identity of radical, labor, or cooperative movements. "1846," that symbolic marker of the birth of liberty and progress, disappeared from the center of historical memory. While the term "the hungry forties" was occasionally used, it no longer called forth the liberal narrative of Repeal. By the 1930s, the "hungry forties" had come to invoke memories of Chartism and socialism. Tellingly, in plays of that name, Friedrich Engels, not Richard Cobden, made a guest appearance.[61] The Cobdenite cause fell to smaller and more isolated groups, like a handful of economists around William Beveridge, the anti-collectivist "Friends of Economy," and Ernest Benn's Individualist Bookshop.[62] Formerly an emancipatory vision at the heart of popular politics and civil society, freedom of trade was appropriated by libertarian individualists and conservative free-marketeers and reduced to a matter for economic theory, think tanks, and economic diplomacy.

The introduction of a general tariff in 1931 signaled Free Trade's final loss of its "civilizing" function. This marked the end not only of a policy but also of a chapter in the history of civil society. One part of this story was the gradual dissociation of "freedom of trade" from a belief in the relative autonomy of civil society from the economy. While the Cooperative Party, formed during the war, continued to fight against profiteering, tariffs, and subsidies, it moved away from absolute opposition to trade regulation. "We are living in an age of trusts and monopolies, and for good or ill they seem destined to remain," the Cooperative Congress was told by its president in 1923.[63] The international power of corporations and combinations undermined confidence in freedom of trade as a domestic shelter and catalyst for a cooperative society and raised concerns about "social dumping" and capital flight to cheap-labor countries. For relief, the movement began to look to the international pooling and distribution of resources between agricultural and manufacturing societies. National trade regulation, too, emerged as a desirable tool. By 1930, the movement advocated a monopoly import board for wheat and flour representing the state, producers, and consumers. Two years later, it called for the nationalization of vital industries and the development of home trade, a program it hoped would increase employment by reducing Britain's dependence on foreign trade and prohibiting sweated imports.[64] Some leaders, like A. V. Alexander and J. T. Davies, tried to sustain the wider vision of Free Trade but had to acknowledge its declining popular resonance.[65] Once economic liberalism was linked to corporate monopolies, "social" dumping, and unemployment, it became difficult to imagine the cooperative commonwealth without import and price controls. To survive in an environment of international corporations, the cooperatives now looked beyond civil society to links with the state in matters of trade regulation. The prewar ideological link between freedom of trade and the autonomy of civil society was loosened. The issue was no longer "civil society versus the state" but where to draw the precise balance between voluntary action and collaboration with the state.

To question the separation of economic and civil society was also to question whether Free Trade and social reform necessarily reinforced each other. By the world depression, the industrial labor movement had moved toward conditional support for trade regulation to assist employment.[66] This was indicative of the more general popularity of trade regulation as a means of cushioning civil society from the growing pressure of capitalist combinations. War controls had left their mark on the popular imagination and loosened the association of "cheap food" with "freedom of trade": Free Trade's moral hold on consumer politics was weakened. This process, too, undermined the gendered connection between Free Trade and the interests of wives and mothers in radical politics. Within the women's section of the Labor Party, a quarter of a million strong by the end of the 1920s, the call for "food for the people" began to be echoed by demands for a food council to free the consumer from the grip of traders and profiteers. Instead of Free Trade, they now demanded the socialization of the trade in wheat, meat, and milk as well as a world council to coordinate international rationing.[67]

The social-democratic promises of trade regulation emerged as a new way to think about politics and the economy. For many radicals it was a way out of the matrix of Free Trade politics that had largely contained political economy as a party political struggle between liberal Free Trade and conservative Tariff Reform.[68] Trade controls were increasingly popular because they promised stable, remunerative prices and employment, checking speculators and fluctuations in supply and demand. Most ambitiously, in the program of the Independent Labour Party, national import boards and price regulation ensured the redistribution of the national income to guarantee workers a "living wage."[69] In important parts of the cooperative and labor movements, then, trade regulation took Free Trade's place as an instrument for extending social rights.

There is a striking symmetry between, on one hand, the ideological marginalization of freedom of trade in the domestic sphere of democracy and social justice and, on the other hand, the sphere of international relations. In the course of the First World War and after, Free Trade internationalism gave way to a more critical "new internationalism," which looked to organizing commercial relations and international structures with powers of economic coercion rather than to a natural congruence between commerce, peace, and global welfare.[70] Similarly at home, the older vision that had pictured the autonomy of civil society in terms of distance from the state was superseded by new approaches that sought to strengthen civil society and liberal polity by inserting supporting beams between these structures.

Functional representation, guild socialism, and industrial parliaments were all manifestations of this effort to extend democratic reform to the state and economy themselves. Here Hobson's rethinking of the relationship between state and civil society is particularly interesting because of the tight link between citizenship and consumption discussed above. In light of the growing concentration of labor and capital, many liberals revised the self-acting model of civil society as an independent nursery of democratic citizenship. While Hobson looked toward new areas of democratization after the war, his lifelong ideal of organic humanity also led him to reject vocational parliaments and G. D. H. Cole's social theory for atomizing the harmony of human interests and functions.[71] Hobson began to doubt whether civil society on its own was strong enough to counter the drift toward bureaucracy, class society, and mass culture. The "new industrial order" he saw emerging in 1922 blended state intervention, industrial democracy, and associations with public powers; a national industrial council composed of self-governing industries would arbitrate and standardize wages and working conditions. The relationship between consumers and the state assumed particular importance, because Hobson saw the failure of postwar reconstruction as a failure of effective demand and distribution. Through the state, "citizen-consumers" would be guaranteed full rights in the management of the economy. The state would act as "economic adjuster" with veto powers over wages and profits. Rather than merely attaching to Westminster a parliament of producers, who performed only "single economic functions," a "consumers' State" was needed: only "man ... as a consumer brings into personal unity and harmony the ends of all the economic functions." Equipped with executive and judicial powers, the "consumers' State" would "direct the flow of new productive power into the several industrial channels" and settle conflicts between industries as a "final court of appeal."[72] Political, social, and economic reform, he concluded, all hinged on the democratic integration of citizen-consumers: their success would "largely depend upon the education of the general body of citizen-consumers and their willingness to give serious attention to the central processes of industrial government through an intelligently ordered state."[73]

How was this to be achieved? Before the war, Free Trade had offered itself as a safeguard of the public interest. It excluded social interests from the political sphere, on the one hand, and assigned the role of civic education to the separate sphere of civil society, on the other. This vision had implied a strong congruence between a vibrant civil society and a strong liberal polity. Associations remained essential to preserving an organic community after the war. "Body and soul, man is made and sustained by association, and the process of civilization is nothing else than the progress of the arts of association."[74] At the same time, Hobson noted that associations were "not always a natural growth."

In their increasing modern complexity, they had come in many ways to "outstrip the capacity of men and women to develop a community sense adequate to the new demands." Civil society was no longer equipped to recreate its own associational structure capable of fostering a sense of reciprocity between its members and responsibility toward the rest of society. As experiments in democracy, both the labor movement and the cooperatives were criticized by Hobson for tending toward bureaucracy and for putting their particular interests before the public welfare.[75] How, then, to re-create the "community sense" essential to a liberal society and politics? How to attain a greater symmetry between community, organic human interests, and democratic participation? Part of Hobson's answer was to extend public participation via a consumer-state and workshop democracy. The second part was to widen the constitutional scope for associations themselves.

Rather than operating merely within the limits of civil society, separate from state and economy, associations became conceived as mediators between them, exercising public functions and assuming public responsibilities. Thus in his 1929 study of *Economics and Ethics*, Hobson called upon the state to utilize trade associations, with their "great stores of economic information needed for the purposes of economic government," for "advisory and even for administrative purposes, delegating to them the requisite statutory powers."[76] The transparency, efficiency, and responsibility of democratic government would be enhanced. This was no longer, however, a one-sided strategy aimed solely at reform of the state, in the radical tradition of fighting waste and corruption. Hobson's growing confidence in the state as an efficient agency of economic government—"the chief general organ for collective human welfare"—went hand in hand with a belief in the expanding public powers of associations. It became imperative to link associations more tightly to the state, because "influencing and participating in the State not merely renders the State technically more competent ... but nourishes in the intellectually and morally alert portions of the public a sense of real membership in the State that spreads new confidence in its wisdom and integrity."[77] Social interests did not necessarily breed faction, particularism, or rent-seeking: through participation in state and industry, they could be raised into public-minded interests. While these elements of associative democracy never amounted to a constitutional blueprint, they effectively burst the frame of the prewar Free Trade design.

VI

What implications does a view from civil society have for our understanding of Free Trade? Instead of being a mere function of economic interests or party strategy, Free Trade can be viewed as a normative vision of the good society, shaping collective identities and views of the legitimate relationship between civil society, economy, and political society. From this perspective it is possible to revise explanations of its survival as a liberal success story, whether as a manifestation of its superior theoretical evolution, its economic benefits, or liberal leaders' adjustment to "modernizing" imperatives.[78] Freedom of trade did not draw its public significance from being an agent of either market or modernization. Quite the reverse, one reason for its popular strength was that it could be dissociated from market capitalism and linked to a vision of an expanding civil society. Put differently, taking seriously the social imagination of popular Free Trade helps us move beyond the still-popular narrative of a struggle between free market capitalism and social rights, most brilliantly expounded by Polanyi.[79]

To historicize Free Trade and emphasize its social vision and cultural assumptions allows for a more critical and comparative interpretation of British liberalism and radicalism in this period. A belief in "the purity of politics," part of the inheritance of Free Trade culture, masked an institutional deficit, a limited view of democratic rights and of the possibilities of strengthening civil society through institutional reform of state and economy. In late-nineteenth-century France and Germany, by contrast, tariffs were not only means of state power or social privilege but, in the long run, also provided alternative means of democratic integration to excluded social groups and an institutional stepping-stone toward the welfare state.[80] In Britain the new interest in trade regulation after the war was part of the rediscovery of political economy as an institutional and regulatory source of greater societal rights and democratic participation. This period saw the end of an overlapping consensus built around Free Trade and marked an important turning point in modern British history. The postwar debate about trade eroded popular norms and ideas about the separation between civil society, the state, and a self-regulating economy and assisted the transition from economic laissez-faire to the Keynesian welfare state.

Notes

For generous comments, I should like to thank Mark Bevir, David Blackbourn, Geoff Eley, Jim Epstein, Nicoletta Gullace, Rohan McWilliam, Elizabeth Ruddick, and Steven Young.

1. Broadbent in *John Bull's Other Island* [1904], G. B. Shaw, *Collected Plays with their Prefaces* (London, 1971), 2:898.

2. Russell to Lucy Donnelly, 29 July 1903, cited in Caroline Moorehead, *Bertrand Russell: A Life* (London, 1992), 141; "The Tariff Controversy," *The Edinburgh Review* 199 (1904); see *The Collected Papers of Bertrand Russell*, vol. 7, *Contemplation and Action, 1902–1914*, ed. Richard A. Rempel (London, 1985), 190ff.

3. There is now a large literature on how social movements are culturally as well as politically situated, see, e.g., Hank Johnston and Bert Landermans, eds., *Social Movements and Culture* (Minneapolis, 1995), esp. ch. 7, G. A. Fine "Public Narration and Group Culture," on movements as a "bundle of stories." To avoid misunderstanding: this is not to deny the material significance of food prices, merely to emphasize that this does not of itself explain the historical meanings of Free Trade. For further theoretical discussion, see Frank Trentmann, "Political Culture and Political Economy," *Review of International Political Economy* [RIPE] 5, no. 2 (1998): 217–51.

4. *Manchester and Salford Co-operative Herald*, December 1903.

5. James Epstein, *The Lion of Freedom: Feargus O'Connor and the Chartist Movement, 1832–42* (London, 1982), ch. 7; Gareth Stedman Jones, *Languages of Class* (Cambridge, 1983), 150ff.; Norman McCord, *The Anti-Corn Law League, 1838–1846* (London, 1958), chs. 4–5; Lucy Brown "The Chartists and the Anti-Corn Law League," in *Chartist Studies*, ed. Asa Briggs (London, 1959).

6. Co-operative Union Archive, Manchester, Holyoake Mss, H. W. Massingham to Holyoake, 15 July 1903. Massingham had been commissioned by the Free Trade publisher Fisher Unwin; Greening Mss, box 4/7, T. Fisher Unwin to George Holyoake 2 Nov 1903; box 4/6, Holyoake to Greening 8 Nov 1903.

7. George Holyoake, "In the Days of Protection," in *Labour and Protection*, ed. H. W. Massingham (London, 1903), 112; reprinted in the popular radical *Reynolds News*, 29 November 1903.

8. Cited in *Bolton Co-operative Record* 14, no. 12 (1903): 27.

9. Rosalind Nash, "The Co-operative Housewife," in Massingham, *Labour and Protection*, 203f.

10. *Co-operative Educational Programme* (1916). *Two-Hundred-And-Fifty Good Books for Co-operative Libraries* (1894) included the standard works on Free Trade by Bastable, Farrer, and Fawcett, major works by Smith, Ricardo, J. S. Mill, Marshall, and Giffen, as well as Morley's biography of Cobden and, for balance, Marx's *Capital* and List's *National System of Political Economy*.

11. Co-operative Union Archive, Manchester, Parliamentary Committee of the Co-operative Congress Minutes, 25 July 1903, 1 August 1903, 7 November 1903, 9 November 1903, 11 January 1904, 20 March 1905. Only a few co-operators opposed collaboration for compromising the movement with the "system of legalized robbery"; *The 36th Annual Co-operative Congress* (London, 1904), 331. Helped by his cooperative background, the Cobden Club's controversial secretary, Harold Cox, was crucial in securing help. As the chairman of the Cobden Club acknowledged to Herbert Gladstone, "[h]e has been useful in keeping us in touch with the bodies cooperative which will not look

at you, or anything akin to Liberal organization." British Library, London [B.L.], H. Gladstone MS 46,061, Welby to H. Gladstone, 10 January 1904. The Cooperative arrangement rescued the Cobden Club, which was starved for funds and divided over strategy; see A. C. Howe, "Hungry Forties" in *Citizenship and Community: Liberals, Radicals and Collective Identities in the British Isles, 1865–1931*, ed. E. Biagini (Cambridge, 1996), ch. 8.

12. G. H. Wood, "Social Movements and Reforms of the Nineteenth Century," *The Co-operative Annual*, 14, no. 8 (1903): 4. A less "progressive" narrative, presenting Cobdenism as the killer of Chartism and social emancipation, was used by the Social Democratic Federation, e.g., *Justice*, 4 June 1904. Recent historians have stressed the more gradual, long-term growth of associational life from the late seventeenth century; see R. J. Morris "Clubs, Societies and Associations," in *The Cambridge Social History of Britain, 1750–1950*, vol. 3, ed. F. M. L. Thompson (Cambridge, 1990), 395–443; for the cooperative movement, see now Peter Gurney, *Co-operative Culture and the Politics of Consumption in England, c. 1870–1930* (Manchester, 1996).

13. Brougham Villiers [F. J. Shaw] in J. Cobden Unwin, ed., *The Hungry Forties: Life under the Bread Tax* (London, 1904), 274. For publication figures, see *The Land Hunger*, ed. J. Cobden Unwin (London, 1913). In England the 1840s were not a decade of hunger: the depression had been limited to 1840–42; see W. H. Chaloner, *The Hungry Forties* (London, 1957). For melodrama, see Patrick Joyce, "The Narrative Structure of Victorian Politics," in *Re-reading the Constitution*, ed. James Vernon (Cambridge, 1996), 179–203.

14. Massingham introduced *Labour and Protection* hoping it would show "that a parallel to the misery inflicted by our Corn Laws exists in modern Germany, the European country in which the Protective system has been most thoroughly set up," xv f. For recent reassessments, see Hans-Ulrich Wehler, *Deutsche Gesellschaftsgeschichte*, vol. 3, *Von der "Deutschen Doppelrevolution" bis zum Beginn des Ersten Weltkrieges, 1849–1914* (Munich, 1995), 637–61.

15. House of Lords Record Office, London, Lloyd George MSS, A/13/1/4, 30 January 1905.

16. The debate was never dominated by theoretical issues or by the economics profession, which was still in its infancy, deeply divided, and, not infrequently, ridiculed. See A. W. Coats, "Political Economy and the Tariff Reform Campaign of 1903," *Journal of Law and Economics* 11 (1968): 181–229.

17. *Daily News*, 6 June 1904.

18. Ross McKibbin, *The Ideologies of Class: Social Relations in Britain, 1880–1950* (Oxford, 1994), 32. McKibbin's analysis has been seminal in stressing Free Trade's function in separating economic and political systems but has done little to explore its popular meanings. We need to take the Free Trade imagination more seriously, instead of reducing it to a liberal gospel of "Free trade finance" disseminated from above or a defensive strategy that "permitted the relative autonomy and propriety of working-class politics," 31f.

19. "A. J. M.," in *Hungry Forties*, 77.

20. The number of employees in agriculture fell from 2 million to 1.5 million between 1860 and 1911. For the failure of resettlement schemes, see Johannes Paulmann "'Ein Experiment der Sozialökonomie,'" *Geschichte und Gesellschaft* 21 (1995): 506–32.

21. Montesquieu, *Esprit des Lois* (1748), book 20; Adam Ferguson, *An Essay on the History of Civil Society* [1767], ed. Fania Oz-Salzberger (Cambridge, 1995), 207.

Albert O. Hirschman, *The Passions and the Interests* (Princeton, 1977); Richard F. Teichgraeber III, *"Free Trade" and Moral Philosophy* (Durham, 1986).

22. R. Bailey Walker, "Three Laws of a Healthy State," *Co-operative News*, 20 March 1880, leader.

23. Herbert Gladstone's works proposal for dealing with cyclical unemployment, for example, quickly encountered skepticism, because it failed to meet the criteria that works would become "reproductive." Schemes for technical education by Haldane or canal reform by Brunner targeted the infrastructure, not the mechanism of the economy, and did not go beyond the revised presentation of Free Trade by J. S. Mill half a century earlier. Asquith to Campbell-Bannerman, 1 January 1905; Spencer to Campbell-Bannerman, 16 December 1904; B. L., Campbell-Bannerman papers, MS 41,210; MS 41,229.

24. House of Lords Record Office, Lloyd George MSS, B/4/1/3, 22 December 1905 speech at Bangor. Kenneth O. Morgan has recently reemphasized Germany's influence on Lloyd George in creating a fellow "modernizer," "Lloyd George and Germany," *Historical Journal* 39 (1996): 755–66. There is some truth to this, especially for social reform, but it is equally important not to lose sight of the selective nature of these influences. In the fiscal controversy Lloyd George's views were predominantly "radical"; his enthusiasm for excluding business associations from politics was as strong as that for land reform. His speeches helped to cement notions of continental political economy as reactionary misdevelopment not "modernization." For his distorted view of German social insurance, see E. P. Hennock, *British Social Reforms and German Precedents* (Oxford, 1987).

25. Eugenio F. Biagini and Alastair J. Reid, eds., *Currents of Radicalism: Popular Radicalism, Organised Labour and Party Politics in Britain, 1850–1914* (Cambridge, 1991).

26. Frank Trentmann, "Wealth versus Welfare: the British Left between Free Trade and National Political Economy," *Historical Research* 70 (1997): 70–98.

27. Ferguson had warned that some of the "ultimate effects" of commercial progress and the "separation of professions" might tend to "break the bands of society, to substitute form in place of ingenuity, and to withdraw individuals from the common scene of occupation, on which the sentiments of the heart, and the mind, are most happily employed"; *Civil Society*, 206f. Hobson feared an erosion of individuals' "social will" to participate in political life; *Evolution of Modern Capitalism* (London, 1894 ed.), 365ff.; *Work and Wealth: A Human Valuation* (London, 1914).

28. Hobson, *Evolution of Modern Capitalism* (1897 ed.), 380. Interestingly, his analysis of the dehumanizing transformation of the consumer into a passive object and the anti-Enlightenment effects of an industrial mass production of standardized desires anticipates aspects of the more famous critique of "culture industry" by the Frankfurt School, e.g., Theodor W. Adorno, "Culture Industry Reconsidered," *New German Critique* 6 (1975): 12–19.

29. Hobson, *Evolution of Modern Capitalism*, 368ff., 377. For a similar critique of the "spirit of competition," see L. T. Hobhouse, *The Labour Movement* (1893).

30. Anson Rabinbach, *The Human Motor: Energy, Fatigue, and the Origins of Modernity* (Berkeley, 1990), 205. See also Charles S. Maier, "Between Taylorism and Technocracy," in his *In Search of Stability* (Cambridge, 1987), ch. 1; Stefan-Georg Schnorr, *Liberalismus zwischen 19. und 20. Jahrhundert: Reformulierung liberaler politischer Theorie in Deutschland und England am Beispiel von Friedrich*

Naumann und Leonard T. Hobhouse (Baden-Baden, 1990); Dieter Langewiesche, *Liberalismus in Deutschland* (Frankfurt a.M., 1988), 187–227.

31. This echoed radical assumptions of the late eighteenth century; John Keane, "Despotism and Democracy," in John Keane, ed., *Civil Society and the State: New European Perspectives* (London, 1988), 48.

32. Hobson, *Work and Wealth*, 221; 212ff. for the above.

33. In addition to his attack on jingoist media in *Imperialism: A Study* (1902), see also Hobson's contempt for new mass sports as part of a "new bastard culture," e.g., *Manchester Guardian*, 3 February 1900, and *Work and Wealth*, ch. 11.

34. See Cobden, "Protection of Commerce" (1836), in The *Political Writings of Richard Cobden*, with a Preface by Lord Welby, Introductions by Sir Louis Mallet and William Cullen Bryant (London, 1903), 1: 217–59. The elevation of the trader into a gentle, pacific agent continued an eighteenth-century idea, see Hirschman, *Passions*, esp. 56ff.

35. See the essays in *Reappraising J.A. Hobson: Humanism and Welfare*, ed. Michael Freeden (London, 1990). The static construct of Cobdenism has also come under attack for his own time; see Miles Taylor, introduction to *The European Diaries of Richard Cobden* (Aldershot, 1994).

36. Hobson, *Evolution of Modern Capitalism* (1897 ed.), 375.

37. This was part of the Treasury argument against "anti-dumping" measures, P.R.O. Cab 37/66 "The Fiscal Problem," 25 August 1903.

38. *Daily News*, 19 December 1903, 10. The People's League was started by radicals, liberals, and laborites to organize workers in the aftermath of the Dulwich and Lewisham by-elections. Its president was W. C. Steadman of the London County Council; other leading members included the MPs James Bryce and John Wilson, Councillor Barrass (Amalgamated Society of Toolmakers, Engineers and Machinists), H. A. Fuller (Metropolitan Radical Federation), and G. K. Chesterton.

39. H. Bell, in *British Industries under Free Trade*, ed. Harold Cox (London, 1904), 282.

40. *Daily News*, 18 July 1903; *Daily News*, 7 July 1903.

41. Cobden Unwin, *Hungry Forties*, 150.

42. Pierre Rosanvallon, "The Decline of Social Visibility," in Keane, *Civil Society and the State*, 199–220.

43. William Glazier in Cobden Unwin, *Hungry Forties*, 212.

44. Bertrand Russell, *The Selected Letters of Bertrand Russell*, vol. 1, *The Private Years, 1884–1914*, ed. N. Griffin (London, 1992), 273.

45. This idea remained interwoven with a nationalist faith in Britain's providential "leadership of the human race" in Lloyd George's words at a mass rally in Aberdeen: "Providence has selected the people—the people inhabit[ing] these islands—from among the peoples of the earth to carry through to victory this one idea [Free Trade], the banner of freedom in [*sic*] commerce, brotherhood through commerce, and good will through commerce," 13 November 1903, House of Lords Record Office, Lloyd George MSS, A/11/2.

46. Jose Harris, "Political Thought and the Welfare State 1870–1940," *Past and Present* 135 (1992): 116–41; Schnorr, *Liberalismus*, 431ff.

47. Note that this is the very reverse of the contemporary critique of Free Trade for eroding social and democratic networks.

48. Jean L. Cohen and Andrew Arato, *Civil Society and Political Theory (Cambridge, MA, 1992)*; as opposed to a strategy of power or "politics of inclusion," such as through electoral reform, a "politics of influence" aims at "altering the

universe of political discourse to accommodate new need-interpretations, new identities, and new norms," 526.

49. Women's Cooperative Guild, 1903 congress, cited in *Bolton Co-operative Record* 14, no. 8 (1903): 22f.

50. B.L.P.E.S., Coll. Misc. 519, poster 46.

51. A. Tyrrell, "'Woman's Mission' and Pressure Group Politics in Britain (1825–60)," *Bulletin of John Rylands University Library* 63 (1980): 194–230; Martin Pugh, "Women, Food and Politics, 1880–1930," *History Today* 41 (1991): 14–20.

52. *Manchester and Salford Co-operative Herald*, December 1903, 199; this demand was also issued by Alison Garland of the Women's Free Trade Union. The guild held rallies and sent resolutions to MPs; *Souvenir of Co-operative Congress at Stratford* (1904), 68f. Its members were largely wives of artisans and skilled laborers; see Miss Llewelyn Davies cited in Jean Gaffin and David Thomas, *Caring & Sharing: The Centenary History of the Co-operative Women's Guild* (Manchester, 1983), 20.

53. [Free Trade Union], *Tales of the Tariff Trippers: An Exposure of the Tariff Reform Tours in Germany* (London, 1910), 50f.

54. Hobson, *Evolution of Modern Capitalism* (1897 ed.), 320.

55. Hobson put the blame for unfit parenting on economic pressures forcing women into marriage. While he supported greater economic freedom for women, his ideal remained that of a "complete home life," which, he thought, would guarantee the highest birth rate in families with the highest physical and mental qualities; *Work and Wealth*, 318f.

56. Judith R. Walkowitz, *City of Dreadful Delight: Narratives of Sexual Danger in Late-Victorian London* (Chicago, 1992), esp. 46ff; Pierre Bourdieu, *Distinction: A Social Critique of the Judgement of Taste* (1979; reprint, Cambridge, MA, 1984).

57. Hobson, *Work and Wealth*, chs. 9–11.

58. "Free Trade," Mrs. Bury, a cooperator and Poor Law Guardian for Darwen, explained in a public lecture in October 1903, "was an everyday question to the wives and mothers of England; and if their sons would devote as much time to the study of the history of the past fifty years as they now do to football and other athletic games, a better judgement of fiscal arrangements was possible." *The Manchester and Salford Co-operative Herald*, December 1903, 201.

59. Robert Cecil to Edward Clarke, 29 May 1906, B.L., Cecil MS 51158. To Arthur Elliot, a Unionist Free Trader, Parliament was "the authorized exponent of the National Will," which was threatened by tariff reform and social reform alike; Elliot to Dicey, 11 December 1912, National Library of Scotland (Edinburgh), Elliot MS 19567.

60. West Sussex Record Office, Cobden MS 1197, Cobden Club subscription book; note the high number of resignations after the war; Cobden MS 1190: general meetings in 1926 and 1934 stressed the imperative of adding new members "if possible younger ones."

61. Mary D. Stocks, *Doctor Scholefield: An Incident of the Hungry Forties* (Manchester, 1936); Lilian Dalton, *Sons of Want: A Story of The Hungry Forties* (London, 1930).

62. William Beveridge, ed., *Tariffs: the Case Examined* (London, 1931); Deryck Abel, *Ernest Benn* (London, 1960); Richard Cockett, *Thinking the Unthinkable: Think-Tanks and the Economic Counter-Revolution, 1931–1983* (London, 1994).

63. Robert Stewart, *Inaugural Address, Co-operative Union* (Manchester, 1923), 9.

64. *Britain Reborn No.4: Buy British* (Manchester, 1932); J. H. Bingham, "Fundamentals of Planning," *The Co-operative Review* 6, no. 35 (1932): 206–10; the editors also gave Mosley space to advertise his import control scheme, "Co-operators

and the Manifesto," *The Co-operative Review* 5, no. 25 (1931): 21–24; G. D. H. Cole, *A Century of Co-operation* (London, 1944), 276f.

65. J. T. Davis, *Free Trade and the Consumer* (Manchester, 1934), 18; A. V. Alexander, "Tariffs and Quotas," *Co-operative Review* 6, no. 31 (1932): 7–10.

66. [Trades Union Congress] *Commonwealth Trade: A New Policy* (London, 1930).

67. *Report of the Eighth National Conference of Labour Women*, 1927, 57ff; *Report of the Tenth National Conference of Labour Women*, 1929, 46ff. See also labor women's resolutions, *ILP Report*, 1927, a6; ILP women's charter, point 6, *ILP Report*, 1930. For the reconfiguration of citizenship and consumption, see Frank Trentmann, "Bread, Milk, and Democracy in Twentieth-Century Britain," in *Material Politics: Citizens, Consumers, and Political Cultures*, ed. Martin Daunton and Matthew Hilton (Oxford and New York, forthcoming).

68. See, e.g., George Edwards, *From Crow-scaring to Westminster: An Autobiography* (London, 1922). Edwards had been a rural radical and organizer for the Free Trade Union, but during the war came to support controls in agriculture and, in 1920, became Labour M.P. for South Norfolk.

69. *The Living Wage* (London, 1926). Import boards figured not only in Mosley's New Party but also in Labour's program advocated by Graham in October 1931, Labor Party, *Report of the 31st Annual Conference* (1931).

70. See Frank Trentmann, Center For European Studies, Working Paper no. 66 (1997), 27 ff.; and now, at greater length, Frank Trentmann, "The Erosion of Free Trade: Political Culture and Political Economy in Great Britain, c. 1897–1932 (Ph.D. thesis Harvard University, 1999), chs. 5, 6.

71. J. A. Hobson, *Incentives in the New Industrial Order* (London, 1922), 147ff.

72. Hobson, *Incentives*, 151f.

73. Hobson, *Incentives*, 160.

74. J. A. Hobson, *Economics and Ethics: A Study in Social Values* (London, 1929), 43.

75. J. A. Hobson, *Incentives*, 135f.; see also Hobson, *Economics and Ethics* (1929), 381. Note that the "citizen-consumers" included both industrial and private ones.

76. Hobson, *Economics and Ethics*, 388f.

77. Ibid., 389. Along similar lines, Hobson argued that to give labor a share in the government of industry at the immediate level of the workshop would not merely make for greater economic justice but would "liberate and educate a wider and more conscious sense of the solidarity and social value of the economic system as a whole, and may make it more feasible to regulate its processes by considerations of human welfare," 267.

78. Jagdish Bhagwati, *Protectionism* (1988; reprint, Cambridge, MA, 1989); Douglas Irwin, *Against the Tide: An Intellectual History of Free Trade* (Princeton, 1996); Irwin, "Political Economy of Free Trade"; Howe, "Hungry Forties."; see now also A. C. Howe, *Free Trade and Liberal England, 1846–1946* (Oxford, 1998).

79. Karl Polanyi, *The Great Transformation* (Boston, 1944).

80. Alan Milward, "Tariffs as Constitutions," in *The International Politics of Surplus Capacity*, ed. Susan Strange and Roger Tooze (London, 1981); Wehler, *Gesellschaftsgeschichte*, vol. 3, 637–80.

– 14 –

SOCIALISM, CIVIL SOCIETY, AND THE STATE IN MODERN BRITAIN

Mark Bevir

A NY ADEQUATE DISCUSSION of the changing nature of western European states during the twentieth century should include accounts of both the expansion of their role and the democratization of their structure. On one hand, they became increasingly centralized and took on new functions in ways that strengthened them in relation to civil society. The British state concentrated decision making in itself, added to its jurisdictions, increased taxation, extended its powers of surveillance, developed new strategies of economic management, oversaw massive growth in the public sector, and accepted some responsibility for the welfare of its citizens. On the other hand, however, many western European states, especially after 1945, granted new political and social rights to their citizens in ways that made them increasingly subject to popular, democratic control. The British state was transformed by the growing power of representative institutions, the establishment of universal adult suffrage, the introduction of legal protections for trade unions, and the embodiment of social rights within the welfare state.

These changes in western European states have been explored mainly in relation to theories of economic development: Marxists have emphasised the rise of monopoly capitalism, non-Marxists the rise of corporate capitalism. Similarly, the conterminous changes in civil society, including the economy, have been explored mainly in relation to theories of the state: scholars have emphasized the impact on social life of the way states mobilized their citizens for war, the extension of disciplinary power from state institutions to social practices, and the growth of rational bureaucracies.[1] Another way of approaching these changes, however, is in the context of changes in ideas or culture. This approach will have the great advantage of enabling us to explain the apparent paradox of an expansion of state power being accompanied by a wave of democratization. This essay, then, will make two main arguments. The first is that socialist theories criticized the free market and thereby undermined the intellectual foundations of the liberal ideal of civil society. Socialists argued that the market was not a naturally harmonious system, so either the state or associations in civil society had to work to correct its defects. The second thesis is that as socialists rejected the free market, they looked to associations in civil society and popular democratic control of the state to protect the interests of the individual. The spread of socialist ideas therefore led both to new powers being taken on by the state and to an extension of the rights of the citizen against the state.

To relate the changing nature of the state and civil society to socialist ideas is to complicate our understanding of the relationship of political, social, and intellectual forces. Civil society incorporates beliefs, meanings, and debates that inform the public activities of individuals, groups, and institutions in ways that transform the political sphere. Equally, however, because these beliefs, meanings, and debates arise from reflections on social and political forces, the state and associations in civil society act in ways that transform the intellectual inquiries found in civil society. The suggestion here is that we can not analyze the dialectical relationship between civil society and the state in terms of objective social and political categories. Rather, we have to see civil society and the state as moderating one another within the context of evolving intellectual traditions. Different forms of civil society and the state develop together as the historical products of beliefs and debates. Here the Enlightenment promoted a faith in a market economy as a harmonious and self-regulating system. A liberal commitment to the minimal state, laissez-faire, and free trade inspired many people to try, with some success, to withdraw the state from the economic sphere of civic life. But the attempt to realize the liberal ideal, including an experience of a market economy, led socialists and others to reconceptualize the state and civil society. These new analyses of the state and civil society then set the scene for the rise of social-democratic states.

In what follows, civil society will be understood broadly to include all groups and institutions that lie between, on one hand, household and kinship groups and, on the other, the state.[2] Because civil society exists alongside the family and the state, it overlaps with them in ways that prevent us from making any rigid distinctions here. Still, the general contours of a broad concept of civil society are clear. Under this broad concept, moreover, economic institutions, including a market economy, are part of civil society, though not constitutive of it. A broad concept of civil society embraces liberal instances in which a market economy plays an important role, other instances in which there is little market activity, and a range of possibilities between these two extremes. Indeed, the shift from classical liberalism to socialism centered on the extent to which the market could contribute to the good of society. Liberals and socialists alike typically believed in the benefits of a strong associational culture, though within both camps there were disagreements about the merits of particular associations, such as churches and trade unions. But whereas classical liberals usually advocated a large role for the market economy as part of civil society, socialists did not. Debates about the workings of the market economy were, therefore, central to the shift from classical liberalism to social democracy.

Classical Liberalism: The Benefits of the Market Economy

The establishment of a civil society placed outside of the legitimate demands of the state was a specific historical achievement. The cultural roots of this achievement lay in moral and pragmatic claims for religious liberties and in the claims of merchants and artisans to similar liberties. Claims to personal freedom were extended from intimate matters to religion and also to economic activities. Moreover, these latter claims arose as states undertook increasingly onerous military functions in part to open-up and then protect foreign trade. A Puritan emphasis on personal conduct fed into a new capitalist discourse focused on the productive citizen so as to generate a vigorous defense of a liberal civil society.[3] In the eighteenth century, various social theorists reworked this defense to incorporate the Newtonian idea of the universe as a system of forces. Civil society, and more especially economic activity, was seen as a harmonious and self-regulating system akin to the planets. Theorists of the Scottish Enlightenment, such as Adam Smith, and later on utilitarians, including J. S. Mill, argued that private activity, whether based on habit or self-interest, could optimize wealth and happiness as well as secure peace and prosperity. Classical liberalism asserted that the economic sphere within civil society could be left to itself. A market economy would bring not an anarchic muddle but a near perfect social system.

It is possible, of course, to overstate the extent to which classical liberals put their faith in an unregulated civil society. For a start, many classical liberals were as profoundly concerned with civic virtue as with individual freedom, and they looked to associations within civil society to sustain and to embody such virtue.[4] Mill saw civic activities, especially participation in local government, as vital to ensure social solidarity. Indeed, he sympathized with Samuel Coleridge's notion of a clerisy and Auguste Comte's notion of a religion of humanity to such an extent that we can describe him as an aristocratic liberal anxious to ameliorate the possible effects of democracy.[5] He argued that representative government required a particular type of political culture, which, therefore, should be promoted as a civic religion. "Hardly any language," he wrote, "is strong enough to express the strength of my conviction—on the importance of that portion of the operation of free institutions, which may be called the public education of the citizens."[6] In addition, many classical liberals expressed serious concerns about the impact of the market upon civic culture. The thinkers of the Scottish Enlightenment, notably Sir James Steuart and Adam Ferguson, were worried about the public effects of the place that luxury acquired within modern economies.[7] Later Mill actually argued "that the most serious danger to the future prospects of mankind is in the unbalanced influence of the commercial spirit."[8] He believed that only thorough participation in the detailed business of government could prevent the commercial spirit from creating a mean populace bereft of civic virtue. Despite such forebodings, however, classical liberals generally extolled the benefits of the market economy. The thinkers of the Scottish Enlightenment, most famously Adam Smith, were modernizers who sought to show how the operation of the market transformed self-interested actions into public goods. Likewise, Mill defended a basic adherence to the market rather than state intervention on grounds that were common among the philosophical radicals. He wrote: "the great majority of things are worse done by the intervention of government, than the individuals interested in the matter would do them, or cause them to be done, if left to themselves."[9] When all the necessary caveats have been made, therefore, we are left with the fact that classical liberals placed their faith in the market. They defended the market in debates with their contemporaries, and they believed, more than any group of thinkers before them, that an unregulated economy could provide prosperity, peace, and happiness. Classical liberalism is rightly associated with advocacy of a large role for a market economy. No doubt we can debate the extent to which the nineteenth-century state actually did withdraw from the economy, let alone other areas of civil society, but the fact remains that the dominant discourse and broad thrust of public policy pointed in such a direction. Victorian Britain came to stand for the classical-liberal vision of a minimal state, laissez-faire, and free trade.

However, even as classical liberalism became a dominant belief system in British society, so people began to conceive of dilemmas within its account of the world. Not everybody recognized the salience of the dilemmas, let alone understood them to require a rejection of liberal doctrine. But socialists did so, and even liberals often recognized their import and sought to modify their beliefs accordingly. Three main dilemmas stand out. The first was a moral concern with the way the market economy undermined the traditional values and associations that made for a stable society. Romantics and radical Tories often argued that liberalism actually promoted disharmony and discord. They called for a more orderly and just civil society, with the state both sponsoring associations, such as Coleridge's clerisy, designed to promulgate civic virtue, and also intervening to protect vulnerable industries and communities.[10] The second dilemma arose in classical economics. In the 1850s and 1860s, trade unions expanded, wages and living standards rose, and there was a population boom. Such conjunctions made a mockery of the classical theory of distribution. If trade unions could raise wages, one had to reject the wages-fund theory according to which in the short term there was a fixed amount of savings to pay wages. And if population and living standards could rise simultaneously, one had to reject the law of "natural" subsistence wages, according to which population growth responded to wage rates so as to bring them back to subsistence level. Economists experienced a crisis within their discipline— even J. S. Mill rejected the wages-fund theory.[11] The final dilemma appeared in the widespread belief that trade cycles produced inevitable slumps. Many observers believed that Britain experienced just such a slump from the early 1870s to the early 1890s.[12]

They often complained that the British economy suffered from a range of ills, including technological obsolescence, insufficient investment, myopic entrepreneurs, poor management, and, most significantly, a lack of support from the state. Although reflecting on these dilemmas did not require one to reject classical liberalism, let alone to adopt socialism, the socialist critique of classical liberalism did arise in large part out of reflections on these dilemmas. Indeed, we might almost say that British Marxism embodied a concern with economic cycles, Fabianism a concern to rework classical economics, and ethical socialism a moral critique of the disruptive effects of the market.

Socialist Theories: The Failings of the Market Economy

In the mid- and late-Victorian age, radicals more or less accepted the classical-liberal vision of a harmonious and self-regulating market economy. Their critique of British society drew on a republican tradition in which social ills appeared as products of a corrupt political system rather than the inner workings of the economy.[13] Radicals argued that the undemocratic, oligarchic nature of the British state enabled landlords and moneylords to institutionalize an unnatural and unjust distribution of land and thereby to keep a virtuous people in poverty. During the 1880s, however, popular radicals began to turn to Marxism in a way that led them to break with this republican tradition. Certainly the Marxists of the Social Democratic Federation (SDF), the Socialist League, and the Bloomsbury Socialist Society began to describe social ills as products of an exploitation integral to capitalism.[14] Early British Marxists adopted Marx's catastrophist vision of capitalist development. They argued that the market economy was leading not to happiness, wealth, and peace but to crises of overproduction, the immiserization of workers, and imperial rivalries.[15] Capitalist competition led to the accumulation and concentration of capital, which then increased productive capacity. But because this increased production soon outstripped demand, capitalists were then forced into ever harsher competition, which soon led to a crisis characterized by bankruptcies, cutbacks, and unemployment. Here the growth of fixed capital, the pressure to reduce costs, and unemployment all forced wages down, thereby leading to the immiserization of the workers and the further accumulation of capital. Similarly, the intensity of competition prompted capitalists both to use the state to secure markets through imperialism and to seek refuge in trusts and cartels that further concentrated capital. Before long, however, the further accumulation and concentration of capital led to an even worse economic crisis. The free market was self-destructive, not self-regulating.

British Marxists rejected the idea of the market economy as a harmonious and self-regulating sphere. Indeed, many of them believed that the failings of capitalism made state intervention in civil society essential. H. M. Hyndman evoked a "principle of State management" in 1881 just after reading Marx.[16] Soon afterwards, at the founding meeting of the SDF, he issued a pamphlet with the significant title *The Text Book of Democracy*. The pamphlet argued that "the time is coming when all will be able to recognise that its [the state's] friendly influence is needed to prevent serious trouble, and lead the way to a happier period."[17] When British Marxists rejected the idea that the market economy guarantees individual liberty and social cohesion, they argued not only that the state had to intervene in civil society to secure a just and stable society but also that freedom had to be secured by a democratic political system. Hyndman insisted that "a great democratic English Republic has ever been the dream of the noblest of our race," and "to bring about such a Republic is the cause for which we Socialists agitate to-day."[18] The program of the SDF called not only for a parliament based on universal suffrage but for popular control of this parliament to be reinforced through measures such as annual elections, referenda, a principle of delegation, abolition of the House of Lords, and even an elected civil service.

Although Marxists often accepted the need for a more interventionist state, their economic theory did not compel them to do so. Because the evils of capitalism arose from private ownership of the means of production, a civil society without such ownership might conceivably come to resemble the liberal ideal of a harmonious and self-regulating system. The crucial question for Marxists, therefore, was what form common ownership of the means of production should take. While members of the SDF generally believed that a democratic state could act as a suitable vehicle for common ownership, other Marxists were more hostile to the state. Socialist, poet, and designer William Morris, for example, defended a form of anarcho-communism. The absence of private property would remove almost all cause for disagreement so that civil society could become a self-regulating sphere from which politics would be more or less absent.[19] Other Marxists, notably Tom Mann, favored a form of syndicalism: they gave an extended role to the state, while unpacking its democratic structure in terms of industrial units composed of producers, not geographical units composed of citizens.[20]

The SDF appealed almost exclusively to popular and Tory radicals. Liberal radical converts to socialism, in contrast, often joined the Fabian Society. They did so in the context of the collapse of classical economics.[21] During the 1870s and 1880s, economists such as W. S. Jevons and Alfred Marshall developed various versions of marginalist economics. Fabians such as George Bernard Shaw and Sidney Webb then drew on marginalism to construct theories of rent as exploitation.[22] Shaw argued that capitalists exploited workers in part by the exercise of their monopoly of the means of production and in part because as landlords they appropriated the rents arising from natural advantages of fertility. Webb argued that interest was strictly analogous to land rent since it derived from an advantageous industrial situation. Both Shaw and Webb believed, therefore, that any economy necessarily produced rent understood as a social surplus. Rent was unearned in that it reflected natural or social variations of fertility or industrial situation. Moreover, rent did not contribute to the maintenance of the supply of land or capital necessary to the efficient functioning of the economy but, rather, appeared when there was a permanent or temporary quasi monopoly. As Webb explained, "an additional product determined by the relative differences in the productive efficiency of the different sites, soils, capitals and forms of skill above the margin has gone to those exercising control over those valuable but scarce productive forces."[23] Indeed, the Fabians believed that rent promoted economic inefficiencies. According to Sidney and Beatrice Webb, child labor, variable local rates, and so forth generated forms of rent or "bounties" that enabled inefficient companies to flourish.[24] The free market led to an uncoordinated industrial system composed of numerous fragmented centers of management that knew little about each other's activities. The anarchic nature of capitalism resulted in duplication, temporary blockages, and other unnecessary forms of waste. Capitalism, the Fabians concluded, was unjust and inefficient, not harmonious and self-regulating.

Fabian economic theories, unlike those of the Marxists, virtually compelled their adherents to call for a more interventionist state. Crucially, rent arose not just under capitalism but within any economy. The surplus value evoked by Marx arose from the buying and selling of labor in a capitalist economy, so collective ownership of the means of production would eliminate it irrespective of the particular role given to the state. The rents evoked by the Fabians, in contrast, arose from the variable productivity of different lands and, arguably, capitals. The solution, therefore, was for the state to appropriate rent.[25] As Shaw explained, "economic rent, arising as it does from variations of fertility or advantages of situation, must always be held as common or social wealth, and used, as the revenues raised by taxation are now used, for public purposes."[26] The Fabians did not believe that the extended role they advocated for the state need bring an increase in bureaucracy. On the contrary, they suggested that state action would eliminate the wasteful inefficiencies of a market economy. The Fabians acknowledged, however, that socialism would make the integrity and efficiency of the state absolutely vital, and they saw democracy as the best means to secure an honest state. They hoped "through Democracy to gather the whole people into the State, so that the State may be trusted with the rent of the country."[27] Yet because the Fabians generally drew on the liberalism of Bentham and Mill, not the republicanism that fed into the SDF, they defined democracy as representative government almost to the exclusion of other forms of popular control over the executive.

The third strand to make up British socialism was an ethical one based principally on a moral critique of capitalism. Ethical socialists, following Thomas Carlyle and John Ruskin, denounced the free market and competition in favor of a moral economy and cooperation.[28] Proponents of the moral economy rejected the classical-liberal view of the market economy as a road to prosperity, happiness, and peace. They associated it instead with poverty, urban squalor, immorality, and social dislocation. Even if it did bring material benefits, these were outweighed by its social costs. Besides, many of the commodities produced in a market economy met artificial wants, not genuine needs, since production in it responded primarily to the changing whims and fashions of the wealthy. Perhaps the worst facet of the market, however, was its promotion of individualism and competition; it brought to the fore people's mean and selfish instincts as opposed to their generous and sharing ones. Edward Carpenter complained of self-consciousness being "almost a disease; when the desire of acquiring and grasping objects, or of enslaving men and animals, in order to administer to the self, becomes one of the main motives of life."[29] Capitalism elevated material greed above human relationships.

Ethical socialists rarely evoked sophisticated economic theories to reveal the unjust or inefficient nature of capitalism. Indeed, Carpenter dismissed the debate over the nature of value as akin to disputes among medieval scholastics.[30] The important thing was not to provide some formal theory of abstract economic processes but to examine the actual results of these processes and then to assess their moral acceptability. Ethical socialists wanted everyone to acknowledge that, in Wilfrid Richmond's words, "economies are within the sphere of conscience."[31] For many of them, the appropriate sphere of conscience derived from an immanentist Christianity, as with Richmond, or a mystical belief in the unity of all things, as with Carpenter. God was present in all of us, uniting us in a single brotherhood, the ethical expression of which was a social fellowship that required us to concern ourselves with others in all our daily activities. The welfare of others constituted the central focus of the moral economy.[32] Capitalists, consumers, and workers alike had to put the well-being of their fellows before selfish concerns with profits, prices, and wages. The liberal view of civil society, with the powerful role it ascribed to the market, stood condemned, therefore, for its failure to ground economics on an ethic of co-operative fellowship.

The idea of a moral economy had perilously little to say about the role of the state under socialism. Ethical socialists typically defined socialism as the enactment of a spirit of democracy, fellowship, or brotherhood. Carpenter spoke of realizing the "instinct of loving Union which lies at the root of every human Soul."[33] The Christian Social Union, more concretely, promoted "white lists" of producers and retailers who met specified criteria with respect to fair wages, decent working conditions, and so forth.[34] By dealing exclusively with such producers and retailers, socialists put the welfare of others before their own wealth and thus laid the foundations for the moral economy. The ethical socialists' ideal centered on a personal democracy in which relationships were based on equality and love. The particular role of the state was of little importance compared to personal transformations and the consequent revolution in civil society. On one hand, if economic interactions were governed by suitable moral values, there would be little need for the state to intervene. Thus, Carpenter advocated a nongovernmental society based on cooperative units of production.[35] On the other hand, however, debates about the economic role to be played by the state should not be allowed to detract from the vital need for a moral revolution within civil society. Thus, Carpenter argued that all forms of socialism and anarchism embodied the same ideal, and the key thing was to spread the ideal without worrying about the material form it might take.[36] Similarly, Christian socialists evoked the example of Christ: "Our

Lord ... preached no system of political economy. He never for a moment would allow us to suppose that changes in the machinery of political life or in the distribution of wealth would remedy the fundamental evils of society. What he required was a profound ethical change based on thoughts about God and about man."[37]

A Socialist Debate: The Role of the State

Socialists reconceptualized the market economy in ways that led them to reject the classical liberal vision of civil society. Some socialists, notably the Fabians and many Marxists, argued that the state had to take on new functions and play a more active role in civil society. They called for an extension of democracy to ensure that a more active state remained trustworthy. Other socialists, notably the ethical socialists and some Marxists, argued that civil society needed to be purged of abuses associated with competitive individualism and capitalism. They called for the democratization of civil society itself: for the ethical socialists, civil society needed to embody the democratic spirit of true fellowship; for Marxists attracted to syndicalism, the associations in civil society needed to be made thoroughly democratic.[38] One of the main debates among British socialists, therefore, concerned the relative roles to be played under socialism by a democratic state and democratic associations in civil society. To simplify, we might say that the dominant outlook in the Independent Labour Party and the Labour Party fused ethical socialism with Fabian economics to emphasize the role of the state, but that this dominant outlook was criticized by socialists influenced by syndicalist forms of Marxism and nongovernmental forms of ethical socialism.

Leading figures in the Labour Party—Keir Hardie, Philip Snowden, and Ramsay MacDonald—condemned capitalism in much the same terms as the ethical socialists. Snowden condemned the competitive market for bringing out our "animal instincts," not our moral ones: "it makes men hard, cruel, selfish, acquisitive economic machines."[39] MacDonald defended the idea of "buying in the best market," where the idea of "the best" had to include the welfare of producers, not just cheapness.[40] And Hardie evoked the Sermon on the Mount and spoke of the coming of the Kingdom of God. Within the framework of ethical socialism, however, leading figures in the Labour Party turned to the Fabians to provide them with an economic analysis of the market economy. Snowden followed Webb's theory of interest as analogous to land rent, arguing that "just as the landlord gets an unearned income from the increase in the value of land, so the capitalist gets an unearned increment from improvements in productive methods and in other ways not the result of his own efforts or abilities."[41] And MacDonald followed the Webbs's denunciation of the uncoordinated nature of the market, arguing that, whereas capitalism relied on a haphazard and chaotic clash of individual interests, socialism would eliminate waste by organizing economic life on a scientific basis.[42]

The Labour Party's reliance on Fabian economics led it to reject the ideal of an unregulated civil society and instead to demand various forms of state intervention. For a start, the existence of an unearned increment present in all economies suggested that the state should be in charge of collecting this surplus and using it for the benefit of the community. The Labour Party's mock budget of 1907, for example, spoke of introducing "taxation" so as to collect "unearned ... increments of wealth" and use them "for communal benefit."[43] Hardie, MacDonald, and Snowden advocated a range of measures to deal with the social surplus in the economy. To secure the surplus, they wanted not only taxation but also legislative restrictions on property rights and eventually public ownership of the means of production. To deploy the surplus for communal benefit, they wanted a considerable extension of social welfare legislation. In addition, they advocated public ownership of the means of production in order to end the anarchic nature of capitalist production. The solution to both overproduction and unemployment lay in the state taking control of the economy and regulating supply in relation to demand.

The leading figures in the Labour Party turned to the state to correct the failings they believed were inherent in the market economy. They rejected·traditional fears about a too powerful state by stressing the ethical nature of a truly democratic state. Liberals had been right to oppose state intervention when the state had been a corrupt aristocratic one, but the establishment of democracy would make the state trustworthy. As MacDonald explained, "the democratic State is an organisation of the people, democratic government is self-government, democratic law is an expression of the will of the people who have to obey the law."[44] The leading figures within the Labour Party defined democracy in terms taken again from the ethical socialists and the Fabians. They equated democracy with a spirit of fellowship and representative institutions, rarely showing enthusiasm for other forms of popular control of the state. A social-democratic state provided a vehicle for freedom. The liberal view of liberty as based on individual activity in a civil society undisturbed by the state made sense when such activity was believed to yield justice, wealth, peace, and happiness. But once socialists questioned the efficacy of the market as a deliverer of such goods, they had to redefine the value of liberty. Typically they redefined it as dependent on factors such as employment, a minimal standard of welfare, and even participation in a polity aiming at the common good. The state became a vehicle for promoting liberty.

While the dominant outlook in the Labour Party drew on Fabian economics, socialist opposition to this outlook often drew on forms of Marxism drifting towards syndicalism and forms of ethical socialism incorporating a nongovernmental ideal. The leading British syndicalists, including Mann and James Connolly, were Marxists who had belonged to the SDF.[45] They emphasised two themes. They argued, first, that the cure for capitalism lay in a transformation of industry and society without any involvement by the political realm. Because Marxist economics did not compel one to call for a greater role for the state, syndicalists were able to envisage a harmonious civil society in which the capitalist system of private property had been replaced by one based on worker-owned industrial units. The syndicalists rejected the Labour Party's commitment to realizing socialism through a parliamentary party and, instead, looked toward the industrial action of trade unions. The syndicalists argued, second, that any leadership soon became a self-serving bureaucracy unless it were subject to strong democratic control. Even worker-owned industrial units had to be subject to popular control through a principle of delegation and so forth. The syndicalists, and many other Marxists, opposed the Labour Party's restricted view of democracy as requiring little other than representative government.[46] They wanted to extend popular control by introducing the initiative and referenda into the institutions with which they were concerned.

Ethical socialism, with its debt to Ruskin, often incorporated a romantic medievalism in which craftsmen conjoined in guilds were seen as an approximation to the ideal of a social fellowship. A. J. Penty developed this medievalism in his *The Restoration of the Gild System*, which in its preface acknowledged a debt to Ruskin and to Carpenter and which inspired the other begetters of guild socialism, A. R. Orage and S. G. Hobson.[47] The early guild socialists drew on two themes central to the ethical socialist tradition. They argued, first, that the ideal of fellowship consisted of a social spirit of democracy. Individuals would exercise full control over their own daily activities in a cooperative and decentralized society. As

Penty explained, "it is necessary to transfer the control of industry from the hands of the financier into those of the craftsman."[48] The guild socialists argued, second, that the cure for capitalism lay in this moral ideal of fellowship, an ideal to which the political realm was largely irrelevant and perhaps even detrimental. Because the moral economy did not require state intervention, indeed because state-owned industries were capable of retaining the commercial ethic of private companies, the Labour Party should focus not on parliamentary politics but on the creation of the ideal of fellowship. The guild socialists rejected the Labour Party's view of democracy as representative government. Democracy, they insisted, entailed local control over the institutions within civil society and these institutions being largely autonomous from the state.

The Labour Party called for an extension of the state to eliminate the inequities and inefficiencies associated with capitalism. Socialist hostility to this position, from both within and without the Party, drew on the economics of the Marxists and ethical socialists to defend socialist visions based on voluntary associations rather than the state.[49] Although all socialists rejected the classical-liberal ideal, there was a division between those who looked to the state to correct the failings of the market and those who sought to transform civil society from within itself in a way that would make state intervention superfluous. The latter group long continued to criticize the Labour Party for the statist nature of its ideal and its limited concept of democracy. Not long after the end of the First World War, for instance, pluralists such as G. D. H. Cole and Harold Laski fused guild socialism with syndicalism, and also some Fabian themes, in an attempt to revitalize the democratic impulses within the Labour Party.[50]

Social-Democracy and Its Discontents

By the outbreak of the First World War, the Labour Party had accepted socialist doctrines that committed it to an extended role for the state. These doctrines transformed state and society over the next half-century. To understand why these doctrines did so, however, we have to recognize that closely related ones gained ground among nonsocialists.[51] Liberals and conservatives, too, reflected on the dilemmas posed by economic cycles, marginalism, and a moral disquiet at the effects of the market. When they did so, they often adopted ideas resembling those of the socialists. Thus, J. A. Hobson explained cycles in the economy as products of a form of underconsumption endemic to the free market, while Marshall introduced the concepts of producer's and consumer's surpluses into neoclassical economics.[52] Numerous theorists began to challenge the idea that the market constituted a harmonious, self-regulating system. Moreover, they often turned to the state to put right the failings of the market, and to democracy to ensure the state could be trusted to play such a role. It is not surprising, therefore, that the twentieth century has witnessed both an expansion of state power and a growth of democracy. The state increased taxation, took an increasingly active role in economic management, and accepted some responsibility for the welfare of its citizens precisely because the market economy was now conceived as incapable of dealing adequately with such matters. Equally, the suffrage was extended, legal protections were granted to institutions in civil society such as trade unions, and citizens acquired greater social rights against the state precisely because an extended state was conceived as being trustworthy only if it were subject to democratic control.

The changes in the nature of the state and civil society therefore have to be located against the relevant intellectual background. No doubt the rise of corporate capitalism, the need of the state to mobilize the population for war, and similar factors played a role in bringing about the changes. Nonetheless, these developments were not given to people as brute facts; rather, they were developments that people made sense of through beliefs and debates that constituted part of the intellectual background. Certainly one need not conceive of trusts and cartels as in need of regulation, let alone as evidence of the need for state ownership. Socialists and others argued in this way only because public debate, private discussion, and personal reflection led them to reject the liberal view of civil society that dominated Victorian Britain. Similarly, politicians would not have mobilized people for war through the state if they had believed the state could not play such a role, and they would not have seen the experience of war as relevant for peace had they not been convinced there were problems with a market economy. The First World War mattered because it was interpreted as further evidence of the failings of a classical liberalism that already had been rejected. MacDonald said that the war provided "a wonderful proof" of the socialist argument, not that the war constituted the socialist argument.[53] The war reinforced arguments about the inequity and inefficiency of the free market, arguments that pointed the way to a shift in vision from a market economy and night-watchman state to social democracy.

Of course, the process of historical change has continued throughout the twentieth century. The emergence of new ideas and institutions produced new debates. Social theorists theorized dilemmas in the theory and practice of social democracy, and these theories inspired further changes in both state and civil society. Social theorists began to suggest that social democracy had undermined civil society. Many of them went on to equate the alleged decline of civil society with an apparent lack of social cohesion. Moreover, worries about the erosion of social cohesion were compounded by a growing unease over the operation of the welfare state. Social theorists began to highlight the emergence of an underclass trapped in a cycle of welfare dependency. Some theorists also argued that the bureaucratic nature of the welfare state undermined the spirit of independence and self-help among many of its beneficiaries. The solution to all of these problems often has been seen to lie in a vigorous civil society. In this view, the welfare state needs to be superseded, at least to some extent, by voluntary associations based on local initiatives. Some of the theorists who call for a revitalized civil society are part of the new right; people like David Green generally adopt a neoliberal vision that relies heavily on the market.[54] Others, however, are inspired by the arguments with which syndicalists and guild socialists once challenged the dominant ideas in the Labour Party. Paul Hirst, for example, has drawn on Cole, J. N. Figgis, and Laski to argue for a shift from the state to a more pluralist society. He wants to revitalize civil society by returning to it tasks currently undertaken by the state and by thoroughly democratizing its institutions and practices.[55] In Britain, however, most critics of the existing social-democratic state still allow, albeit tacitly, some validity to the arguments of the early Fabians and ethical socialists. Certainly neither Green nor Hirst wants to do away with the welfare state altogether. Rather, they want to see the state doing more through and alongside markets or democratic associations. Therefore, the arguments of the early socialists still constitute a part of the accepted background against which current disputes are conducted.

Notes

1. See, respectively, Theda Skocpol, *Protecting Soldiers and Mothers: The Political Origins of Social Policy in the United States* (Cambridge, Mass., 1992); Michel Foucault, *Discipline and Punish: The Birth of the Prison*, trans. A. Sheridan Smith (London, 1977); Max Weber, *On Capitalism, Bureaucracy, and Religion*, ed. S. Andreski (London, 1983).

2. Some scholars define civil society in contrast to the market. See, e.g., Jean Cohen and Andrew Arato, *Civil Society and Political Theory* (Cambridge, Mass., 1992). While we should not confuse issues of definition with those of substance, I am worried that this way of defining the term encourages certain assumptions about clear-cut differences between the market and other aspects of civil society. Consider, for instance, three plausible reasons for defining civil society in contrast to the market. First, one might say the market lacks the personal immediacy, or face-to-face interactions, of some associations. Surely, however, the market entails such interactions when consumers buy items in shops or workers negotiate with managers; and surely a number of churches are constituted more by television and radio programs than by physical meetings. The level of personal intimacy in an institution depends on the technology associated with it as much as on any properties allegedly intrinsic to it. Second, one might say people do not join the market in the way they do other associations. But surely people are brought into both churches and markets by learning and repeating appropriate patterns of behavior in a process of socialization. Likewise, to suggest that people choose to join other associations in a way they do not the market is to come perilously close to assuming a view of the human subject as autonomous, when such a view is at best ethnocentric and at worst unsustainable. Third, one might suggest that other associations perform functions different than the market performs in society. Surely, however, all sorts of associations are capable of performing all sorts of functions. To equate certain associations with certain functions is, therefore, again to run the risk of creating a theory that is at best ethnocentric and at worst unsustainable. Cf. Chris Hann and Elizabeth Dunn, eds., *Civil Society: Challenging Western Models* (London, 1996). No doubt there are differences, at least of degree, here. But by insisting on including the market within civil society, we help to dispel some of the mythic qualities ascribed to the market by both its proponents and its critics.

3. The classic study of the process remains Max Weber, *The Protestant Ethic and the Spirit of Capitalism*, trans. T. Parsons, intro. R. Tawney (London, 1930).

4. Donald Winch, *Adam Smith's Politics* (Cambridge, 1978); Eugenio Biagini, "Liberalism and Direct Democracy: John Stuart Mill and the Model of Ancient Athens," in *Citizenship and Community: Liberals, Radicals, and Collective Identities in the British Isles, 1865–1931*, ed. E. Biagini (Cambridge, 1996), 21–44. It should be said, however, that by the time we reach Mill the idea of virtue has been transformed to highlight self-development and responsible public participation.

5. Alan Kahan, *Aristocratic Liberalism: The Social and Political Thought of Jacob Burckhardt, John Stuart Mill, and Alexis de Tocqueville* (Oxford, 1992).

6. J. S. Mill, "Considerations on Representative Government," in *Collected Works of J.S. Mill* (London, 1963–89), 19:535.

7. Istvan Hont, "The Rich Country-Poor Country Debate in Scottish Classical Political Economy," in *Wealth and Virtue: The Shaping of Political Economy in the Scottish Enlightenment*, ed. I. Hont and M. Ignatieff (Cambridge, 1983).

8. J. S. Mill, "De Tocqueville on Democracy in America [II]," in *Collected Works*, 18:198.

9. J. S. Mill, "Principles of Political Economy," in *Collected Works*, 3:941.

10. Jonathan Mendilow, *The Romantic Tradition in British Politics* (London, 1986); Raymond Williams, *Culture and Society, 1780–1950* (London, 1987).

11. J. S. Mill, "Thornton on Labour and Its Claims," in *Collected Works*, 5:631–68. Examples of economists decrying the state of their discipline include William Cunningham, "Political Economy as a Moral Science," *Mind* 3 (1878), 369–83; H. S. Foxwell, "The Economic Movement in England," *Quarterly Journal of Economics* 2 (1888): 84–103; Henry Sidgwick, *The Principles of Political Economy* (London, 1883), 1–7.

12. Historians have been skeptical about the depth of the depression, restricting it at most to certain sectors: see S. B. Saul, *The Myth of the Great Depression 1873–1896* (London, 1969). The fact remains, however, that most contemporaries believed they were living through a depression.

13. The alliance between radicals and liberals has been emphasized by Eugenio Biagini and Alastair Reid, eds., *Currents of Radicalism: Popular Radicalism, Organised Labour and Party Politics in Britain, 1850–1914* (Cambridge, 1991). On the discourse of popular radicalism, see Patrick Joyce, *Visions of the People: Industrial England and the Question of Class* (Cambridge, 1991); Gareth Stedman Jones, "Rethinking Chartism," in *Languages of Class: Studies in English Working Class History 1832–1982* (Cambridge, 1983), 90–178.

14. Mark Bevir, "The British Social Democratic Federation 1880–1885: From O'Brienism to Marxism," *International Review of Social History* 37 (1992): 207–29; Mark Bevir, "Republicanism, Socialism, and Democracy in Britain: The Origins of the Radical Left," in *Journal of Social History* (forthcoming).

15. See, e.g., H. M. Hyndman, *The Economics of Socialism* (London, 1896); William Morris and Ernest Bax, *Socialism: Its Growth and Outcome* (London, 1893).

16. H. M. Hyndman, "The Dawn of a Revolutionary Epoch," *Nineteenth Century* 9 (1881): 17.

17. H. M. Hyndman, *The Text Book of Democracy: England for All* (London, 1881), 31.

18. *Justice*, 14 June 1884.

19. William Morris, *News from Nowhere*, in *The Collected Works of William Morris* (London, 1910–15), vol. 16.

20. Joseph White, *Tom Mann* (Manchester, 1991).

21. On the Fabians and their intellectual ancestry, see Norman and Jean MacKenzie, *The First Fabians* (London, 1977); Willard Wolfe, *From Radicalism to Socialism* (New Haven, 1975).

22. Mark Bevir, "Fabianism and the Theory of Rent," *History of Political Thought* 10 (1989): 313–27.

23. Sidney Webb, "English Progress towards Social Democracy," *Fabian Tract, no. 15* (1892), 5.

24. Sidney and Beatrice Webb, *Industrial Democracy* (London, 1902), esp. 863–72.

25. At first Webb advocated the positivist solution of moralization of the capitalist: see Sidney Webb, "The Economics of a Positivist Community," *Practical Socialist* 1 (1886): 37–39. Before long, however, he rejected this solution on the grounds that it would not address the inefficiencies of the free market: see Sidney Webb, "Rome: A Sermon in Sociology," *Our Corner* 12 (1888): 53–60 and 79–89.

26. George Bernard Shaw, "The Economic," in *Fabian Essays in Socialism*, ed. G. Shaw (London, 1890), 27.

27. George Bernard Shaw, "The Transition to Social Democracy," in ibid., 182.

28. On the importance of Carlyle and Ruskin for ethical socialism, see Stanley Pierson, *Marxism and the Origins of British Socialism* (Ithaca, 1973); and Mendilow, *Romantic Tradition*. On ethical socialism, also see Stephen Yeo, "A New Life: The Religion of Socialism in Britain, 1883–96," *Historical Workshop* 4 (1977): 5–56.

29. Edward Carpenter, *The Art of Creation* (London, 1904), 50.

30. Edward Carpenter, "The Value of the Value Theory," *To-day* 11 (1989): 22–30.

31. Wilfrid Richmond, *Christian Economics* (London, 1888), p. 25.

32. Frank Trentmann, "Wealth versus Welfare: The British Left between Free Trade and National Political Economy before the First World War," *Historical Research* 70 (1997): 70–98.

33. Edward Carpenter, *Angel's Wings* (London, 1898), 226.

34. E.g., "Preferential Dealing," in Christian Social Union (Oxford Branch), Leaflets, Bodleian Library, Oxford.

35. Edward Carpenter, "Transitions to Freedom," in *Forecasts of the Coming Century*, ed. E. Carpenter (Manchester, 1897), 174–92.

36. *Commonweal*, 5 December 1891.

37. Charles Gore, *Strikes and Lock-Outs: The Way Out* (London, 1926), 12.

38. Of course, the divisions were never as clear-cut as this suggests. So, for example, Sydney Olivier, a Fabian, held views remarkably close to those described as ethical socialism: see Sydney Olivier, *Sydney Olivier: Letters and Selected Writings*, ed., M. Olivier (London, 1948). Likewise, many of the early socialists changed their beliefs somewhat, often under one another's influence. So, for example, the Webbs and Carpenter briefly showed signs of being influenced by syndicalism: see Sidney and Beatrice Webb, *A Constitution for the Socialist Commonwealth of Great Britain* (London, 1920); Edward Carpenter, *Towards Industrial Freedom* (London, 1917).

39. Philip Snowden, *Socialism and Syndicalism* (London, 1913), 84.

40. Ramsay MacDonald, *The Zollverein and British Industry* (London, 1903), 163.

41. Snowden, *Socialism and Syndicalism*, 117.

42. E.g., Ramsay MacDonald, "Socialism," in *Ramsay MacDonald's Political Writings*, ed. B. Barker (London, 1972).

43. Philip Snowden, "The Socialist Budget 1907," in *From Socialism to Serfdom*, ed. J. Hardie (Hassocks, 1974), 7.

44. Ramsay MacDonald, *Socialism and Society* (London, 1905), 70.

45. R. J. Holton, *British Syndicalism, 1900–14: Myths and Realities* (London, 1976). On Connolly's political thought, see David Howell, *A Lost Left* (Manchester, 1986).

46. On socialist debates about the nature and role of democracy, see Logie Barrow and Ian Bullock, *Democratic Ideas and the British Labour Movement, 1880–1914* (Cambridge, 1996).

47. A. J. Penty, *The Restoration of the Gild System* (London, 1906). For discussion of the movement, see S. T. Glass, *The Responsible Society: The Ideas of the English Guild Socialists* (London, 1966).

48. Penty, *Restoration*, 57.

49. Once again, of course, the division was not as clear-cut as this suggests. So, e.g., Orage and Hobson were themselves members of the Fabian Society, albeit part of an internal opposition to Shaw and the Webbs; while the leading figures in the Labour Party, including MacDonald, were influenced at times by doctrines such as syndicalism. See Ramsay MacDonald, *Socialism: Critical and Constructive* (London, 1921).

50. A. W. Wright, *G. D. H. Cole and Socialist Democracy* (Oxford, 1979); Michael Newman, *Harold Laski: A Political Biography* (Basingstoke, 1993).
51. Cf. Frank Trentmann, "The Strange Death of Free Trade: The Erosion of 'Liberal Consensus' in Great Britain, c. 1903–1932," in *Citizenship and Community*, ed. E. Biagini (Cambridge, 1996), 219–50.
52. J. A. Hobson and A. F. Mummery, *The Physiology of Industry* (London, 1889); Alfred Marshall, *Principles of Economics*, ed. C. Guillebaud (London, 1961).
53. Ramsay MacDonald, *Socialism after the War* (London, 1918), 8.
54. David Green, *Reinventing Civil Society: The Rediscovery of Welfare without Politics* (London, 1993); David Green, *Community without Politics: A Market Approach to Welfare Reform* (London, 1996).
55. Paul Hirst, ed., *The Pluralist Theory of the State: Selected Writings of G. D. H. Cole, J. N. Figgis, and H. J. Laski* (London, 1989); Paul Hirst, *Associative Democracy: New Forms of Economic and Social Governance* (Cambridge, 1994); Paul Hirst, *From Statism to Pluralism: Democracy, Civil Society, and Global Politics* (London, 1997).

CIVIL SOCIETY IN THE AFTERMATH OF THE GREAT WAR

The Care of Disabled Veterans in Britain and Germany

Deborah Cohen

DISABLED VETERANS were the Great War's most conspicuous legacy. At the Armistice, there were eight million disabled veterans in Europe, each of whom required, often in the most literal sense, reconstruction.[1] Casualties of Europe's bloodiest war, disabled soldiers had suffered the worst injuries ever seen. Shrapnel from exploding shells tore a ragged path through flesh and bone, leaving wounds, one British surgeon acknowledged, "from which the most hardened might well turn away in horror."[2] Under the threat of constant shellfire and ubiquitous death, some men lost their minds. Others contracted debilitating illnesses that stole their breath and shortened their lives. Years after their demobilization, disabled veterans still bore the sufferings war inflicted. Like bank clerk Erich Reese, they lived with injuries that robbed independence. Both hands amputated, blind in one eye, Reese found himself unable even to hold an umbrella.[3] Former infantryman Albert Bayliss, gassed in France, could not sleep for his racking cough. Unemployed for thirteen months, his rent severely in arrears, Bayliss despaired. "I am only 31," he wrote, "what will I be in a few years time."[4] Keen sportsmen became invalids unable to climb staircases. A drummer boy lost both of his hands. Each disabled man brought the war's horrors home with him.

Throughout Europe, the care of disabled veterans posed one of the most important challenges to postwar reconstruction. Although the war's chief belligerents faced the same dilemma, they sought to resolve the problem in strikingly different ways. In Britain, rehabilitation was left largely to philanthropy and the generous public. In Germany, on the other hand, the state embraced the care of disabled veterans as its highest duty, and charity was all but eliminated. In the latter half of the 1920s, Germany's first democracy spent approximately 20 percent of its annual budget on war victims' pensions; in Britain, by contrast, war pensions accounted for less than 7 percent of the annual budget from 1923 onwards.[5] Yet the British state's neglect, and the German state's attentiveness, had paradoxical effects. Despite comparatively generous pensions and the best social services in Europe, disabled veterans in Germany came to despise the state that favored them. In contrast, their British counterparts remained devoted subjects though they received only meager compensation.

Why did those who had profited from a state's generosity become its implacable foes? Why did Britain's heroes, treated so shabbily by successive governments, never force the state to pay for its negligence? The answers to these questions are complicated. The consequences of victory and defeat, on one hand, and the broader political cultures of interwar Germany and Britain, on the other, frame my inquiry. However, the war's resolution and political culture cannot fully account for the very different responses of veterans in Britain and Germany. Veterans' attitudes toward their fellow citizens left an indelible imprint on ex-servicemen's political movements. In both countries, broad public participation in the resolution of the war victims' problems— through voluntary organizations and charities—led veterans to believe that their fellow citizens had honored their sacrifices. Voluntarism brought about a reconciliation between the war's most visible victims and those for whom they had suffered. Veterans' demands on the state reflected what they believed they could expect from their fellow citizens.

In the absence of state involvement, British philanthropists brokered a lasting social peace between the disabled and their fellow citizens. Shoddy treatment at the hands of the state never shook disabled veterans' belief that the public had appreciated their sacrifices. Fearful of alienating their fellow citizens, British veterans—alone among their European counterparts—retreated from politics. No such reconciliation between the public and veterans occurred in Germany. It was not, as veterans later came to believe, that the public scorned their sacrifices. State authorities in postwar Germany eliminated most avenues for the country's citizens to demonstrate their gratitude. Intent upon preserving the new republic's monopoly on benevolence, German civil servants viewed charities for the disabled as a threat to the state's own claim to legitimacy. They closed most philanthropies down, hounding the oldest and most reputable into submission. Yet as a result of the suppression of charity, the Weimar state ended up bearing not only the burden of thanks for the entire Fatherland but the full brunt of veterans' discontent.

This chapter begins with an analysis of care for the disabled in Britain and Germany, focusing on the parallel development of two very different systems of care, one driven by voluntary effort, the other the crowning achievement of a new state. Each system, the second part of the essay will argue, fostered a particular type of ex-servicemen's movement. In Britain, veterans' associations cultivated the public and considered their fellow citizens the best allies against the negligent state. In Germany, by contrast, veterans turned against a public they believed had scorned their sacrifices. German veterans' sense of alienation fueled their unceasing demands on the state. Part three will assess the benefits and costs to individual veterans of social reconstruction in both countries. As the state's favored wards, German veterans enjoyed a privileged place in the turbulent post-war economy. Left to the mercy of charity, by comparison, British veterans paid a high price for their country's stability and democratic survival.

I

Despite high expectations raised during the war and promises of "a land fit for heroes," the British state offered only modest compensation to its disabled. Civil servants in the Ministry of Pensions, founded 1917, were more concerned to limit the state's liabilities than to ensure veterans' well-being. Even the seriously disabled were paid pensions that fell short of the minimum they needed for survival. In 1920, a paraplegic received two pounds a week, not even half of what unskilled building (84s.4d.) and coal mining laborers (99s.3d.) could expect that year.[6] As the cost of living fell in the early 1920s, the buying power of pensions increased. However, the amount paid was not enough to allow men to live with a measure of comfort—or enjoy family life. In France and Germany, men received higher pensions when they married and had children. Citing the prohibitively high cost of marital allowances (£30 million), British authorities compensated the disabled only for familial "responsibilities" they had "incurred" before disablement.[7]

Most importantly, successive British governments proved extremely reluctant to institute programs that would provide disabled men with a chance at gainful employment. At the end of the war, the government had few plans for rehabilitation. In early 1920, the British Ministry of Labor trained only 13,000 disabled men, while another 65,000 waited on placement.[8] Less than two years later, with an estimated 100,000 disabled ex-servicemen unemployed, the government closed admission to the rehabilitative training programs altogether.[9] Because of the postwar slump, the Ministry of Labor could not find employment for those disabled who had already been retrained. There was no room for others. In response to the plight of the severely disabled, the German, French, and Italian states mandated the compulsory employment of badly disabled men; in Britain, the war's victims were left to the mercy of their fellow citizens.

Historians often have noted the unwillingness of the interwar British state to intervene in intractable social problems.[10] Less well understood, however, is the role that voluntarists played in assuming duties that many contemporaries regarded as the state's responsibility.[11] In Britain, the reintegration of disabled veterans proceeded primarily through voluntary and philanthropic efforts. Philanthropists ran most initiatives for the long-term treatment or rehabilitation of wounded serviceman, from the country's largest artificial limb-fitting center at Roehampton to the comprehensive program for the war-blinded, administered through St. Dunstan's Hostel. Before their discharge from hospital, every blinded veteran in Britain received a Braille watch and an invitation to train at St. Dunstan's.[12] Similarly, voluntarists administered all organized employment for severely disabled men, whether in settlements for neurasthenics, through the ten local Lord Roberts' Workshops, or in factories such as Bernard Oppenheimer's specially outfitted diamond-cutting facility in Brighton. Capitalizing on public indignation about the government's inaction, philanthropists raised money as never before. In just six months (July to November 1916), the British Women's Hospital Committee raised £150,000 to build a home for paralyzed men.[13] Every home for the permanently disabled—and there were eight such institutions in the London area alone—owed its founding to private munificence.

Philanthropists did not wish to replace the state. But in essence, their success encouraged the Ministry of Pensions to do even less for its disabled than it had originally pledged. Ministry officials saw no reason why the state should provide for war victims when philanthropists had produced a Lord Roberts', a St. Dunstan's, and a Roehampton. Charitable institutions that themselves reflected the state's unwillingness to provide for the disabled thereby served to justify further governmental neglect.

By relying on charity, the Ministry of Pensions expected to save money. But fiscal conservatism was not its sole consideration. Between 1920 and 1922, when tens of thousands of men waited for rehabilitation, the ministry underspent special Treasury grants for the purpose by more than one-third.[14] What was at stake for the ministry's senior civil servants was their conception of the state's proper sphere. To the Ministry of Pensions' way of thinking, the state did not represent the nation but was only one actor among many, and a beleaguered one at that.[15] The state could not take on too much. The British public, or so ministry officials believed, wanted the state to accept an infinite amount of responsibility for the disabled—whether or not it could afford to do so. By contrast, the Ministry's officials thought it their duty to divest the state of as many tasks as they could. Eager to restrict the state's purview, and increasingly subject to Treasury restrictions, senior civil servants in the Ministry of Pensions delegated responsibility for the most severely injured disabled—the most expensive of cases—to voluntary initiative.

The case of disabled ex-servicemen shows that in a period often conceived of in terms of the state, voluntarism proved a more significant force than is generally acknowledged. As the state demobilized between 1919 and 1921, those ex-servicemen to whom successive governments owed the most—the paralyzed, the insane, the tubercular—instead found themselves dependent on the public's philanthropy. Rare was the disabled ex-service man who, by the end of the war, had not been served by charitable enterprise. Of course, charities could help only a fraction of the needy over the long term. Total war wrought destruction far beyond the resources of voluntarism. All told, the number of men employed by sheltered workshops may have approached 2,000 at any one time; according to the government's figures, that was only a fraction of those who needed work.[16] Nevertheless, the public's role was prominent and long lasting. Throughout the 1920s, donations to the charities for the disabled remained strong, and while there was a general decline during the Slump, some institutions actually recorded improvements. In 1932, donations to the Village Centre at Enham, a rehabilitative training colony for neurasthenics and other "difficult" cases, were higher than they had been in 1921; at the height of the Slump in 1933, Enham managed to collect more subscriptions than in the preceding year.[17]

In sharp contrast to its British counterpart, the postwar German state provided its disabled with the best benefits in Europe. Not only did pensions for the most severely disabled approximate the wages of skilled workmen, but they included provisions for wives and children.[18] Unlike the British government, which limited its responsibilities to the distribution of pensions, German authorities aimed to return even the most incapacitated to work, preferably to their former occupations. Weimar's National Pension Law (1920) accorded the disabled more than a right to pensions; they were also entitled to an occupational retraining course and free medical care for their service-related ailments. After 1919, severely disabled veterans were practically assured work by the Labor Ministry. Under the Law for the Employment of the Severely Disabled, most employers were required to hire and keep them.[19] At the height of the Great Depression, severely disabled workers were twice as likely as their able-bodied counterparts to retain their jobs.[20] Despite half a million unemployed, Berlin's welfare office maintained 30,000 of the severely disabled in work. In 1932, 28 percent of the German capital's male workers were unemployed, as opposed to 15 percent of its severely disabled.[21]

The Weimar Republic created Europe's most comprehensive programs for disabled veterans. However, for most of the war, Germany, like Britain, had relied upon voluntary effort. During the war, a dynamic charitable culture thrived in Germany, even briefly surviving the defeat. In most regions, voluntary and local organizations assumed the lion's share of responsibility for the disabled. In Cassel, for example, citizens' committees found work for the disabled, while in Frankfurt am Main a war time coalition of private charities directed vocational retraining efforts. For blinded men, there were vacation homes and retraining schools, among others, Berlin's School for the War Blinded, founded by optician Paul Silex in October 1914. Those who had lost hands could attend workshops for retraining, including the Saxon One-Armed School founded in 1915.[22] In 1916, the authoritative welfare periodical *Social Practice* reported that in the greater Berlin area alone thirty-four new organizations had been founded to benefit the war disabled, a development that established philanthropists criticized from the standpoint of practicality, but the fact of which nevertheless testified to public enthusiasm.[23]

Following a 1917 decree by the Bundesrat (Federal Council), however, the state required charities that sought to raise funds or solicit new members to secure the permission of the authorities. Desperate for scarce resources, the rapidly expanding and militarized state demanded a thorough rationalization of philanthropic efforts.[24] Only a handful of charities were granted a permit to raise funds, and only on the condition that they submit to government control of their expenditures. As Germany's authorities gained unprecedented control over charity, many new or small philanthropies folded, and their more prestigious counterparts entered into junior partnerships with the state. In the early Weimar Republic, the regulation of charity proceeded dramatically; in Prussia alone, the newly appointed State Commissioner for the Regulation of Charity refused more than 300 charities for the war's victims permission to collect in the years 1919–1924.[25]

By 1924, nearly every charity for the disabled had been shut down or relinquish its funds to the government. Even the oldest and most reputable of organizations ran into trouble if the methods or aims of their application violated official dogma. On behalf of the Red Cross, no less a personage than the general of the cavalry appealed to the State Commissioner for the Regulation of Charity for permission to sell a commemorative chest priced at 37 marks.[26] On principle, state officials opposed the sale of products to benefit charity, fearing the possibility of fraud; the Commissioner rejected the application. Similarly, state officials vetoed nearly every proposal for veterans' homes. Before 1918, the citizens of the university town of Marburg raised 250,000 marks to build a home for disabled soldiers.[27] They put the foundations in the ground, but could not afford to finish the home without an additional 150,000 marks. Between 1918 and 1922, the authorities consistently refused permission to collect, on the grounds that segregation of the disabled ran contrary to the Labor Ministry's principles. State officials were willing to allow the building to remain unfinished—and the money already collected from the generous public to be wasted—rather than make an exception.

Historians of the Weimar Republic have generally accepted the restriction of philanthropy's role as self-evident, even ineluctable, a product of the socialist revolution of 1918–19 and the economic exigencies of the 1920s.[28] The causes of charity's eclipse are more complex. Justified during the war as a necessary measure against waste, the regulation of charity became, in the early Weimar Republic, a critical means of establishing the state's authority. To secure the loyalty of its skeptical citizenry, the Weimar state sought to establish a monopoly on benevolence; centerpiece of a compromise among Social Democrats, the Catholic Center Party, and the left-liberal Democrats, Weimar's comprehensive welfare programs included initiatives for youth, the unemployed, and women.[29] In a state that guaranteed the well-being of its citizenry, charity, more than merely a hindrance, threatened the state's legitimacy. Armed with decrees to regulate charity, Germany's civil servants put an end to philanthropic efforts on behalf of the disabled.

Even before the war ended, then—before there were winners and losers—care for the disabled had diverged markedly in Great Britain and Germany. In Britain, the rehabilitation of the disabled remained the business of voluntarists. In Germany, it became a cornerstone of the new democratic order. Unlike British civil servants in the Ministry of Pensions, who deemed disabled veterans an unnecessary burden for the state, German officials regarded the "war victims problem" as an opportunity. They envisioned programs for wounded soldiers, as well as those for youth and the unemployed, as showpieces of post war social policy. The Revolution of 1918–1919 gave their plans for state control of war victims' care new urgency. Wielded by civil servants convinced of the necessity of generous and comprehensive programs controlled solely by the state, the power to regulate philanthropy ended up isolating the very institutions of governance it was intended to protect.

II

What were the practical implications of the British and German solutions to the problem of the disabled? Generous pensions and comprehensive rehabilitation programs did not secure German veterans' loyalty. The German disabled came to despise the state that favored them. The British disabled, on the other hand—despite the state's ill-treatment—remained loyal subjects.

British ex-servicemen never received the "land fit for heroes" that Lloyd George had promised them, but they blamed that on the government, not the public at large. Individual philanthropists, supported by the charitable public, had done what they could. As one disabled man wrote the philanthropist Oswald Stoll in 1932, "To lose you, Sir, would be to lose the Greatest Friend the British Soldier ever had," adding that "it is to me Sir very difficult to express in writing my appreciation for your kindness in thinking of my comfort and happiness, also that of my wife and children."[30] Only the wealthy such as Oswald Stoll could build "Homes for

360 | *Deborah Cohen*

Heroes," but there were other sorts of voluntarism, equally appreciated if less spectacular. Patients at the Star and Garter Home reserved their highest praise for the women who accompanied them on their Sunday strolls. It was that kind of personal attention, said one disabled man, remembering the care he had received in a private convalescent home, that made him believe—as he put it—"life was worth living again."[31]

Scholars have often written of British ex-servicemen's hostility towards their fellow citizens, drawing on the writings of the War Generation's literati, Robert Graves and Siegfried Sassoon among them. My research does not support that conclusion. However much the disabled ex-serviceman distrusted the Ministry of Pensions or the government or the state, he believed the charitable public had done their best by him. The enormous sums raised to build the Star and Garter Home for Totally Disabled Ex-Servicemen, the Roehampton Hospital for amputees, Lord Roberts' Workshops (and many others) testified to the public's appreciation. Disabled men directed their anger at the state, usually the Ministry of Pensions, rarely against their families, and almost never against the public at large. The Home Front could not understand what soldiers had endured in the trenches; however, that did not prevent the public from helping disabled veterans rebuild their lives. Most men appreciated the distinction. They had not wanted charity, of course, but philanthropists conveyed the public's gratitude.

The British Legion, founded 1921 as the country's largest veterans' organization, erected gratitude to the public as one of its foremost principles. According to the organization's ethos, disabled veterans occupied an honored position in their society, a result not only of their own role in the war but of their fellow citizens' appreciative response to their sacrifices. The Legion filled the pages of its journal with praise for voluntary initiatives. As one commentator noted: "What would these poor fellows do but for the help of the various voluntary associations?"[32] Delegates at the Legion's annual conferences invoked the "generous public" in near-reverential tones. Urging that the Legion's financial transactions be disclosed, a delegate in 1929 referred to the importance of "keeping faith" with the public: "It was impossible to tell the public too much, and the more they were allowed to know the more they would help."[33] In 1931, the Sandhurst delegate expressed his conviction that time limits on pensions' claims might be overturned if only the public could be "rightly informed."[34] The Duncannon delegate reminded his fellow veterans, "When the public failed them, the Empire, and not only the Government would fall."[35]

As the Legion's leaders recognized, the knowledge that the public was on their side defused veterans' anger toward the negligent state. According to the Legion's officials, the problem of obtaining fair compensation was not "social" in nature. It did not, in other words, reflect the country's denial of disabled men's suffering but had to be attributed to administrative failure, bureaucratic red tape, and official hard-heartedness. The Legion's diagnosis of the problem implied its solution. Demonstrations, boycotts, and veterans' candidates would not improve ex-servicemen's lot, because, as the Legion's officials emphasized, bureaucratic failings required bureaucratic remedies. The best that ex-service men could do was to put their faith in the "generous public." Only if veterans defended their society's well-being in peace as in war—by refraining from demonstrations and by proclaiming their "apoliticism"—could they maintain the privileged status gained between 1914 and 1918. Ex-servicemen owed the British public "Service, not Self," as the Legion's motto proclaimed. Instead of mere interest politics, then, the Legion promised ex-servicemen something higher: a moral and patriotic community.

In Britain, philanthropy fostered a sense of belonging among the war's most visible victims. In Germany, by contrast, the disabled grew alienated from the rest of society, depriving the Weimar Republic of a much-needed source of support. Disabled veterans were among the most embittered of the republic's discontented. In the years 1918–1921, they formed scores of local associations to represent their interests. By 1922, there were six national organizations of disabled veterans with an estimated total membership of 1.4 million, largest among them the Social Democratic *Reichsbund*.[36] In the cities, thousands of disabled marched to secure their rights, but even the smallest towns witnessed protests. Demonstration followed demonstration—for higher pensions, for secured employment, for free or reduced fares on public transportation. Even as pension costs swelled to 20 percent of the Republic's total expenditure, veterans' organizations took to the streets to protest the state's neglect.

Veterans' bitter discontent requires explanation. Although the German disabled received pensions that were as good as their European counterparts, if not better, superior social services, and secured employment, most came to despise the republic. While lauding the state's material provisions as "exemplary," historians have blamed Weimar's welfare bureaucracy for veterans' alienation.[37] If the state succeeded in the realm of material compensation, it failed, in Robert Whalen's words, "to show human sympathy," to consider men's psychological needs, as James Diehl has argued, and to incorporate its intended clients in decision making, in Michael Geyer's formulation.[38] Yet judged by any criterion, the British state was just as inflexible, bureaucratic, stingy, and inhuman as its German counterpart, if not more so. Yet successive British governments not only dodged their responsibilities to the disabled, but remained largely immune from veterans' protests.

What was significant about German veterans' attitudes was not their anger at the state but their antipathy toward the public. At the war's end, many disabled veterans in Germany still believed in the goodwill of their fellow citizens. The public might have to be "enlightened," but once people realized how soldiers were suffering, they would respond sympathetically. In 1920, the conservative veterans' organization, the *Zentralverband*, observed that "the widest sections of the population have full sympathy for the situation of war disabled and war dependents"; it commented particularly on the public's "sense of honor and obligation, and their will" to help war victims.[39] By the mid-1920s, hope had turned to hostility. The public, or so veterans believed, was not merely ungrateful but grudged war victims their rightful due. The animosity became mutual: most people thought that the disabled were the favored wards of the welfare state, and could not understand why they should complain so incessantly. Whereas the British disabled could take pride in their fellow citizens' gratitude, German veterans complained that the public did nothing to help them. "It will not be much longer," warned one severely war-disabled man, "and we will be complete outcasts and pariahs, although it was this ruthless society that sent our bodies to be smashed up."[40]

In Germany, the process of state consolidation of war victims' care elided gratitude and compensation. For disabled veterans, the granting of ever higher pensions and better social services signified that the nation was grateful. When social services were returned to the local level (after the hyperinflationary year of 1923) or pensions were cut (as in the Depression), they assumed that their fellow citizens had forgotten them, even spurned their sacrifices. In interwar Britain, pensions were nothing more than compensation, inadequate, as everyone acknowledged, to repay what had been lost; the nation's thanks was expressed in other ways, chiefly by means of philanthropy and sympathetic public opinion. When German authorities suppressed private and local initiatives for disabled veterans, they established a monopoly on much more than welfare programs. The state unwittingly ended up bearing the burden of thanks for the entire Fatherland. However, if the state could deliver legitimation in the form of increased pensions and better social services, the peace it bought was fragile, dependent upon the republic's financial prosperity.

III

In Britain, the state escaped veterans' wrath, whereas in Germany a newly founded republic bore its heroes' full fury. And yet, individual British veterans paid a high price for their country's stability. Never reintegrated into the economy, disabled men existed figuratively, as well as literally, on the margins of British society. Although the charitable public championed the veteran's cause, philanthropy did little more than rescue men from penury. It did not promote their return to society. Disabled veterans were segregated: in sheltered workshops, in veterans' homes in outlying suburbs, in rehabilitation centers. They rarely took part in Armistice Day parades. The Great War's most conspicuous legacy, they became its living memorials. When journalists wanted to write about the war's aftermath, they visited the disabled.[41] But not otherwise. Veterans' stories were feature articles, not front-page news. Touching, occasionally also uplifting, they were irrelevant to the economy and politics.

Abandoned to the mercy of charity, British veterans suffered the indignity that those without rights must bear. As the inmates of philanthropic institutions soon learned, they were to eat the food served them, remain compliant on visiting days, and bury their sorrow in embroidery or chess. Dependent upon philanthropic goodwill, disabled veterans in Britain had no choice but gratitude. Above all, the objects of charity had to eschew bitterness and remain cheerful, at least publicly. Philanthropists might appeal on behalf of the war's "human wreckage," but, when visitors arrived, the wreckage had to behave like the brave Tommies of 1914. No one wanted to support a malcontent, a depressive, or an amputee who mourned his lost limb. While some men were good-humored, there were many others for whom helplessness, institutional life, and separation from their families proved intolerable. They got drunk and violent, or retreated into isolation. Unless they committed suicide, few outside of the veterans' homes knew about their despair. The unrepentantly disgruntled were discharged.

In comparison, the German disabled—as individuals—fared well in material terms. Despite the massive upheaval caused by hyper-inflation and Depression, the Labor Ministry and its local

---

welfare offices returned the vast majority of disabled to self-sufficiency and family life. In state-sponsored rehabilitative training programs, they learned the skills they needed to return to their prewar occupations or, if necessary, to embark on another career. Local welfare offices ensured that their severely disabled clients secured and kept jobs. For those veterans too badly disabled to work, the state provided pensions that allowed recipients to live at home with their families. Disabled veterans in Germany were integrated into the workplace; they were the welfare state's favored wards; their protest carried power. They became self-confident and assured of the justice of their cause. Their British counterparts—triumphant heroes of western Europe's bloodiest war—became the objects of charity, relegated to the periphery of their society, bound by desperation to a "grateful public" that diminished daily.

As the memory of the war receded, disabled veterans in Britain began to regret their "apoliticism." In a 1932 *Sunday Express* article, Viscount Castelrosse, who served with the Guards on the Western Front, condemned the state for neglecting ex-servicemen but acknowledged that he and his comrades also had failed: "We have never demanded our rights.... Instead of demanding our rights, we went hat in hand asking for charity. We ought to have gone bayonet in hand demanding our rights. We behaved sweetly, and were swindled accordingly."[42] Philanthropy could go a long way toward easing hard feelings, but it was never enough to provide for disabled men's reintegration. It helped keep the war's victims out of politics, not off of the public assistance rolls.

* * * *

SCHOLARS HAVE REGARDED POSTWAR RECONSTRUCTION as a task for states and their corporate partners in industry and labor, judging its success or failure on the basis of governments' responses to the problems bequeathed by war. But reconstruction after the Great War was not simply a matter of demobilizing armies, rebuilding cities, and reestablishing industry. Equally important were less concrete aspects of reconstruction, including the development of social solidarity. After this century's first total war, there was peace to be made not only abroad but at home as well. It was a peace between those who had fought and those who had stayed at home, between those who lost loved ones and those who were spared, between the disabled and those for whom they sacrificed.

In Britain, voluntarism shielded the state from the consequences of its unpopular policies. Philanthropy bound veterans closer to their society and diminished their rightful claims on the victorious state. In Germany, by contrast, the state's suppression of charity isolated the disabled from their public. As a result of its elimination of voluntarism, the Weimar state became solely responsible for the fulfillment of veterans' demands. In both nations, reconstruction required the full participation of civil society. The Weimar Republic's framers had believed that they could heal the war's rifts through the distribution of generous benefits. Theirs was a terrible error, for the state alone could not promote successful social reconstruction.

Notes

This chapter provides an overview of an argument developed in my forthcoming book, *The War Come Home: Disabled Veterans in Britain and Germany, 1914–1939* (Berkeley: University of California Press).

1. International Labor Office, *Employment of Disabled Men: Meeting of Experts of the Study of Methods of Finding Employment for Disabled Men* (Geneva, 1923), 16.
2. Henry Cedar, *A Surgeon in Belgium* (London, 1915), 22.
3. Herr Erich Reese to the Labor Ministry, 4 June 1921, Bundesarchiv Lichterfelde (hereafter BAL), RAM 7757.
4. Albert Bayliss to Lord Derby, 31 March 1922, Liverpool Record Office, 920 DER (17) 21/5.
5. Approximately 752,000 British men (from a total prewar population of 45,221,000) and 1,537,000 German (from a total prewar population of 67,800,000) were permanently disabled in the First World War. See Boris Urlanis, *Bilanz der Kriege* (Berlin, 1965), 354; J. M. Winter, *Great War and the British People* (Basingstoke, 1985), 73, 75; International Labor Office, *Employment of Disabled Men* (Geneva, 1923), 15; Katherine Mayo, *Soldiers, What Next* (London, 1934), 555; L. Grebler and W. Winkler, *The Cost of the World War to Germany and to Austria-Hungary* (New Haven, 1940), 78. On budgets: for Germany, Peter-Christian Witt, "Auswirkungen der Inflation auf die Finanzpolitik," in *Die Nachwirkungen der Inflation auf die deutsche Geschichte,* ed., Gerald Feldman (Munich, 1985), table 9, p. 93; Robert Weldon Whalen, *Bitter Wounds: German Victims of the Great War, 1914–1939* (Cornell, 1984), 16; Reichstag, Reichshaushaltsetat für das Rechnungsjahr 1932. For Britain, Sir Bernard Mallet and C. Oswald George, *British Budgets: Third Series, 1921–2 to 1932–3* (London, 1933), 558–59. These figures represent the total pension budget for disabled veterans and war dependents.
6. Guy Routh, *Occupation and Pay in Great Britain, 1906–1979* (London, 1965; 2nd ed., 1980), 120. See also Oksana Newman and Allan Foster, *The Value of a Pound: Prices and Incomes in Britain, 1900–1993* (New York, 1995), 51, 78.
7. Questions and Answers, 21 April 1921, Mr. Macpherson, Public Record Office, London (hereafter PRO), PIN 14/41.

8. James Currie to the Minister of Labour, Minute Note of 26 July 1919, PRO, Lab 2/523/TDS/5354/1010.

9. *Times of London*, 25 July 1921; *British Legion Journal*, August 1921, 37; Rehabilitation Committee Paper no. V.T. 8, Draft Report on Vocational Training, 22 September 1928, Modern Record Office, MSS 292/146.9/2.

10. See, e.g., James Cronin, *Politics of State Expansion* (London, 1991), chs. 6 and 7; Anne Crowther, *British Social Policy, 1914–1939* (London, 1988), 40–74; F. M. Miller, "The Unemployment Policy of the National Government 1941–1936," *Historical Journal* 19 (1976); Robert Skidelsky, "Keynes and the Treasury View: The Case For and Against an Active Unemployment Policy in Britain, 1920–1939," in *The Emergence of the Welfare State in Britain and Germany*, ed. W. J. Mommsen (London, 1981); John Stevenson, "The Making of Unemployment Policy 1931–1935," in *High and Low Politics in Modern Britain*, ed. Michael Bentley and John Stevenson (Oxford, 1983), 182–213.

11. Geoffrey Finlayson, *Citizen, State, and Social Welfare in Britain, 1830–1990* (New York, 1994), 201–86; Frank Prochaska, "Philanthropy," in *The Cambridge Social History of Britain, 1750–1950*, vol. 3, ed. F. M. L. Thompson (Cambridge, 1990).

12. Committee on Employment of the Severely-Disabled Ex-Service Man, 3 November 1920, PRO, PIN 15/37.

13. British Women's Hospital Committee, Final Report, 1918, Star and Garter Collection, British Red Cross Archive.

14. Parl. Papers 1922, xi, 406–7: Report from the Select Comm on Training and Employment of Disabled Ex-Service Men, 2 August 1922.

15. See esp. C. F. A. Hore, "State-Aided Provision of Employment—An Act of Obligation or Charity," 16 December 1920, PRO, PIN 15/37.

16. Peter Reese, *Homecoming Heroes: An Account of the Reassimilation of British Military Personnel into Civilian Life* (London, 1992), 95.

17. Report on the 1933 Accounts; Minutes, Executive Committee, Enham. As Macadam noted, "Voluntary charities are less liable than public schemes to fluctuations of policy or economy scares …" (267)

18. Benckendorff et al., *Kommentar von Reichsversorgungsbeamten zum Reichsversorgungsgesetz vom 12.5.1920* (Berlin, 1929), 748–65; Reichsarbeitsministerium, *Handbuch der Reichsversorgung* (Berlin, 1932), 356–68; for wage statistics, Gerhard Bry, *Wages in Germany, 1871–1945* (Princeton, 1960), 341, 352, 379.

19. Christopher Jackson, "Infirmative Action: The Law of the Severely Disabled in Germany," *Central European History* 26:4 (1993): 417–55.

20. Dr. Bruno Jung, *Der Einfluss der Wirtschaftskrise auf die Durchführung des Schwerbeschädigten-Gesetzes* (Mannheim, 1932), 32–33, 39.

21. *Statistisches Jahrbuch der Stadt Berlin* (1933), 105, 229.

22. "Die Einarmigenschule zu Dresden," Eine Denkschrift von Gustav Curt Beyer, Dresden, am Sedantag 1917, Sächsisches Hauptstaatsarchiv, Curt Beyer Collection.

23. "Planlose Wohlfahrtspflege," letter from the Zentralstelle für Volkswohlfahrt, die Zentrale für private Fürsorge, and the Bureau für Sozialpolitik, *Soziale Praxis* 25: 22 (2 March 1916): 2. See also "Die Organisation der Kriegsinvalidenfürsorge," *Concordia*, 22: 24 (15 December 1915): 427.

24. Wilhelm Groener, Minutes, National Ausschuss für Frauenarbeit im Kriege, 29 January 1917, Archiv des deutschen Caritasverbandes, CA XIX 15.

25. Index, Rep. 191, Geheimes Staatsarchiv Preußischer Kulturbesitz (hereafter GStAB).

26. Zentralkomitee der deutschen Vereine vom Roten Kreuz [General der Kavallerie v. Pfuel] to the Herrn Staatskommissar für die Regelung der Wohlfahrtspflege, November 1918. Response dated 20 November 1918, GStAB, Rep. 191, 3577.

27. Contributions Lists; Der Regierungspräsident Cassel [v. Hartmann] to the Herrn Staatskommissar, 9 August 1920, GStAB, Rep. 191, 3365 (unfoliated).

28. Christoph Sachsse and Florian Tennstedt, *Geschichte der Armenfürsorge in Deutschland, vol. 2: Fürsorge und Wohlfahrtspflege, 1871 bis 1929* (Stuttgart, 1988), esp. 160–161; Gerhard Buck, "Die Entwicklung der freien Wohlfahrtspflege von den ersten Zusammenschlüssen der freien Verbände im 19. Jahrhundert bis zur Durchsetzung des Subsidiaritätsprinzip in der Weimarer Fürsorgegesetzgebung," in *Geschichte der Sozialarbeit*, ed. Rolf Landwehr and Rüdiger Baron (Weinheim, 1983), 166–71. An important exception and the best account of changes in the private welfare sector is Young-Sun Hong's *Welfare, Modernity, and the Weimar State, 1919–1933* (Princeton, 1998), esp. 44–75, 181–202.

29. Tennstedt and Sachsse, II, 68–87; Detlev Peukert, *Die Weimarer Republik: Krisenjahre der klassischen Moderne* (Frankfurt am Main, 1987), 46–52; David Crew, *Germans on Welfare* (Oxford, 1998), 16–31; Elizabeth Harvey, *Youth and the Welfare State in Weimar Germany* (Oxford, 1993), 152–85; Young-Sun Hong, *Welfare, Modernity, and the Weimar State, 1919–1933* (Princeton, 1998), 44–75; Ludwig Preller, *Sozialpolitik in der Weimarer Republik* (Düsseldorf, 1978), 34–85; Werner Abelshauser, "Die Weimarer Republik—ein Wohlfahrtstaat?" in *Die Weimarer Republik als Wohlfahrstaat*, ed. Abelshauser (Stuttgart, 1987), Edward Ross Dickinson, *The Politics of Child Welfare from the Empire to the Federal Republic* (Cambridge, MA, 1996).

30. Mackenzie to Stoll, 29 January 1932, Box 6, War Seal Mansions, Hammersmith & Fulham Local Record Office.

31. Recording of Bill Towers, Taped 29 November 1989, Imperial War Museum—Sound Records, R9.

32. A. G. Webb, *British Legion Journal*, August 1922, 45.

33. Verbatim Report of the Annual Conference, 20 May 1929, 20, British Legion Archives. Charles Kimball, "The Ex-Service Movement in England and Wales, 1916–1930." Unpub. Ph.D. diss., Stanford University, 1991, 9–18, 150–51.

34. Verbatim Report of the Annual Conference, 25 May 1931, 13, British Legion Archives.

35. Verbatim Report of the Annual Conference of the British Legion, 20 May 1929, 15. British Legion Archives.

36. The Social Democratic Reichsbund (founded 1917) had 639,856 members in 1921. The Kyffhäuser Bund, a prewar veterans' organization, followed, with 225,392. The moderate Einheitsverband (founded in 1919) had 209,194 members. The conservative Zentralverband (1919) had 156,320 members; the communist Internationaler Bund (1919), 136,883; Deutscher Offiziersbund, 27,435; the Bund erblindeter Krieger (1916) founded 1916, 2,521. Throughout the Republic, membership in war victims' organizations fluctuated significantly, declining in most cases from 1922. In January 1924, for instance, the Reichsbund had only 245,410 members in 4,075 local branches. By December 1926 it had 324,580 members organized in 5,156 branches. Geschäftsbericht des Bundesvorstandes und Bundesausschusses für die Zeit vom 1.Januar 1924 bis 31 März 1927. *Reichsbund*, 1927, p. 5, 351–10 I, Sozialbehörde I, KO 80.11, f. 42, Staatsarchiv Hamburg. There is a large literature on Weimar veterans. Among

others, Volker Berghahn, *Der Stahlhelm: Bund der Frontsoldaten, 1918–1935* (Düsseldorf, 1966); James Diehl, *Paramilitary Politics in Weimar Germany* (Bloomington, 1977); Karl Rohe, *Das Reichsbanner Schwarz-Rot-Gold* (Düsseldorf, 1966); Kurt Schuster, *Der rote Frontkämpferbund, 1924–1929* (Düsseldorf, 1975).

37. Ewald Frie, "Vorbild oder Spiegelbild? Kriegsbeschädigtenfürsorge in Deutschland, 1914–1919," in *Der erste Weltkrieg,* ed. Wolfgang Michalka (Piper, 1993), 564.

38. Robert Whalen, *Bitter Wounds*, 107–24; James Diehl, "Victors or Victims? Disabled Veterans in the Third Reich," *Journal of Modern History* 59 (December 1987): 718, 719; Michael Geyer, "Ein Vorbote des Wohlfahrtsstaates: Die Kriegsopferversorgung in Frankreich, Deutschland und Großbritannien nach dem ersten Weltkrieg, *Geschichte und Gesellschaft* 9 (1983): 230–77, esp. 257–58.

39. "Aufruf an das deutsche Volke!" *Zentralblatt für Kriegsbeschädigte und Kriegshinterbliebene,* 1 February 1920, 2.

40. "Zustände beim städtischen Fürsorgeamt für Kriegsbeschädigte," *Arbeiter-Zeitung,* 11 January 1923, Frankfurt City Archive, Mag. Akte V/65.

41. See, e.g., "The Man Who Lay Still for 20 Years," *Sunday Express,* 30 January 1938, Press Cutting Book IV, Roehampton, Greater London Record Office; "Shall They Be Forgotten," *Evening Standard,* 9 May 1931, PH 10, Star and Garter Collection, British Red Cross Archive; "Salvaged Lives Wrecked in Battle: Hope Winning," *Daily Chronicle,* 20 May 1930, Cutting Book II, Stoll Foundation, London; Gordon Laws, "Hang Disability: We'll Show 'Em How to Smile through," *London Opinion,* 15 November 1930, PH 10, Star and Garter Collection, British Red Cross Archive.

42. Quoted in the *British Legion Journal,* January 1933, 235.

CONTRIBUTORS

John Abbott is adjunct lecturer at Dominican University in River Forest, Illinois. He is completing a study on sociocultural change and political behavior in rural Bavaria, 1871–1933.

Robert Beachy is Visiting Assistant Professor of History at Wake Forest University. His work focuses on commercial and civic culture in eighteenth- and nineteenth-century Germany.

Mark Bevir teaches political theory at the University of California at Berkeley. His work ranges from the history of socialism and religion to studies in political thought and historical method. He is the author of *The Logic of the History of Ideas* (1999).

Deborah Cohen is Assistant Professor of British History at American University in Washington, D.C. She is the author of *The War Come Home: Disabled Veterans in Britain and Germany, 1914–39* (forthcoming).

Elisabeth Ellis is a doctoral candidate in the Political Science Department at the University of California at Berkeley. Her research focuses on Kant's concept of publicity.

Rupert H. Gordon is a postdoctoral fellow in the Department of Political Science at the University of Toronto. He works on Hegel and the politics of difference.

John A. Hall is Professor of Sociology at McGill University, Montreal. He is the author of many books in historical sociology and social theory, including *Powers and Liberties: The Causes and Consequences of the Rise of the West* (1985) and *International Orders* (1996). He is also the editor of *Civil Society: Theory, History, Comparison* (1995), and, most recently, of *The State of the Nation: Ernest Gellner and the Theory of Nationalism* (1998).

Róisín Healy is Lecturer in the Department of History at the National University of Ireland, Galway. She is completing a book on anti-Jesuitism and the Protestant bourgeoisie in Imperial Germany.

Madeleine Hurd is Assistant Professor of History at the University of Pittsburgh. She is the author of *Public Spheres, Public Mores, and Democracy in Hamburg and Stockholm, 1870–1914* (2000).

Charles S. Maier is the Director of the Center for European Studies and Krupp Foundation Professor of European Studies at Harvard University. He is the author of several prize-winning works, including *Recasting Bourgeois Europe: Stabilization in France, Germany, and Italy in the Decade After World War I* (1975), and, most recently, *Dissolution: The Crisis of Communism and the End of East Germany* (1997).

Steven S. Maughan is Associate Professor of History at Albertson College. He is completing a book on Anglican missions and imperial culture in Victorian and Edwardian Britain.

Daniel A. McMillan is Assistant Professor in the Department of History at Eastern Illinois University. He is is completing a manuscript entitled *Germany Incarnate: Politics, Gender and Sociability in the Gymnastics Movement, 1811–1871.*

Ian F. McNeely, a Junior Fellow at the Society of Fellows at Harvard University, is completing a book entitled *Scribes and Citizens: Writing and the Making of Civil Society in Germany, 1790s–1820s.*

Mary Catherine Moran is a postdoctoral fellow at the University of Edinburgh. She received her Ph.D. from Johns Hopkins University where her dissertation examined the role of gender in Scottish Enlightenment discourse.

Julia Roos is completing a dissertation in social history at Carnegie Mellon University and has published on emigration and prostitution.

Frank Trentmann is Assistant Professor of History at Princeton University. He has written on Free Trade in Britain, and on nature movements in the twentieth century. He is completing a book on the transformation of political culture and political economy in twentieth-century Britain.

SELECT BIBLIOGRAPHY

Arato, Andrew, and Jean L. Cohen. *Civil Society and Political Theory*. Cambridge, MA: MIT, 1992.

Ash, Timothy Garton. *The Uses of Adversity*. London: Jonathan Cape, 1983.

Avineri, Shlomo. *Hegel's Theory of the Modern State*. Cambridge: Cambridge University, 1971.

Becker, Marvin B. *The Emergence of Civil Society in the Eighteenth Century*. Bloomington: Indiana University, 1994.

Berman, S. "Civil Society and the Collapse of the Weimar Republic." *World Politics* 49 (1997): 401–29.

Biagini, Eugenio, ed. *Citizenship and Community: Liberals, Radicals and Collective Identities in the British Isles, 1865–1931*. Cambridge: Cambridge University, 1996.

Blackbourn, David, and Richard J. Evans, eds. *The German Bourgeoisie: Essays on the Social History of the German Middle Class from the Late Eighteenth to the Early Twentieth Century*. London: Routledge, 1991.

Bödeker, Hans Erich, ed. *Aufklärung der Politisierung-Politisierung der Aufklärung*. Hamburg: F. Meiner, 1987.

Brewer, John. *Party Ideology and Popular Politics at the Accession of George III*. Cambridge: Cambridge University, 1976.

———. *Pleasures of the Imagination: English Culture in the Eighteenth Century*. London: HarperCollins, 1997.

Burchell, Graham. "Peculiar Interests: Civil Society and the Governing System of Natural Liberty." In Graham Burchell, Colin Gordon, and Peter Miller, eds., *The Foucault Effect: Studies in Governmentality*. Chicago: Chicago University, 1991: 119–50.

Burton, Antoinette. *Burdens of History: British Feminists, Indian Women, and Imperial Culture, 1865–1915*. Chapel Hill: University of North Carolina, 1994.

Caffentzis, George C. "On the Scottish Origin of 'Civilization.'" In Silvia Federici, ed., *Enduring Western Civilization: The Construction of the Concept of Western Civilization and its "Others."* Westport: Praeger, 1995: 13–36.

Calhoun, Craig, ed. *Habermas and the Public Sphere*. Cambridge, MA: MIT, 1992.

Clark, Anna. *The Struggle for the Breeches: Gender and the Making of the British Working Class*. Berkeley: University of California, 1995.

Clark, Peter. *Sociability and Urbanity: Clubs and Societies in the Eighteenth Century City*. Leicester: Victorian Studies Center, 1986.

Cohen, Joshua, and Joel Rogers, eds. *Associations and Democracy*. New York: Verso, 1995.

Colas, Dominique. *Civil Society and Fanaticism: Conjoined Histories*. Stanford: Stanford University, 1997.

Cooper, Frederick, and Ann Laura Stoler, eds. *Tensions of Empire: Colonial Cultures in a Bourgeois World*. Berkeley: University of California, 1997.

Cox, Jeffrey. "The Missionary Movement." In D.G. Paz, ed., *Nineteenth Century English Religious Traditions*, Westport, CT: Greenwood, 1995.

Dahrendorf, Ralf. *After 1989: Morals, Revolution, and Civil Society*. New York: St. Martin's, 1997.

Dann, Otto, ed. *Lesegesellschaften und bürgerliche Emanzipation: Ein europäischer Vergleich*. Munich: C.H. Beck, 1981.

———. *Vereinswesen und bürgerliche Gesellschaft in Deutschland*. Munich, 1984.

Davidoff, Leonore, and Catherine Hall. *Family Fortunes: Men and Women of the English Middle Class, 1780–1850*. Chicago: University of Chicago, 1987.

Davis, Deborah S., et al., eds. *Urban Spaces in Contemporary China: The Potential for Autonomy and Community in Post-Mao China*. Cambridge: Cambridge University, 1995.

Dwyer, John, and Richard B. Sher, eds. *Sociability and Society in Eighteenth-Century Scotland*. Edinburgh: Mercat, 1993.

Elias, Norbert. *The Civilizing Process: The History of Manners and State Formation and Civilization*. Oxford: Blackwell, 1994.

Fine, R. and Shirin Rai, eds. *Civil Society: Democratic Perspectives*. London: Frank Cass, 1997.

François, É., ed. *Sociabilité et Société Bourgeoise en France, en Allemagne et en Suisse, 1750–1850*. Paris: Ed. Recherche sur les Civilisations, 1986.

Freudenthal, Herbert. *Vereine in Hamburg: Ein Beitrag zur Geschichte und Volkskunde der Geselligkeit*. Hamburg: Museum für Hamburgische Geschichte, 1968.

Frevert, Ute. *Bürgerinnen und Bürger*. Göttingen: Vandenhoeck & Ruprecht, 1988.

Gall, Lothar. *Bürgertum in Deutschland*. Berlin: Siedler, 1989.

Gall, Lothar, ed. *Vom alten zum neuen Bürgertum: Die mitteleuropäische Stadt im Umbruch 1780–1820*. Munich: R. Oldenbourg, 1991.

Gellner, Ernest. *Conditions of Liberty: Civil Society and its Rivals*. London: Allen Lane, Penguin, 1994.

Gobetti, Daniela. *Private and Public: Individuals, Households, and the Body Politic in Locke and Hutcheson*. New York: Routledge, 1992.

Gosden, P. *Self-Help: Voluntary Associations in the Nineteenth-Century*. London: Batsford, 1973.

Gray, John. *Post-Liberalism. Studies in Political Thought*. New York: Routledge, 1993.

Grell, Ole Peter, Jonathan I. Israel, and Nicholas Tyacke, eds. *From Persecution to Toleration: The Glorious Revolution and Religion in England*. Oxford: Clarendon, 1991.

Grossman, Atina. *Reforming Sex: The German Movement for Birth Control and Abortion Reform, 1920–1950*. Oxford: Oxford University, 1995.

Gutmann, A. Ed. *Freedom of Association*. Princeton: Princeton University, 1998.

Habermas, Jürgen. *The Structural Transformation of the Public Sphere*. Cambridge, MA: MIT, 1989.

———. *Between Facts and Norms: Contributions to a Discourse Theory of Law and Democracy*. Cambridge, MA: MIT, 1996.

Hall, John A., ed. *Civil Society: Theory, History, Comparison*. Cambridge: Polity, 1995.

Haltern, U. *Bürgerliche Gesellschaft: Sozialtheoretische und sozialhistorische Aspekte*. Darmstadt: Wissenschaftliche Buchgesellschaft, 1985.

Hann, C. and E. Dunn, eds. *Civil Society: Challenging Western Models*. London: Routledge, 1996.

Hardtwig, W. *Genossenschaft, Sekte, Verein in Deutschland*. Munich: Beck, 1997.

Harris, Jose. *Private Lives, Public Spirit: A Social History of Britain, 1870–1914*. Oxford: Oxford University, 1993.

Harrison, Brian. *Peaceable Kingdom: Stability and Change in Modern Britain*. Oxford: Clarendon, 1982.

Hefner, Robert W., ed. *Democratic Civility: The History and Cross-Cultural Possibility of a Modern Political Ideal*. New Brunswick: Transaction, 1998.

Hein, D., and A. Schulz, eds. *Bürgerkultur im 19. Jahrhundert: Bildung, Kunst und Lebenswelt*. Munich: C.H. Beck, 1996.

Hellmuth, E., ed. *The Transformation of Political Culture: England and Germany in the Late Eighteenth Century*. Oxford: Oxford University, 1990.

Hilton, B. *The Age of Atonement: The Influence of Evangelicalism on Social and Economic Thought*. Oxford: Clarendon, 1988.

Hirschman, Albert O. *The Passions and the Interests: Political Arguments for Capitalism Before Its Triumph*. Princeton: Princeton University, 1977.

Hirst, Paul. *Representative Democracy and its Limits*. Oxford: Polity, 1990.

Hont, Istvan, and Michael Ignatieff, eds. *Wealth and Virtue: The Shaping of Political Economy in the Scottish Enlightenment*. Cambridge: Cambridge University, 1983.

Hübinger, Gangolf. *Kulturprotestantismus und Politik: Zum Verhältnis von Liberalismus und Protestantismus im wilhelminischen Deutschland*. Tübingen: J.C.B. Mohr, 1994.

Hull, Isabel V. *Sexuality, State, and Civil Society in Germany, 1700–1815*. Ithaca: Cornell University, 1996.

Im Hof, U. *Das Gesellige Jahrhundert: Gesellschaft und Gesellschaften im Zeitalter der Aufklärung*. Munich: C.H. Beck, 1982.

Jacob, M.C. *Living the Enlightenment: Freemasonry and Politics in Eighteenth-Century Europe*. Oxford: Oxford University, 1991.

Janoski, T. *Citizenship and Civil Society: A Framework of Rights and Obligations in Liberal, Traditional, and Social Democratic Regimes*. Cambridge: Cambridge University, 1998.

Johnston, Hank, and Bert Landermans, eds. *Social Movements and Culture*. Minneapolis: University of Minnesota, 1995.

Joyce, Patrick. *Visions of the People: Industrial England and the Question of Class, 1848–1914*. Cambridge: Cambridge University, 1991.

———. *Democratic Subjects: The Self and the Social in Nineteenth Century England*. Cambridge: Cambridge University, 1994.

Keane, John. *Civil Society: Old Images, New Visions*. London: Polity, 1999.

———, ed. *Civil Society and the State: New European Perspectives*. London: Verso, 1988.

Kocka, Jürgen, and Allan Mitchell, eds. *Bourgeois Society in Nineteenth-Century Europe*. Oxford: Berg, 1993.

Koo, Hagen, ed. *State and Society in Contemporary Korea*. Ithaca: Cornell University, 1993.

Koselleck, Reinhart. *Preußen zwischen Reform und Revolution. Allgemeines Landrecht, Verwaltung, und soziale Bewegung von 1791 bis 1848*. 3d. ed. Stuttgart: Klett-Cotta, 1981.

———. *Critique and Crisis: Enlightenment and the Pathogenesis of Modern Society*. Oxford: Berg, 1988.

Koselleck, R., U. Spree, and W. Steinmetz. "Drei bürgerliche Welten? Zur vergleichenden Semantik der bürgerlichen Gesellschaft in Deutschland, England und Frankreich." In H.-J. Puhle, ed., *Bürger in der Gesellschaft der Neuzeit: Wirtschaft—Politik—Kultur*, Göttingen: Vandehoeck & Ruprecht, 1991.

Krygier, M. "Virtuous Circles: Antipodean Reflections on Power, Institutions, and Civil Society." *East European Politics and Societies* 11 (1997): 36–88.

Kuehn, Manfred. *Scottish Common Sense in Germany, 1768–1800.* McGill: Queen's University, 1987.

Kuttner, Robert, ed. *Ticking Time Bombs.* New York: New, 1996.

Langford, Paul. *Polite and Commercial People: England, 1727–1783.* Oxford: Clarendon, 1989.

Linebaugh, Peter A. *The London Hanged: Crime and Civil Society in the Eighteenth Century.* Cambridge: Cambridge University, 1992.

Maier, Charles S. *Dissolution: The Crisis of Communism and the End of East Germany.* Princeton: Princeton University, 1997.

Mannheim, Ernst. *Die Träger der Öffentlichen Meinung: Studien zur Soziologie der Öffentlichkeit.* Leipzig, 1933.

Medick, Hans. *Naturzustand und Naturgeschichte der bürgerlichen Gesellschaft: Die Ursprünge der bürgerlichen Sozialtheorie als Geschichtsphilosophie und Sozialwissenschaft bei Samuel Pufendorf, John Locke und Adam Smith.* Göttingen: Vandenhoeck & Ruprecht, 1973.

Mitchell, A. "The Association Movement of 1792–1793." *Historical Journal* 4 (1961).

Morris, R. J. *Class, Sect, and Party: The Making of the British Middle Class, Leeds 1820–1850.* Manchester: Manchester University, 1990.

———. "Clubs, Societies and Associations." In F .M. L. Thompson, ed. *The Cambridge Social History of Britain, 1750–1950*, III, Cambridge: Cambridge University, 1990.

Nipperdey, Thomas. "Verein als soziale Struktur in Deutschland im späten 18. und frühen 19. Jahrhundert." In Thomas Nipperdey, *Gesellschaft, Kultur, Theorie.* Göttingen: Vandenhoeck & Ruprecht, 1976.

Nord, Philip. *The Republican Moment.* Cambridge: Harvard University, 1995.

Norton, Augustus R., ed. *Civil Society in the Middle East.* Leiden: Brill, 1995.

Oz-Salzberger, Fania. *Translating the Enlightenment: Scottish Civic Discourse in Eighteenth-Century Germany.* Oxford: Clarendon, 1995.

Poovey, Mary. *A History of the Modern Fact: Problems of Knowledge in the Sciences of Wealth and Society.* Chicago: Chicago University, 1998.

Porter, Andrew. "Religion and Empire: British Expansion in the Long Nineteenth Century, 1780–1914." *The Journal of Imperial and Commonwealth History* 20 (1992).

Prochaska, Frank. "Philanthrophy." In F. M. L. Thompson, ed. *The Cambridge Social History of Britain, 1750–1950*, III, Cambridge: Cambridge University, 1990.

Putnam, Robert. "Bowling Alone: America's Declining Social Capital." *Journal of Democracy* 6 (1995): 65–78.

Putnam, Robert D., with Robert Leonardi and Raffaella Y. Nanetti. *Making Democracy Work: Civic Traditions in Modern Italy.* Princeton: Princeton University, 1993.

Reinalter, Helmut, ed. *Aufklärung und Geheimgesellschaften.* Munich: R. Oldenbourg, 1989.

Riedel, Manfred. *Bürgerliche Gesellschaft und Staat: Grundproblem und Struktur der Hegelschen Rechtsphilosophie.* Neuwied: Luchterhand, 1970.

———. "Gesellschaft, Bürgerliche." In Otto Brunner, Werner Conze, and Reinhart Koselleck, eds. *Geschichtliche Grundbegriffe.* Stuttgart: E. Klett, 1972.

Seligman, Adam B. *The Idea of Civil Society.* New York: Maxwell MacMillan International, 1992.

Silver, Allan. "'Two Different Sorts of Commerce'—Friendship and Strangership in Civil Society." In Jeff Weintraub and Krishan Kumar, eds., *Public and Private in Thought and Practice: Perspectives on a Grand Dichotomy*. Chicago: Chicago University, 1995: 43–74.

Smith, Helmut. *German Nationalism and Religious Conflict: Culture, Ideology, Politics, 1870–1914*. Princeton: Princeton University, 1995.

Smith, Steven B. "At the Crossroads: Hegel and the Ethics of *Bürgerliche Gesellschaft*." *Laval Theologique et Philosophique* 51, no. 2 (June 1995): 545–62.

Strand, David. "Protest in Beijing: Civil Society and Public Sphere in China." *Problems of Communism* 39 (May-June, 1990): 1–19.

Taylor, B. *Eve and the New Jerusalem: Socialism and Feminism in the Nineteenth Century*. New York: Pantheon, 1983.

Taylor, Charles. "Invoking Civil Society." In Charles Taylor, *Philosophical Arguments*. Cambridge, MA: Harvard, 1995: 202–24.

Tyrell, A. "'Women's Mission' and Pressure Group Politics in Britain (1825/60)." *Bulletin of John Rylands University Library* 63 (1980): 194–230.

van Dülmen, Richard. *Die Gesellschaft der Aufklärer: Zur Bürgerlichen Emanzipation und aufklärerischen Kultur in Deutschland*. Frankfurt a.M.: Fischer, 1986.

Van Horn Melton, James. "The Emergence of 'Society' in Eighteenth- and Nineteenth-Century Germany." In P. J. Corfield, *Language, History and Class*, Oxford: Blackwell, 1991.

Vernon, James, ed. *Re-Reading the Constitution: New Narratives in the Political History of England's Long Nineteenth Century*. Cambridge: Cambridge University, 1996.

Wahrman, Dror. *Imagining the Middle Class*. Cambridge: Cambridge University, 1995.

Walker, Mack. *German Home Towns: Community, State, and General Estate 1648–1871*. Ithaca: Cornell University Press, 1971.

Walkowitz, Judith R. *Prostitution and Victorian Society*. Cambridge: Cambridge University, 1980.

Walzer, Michael, ed. *Toward a Global Civil Society*. Providence: Berghahn, 1995.

Waszek, Norbert. *The Scottish Enlightenment and Hegel's Account of Civil Society*. Dordrecht: Kluwer, 1988.

Weindling, Paul. *Health, Race, and German Politics between German Unification and Nazism, 1870–1945*. Cambridge: Cambridge University, 1993.

Winch, Donald. *Adam Smith's Politics*. Cambridge: Cambridge University, 1978.

———. *Riches and Poverty: An Intellectual History of Political Economy in Britain, 1750–1834*. Cambridge: Cambridge University, 1996.

Yeo, S. *Religion and Voluntary Organisations in Crisis*. London: Croom Helm, 1976.

INDEX